CAROLYN STEEL

Hungry City

How Food Shapes Our Lives

VINTAGE BOOKS
London

Published by Vintage 2013

4 6 8 10 9 7 5

Copyright © Carolyn Steel 2008

Carolyn Steel has asserted her right under the Copyright, Designs and
Patents Act 1988 to be identified as the author of this work

First published in Great Britain in 2008 by
Chatto & Windus

First published in paperback in Great Britain in 2009 by
Vintage

Vintage
Random House, 20 Vauxhall Bridge Road,
London SW1V 2SA

www.vintage-books.co.uk

Addresses for companies within The Random House Group Limited can be found at:
www.randomhouse.co.uk/offices.htm

The Random House Group Limited Reg. No. 954009

A CIP catalogue record for this book
is available from the British Library

ISBN 9780099584476

Penguin Random House is committed to a sustainable future for
our business, our readers and our planet. This book is made from
Forest Stewardship Council® certified paper.

Printed and bound in Great Britain by Clays Ltd, St Ives plc

HUNGRY CITY

Carolyn Steel is a London-based architect, lecturer and writer. Since graduating from Cambridge University, she has combined architectural practice with teaching and research into the relationship between food and cities, running design studios at the LSE, London Metropolitan University and at the Cambridge University School of Architecture, where her lecture series on *Food and the City* was the first of its kind. A visiting lecturer at Wageningen University and director of Kilburn Nightingale Architects in London, Carolyn has been a Rome Scholar, presented on the BBC's *One Foot in the Past,* and gave a talk at TEDGlobal in 2008.

Hungry City won the RSL Jerwood Award for Non-Fiction (for a work in progress) in 2006.

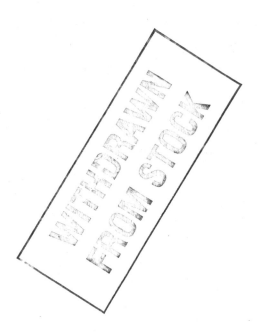

For my mother and father

Contents

Contents

Introduction

Close your eyes and think of a city. What do you see? A jumble of rooftops stretching off into the distance? The chaos of Piccadilly Circus? The Manhattan skyline? The street where you live? Whatever it is you imagine, it probably involves buildings. They, after all, are what cities are made of, along with the streets and squares that join them all together. But cities are not just made of bricks and mortar, they are inhabited by flesh-and-blood humans, and so must rely on the natural world to feed them. Cities, like people, are what they eat.

Hungry City is a book about how cities eat. That is the quick definition. A slightly wordier one might be that it is about the underlying paradox of urban civilisation. When you consider that every day for a city the size of London, enough food for thirty million meals must be produced, imported, sold, cooked, eaten and disposed of again, and that something similar must happen every day for every city on earth, it is remarkable that those of us living in them get to eat at all. Feeding cities takes a gargantuan effort; one that arguably has a greater social and physical impact on our lives and planet than anything else we do. Yet few of us in the West are conscious of the process. Food arrives on our plates as if by magic, and we rarely stop to wonder how it got there.

Hungry City deals with two major themes – food and cities – yet its true focus is on neither. It is on *the relationship between the two*: something no other book has ever directly addressed. Both food and cities are so fundamental to our everyday lives that they are almost too big to see. Yet if you put them together, a remarkable relationship emerges – one so powerful and obvious that it makes you wonder how on earth you could have missed it. Every day we inhabit spaces food has made,

ix

unconsciously repeating routine actions as old as cities themselves. We might assume that takeaways are a modern phenomenon, yet five thousand years ago, they lined the streets of Ur and Uruk, two of the oldest cities on earth. Markets and shops, pubs and kitchens, dinners and waste-dumps have always provided the backdrop to urban life. Food shapes cities, and through them, it moulds us – along with the countryside that feeds us.

So why write about food and cities, and why now? With cities already gobbling up 75 per cent of the earth's resources and the urban population expected to double by 2050, the subject is certainly topical. Yet the real answer is that *Hungry City* is the result of a lifelong obsession. Seven years in the making, it has taken a lifetime to research, although for most of that time, I had no idea that it – or indeed, any book – would be the outcome. *Hungry City* is an exploration of the way we live, from the perspective of someone who decided at the age of ten she wanted to be an architect, and has spent the rest of her life trying to work out why.

Perhaps because I was born and bred in central London, I have always been interested in buildings. However, my interest was never limited to the way they looked, or to their physical form. More than anything else, I wanted to know *how buildings were inhabited*. Where the food came in, how it got cooked, where the horses were stabled, what happened to the rubbish – these details fascinated me as much as the perfect proportions of their facades. Most of all, I loved the unspoken bond between the two: the public/private, upstairs/downstairs divisions within buildings, and the way they were subtly interwoven. I suppose I have always been drawn to the hidden relationships between things.

This predilection probably came from my grandparents' hotel in Bournemouth, where I spent most of my holidays as a child. Wandering around the hotel on my own, I had the excitement of knowing both its 'front of house' and 'backstage' areas at once, and of being able to move between the two at will. I always preferred to lurk in the service quarters: the sculleries full of teapots and hot-water bottles; the laundry room with its piles of freshly ironed, neatly folded linen; the porters' room, with its ancient workbench and the stench of tobacco and furniture polish. But more thrilling by far were the kitchens, with their worn tiled floors and greasy enamel walls, mounds of butter and chopped vegetables, steaming stills and copper pans full of fragrant boiling stock. I loved those rooms, not just for their pragmatic homeliness, but for the fact that they were separated from all the antiques and politeness of the public rooms by the merest swing of a green baize door. The allure of such thresholds has never left me.

Looking back, I suspect my love of food must have begun then, although it was only years later that I realised that my twin passions for food and architecture were really two aspects of the same thing. It was architecture that I pursued as a career, first studying it at Cambridge, and then, two years after qualifying, returning there to teach. By then, I understood architecture to be the embodiment of human dwelling in its fullest sense, with politics and culture as its social contexts, landscape and climate its physical ones, and cities its greatest manifestation. Architecture encompassed every aspect of human life – which made the teaching of it in an architecture school somewhat limiting. I felt increasingly that in order to study architecture, one had to look away from it – only then could one see it for what it really was. It seemed to me that what was missing from the traditional discipline was life itself: the very thing it was supposed to support. I found the same in practice: discussing projects with clients, it was clear to me that I had somehow learnt to think and speak in an architectural code that excluded non-practitioners. This struck me as not only wrong, but potentially disastrous. How could architects expect to design spaces for people to inhabit, if we had no proper dialogue with them?

I began to look for ways of bridging the gap: to bring life into architecture, and architecture to life. My search took me to Rome in the 1990s, where I studied the everyday habits of a local neighbourhood over the course of 2,000 years; and to the London School of Economics, where I was director of the first urban design studio ever held there. My time at the LSE was fascinating: there were architects, politicians, economists, developers, sociologists, housing experts and engineers all gathered together in one room, trying (and failing) to find a common language with which to discuss cities. It was then that I hit on the idea of using food as a common medium. How would it be, I wondered, if one tried to describe a city through food? I was confident that such a thing could be done, but had no idea how one might go about it, or where it would lead. Seven years later, this book is the result.

Hungry City began as an attempt to describe one city – London – through food, but it became much more than that. It was only through writing the book that I realised I had stumbled on a connection so profound that its applications were virtually limitless. Writing it has been a bizarre as well as lengthy process, since it has taken place during a period in which many of the themes I was linking together – food miles, the obesity epidemic, urbanisation, the power of supermarkets, peak oil, climate change – were rising inexorably in the public consciousness. Eventually, it got to a point where I could barely turn on the radio or TV without dashing to my computer to take notes. Food has become a hot topic in contemporary Britain, and a very fast-moving one. I dare say that by the time you are reading this, the scene will have shifted again. No matter. *Hungry City* taps into the zeitgeist, yet its essential themes are as old as civilisation itself.

With a book as horizontal in scope as mine, I have had to thread my arguments carefully. *Hungry City* is not an encyclopaedic book; it is more of an introduction to a way of thinking. It uses London (and other cities in the West) to draw out eternal themes that are global in reach: to trace the critical path of urban civilisation as seen through food, from the ancient Near East, through Europe and America, to modern-day China. The book follows food's journey from land and sea to city, through market and supermarket to kitchen and table, waste-dump and back again. Each chapter begins with a snapshot of contemporary London, exploring the historical roots of that stage of food's journey and the issues it raises. The chapters deal in turn with farming, food transport, shopping, cooking, eating and waste, asking how each affects our lives, and impacts on the planet. The final chapter asks how we might use food to rethink cities in the future – to design them and their hinterlands better, and live in them better too.

Writing *Hungry City* has changed the way I see the world so fundamentally that I now struggle to imagine how I saw it before. To see the world through food, as I now do, is to see it with lateral vision;

to understand how apparently disparate phenomena are in fact connected. I very much hope that reading the book will change the way you see things too – that it will show you how powerfully food shapes *all* our lives, and give you the power and motivation to engage more with food, and through it, to help shape our common destiny.

Chapter 1
The Land

The supply of food to a great city is among the most remarkable of social phenomena - full of instruction on all sides.

George Dodd[1]

Detail of *The Allegory of Good Government* by Ambrogio Lorenzetti. A rare glimpse of city and country in perfect harmony.

Christmas Dinner

In the run-up to Christmas a couple of years ago, anyone with access to British television and some recording equipment could treat themselves to a surreal evening's viewing. At nine p.m. one night, two programmes were broadcast simultaneously about how our Christmas dinners are produced. You had to be a bit keen, even obsessed, to watch both, but if you chose to make a night of it as I did, the effect was truly discombobulating. First up was *Rick Stein's Food Heroes Christmas Special*, in which Britain's favourite champion of high-quality local produce set off in his Land Rover (accompanied by faithful terrier Chalky) to sniff out the finest smoked salmon, turkey, chipolatas, Christmas pudding, Stilton and fizz the nation has to offer.[2] An hour of gorgeous landscapes, uplifting music and mouthwatering fodder later, I could hardly bear to wait six days before tucking into the promised feast for real. But lurking on my DVD recorder was the antidote to all that. While Rick and Chalky had been busy charming millions of us into the festive mood on BBC2, on Channel 4 the *Sun* journalist Jane Moore had been putting off several million others from ever eating Christmas dinner again.

In *What's Really in Your Christmas Dinner*, Moore explored the same traditional meal as Rick Stein, but sourced her ingredients from rather different suppliers. Using secretly shot footage of unspecified industrial units, she showed how most of our Christmas food is produced, and it wasn't a pretty sight. There were pigs on a Polish factory farm confined to sow stalls too narrow to turn around in; turkeys crowded together in massive dark sheds with so little space to move that many went lame.[3] The normally unruffled chef Raymond Blanc was wheeled in to perform a post-mortem on one specimen, revealing its pathetically weak bones and blood-swollen liver (both the result of premature growth) with a zeal that was close to macabre. If life was grim for these birds, the manner of their death was even worse. Slung into trucks by their legs, they were hung upside down from hooks on a conveyor belt, their heads dipped into a stun bath that rendered them unconscious (although not always) before having their throats cut.

Back on BBC2, Rick Stein also touched on what he called the 'unmentionable side of turkeys – slaughtering them'. The subject came up when he visited Andrew Dennis, an organic farmer whose turkeys are reared in flocks of 200 or fewer in natural woodland, where they can forage freely, just as their forebears would have done in the wild. Dennis sees his turkey-rearing enterprise as an exemplar that he hopes will be followed by others. 'Of all farm animals,' he says, 'turkeys are by far the most abused. And that's why we're trying to produce a blueprint for compassionate turkey rearing and breeding.' When the time comes for their slaughter, the birds are taken to an old barn familiar to them and killed individually, out of sight of one another. When his slaughterman failed to turn up in 2002, Dennis practised what he preaches, killing every one of his birds himself. 'It's the quality of life that's so important, and the quality of death,' he says, 'and if you can provide for both those things, I think I'm comfortable with what we do.' So there you have it. If you want to eat turkey for Christmas and still feel good about yourself, you can either shell out about £50 for a 'happy' bird, or you can spend less than a quarter of that and try not to think too hard about how the animal was reared and killed. No prizes for guessing what the majority of us do.

One could be forgiven for feeling confused about food in contemporary Britain. There is almost blanket coverage of it in the media, increasingly polarised between the 'foodie' strand, for which Rick Stein is justly renowned, and the sort of shock-horror exposé delivered that night by Jane Moore. With farmers' markets, speciality food shops and fancy restaurants popping up all over the place, we are supposedly in the midst of a gastronomic revolution, yet our everyday food culture belies this. We have never spent less on food than we do now: food shopping accounted for just 10 per cent of our income in 2007, down from 23 per cent in 1980. Eighty per cent of our groceries

are bought in supermarkets, and when we shop for food
are overwhelmingly influenced by cost, well ahead of tas
healthiness.[4] We are losing our kitchen skills too: half o
the age of 24 say they never cook from scratch, and one i
eaten in Britain is a ready meal. Hardly a revolution.

In truth, British food culture is little short of schizophrenic. To read
the Sunday papers, you would think we were a nation of rampant
gastronomes, yet few of us know much about food, or care to invest
our time and effort in it. Despite the recently acquired veneer of foodie
culture, we remain Europe's leading nation of 'fuellies', happy to let
food take a back seat as we get on with our busy lives, unconscious of
what it takes to keep us fuelled.[5] We have become so used to eating
cheaply that few of us question how it is possible, say, to buy a chicken
for less than half the cost of a packet of cigarettes. Although a moment's
thought – or a brief channel-flick to *What's Really in Your Christmas
Dinner* – would soon tell us, most of us steer clear of such sobering
revelations. It is as if the flesh we put in our mouths bears no relation to
the living bird. We simply don't make the connection.

So how come a country of dog-owning bunny-huggers like us can
be so callous about the critters we breed to eat? It all comes down to
our urban lifestyles. The oldest industrialised nation on earth, we have
been losing touch with rural life for centuries. Over 80 per cent of us
in Britain now live in cities, and the nearest most of us ever get to the
'real' countryside – the working sort, at any rate – is when we see it on
television. We have never been more cut off from farms and farming,
and while most of us probably suspect, deep down, that our eating
habits are having nasty consequences somewhere on the planet, those
consequences are sufficiently out of sight to be ignored.

Even if we wanted to, supplying ourselves with the amount of meat
we eat today with free-range animals would be next to impossible. We
British have always been a carnivorous lot: not for nothing did the
French dub us *les rosbifs*. But a century ago, that meant each of us ate
around 25 kg of meat a year, not the whopping 80 kg we eat today.[6]
Meat was once a luxury food, and leftovers from the Sunday roast – if
you were lucky enough to have one – were eked out during the week.
No longer. Meat today is an everyday commodity; something we

consume without thinking. Every year we eat 35 million turkeys, and at Christmas we get through 10 million birds. That's 50,000 times more than Andrew Dennis produces. Even if we could find 50,000 farmers as dedicated as he is, to rear all our turkeys the Dennis way would take some 34.5 million hectares: double the total amount of farmland the UK currently has in production.[7] And turkeys are just the tip of the iceberg – we currently eat some 820 million chickens every year in the UK. Try rearing those by hand.

The modern food industry has done strange things to us. By supplying us with cheap and plentiful food at little apparent cost, it has satisfied our most basic needs, while making those needs appear inconsequential. That applies not just to meat, but to every type of food. Potatoes and cabbages, oranges and lemons, sardines and kippers; whatever we eat, the scale and complexity of the process of getting it to us is considerable. By the time it reaches us, our food has often travelled thousands of miles through airports and docksides, warehouses and factory kitchens, and been touched by dozens of unseen hands. Yet most of us live in ignorance of the effort it takes to feed us.

No inhabitant of a pre-industrial city could have been so unaware. Before the railways, supplying themselves with food was the biggest headache cities faced, and evidence of the struggle was unavoidable. Roads were full of carts and wagons carrying vegetables and grain, rivers and docksides were packed with cargo ships and fishing boats, streets and back yards were full of cows, pigs and chickens. Living in such a city, there could be no doubt as to where your food came from: it was all around you, snorting and steaming and getting in the way. City-dwellers in the past had no choice but to acknowledge the role of food in their lives. It was present in everything they did.

We have lived in cities for thousands of years, yet we remain animals, defined by animal needs. And therein lies the basic paradox of urban life. We inhabit cities as if that were the most natural thing in the world, yet in a deeper sense, we still dwell on the land. Civilisation may be urban, but the vast majority of people in the past were hunters and gatherers, farmers and serfs, yeomen and peasants, who led predominantly rural lives. Theirs is largely a forgotten history, yet without them, none of the rest of the human narrative would have been possible. The relationship between food and cities is endlessly complex, but at one level it is utterly simple. Without farmers and farming, cities would not exist.

As civilisation is city-centric, it is hardly surprising that we have inherited a lopsided view of the urban–rural relationship. Visual representations of cities have tended to ignore their rural hinterlands, somehow managing to give the impression that their subjects were autonomous, while narrative history has relegated the countryside to a neutral green backdrop, good for fighting battles in, but little else. It is a curious distortion of the truth, yet when you consider the extraordinary power that rural communities could have wielded over cities had they ever realised their potential, an understandable one. For 10,000 years, cities have relied on the countryside to feed them, and the countryside, under various degrees of duress, has obliged. City and country have been locked together in an uneasy symbiotic clinch, with urban authorities doing all in their power to maintain the upper hand. Taxes have been imposed and land reformed, deals done and embargoes issued, propaganda spread and wars waged. The effort has been unceasing, and despite appearances, it still is. The fact that so few of us are aware of it is symptomatic of the political sensitivity of the issue. No government, including our own, has ever wanted to admit its dependency on others for its sustenance. Put it down to the siege mentality: the fear of starvation that has haunted cities through history.

We may no longer live in walled citadels, but we rely just as much on those who feed us as any ancient city-dweller did – arguably more so, since the cities we inhabit today are mostly sprawling conurbations on a scale that would have been unthinkable even a century ago. The ability to preserve food, as well as transport it long distances, has freed cities from the constraints of geography, making it possible for the first time to build them in such unlikely spots as the Dubai desert, or above the Arctic Circle. Whether or not one considers such settlements to be the ultimate in urban hubris, they are far from being the only ones to rely on imported food. Most cities today do precisely that, having long outgrown their local farm belts. London has imported the bulk of its food for centuries, and the modern city is fed by a global hinterland with a combined area more than a hundred times larger than the city itself – roughly equivalent in size to all the productive farmland in the UK.[8]

Meanwhile, the countryside we like to imagine just beyond our urban borders is a carefully sustained fantasy. For centuries, city-dwellers have seen nature through a one-way telescope, moulding its image to fit their urban sensibilities. The pastoral tradition, with its hedgerows and its meadows full of fluffy sheep, is part of that tendency, as is the Romantic vision of nature, all soaring peaks, noble firs and plunging gorges. Neither bears any relation to the sort of landscape capable of feeding a modern metropolis. Fields of corn and soya stretching as far as the eye can see, plastic polytunnels so vast they can be seen from space, industrial sheds and feed lots full of factory-farmed animals – these are the rural hinterlands of modernity. Our idealised and industrialised versions of 'countryside' may be antithetical, but both are products of urban civilisation. They are the Jekyll and Hyde of the natural world as modified by man.

Cities have always moulded nature in their image, but in the past their impact was limited by their size. Back in 1800, just 3 per cent of the world's population lived in towns with 5,000 inhabitants or more; in 1950 that figure was still less than a third.[9] But in the past 50 years, the situation has been changing far more rapidly. Sometime in 2006, the global population became predominantly urban for the first time, and by 2050, the UN predicts the figure will be 80 per cent. That means *three billion* more people will be living in cities in 40 years' time. With cities already consuming an estimated 75 per cent of the world's food and energy resources, it doesn't take a mathematical genius to see that pretty soon the sums won't add up.

Part of the problem is what city-dwellers like to eat. Although meat was always the staple food of hunter-gatherers and tribal herdsmen, in most societies it has been the preserve of the rich; its presence in the diet a sign of prosperity when the vast majority subsisted on grain and vegetables. For centuries, rates of global consumption have been a case of 'the West and the rest', with Americans recently topping the tables at a gut-clenching 124 kg per head per year. But now it seems that the rest are catching up. According to the United Nations Food and Agriculture Organization (FAO), the world is in the grip of a 'livestock revolution', with global consumption rising fast, particularly in the developing world, where diets have traditionally been vegetarian.[10] By

2030, the UN predicts, two thirds of worldwide meat and milk supplies will be consumed by developing nations, and by 2050, global meat consumption will have doubled.[11]

What lies behind the world's increasing carnivorousness? The reasons are many and complex, but in the end they come back to our animal natures. Whether or not we are vegetarians by choice, we are omnivores by nature, and meat, quite simply, is the most privileged food we can eat. Although some religions, notably Hinduism and Jainism, eschew it, most humans who have forgone meat in the past have done so mainly due to lack of opportunity. Now, however, urbanisation, industrialisation and greater prosperity are creating an appetite in many countries for the sort of meat-based diet we have long taken for granted in the West. The most startling changes are taking place in China, where 400 million people are expected to urbanise in the next 25 years. For centuries, the typical Chinese diet has consisted of rice and vegetables, with the occasional morsel of meat or fish. But as the Chinese abandon the countryside, it seems they are abandoning their rural diets too. In 1962, the average Chinese person was eating just 4 kg of meat per year; by 2005 that figure was 60 kg and rising fast.[12] The inexorable rise of burgher and burger go hand in hand.

What, you might ask, is wrong with that? If we in the West have long enjoyed a meat-based diet, why shouldn't the Chinese – and anyone else who wants to – enjoy the same? The problem is that meat is a very environmentally costly food to produce. Most animals we consume today are fed on grain rather than grass, with one third of the world's crop going to feed animals, not people.[13] When you consider that it takes an estimated 11 times as much grain to feed a man if it passes through a cow first, that is hardly an efficient use of resources.[14] It also takes a staggering *thousand* times more water to produce a kilo of beef than of wheat, which, given that fresh water is in increasingly short supply worldwide, is not good news either. According to the UN, animal farming now accounts for a fifth of global greenhouse gas emissions, with forest clearances and methane emitted by cattle high on the list of contributors. Since climate change is a key driver of water shortages, our growing taste for meat is doubly damaging.

The impact of China's urbanisation can already be felt globally. With much of its land mass covered by mountain and desert, China has always struggled to feed itself, and as its population urbanises, it is fast becoming dependent on land-rich countries such as Brazil for its food. China is already the world's largest importer of grain and soya, and its demand is growing exponentially. In the 10 years to 2005, its soya imports from Brazil increased more than a hundredfold, and in 2006, the Brazilian government agreed to add another 90 million hectares to the 63 million already in production.[15] Needless to say, the extra land that is to go under the plough isn't any old scrubland nobody cares about. It is Amazonian rainforest, one of the richest and most ancient natural habitats on earth.

If the global future is urban, as every indication suggests it is, we need to take an urgent look at what that means. Until now, cities have existed largely on their own terms, commanding resources and consuming them more or less at will. That is going to have to change. The feeding of cities has been arguably the greatest force shaping civilisation, and it still is. In order to understand cities properly, we need to look at them through food. That, in essence, is what this book does. It suggests a new way of thinking about cities, not as autonomous, isolated entities, but as organic ones, bound by their appetites to the natural world. We need to put away our one-way telescopes and think holistically: use food to take a fresh look at how we build cities, feed them and dwell in them. In order to do that, we have to understand how we got here in the first place. We need to go back to a time before cities even existed; to a time when it was grain, and not meat, that held everyone's attention.

A New Food

Corn is a necessary; silver only a superfluity.
Adam Smith[16]

The origins of agriculture are obscure, but what can be said with some degree of certainty is that before farming came along, there were no cities. Half a million years before grain came on the menu, our ancestors were nomadic hunter-gatherers who spent their lives tracking the annual migrations of the beasts that formed the basis of their diet. Men had learned to shape the natural world with fire, using it to burn clearings in the forest to improve grazing for animals, and presumably to ward off predators too. Fire also helped our ancestors to survive in inhospitable habitats, such as Europe during the last Ice Age; and it must have provided at least some comfort in an otherwise bleak existence (one presumes woolly mammoth tasted better roast than raw). But despite man's command over fire, his life was still essentially peripatetic. Permanent settlements were about as much use to him as they were to the animals he hunted.

Around 12,000 years ago, all that began to change. As the last Ice Age retreated northwards, it left behind it a swathe of land so rich in natural foods that it has been dubbed 'the Fertile Crescent'. Running northwards from the Nile Delta, along the eastern seaboard of the

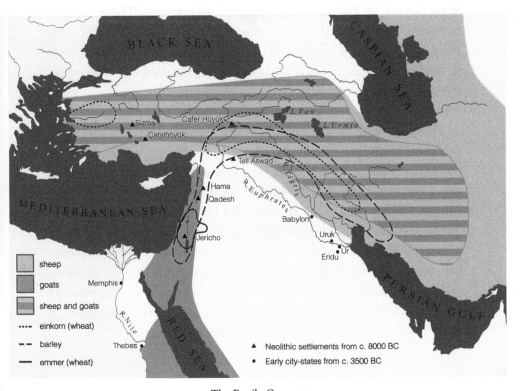

The Fertile Crescent.

Mediterranean as far as southern Anatolia (modern Turkey) and then southwards again through Mesopotamia (Iraq), the territory blossomed into an arcadia of oak forests and wild grasslands (the ancestors of wheat and barley) grazed by the forebears of the modern sheep and goat. The land was bursting with good things to eat, although it may not have seemed that way to its human inhabitants. To people used to a meat-based diet, the idea of eating wild grasses can't have been too appealing. But the growing pressure of population, together with the migration of larger animals northwards, probably forced their hand.

The first attempts of early farmers to harvest wild grain must have been frustrating, to put it mildly. The ears had to be gathered at the exact moment of ripening, or they would burst, scattering their seed and leaving nothing but an inedible husk behind. Pioneer harvesters probably set up temporary camps next to the fields in order to make sure that they were there at the critical moment; a practice that over the course of millennia led to the establishment of settled villages, such as those found in Palestine from around 10,000 BC. These villages, consisting of groups of circular stone-walled huts, suggest that early village life combined hunting and herding with the intensive gathering of wild grain, which would be laboriously processed by winnowing, threshing and stone-grinding, to make the world's first attempt at bread – or its first mashed-up grain paste, at any rate.[17]

The poor state of the villagers' teeth suggests that this earliest of processed foods made somewhat challenging eating – yet its discovery was to prove pivotal. For the first time in history, here was a food (albeit not a very palatable one) that could be gathered and stored in large enough quantities to allow at least some people, some of the time, to live in permanent settlements. Grain, in other words, was the means by which the land could be made to yield a food surplus – one which over the course of two millennia became increasingly secure, as the intensive gathering of wild grasses evolved into the conscious management of crops, through the saving and scattering of seed: until it became, in other words, what we would now describe as farming.

The First Cities

Jericho was an early settlement that characterised this period of transition from rural to urban life. Founded beside an oasis of the River Jordan in Palestine around 8000 BC, its inhabitants fed themselves partly through hunting, and partly through the intensive gathering of wild seeds, which they ground up to make flour. Life in Jericho was seasonal: the town was fully occupied during the harvest, but at other times its inhabitants would abandon it to go foraging in the countryside. The biblical account of Jericho's downfall, which refers to it being 'shut up' by divine intervention prior to Joshua's destruction of its walls, alludes to its heavy dependence on its rural links.[18] Without being able to lay aside emergency reserves of grain, being cut off from its food supply was fatal. Nobody is quite sure what finally did for Jericho, but whether earthquake, famine, or the playing of magic trumpets spelt its end, the event took place sometime around the late fourteenth or thirteenth century BC, by which time the town had survived for some 6,500 years. Not bad for a semi-rural mixed farming community.

Whether or not settlements such as Jericho count as cities is a matter of debate among archaeologists. The consensus is that they don't, because they fail to display the division of labour characteristic of urbanity. Nevertheless, Çatalhöyük in Anatolia, dating from about 7000 BC, at least marks the beginnings of urban civilisation. Çatalhöyük's many decorated shrines and elaborate craftwork suggest it had a rich cultural and religious life, indicating that having a stable, reasonably predictable food source gave people the freedom to indulge in non-essential creative pursuits: the characteristic activities of urban man.

Uruk, founded by the Sumerians in southern Mesopotamia around 3500 BC, is the first settlement that even the strictest of archaeologists agree was a proper city. Along with its neighbours Ur, Larsa and Nippur, it had what is now considered to be the *sine qua non* of fully fledged urbanism: zoning. Not the most exciting sounding attribute perhaps, but critical to the way the city was run. Uruk can claim to be the world's first true city, not because of its magnificent temples and monuments, but because its citizens were employed in specialised tasks, including the running of a civic administration.[19] To judge from its records, the latter was devoted almost entirely to managing the agricultural hinterland, and many experts believe it was the complexity of this task that led the Sumerians to invent writing.

In many ways, the location of this first attempt at full-blown urbanity was far from ideal. The land's fertility relied on the annual flooding of the Tigris and Euphrates rivers, which although rich in minerals from the northern hills were also highly unpredictable. The spring floods came too late for the growing season, so the floodwater had to be stored for later use. The city solved this problem by building a series of massive levees – the first municipal public works ever undertaken – to contain the river, and sophisticated irrigation systems to distribute the water evenly between outlying farms. The earthworks required constant upkeep and a massive investment of time and effort, but they were the means by which the flood-ravaged semi-desert was transformed into a blossoming oasis. Date palms flourished on the levees, along with a range of vegetables and legumes to keep any modern chef happy: chickpeas, lentils and beans; onions, garlic and leeks; cucumbers, cress, mustard and lettuce; dates, figs and grapes. Hardier crops such as wheat, barley and sesame grew further afield in irrigated paddocks.[20]

By moulding the natural world to suit their needs, Sumerian cities established the basic ground rules of urban civilisation. Their municipal market gardens were the world's first artificial landscapes, showing how nature might be modified to serve urban man. City and country combined to form a single entity, the city-state, and their mutual dependence, so clear in the ancient world and so obscure in ours, has underpinned urban existence ever since.

Man and Grain

Nobody in the ancient world ever took their food for granted. The fact that our words 'culture' and 'cultivate' share the same stem (the Roman *cultus*) tells its own story. Cultivation and civilisation in the Graeco-Roman world were inextricably linked. The ancient Greek word *sperma* referred to the seed of both man and grain, and the two were bound together in reality and myth. To Homer, man was, simply, 'bread-eater': a creature whom agriculture had transformed from a savage beast into a cultured, thinking being.

The bond between man and grain dominated life in the ancient city, with festivals that mirrored the agricultural calendar. Every year at harvest time, Athenians would decamp to Eleusis (the mythical 'original fields' where the earth goddess Demeter was said to have first taught man to cultivate) to celebrate the Eleusinia, a nine-day-long ritual of ceremony, fasting and feasting. Every four years the festival included inter-regional games, a sort of agrarian Olympics at which the victors were given not medals, but sacred ears of corn to take home to sow. Agrarian rites were also performed in the city. The Thesmophoria was a ritual in which women buried pig carcasses to ferment over the summer, returning in autumn for a three-day fast, after which they would mix the putrid remains with new seed to create a 'sacred compost' for the following year's sowing.[21] The importance of the ritual can be gauged from the fact that it took place on the Pnyx Hill, right under the noses of the all-male Athenian assembly. Women took part in similar fertility rites all over the ancient world. The figure of the Earth Mother was common to many archaic cultures, representing the female embodiment of the earth's mysterious power to nurture life. But the bounty of the earth could never be taken for granted. The success of the harvest was the gift of the gods, who must be appeased by ritual sacrifice. Death was necessary to bring forth new life; blood spilt to make the soil fertile.

For the Greeks and Romans, the bond between city and country would take on greater significance as their empires spread. With new cities to be founded in distant territories, choosing the right sites, and ensuring their capacity to support life, was vital. Sites for new Roman cities were chosen by augurs, who made careful observations of natural phenomena such as prevailing winds and the movements of animals before choosing the right spot. The city was then bound to the ground by the digging of a pit, the *mundus*, into which sacrifices to the gods of the underworld were thrown. The *mundus* marked the city's symbolic centre, through which it was 'married' to the soil.[22] In Rome itself, the *mundus* was in the Forum Romanum, guarded night and day by Vestal Virgins, whose sacred duty it was to tend the fire that burned there. The boundaries of Roman cities were also established by agrarian rites, with the ploughing of a sacred furrow, the *pomoerium*, along the line the walls would later follow. To cross the *pomoerium*, other than through its gates (where the plough was duly lifted), was a crime punishable by death; yet in Rome's foundation myth, that is precisely what Remus does, forcing his older brother Romulus to kill him. Remus' blood, of course, provided the necessary sacrifice to ensure the soil's fertility, and thus the city's future prosperity.

Through such rites, the ancients recognised their debt to farming, but also revealed its darker side. Grain may have liberated man, but its production had also imprisoned him in a life of toil; one that was chiefly viewed as the punishment of the gods. Myths abounded of an earlier, happier time, when food grew on trees and men did not have to labour in order to feed themselves. The Garden of Eden, partly derived from eighth-century Sumerian texts, was one such myth, as was the ancient Greek notion of a former Golden Age, described by the poet Hesiod as a time when men had dwelt in a 'fruitful grainland' that 'yielded its harvest to them of its own accord'.[23] Farming, according to Hesiod, was the punishment handed to man by Zeus in return for Prometheus' having stolen fire. The story is echoed in the Old Testament, in which Adam and Eve are banished from paradise as soon as they acquire self-knowledge. Agriculture, according to the Bible, is man's punishment for being human.

Taming Nature

Whatever their opinion of farming, the ancients accorded it a status equal to that of the cities it served. The fields and vineyards of ancient city-states were considered just as important as their streets and buildings, and rural citizens of the *polis* (city-state) of Athens enjoyed the same rights as their urban counterparts. Many Athenians owned farms, and farmers came frequently to town in order to vote, or carry out other business. Similarly, the cultivated land around Roman towns, the *ager*, was considered an extension of the *civitas*, the city. The *ager* was distinguished from *saltus*, wild and unproductive nature, which the

Romans viewed with disdain, or even dread. To Roman eyes, nature was split into two: the tame and the untamed, the productive and the unproductive, the good and the bad. It was a view that would persist as urbanity strengthened its hold on Western culture, but despite the Romans' best efforts, it never convinced the tribes of northern Europe.

Away from the Mediterranean, Europe was still covered in dense forest, and Teutonic myth bound men to trees, not grain. Northern forests were imbued with the spirit of the hero Wotan, whose self-sacrifice, hanging himself on a tree, led to his miraculous rebirth as a life-giving god. The event was celebrated by Germanic tribes with blood sacrifices; a practice the Roman historian Tacitus, rather two-facedly, declared repellent. Celts and Germans spent their lives hunting and fishing, and pasturing horses, cows and pigs in the forest. Indeed, pigs were so important to the northern economy that from the seventh century onwards, forests were measured not in terms of their physical dimensions, but by the number of animals they could sustain. With all this natural bounty, there was little need to build cities or engage in the tedious business of tilling the earth. As Caesar remarked of the Germans, 'for agriculture they have no zeal, and the greater part of their food consists of milk, cheese and flesh.'[24] Tacitus noted that the northerners preferred to live close to nature: 'None of the German tribes live in cities,' he wrote, 'they live separated and scattered, according as spring water, meadow or grove appeals to each man.'[25] Yet as Seneca observed, this natural lifestyle seemed to suit the Germans: 'They nourish themselves on the wild beasts which they hunt in the forest. Are they unhappy? No, there is no unhappiness in that which has become natural through habit; what has become necessity soon becomes pleasure . . .'[26]

The Roman view of Germania, a mixture of repulsion and admiration, summed up the cultural tensions between north and south. While life in the forest appeared uncivilised to the orderly Roman mind, it clearly offered protection from the urbane decadence to which Rome was then succumbing. The disdain was mutual, even if the admiration wasn't: when the 'barbarian' hordes came sweeping down across Rome's carefully manicured landscapes, they saw little there to engage them. Cities held no value for the forest-dwelling Germans, nor for the nomadic horsemen of the eastern Steppes, the Huns, who plundered them for portable treasures before sacking them and riding on.[27]

Who Owns the Land?

> The first man who, having enclosed a piece of ground, bethought himself of saying *This is mine*, and found people simple enough to believe him, was the real founder of civil society.
>
> Jean-Jacques Rousseau[28]

Cities may not have been universally appealing to early Europeans, but land was a commodity that everybody valued, whether hunter, nomad or city-dweller. The difference was in the way they used it. A German tribesman might keep a few cows and pigs, but he made little investment in feeding them. He might make a clearing in the forest to create pasture for cattle, or encourage wild deer to come there to graze, but that was about it. The vastness of the forest belonged to nobody. It was common territory, in which everyone was free to go and forage, raise pigs or hunt. But such an open-ended approach could never have worked in the agricultural south. Cultivated land didn't just offer up nuts, berries and pigs out of the blue – it required constant hard work, and needed to be protected. It had to be owned.

From the beginning, the cultivated farm belts around cities were owned by urban elites. Rich Sumerians leased out land to tenant farmers in return for rent or labour, the latter being especially valuable during the harvest, when there was invariably a shortage of manpower.[29] Similarly, pre-democratic Athens' rural hinterland was controlled by a land-owning elite, the Areopagoi, who used slave labour to produce oil and wine, much of it for export. The arrangement nearly caused the city's downfall, since the Areopagoi didn't generally bother with growing the less lucrative, yet far more necessary, grain. Yet despite their greed, the Areopagoi managed to hang on to power after the city became a democracy, largely because the law-giver Solon was one of their kind, and decreed that only the wealthiest citizens (i.e. landowners) should be allowed to hold public office.

In Rome, land ownership was not a prerequisite to power, but in a city obsessed with social prestige, it certainly helped. Many powerful Romans owned villas close to the capital, allowing them to enjoy the contemplative life in the countryside, as well as to attend to business in the city. Pliny the Younger's description of his seaside villa near Ostia, with its shady porticoes, fragrant vines and gentle sea breezes, reads like something out of a modern holiday brochure. But Roman villas were not just pleasant retreats: the majority were also working farms that used slave labour to produce high-value crops such as fruit and vegetables, poultry, fish and snails for the urban market. The agronomist Varro hailed the huge profits to be made from this *pastio villatica* (villa farming), advising farmers to focus on supplying 'a public banquet or somebody's triumph . . . or the *collegia* dinners that are now so numerous that they make the price of provisions go soaring'.[30] By Augustus' day, the suburbs of Rome were an endless sprawl of commercial farms, described by the Greek visitor Dionysius of Halicarnassus as merging seamlessly with the city:

> If anyone wishes to estimate the size of Rome by looking at these suburban regions, he will necessarily be misled for want of a definite clue by which to determine up to what point it is still the city and where it ceases to be the city; so closely is the city connected with the country, giving the beholder the impression of a city stretching out indefinitely.[31]

Rome, of course, was a monstrous aberration. For a thousand years after its fall, urban civilisation would wane in Europe, as 'barbarian' hunting cultures restored the concept of forest as privileged territory. However, by the ninth century, the forest no longer seemed limitless. Clearances for agriculture had encroached on its vastness, and influxes of tribes from the east brought new pressures to bear. Disputes over territory became increasingly common as various powers, including the monasteries, tried to secure exclusive rights over the forest for themselves.

The spread of Frankish and Gothic tribes brought a new understanding of the forest to northern Europe. Both cultures took hunting very seriously indeed, linking social prestige directly to its rituals. The right of Norman kings to hunt was considered a sacred privilege, and to meddle with their aim was a treasonable offence. Once William the Conqueror had defeated Harold at Hastings, he lost no time in annexing a quarter of his new kingdom as 'royal forest', which, as the name suggests, was territory in which the king, and only he, was allowed to hunt. Punishments for foraging and poaching were severe, ranging from the removal of one's eyes and testicles for the killing of a deer, to the less imaginative but undeniably effective penalty of death. All this would have been harsh enough, were it not for the fact that William's 'forest' included great swathes of countryside (including the entire county of Essex) which were not wooded at all, but included, as the historian Simon Schama has pointed out, 'tracts of pasture, meadow, cultivated farmland, and even towns'.[32] Quite what Essex Man, used to snaring himself the odd rabbit for the pot, was supposed to do under this draconian regime was anyone's guess. It was tantamount to a life sentence of covert criminality to those who had always made their living from the woods.

The Norman land-grab signalled the start of feudalism in England, and a system of land management that would dominate in some parts of Europe until well into the nineteenth century.[33] Feudalism came in many forms, but typically it consisted of large manorial estates or strips of land around villages or towns, which were owned by lords and worked by peasants, whose privileges depended largely on how their numbers matched up to the demand for labour. After a major plague, such as the Black Death, which wiped out a third of the population in Europe during the 1340s, a peasant's life could be tolerable. At such times, landowners might see their way to extending peasants' rights, allowing them to keep a proportion of their own produce, or even granting them ownership of their land, in exchange for military or other obligations. But when labour was plentiful, peasants' lives could be bleak, and they were often treated as little better than slaves. The serfs who worked on Russian grain estates, for instance, could be branded or sold at public auction, and one law of 1649 allowed the torture of children who denied their feudal bond to lord and land.[34]

Feudalism didn't spread much happiness, nor was it very good at producing food; it was the latter failing, rather than the numerous peasant revolts that characterised its history, that would eventually prove its downfall. As a system of land management, feudalism was just about capable of sustaining an essentially rural population. As a means of feeding cities, it was next to useless.

Town and Country

By early medieval times, urban civilisation was making a comeback in Europe. Ever since the fall of Rome, monasteries had provided some civilised sanctuary amidst the lawlessness that raged over the continent, and by the ninth century, thanks chiefly to the Christian conversion of the Frankish king Charlemagne, they had gained an impressive foothold. Some were so large, they were effectively towns in their own right: the monastery of Tours, with a population of 20,000, was one of the largest settlements in Europe.[35] With their close-knit, self-sufficient communities, protective walls and market gardens, monasteries provided the template for a new kind of city. From the eleventh century onwards, fortified 'communes' began to appear in northern Italy and Spain, France, Germany and the Low Countries, reviving the ancient city-state in a new, Christian configuration.

One such commune, Siena, has a council chamber with one of the finest views in all of Italy. A large rectangular room set high within the city's thirteenth-century town hall, the Sala dei Nove has a great window that looks out over a classic Tuscan landscape, with its gently rolling patchwork of vineyards, olive groves, villas and cypresses. That the landscape has barely changed in nearly 700 years becomes evident when one looks at the frescoes decorating the room, painted by Ambrogio Lorenzetti in 1338. To the left of the window is a fresco entitled *The Effects of Good Government on City and Country*, depicting a tidy, well-maintained Siena surrounded by a neat landscape just like the one outside. Peasants till the fields, two huntsmen set off with a pack of orderly hounds, a farmer enters the city with mules laden with corn, and another drives a flock of sheep to market. City and country exude peace and prosperity – which is more than can be said for the scenes on the opposite wall. In *The Allegory and Effects of Bad Government*, war is raging in the countryside, the fields are a burnt-out wasteland, and Siena itself resembles a medieval sink estate, with broken windows, dilapidated buildings, and a populace intent on robbing and fighting one another. Even if the Council of Nine never uttered a word in that room, the walls themselves – and the view outside – would have carried the argument for them. Look after your countryside, and it will look after you.

The Lorenzetti fresco captures a unique moment in urban history: one in which city and country co-existed in relative harmony. Unlike ancient city-states, whose rural hinterlands were owned almost exclusively by urban elites, the farmland around Italian communes was managed by city councillors, whose mercantile instincts brought a completely new perspective to farming. Recognising the value of maximising agricultural yields, many communes released their serfs to become land-owning peasants, or *contadini*, encouraging them to work the land far harder. In 1257, Bologna freed 6,000 serfs in one go in exchange for the receipt of half their produce every year – a move considered by the sociologist Henri Lefebvre to have marked the arrival of the world's first capitalist agriculture.[36]

Italian communes were in many ways ahead of their time, but their intimate involvement with their rural hinterlands was far from unique in the pre-industrial world. City-dwellers all over Europe retained close links with the countryside. Rich townsfolk often had country estates from which they kept themselves supplied with grain, poultry and vegetables, while poorer ones had smallholdings that they would periodically leave the city in order to farm. When the merchant classes, or bourgeoisie, came on the scene, they operated somewhere in between, building themselves country houses in order to imitate the lifestyles of the rich, but also making money from commercial farming. As a result, the suburbs of Renaissance Rome were almost as full of farms and villas as they had been in ancient times, with the difference that the typical fifteenth-century farmer possessed his own olive grove or vineyard and tended it himself. The city became so deserted at harvest times that a statute had to be passed suspending civic justice during those periods.[37]

Not only did pre-industrial city-dwellers go regularly into the countryside, many also brought the country to the city. People commonly kept pigs and chickens in their houses, and grain and hay were often stored in yards too. Many houses resembled urban farms – an appearance that was not to everyone's taste. The eighteenth-century German economist Ernst Ludwig Carl deplored the 'piles of dung' clogging up the nation's cities, suggesting it would be far preferable 'to ban all farming in towns, and to put it in the hands of those suited to it'.[38] But despite such protestations, people continued to farm in cities until well into the nineteenth century – even those as large as London. In 1856, the Victorian historian George Dodd described one 'extraordinary piggery at Kensington' as follows:

> A group of wretched tenements, known as 'The Potteries', inhabited by a population of 1000 or 1200 persons, all engaged in the rearing of pigs; the pigs usually outnumbered the people three to one, and had their sties mixed up with the dwelling-houses; some of the pigs lived in the houses and even under the beds.[39]

Whatever they might have thought of farming, no pre-industrial city-dweller could forget it existed. As the social historian Fernand Braudel remarked, 'Town and country never separate like oil and water. They are at the same time separate yet drawn together, divided yet combined.'[40]

Good City, Bad City

Despite the close links between town and country in early modern Europe, the idea that urban life was civilised and rural life boorish frequently prevailed. Although the vast majority lived on the land, social life in Tudor England revolved increasingly around cities, with the landed gentry deserting their estates every winter for London; the beginnings of the so-called 'London Season'. Urban life was compared favourably to the 'great rudeness and barbarous custom of dwelling in the country', while cities themselves were small and, in the opinion of their inhabitants, perfectly formed, often being described as 'fair' and 'pretty'.[41]

However, things were about to change. As cities grew larger (and smoggier, thanks to the increasing use of coal), their perceived moral stock began to decline. In 1548, Hugh Latimer, Bishop of Worcester, delivered a lacerating sermon on the steps of St Paul's, accusing Londoners of 'pride, covetousness, cruelty, and oppression', and assuring them that 'if the ploughmen in the country were as negligent in their office as prelates be, we should not long live, for lack of sustenance'.[42] Latimer's use of the plough as an image of virtue was to become a recurrent theme in centuries to come. As cities prospered and glittered, the rural view of them became increasingly jaundiced, as the admirably succinct 1630 ditty 'The Poor Man Paies for All' suggests:

> The King he governs all,
> The Parson pray for all,
> The Lawer plead for all,
> The Ploughman pay for all,
> And feed all.[43]

By the seventeenth century, it wasn't just country folk who found cities distasteful. Poets and philosophers were also starting to show a preference for the countryside; for, as the prominent Quaker William Penn put it, 'there we see the works of God; but in cities little else but the works of men'.[44] Penn demonstrated his love of nature by departing for somewhere he could get his paws on plenty of it: North America, a large tract of which (Pennsylvania) still bears his name.[45] While Penn and others sailed off to pastures new, the nation they abandoned remained in the grip of a pastoral obsession. The purity and innocence of the countryside were extolled in paintings, poetry and plays, such as John Fletcher's *The Faithful Shepherdess*, performed at court in 1633 with the inclusion, at the author's insistence, of real shepherds and sheep. But as the historian Keith Thomas pointed out in his book *Man and the Natural World*, such fantasies were born of the increasing distance between town and country: '. . . the growing tendency to disparage urban life and to look to the countryside as a symbol of innocence rested on a series of illusions. It involved that wholly false view of rural social relationships which underlies all pastoral.'[46]

Meanwhile, the countryside of Stuart England was fast becoming a manmade landscape, as it scrambled to meet the cities' growing demand for food. Agricultural improvement was the new moral imperative; the question was, how was it to be achieved? The answer came from the one nation that was predominantly urban earlier than England: the Netherlands. By the mid seventeenth century, more than half the Dutch lived in towns, and the land (much of which had been reclaimed from the sea) was working overtime to feed the population. Dutch farms consisted of small, sandy plots made fertile by deep digging, constant weeding and plenty of fertiliser, much of the latter provided by the towns in the form of wood ash and manure. Country and city were linked by a close network of canals, which carried waste from the towns to the farms and brought food back in the opposite direction. But perhaps the most important legacy of Dutch farming was the use of fodder crops, both to improve the soil and to provide winter feed for animals, which hitherto had to be slaughtered in late autumn. The value of these techniques was noted by English farmers, particularly those in the south-east, who enjoyed close trading links with the Dutch. The planting of fodder crops, popularised by Charles 'Turnip' Townshend at the start of the eighteenth century, was a symbol of the English Agricultural Revolution, but it had been practised in the Netherlands – and parts of East Anglia – for decades before he was even born.

Robbing the Commons

As Jean-Jacques Rousseau would later note, when men invest a lot of effort in land, they tend to want to own it. As marshes were drained and trees felled in England after the Civil War, the enclosure of common land was actively encouraged by Parliament, with the result that the traditional feudal landscape – large, open fields with village-based strip-farming – began to disappear under thousands of acres of neatly hedged, privately owned rectangles. The rural scenes that we think of today as typically English were the result of this particular land-grab, the like of which had not been seen since the days of the Normans. The comparison was not lost on those who witnessed it, as one contemporary verse suggests:

> The law locks up the man or woman,
> Who steals the goose from off the common,
> But leaves the greater villain loose
> Who steals the common from the goose.[47]

To make matters worse, this second dispossession of rural England was not being perpetrated by some foreign despot, but by the nation's own parliament. Although the changes were arguably necessary in order to feed the expanding urban population, the speed of change, and the manner of it, was brutal.

The upheavals brought the 'land question' once more to the fore, with battle lines drawn between Sir Robert Filmer, champion of the 'Divine Right' school of thought, and John Locke, co-founder of the Whig Party and one of England's foremost political philosophers. Filmer's logic, published in his treatise of 1680, *Patriarcha, or the Natural Power of Kings*, went thus: God had given the earth to Adam, and since Adam was the 'first monarch' of mankind, all monarchs who succeeded him inherited the earth by divine right. Stuff and nonsense, said Locke: Adam may have inherited the earth, but he did so on behalf of *all* mankind, not just on behalf of himself and his offspring. Locke's refutation of Filmer took up the whole of the first of his *Two Treatises of Government*, written in 1690. Having demolished Filmer in the first volume, Locke spent the second pondering how, if the earth belonged to everyone, any individual could claim a piece of it for himself. The answer, he concluded, was by investing labour in it:

> He that is nourished by the acorns he picked up under an oak, or the apples he gathered from the trees in the wood, has certainly appropriated them to himself. Nobody can deny but the nourishment is his. I ask, then, when did they begin to be his? when he digested? or when he ate? or when he boiled? or when he brought them home? or when he picked them up? And it is plain, if the first gathering

made them not his, nothing else could. That labour put a distinction between them and common.[48]

It followed that if a farmer tilled the land, he earned the right to call it his own. However (and here was the rub), this was only true *provided each man took only what he needed*, and no more. A farmer could enclose his land, so long as he was not greedy, and left enough for others. Locke's ideas – that each man had the natural right to liberty, freedom and subsistence – would form the basis of the social contract at the heart of liberal democratic thought; and they were about to be put to the test in America, where, theoretically at least, there should have been enough land to go round. As it turned out, there wasn't. The invidious treatment by European settlers of the Native Americans (who, thanks to their hunter-gatherer lifestyles, had never felt the need to lay claim to their land by planting hedges around it) soon put paid to any notion that the New World might deal with the land question any more equably than the old one had.

Part of the problem, of course, was that Locke's ideas were formulated from a farming perspective, not that of a hunter-gatherer. While Locke's concept of liberty was eventually bound into the American Constitution through Thomas Jefferson's 1776 Declaration of Independence, Native Americans forfeited their right to land because they lived *on* it, not off it. They trod too lightly to put down markers that Europeans might have recognised or understood. As it was, the concept of common land was as doomed in the vastness of North America as it was in the tiny island nation that sought to colonise it.

War of the Wens

While Native Americans were being robbed of their land in the New World, the peasant dream of a plot of one's own was fast disappearing in the old one. The process of enclosure in England accelerated rapidly during the eighteenth century, resulting in the annexing of some million hectares by the century's end.[49] Yet progress was still too slow for the nation's greatest champion of agricultural reform, Arthur Young. Surveying the country in 1773, Young declared the amount of land that remained uncultivated 'a disgrace', announcing his intention to bring 'the wastelands of the Kingdom into culture' and 'cover them with turnips, corn and clover'.[50] Although not raised a farmer, Young acquired an Essex farm in 1767, where he conducted a series of technical experiments, publishing the results in his *Annals of Agriculture*, which were so well received they ran to 45 volumes, and even enjoyed the occasional anonymous contribution from King George III. As his fame spread, Young took to travelling, preaching agricultural reform throughout Britain, France and Italy, lecturing to rapt audiences wherever he went.

For Young and his followers, the growth of cities represented a fabulous opportunity for farmers to modernise; to develop what Young called 'agriculture animated by a great demand'.[51] But his enthusiasm was not universally shared. To William Cobbett, gentleman farmer, political essayist and tireless campaigner on behalf of the rural poor, cities were 'wens': parasitical boils that consumed everything in their path. Those who lived in them were little better: they were the undeserving and ungrateful beneficiaries of others' sweat and toil. 'We who are at anything else,' he wrote, 'are deserters from the plough.'[52] Cobbett, unlike Young, was the son of a Surrey smallholder, and he identified personally with the agricultural labourers he considered 'the very best and most virtuous of all mankind'.[53] He dedicated himself to their cause, publishing a stream of invective in his paper, the *Political Register*, against the systems and policies that were destroying rural life. Cobbett's disgust for London was such that he could barely bring himself to mention it by name, dubbing it instead 'the Great Wen'. Yet since his political life forced him to spend a considerable amount of time there, he put it to good use, going on a series of exploratory journeys to see the effects of urbanisation for himself. His subsequent account, published as *Rural Rides* in 1830, emerged as a bitter diatribe against cities:

> Have I not, for twenty years, been regretting the existence of these
> unnatural embossments; these white-swellings, these odious wens,

Highgate in the late eighteenth century, looking towards London. The idyllic scene masks the growing tensions between city and country.

produced by Corruption and engendering crime and misery and slavery? But, what is to be the fate of the greatest wen of all? The monster, called, by the silly coxcombs of the press, 'the metropolis of the empire'?[54]

Cobbett's solution was simple. He wanted to 'disperse' all the wens in England: literally lance them like boils, and return the countryside to its former state. He would be far from the last person to have such a wish, but, sadly for him, the urban tide was already flowing unstoppably in the opposite direction.

Across the Channel, however, people watched the 'English miracle' with interest. While the Dutch and English had been engaging in land reform and inventing newfangled farming techniques, the French had remained mired in the past, with unimproved wastelands, crippling peasant taxes and convoluted patterns of ownership all serving to hamper agricultural production. Just as English farmers in the previous century had learned from the Dutch, French envoys now travelled to

England to gain desperately needed farming knowledge. Uneasy relations between the two countries meant that agricultural espionage was rife: in 1763, the French government defied the English ban on exporting animals, paying for three Lincolnshire rams and six ewes to be smuggled illegally into France; while English turnip seeds made an unexpected appearance at the Parisian Royal Agricultural Society in 1785, where they were distributed among its members.[55] As enthusiasm for agricultural reform took hold, a new wave of pastoralism hit the French. Painters such as Fragonard and Boucher portrayed the country-side as a sort of idealised picnic-ground populated by creamy-fleshed nymphs, and Marie-Antoinette famously dressed up as a shepherdess to keep company with her sheep in Le Hameau de la Reine, a rustic retreat constructed for her in the gardens at Versailles.

But for one member of Parisian society, such pastoralist fantasies were symptomatic of a deep malaise. Jean-Jacques Rousseau was raised in the mountains around Geneva, but had moved to Paris as a young man, and found it not to his liking. For him, city and country were bound together on a path towards self-destruction, fuelled by the call to 'progress' that drove them on. His 1755 *Discourse on the Origin and Basis of Inequality Among Men* was a paean to man's lost innocence:

> So long as men remained content with their rustic huts, so long as they were satisfied with clothes made of the skins of animals and sewn together with thorns and fish-bones . . . they lived free, healthy, honest and happy lives . . . but from the moment it appeared advantageous to any one man to have enough provisions for two, equality disappeared, property was introduced, work became indispensable, and vast forests became smiling fields, which man had to water with the sweat of his brow, and where slavery and misery were soon seen to germinate and grow up with the crops.[56]

By swapping the pastoralist fantasy for that of the noble savage, Rousseau's *Discourse* was tantamount to a critique of civilisation itself. Like Seneca before him, Rousseau believed that the life of primitive man in the 'vast forests' must once have been happy, but Seneca, good Roman that he was, could hardly have approved of Rousseau's conclusion that it 'was iron and corn which first civilised men, and ruined humanity'. For Rousseau, agriculture was as much to blame for man's misfortune as cities were. He warmed to his theme with a series of romantic novels: thinly disguised polemical tracts whose innocent heroes and heroines led lives of exemplary purity in the mountains, living on fruit, milk and honey.[57] Unsurprisingly, these forerunners of Heidi didn't go down too well with some of Rousseau's Parisian contemporaries, Voltaire among them, who greeted the author's announcement that he was heading for the mountains in order to practise what he preached with howls of derision. But it was Rousseau's view that would prove the more enduring. By disparaging cultivated landscape in favour of wilderness, he paved the way for Romanticism, creating a schism in the urban view of nature that helped to shape the modern world.

The Invisible Land

Any remaining pastoral fantasies in England were soon to be swept away by the onset of industrial farming. Half the iron produced during the eighteenth century went to make ploughs and horseshoes, and from the mid nineteenth century onwards, farm machinery began to transform English agriculture. Horse-drawn drills and reapers, and later steam-driven threshers, drastically reduced the number of people needed to work on the land, while various industrial by-products, such as the lime-rich slag created by steel production, allowed the manufacture of artificial fertilisers that could double farmers' yields. Food was being produced in larger quantities than ever before, and by fewer people; and as rural workers headed to the cities, the social bonds that held rural communities together – and linked city to country – began to disintegrate. The gap between the feeders and the fed was widening, and it was about to get a whole lot wider.

Ten years after Cobbett's *Rural Rides* came an invention that would render all resistance to urban expansion useless. In the space of a few years, the railways removed all the constraints that had hitherto chained cities to their rural back gardens. From now on, cities would be able to get their food from more or less anywhere. The food economy was about to go global, and nowhere was the effect more dramatic than in the American Midwest, a vast prairie ripe for exploitation. By the mid nineteenth century there were some million and a half farmers in North America, most of them European settlers who had acquired their land along Lockean principles, by investing years of labour in it. Their combined grain-producing potential was enormous, but with the Appalachian Mountains in the way, there was no easy way of transporting the grain to the East Coast. The Erie Canal, a 360-mile-long, 83-lock 'eighth wonder of the world', completed in 1825, had shown the potential of such a connection, providing a water passage from the interior to New York. Thanks to its inland empire, New York soon outstripped its rivals Boston and Philadelphia, earning itself the nickname 'Empire State'. But it was only when the Appalachians were breached by the railroads during the 1850s that the true impact of American grain would be felt on the global stage.

The railroads brought thousands of acres of previously inaccessible farmland into the food chain for the first time, delivering efficiencies of which Arthur Young could only have dreamt. The American prairies weren't worked by serfs enslaved by a noble lord or obliged to feed their local populace. They were commercial enterprises whose temples were the towering elevators that transferred their grain into ships bound for distant markets. Limitless quantities of cheap grain began to arrive in Europe in the 1870s, sparking an agricultural depression from which the continent would never fully recover. Rural Britain was hit particularly hard: with more than half the British population living in cities, food shortages were acute, and feeding the urban poor was a more urgent government priority than protecting local farmers. While most other European countries imposed import tariffs on American grain (Bismarck tripled import duties in Germany in order to protect its powerful land-owning classes), Britain went the other way. Having abandoned protectionism with the repeal of its Corn Laws in 1846, it once again felt the pain of agricultural reform as a short sharp shock, rather than dragging out the inevitable.

Grain wasn't the only cheap food coming out of America. The expense and difficulty of feeding cattle had always meant that meat was a luxury food, but with a surplus of feed available, it now became possible to raise animals in artificial feed lots, preserving their carcasses after slaughter by 'packing' them with grain and salt. By the early nineteenth century, Cincinnati was the centre of the new 'meat-packing' industry, processing thousands of hogs and dispatching them down the Ohio River to the East Coast. The hogs were 'disassembled' in purpose-built slaughterhouses, where they were slaughtered, butchered, cured and canned, all along a single conveyored production line. There was no room for sentimentality in such a process: the animals were treated brutally, shackled to a wheel by their hind legs and dragged backwards before being hoisted up in the air to have their throats cut without prior stunning. Cruel though it was, the automated

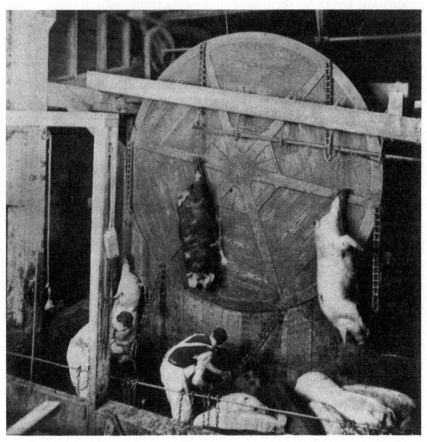

A state-of-the-art Chicago packing house, early twentieth century.

disassembly line was certainly efficient: by 1848, Cincinnati (or 'Porkopolis', as it became known) was the undisputed meat-packing capital of the world, processing half a million hogs a year. Its position seemed assured – until the railroads came along and nullified its strategic advantage at a stroke. Cincinnati was forced to cede its mantle to Chicago, whose Union Stockyards took meat-packing to a whole new level. Covering more than a square mile and employing some 75,000 people, they were a city within a city, with their own water and electricity supply, bank, hotel and even newspaper, the *Drovers' Journal*. According to the *Chicago Tribune*, the Stockyards were the 'eighth wonder of the world' (which perhaps should have been the ninth, since the Erie Canal had already been built). In any case, they were certainly prodigious. By 1872, they were processing three million cattle, hogs and sheep annually, rising to 17 million by 1905.

Grain was the food that made the ancient city, but meat made the industrial one. Factory workers needed higher-octane fuel to get them through the day, and meat was what they demanded for their dinner. British meat consumption increased threefold in the 20 years after 1870, with most of the increase accounted for by imported meat. Meat-packing made cheap meat widely available for the first time, so setting the scene for modern urban consumption, and the ruthless efficiencies and economies of scale necessary to satisfy it. America wasn't the only nation getting into factory food production either. Two European nations, Denmark and the Netherlands, saw an additional opportunity presented by cheap American grain. Both countries began to build factory farms in which pigs and chickens could be reared intensively on imported feed, exporting the results to the British in the form of bacon and eggs, as both still do today.

For the first time, cities had a cheap, reliable source of food. Prices plummeted, revolutionising living standards for the urban poor. So, did city-dwellers burst with gratitude, composing grateful sonnets to the glorious meat-packers of the New World? Not a bit of it. Perhaps understandably, people preferred to marvel at the engineering feats of the age, rather than contemplate the industrialised rendition of pork fat, even though the latter was having just as great an impact on their standard of living. Industrialisation might have brought people cheap food, but by denaturing farming, it also created an irreparable gulf between the feeders and the fed. That left just one kind of 'nature' capable of capturing the urban imagination: wilderness. Rousseau had been ahead of his time.[58]

Back to the Woods

By the mid nineteenth century, the cities that were once extolled as centres of beauty had descended into smog-ridden hell-pits. While writers such as Dickens, Hugo and Zola chronicled the degradations of industrial urbanity, others took a leaf out of Rousseau's book, wandering off to rediscover the wild. Prominent among them was the American proto-environmentalist Henry David Thoreau, who spent two years living in a rustic cabin in the Massachusetts woods, recording his experiences in *Walden, or Life in the Woods*, published in 1854. The book's central theme was a plea for men to abandon the complexities of urban existence and embrace a simpler life closer to nature. Thoreau tried to lead by example, detailing his uneventful days spent cultivating his bean patch, listening to birds, and bathing in the eponymous Walden Pond, while ruminating on the shortcomings of the civilised society he had left behind: 'Our life is frittered away by detail. Simplicity, simplicity, simplicity! I say, let your affairs be as two or three, and not a hundred or a thousand.'[59]

Although Thoreau made much of his self-imposed exile, in reality his hut was only a mile and a half from his native town of Concord, where he would repair occasionally for a bit of human company, or to pick up supplies. Not that such details made any difference to his readers. To them, Thoreau was the true prophet of living wild, his example a clarion call to lead a purer, truer life. *Walden* might not have been the instant success Thoreau had hoped for, but after his death, its popularity grew steadily, as its message, 'in wilderness is the preservation of the world', struck the perfect chord with the nascent environmental movement.

Thoreau may have heard the call of the wild, but it was the Scottish-born geologist John Muir who became its most effective mouthpiece.

Yosemite Valley – nature reconfigured as temple.

Muir's credentials as a woodsman were rather more impressive than were Thoreau's: his induction in the 'university of the wilderness' consisted of a 1,000-mile walk from Indiana to Florida, and he spent most of his life in the wild, including what became a revelatory sojourn in the Yosemite Valley, Sierra Nevada. On his first visit there in 1868, Muir was struck by the natural beauty of what he called 'the grandest of all special temples of Nature', and he immediately accepted a series of casual jobs that would allow him to remain there. Over the next five years, he lived rough in the mountains, earning his keep as a shepherd, sawmill operator and ferryman, all the while studying the craggy rocks that he was increasingly coming to resemble. Over time, he became convinced that Yosemite should be protected from man's influence, and in 1889 he wrote two articles in *Century* magazine, advocating that it should be made into a national park, from which all human activity was excluded. (The sheep he had gladly tended 20 years earlier were now described as 'hooved locusts'.) Muir attracted some powerful friends to his cause, including President Theodore 'Teddy' Roosevelt, whose conversion came on a 1903 camping trip with Muir during which the president had to be dug out of a snowdrift. Muir's efforts were rewarded in 1905, when Yosemite was granted the status of a national park.

The idea that 'proper' wilderness should be untouched by human hand was a curious legacy of Thoreau and Muir, since both men recognised the role of man in creating the landscapes they so admired. Muir's early writings described how the Ahwahneechee Indians had helped to shape Yosemite, and he wondered, not without a hint of jealousy, at their deep knowledge of their natural habitat: 'Like the Indians, we ought to know how to get the starch out of fern and saxifrage stalks, lily bulbs, pine bark etc. Our education has been sadly neglected for many generations.' Muir also noted approvingly how the Indians lived alongside nature – 'Indians walk softly and hurt the landscape hardly more than the birds and squirrels' – but as he got older, he could condone less and less the thought of any human intervention in his precious wilderness. As the historian Simon Schama remarked, the Indians' memory at Yosemite was 'carefully and forcibly edited out of the idyll'.[60]

Like Thoreau before him, Muir created a reverence for wilderness that became the equivalent of a religion. 'Everybody needs beauty as well as bread,' he wrote in *The Yosemite* in 1912, 'places to play in and pray in, where nature may heal and give strength to body and soul alike.' Absolutely. But the question of where that bread was going to come from was something about which Muir had a lot less to say.

The Artificial Soil

> The nation that destroys its soil, destroys itself.
> Franklin D. Roosevelt

By the mid nineteenth century, the age-old struggle to supply cities with food seemed to have been solved. The question was no longer *whether* cities could be fed, but how much it would cost to feed them.

As far as urban consumers were concerned, all the ancient fears about food – the fertility of the soil, the sun and the rain, the strength of the harvest – translated into one concern: the size of their weekly shopping bill. Cut off from the land as never before, city-dwellers began to disassociate food from the very idea of nature.

Which was precisely what farmers were trying to do. The whole point of farming had always been to produce food as cheaply and reliably as possible; a pursuit in which the vagaries of nature were the chief enemy. Farmers had always sought ways to tame their old adversary; now it seemed they had finally found some. In 1836, the German chemist Justus von Liebig had investigated the chief nutrients necessary to plant life, concluding they were carbon dioxide, nitrogen, phosphorus and potassium. Liebig went on to manufacture the world's first mineral fertiliser, earning himself the soubriquet 'father of fertiliser' (although he could equally well have been called 'father of the stock cube', since he also pioneered the meat extraction process and co-founded the OXO company).

At first, results were encouraging. With the help of manmade chemicals, farmers found that yields were steadily rising, and it looked as though hunger would soon be consigned to history. But after a few years, yields began to fall again, and farmers found they were having to use ever more potent cocktails just to maintain their crops.[61] It seemed that artificial fertilisers were no substitute for the natural balance of the soil provided by mixed vegetation – used over long periods, they actually stunted its fertility. Towards the end of his life, Liebig became disillusioned with his efforts. 'I have sinned against the Creator,' he wrote, 'and justly I have been punished. I wanted to improve his work because, in my blindness, I believed that a link in the astonishing chain of laws that govern and constantly renew life on the surface of the earth had been forgotten.'[62] Liebig may have thought better of interfering with nature, but by then the genie was out of the bottle. Towering American silos demanded constant supplies of grain, not a mixed diet of wheat, turnips, barley and clover. Chemical fertiliser had already become a necessary prop to commercial farming.

Worldwide food shortages during the First World War meant there were huge profits to be made from grain, and even marginal farmland in America was ploughed up in order to increase production. American farmers grew rich, but slowly, surely, the land was being exhausted. Stripped of its natural vegetation and continuously exploited year after year, the topsoil was being sucked dry of humus and losing its capacity to retain moisture. Then, during the 1930s, the worst possible thing happened: the rains failed. Eight years of drought turned the Great Plains into a desert. Without any plant fibres to hold it down, the topsoil simply blew away in a series of devastating dust storms known as 'black blizzards'. Four hundred thousand farmers – the 'Okies' of John Steinbeck's *Grapes of Wrath* – lost everything, and were forced to migrate west in search of work.

The Dust Bowl was a massive body blow to the brave new world of commercial farming. Franklin D. Roosevelt responded by setting up the US Soil Conservation Service in 1935, the first such body in the world. The disaster had repercussions across the Atlantic too. It inspired Lady Eve Balfour, one of the first women to graduate from agricultural college, to set up the first comparative study of organic and chemical-based farming methods on her farm at Haughley, Suffolk, in 1939. She ran two mixed farms side by side, one as a closed organic system, and the other using chemical inputs. The experiment confirmed what Justus von Liebig had suspected a century earlier. Balfour found that while the organic farm developed a robust cycle in which soil nutrients peaked naturally during the growing season, the fertilised farm developed a dependency on its chemical 'fix', in what she described as 'a manner suggestive of drug addiction'.[63] Not only did the organic farm maintain nutrient levels as high as those of the fertilised one, but, according to Balfour, the cows that grazed it were 'noticeably more contented' than their chemically dosed-up counterparts, producing 15 per cent more milk. Balfour's account of her findings, published as *The Living Soil* in 1943, remains a classic text of the organic movement, and she went on to co-found the Soil Association three years after its publication.

Soil fertility is not the only perennial source of vexation to farmers. Another is pests. For millennia, farmers have tried everything to control them. The Chinese harnessed ant power in the battle against aphids; the Romans used sulphur to beat the *bestiolae*. Such methods worked to a degree, but eventually the bugs always seemed to get the upper hand. Until, that is, the discovery just before the Second World War of a chemical capable of delivering insect Armageddon: dichlorodiphenyl-trichloroethane, or DDT. The chemical was first manufactured as early as 1873, but its spectacular pesticidal qualities were only discovered in 1939 when the Swiss scientist Paul Hermann Muller had the idea of using it to control insect-borne diseases such as malaria; a piece of work that earned him the Nobel Prize for Physiology and Medicine. Throughout the war, DDT was used by Allied troops to kill mosquitoes and nits. It was only later that people would think of using it on crops.

On the eve of war, farming in Britain remained essentially its old nineteenth-century self. With cheap food imports available from overseas, British farmers had coasted along for years, and the nation's half-million farms were mostly of the small-scale 'Old McDonald' variety, with a few cows, pigs and chickens and some arable land. The nearest most came to progress was a carthorse; there were still 640,000 working the land in 1939, as opposed to just 100,000 tractors.[64] But when German U-boats cut off Atlantic supply lines, the inadequacies of British farming were made all too apparent. The country suffered its worst food shortages in more than a century. The famous 'Dig for Victory' campaign, in which patches of land as unlikely as Kensington Gardens went under the plough, got the nation through the crisis, but after the war, the Attlee government was determined that Britain should never be as vulnerable again. The 1947 Agriculture Act was the result: a licence to slash, dump and spray in the name of increased productivity.

The last great transformation of the British countryside now took place, as the land was cleared of obstacles, enriched with fertilisers and doused in DDT in a bid to make the nation self-sufficient in food. In the 50 years after the war, Britain lost an estimated 190,000 miles of hedgerow, 97 per cent of its flower meadows and 60 per cent of its ancient woodlands.[65] But dramatic though the changes were, they were only half the story. The rest became apparent in 1962 with the publication of *Silent Spring*, an explosive investigation into the effects of DDT by the American biologist Rachel Carson. Carson showed that by indiscriminately killing off virtually all insect life, DDT had a devastating effect not only on its intended victims, but on the rest of the food chain too, passing directly into birds and eventually into humans, causing cancers and other diseases. Carson argued that in the future, the spring would be silent, because there would be no birds left to sing.

The book brought the predictable howls of protest from the chemical lobby, led by the US biochemical company Monsanto, which published a pamphlet entitled *The Desolate Year*, rubbishing *Silent Spring* and describing the devastation that would be caused if pesticides were *not* used. However, Carson's evidence was enough to persuade the American and European governments to ban the use of DDT on crops – which, had this been Hollywood, should have been the end of the story. Instead, it was just the beginning. Far from waning, the use of indiscriminate pesticides, including DDT, has increased in the developing world, with all the predictable side effects. According to the World Health Organisation, between one and five million pesticide poisonings take place every year, leading to 20,000 deaths, virtually all in developing countries.[66]

Mad Cows and Englishmen

For 40 years after the war, British consumers enjoyed ever-cheaper food, blissfully unaware of the crises brewing in the farming industry. Tough times make for tough attitudes, and for a nation recovering from austerity, the prospect of cheap food was too attractive to quibble about how it was produced. Battery farming was introduced with barely a murmur of public protest; the fact that animals were being pumped full of hormones and antibiotics – and fed the ground-up remains of their fellows – went unnoticed. British farming had entered its post-industrial, invisible phase.

For a while, as yields rose and prices fell, everything in the garden seemed rosy. But then it was payback time. From Edwina Currie's salmonella-infected eggs in 1988, to BSE in 1992 and the foot and mouth epidemic in 2001, British farming was hit by a series of scandals and plagues of truly biblical proportions. The crises couldn't have come at a worse time for British farmers, already struggling to survive in the global market, but the Policy Commission on the Future of Food and Farming, chaired by Sir Donald Curry in 2001, wasn't very sympathetic. The Commission delivered a damning verdict on the state of British farming, calling it 'dysfunctional' and 'unsustainable', and blaming subsidies from the Common Agricultural Policy (CAP) for masking its inefficiencies. The CAP should be abolished, the report concluded, and farmers left to sink or swim in the global market. Farmers would have to adapt: become entrepreneurs, salesmen, land managers. Not exactly the skills your typical dairyman or herdsman went into the business for 40 years ago – which is roughly when most of them did. The average age of a British farmer today is 59.

These days, few people outside France have much good to say about the CAP. Set up in 1960 in the aftermath of postwar recovery, it was concerned primarily with ensuring food security in Europe. But the policy was soon attracting critics. Subsidies encouraged farmers to overproduce, creating the notorious 'wine lakes' and 'butter mountains' of the 1970s. By 1975, the Common Market had half a million tonnes of unshiftable butter on its hands: enough, as the Monster Raving Loony Party pointed out, to make a ski slope for Eddie the Eagle.[67] There was a more sinister side to the surpluses too: export subsidies were used to encourage farmers to 'dump' surplus food on developing nations at cut-price rates, so putting their competitors out of business. Subsequent decades saw various attempts to reduce food surpluses in Europe: limits on production were first introduced during the 1980s, and in the 1990s 'set-aside' payments were made to farmers to let their land lie fallow.

For all its labyrinthine muddle, the main effect of the CAP in Britain over the past two decades has been to disguise the fact that the government has lost interest in preserving food production in this country. That has left supermarkets free to engage in a cut-throat 'race to the bottom', screwing farmers to the point of bankruptcy. In the 10 years to 2005, more than half the dairy farmers in Britain went out of business, and livestock producers are finding it increasingly uneconomic to farm here. Much of our meat now comes from Brazil, Argentina and Thailand, where lower welfare standards and cheap labour costs make it up to five times cheaper to produce.[68] Unless something changes soon, there won't be any livestock left in Britain – or any farmers either.

The question of how Europe should feed itself remains unclear. To keep local farmers going by subsidising them to produce mountains of food doesn't make much sense. The trouble is, neither does simply abandoning food production to the global market. Apart from the obvious wastefulness of 'food miles' (and the oft-forgotten issue of food security), urban demand for cheap food is destroying the planet. While producer nations fiercely defend their right to exploit their natural resources, just as we did in the West, the scale of destruction involved in farming today is of an entirely new order. Modern agribusiness is all to do with short-term profit, and nothing to do with stewardship of the land. As the Amazonian rainforest goes up in smoke to make way for beef and soya, or the forests of Borneo (the last natural habitat of the orang-utan) are destroyed to create palm-oil plantations, our cheap food is costing us far more than money. An estimated half of the world's species of anything you care to mention lives in tropical rainforest, including all the countless nameless things we haven't discovered yet. Who is to say what obscure Amazonian toad or Bornean fungus might not possess a natural cure for cancer? It is not just native tribespeople and orang-utans we are destroying, but all the unknown things that live alongside them – all the unknown unknowns, as Donald Rumsfeld might say.[69]

Free trade may have a beautiful economic logic to it, but as history tells us, beautiful economic logic doesn't necessarily make for a beautiful world. Rather the opposite, in fact. An estimated 1.7 million hectares of Amazonian rainforest are currently lost to farmland every year, and a staggering 20 million hectares of existing arable land to salination and soil erosion. Yet despite all that destruction, we aren't managing to feed the world. During the second half of the twentieth century, global food production increased by 145 per cent – the equivalent of 25 per cent extra per person worldwide – yet 850 million people face hunger every day.[70] It doesn't make much sense, but then very little about the modern food industry does.

Constable Country

If you look at Britain from the air, it seems inconceivable that we don't produce most of our own food here. The landscape is overwhelmingly green; the cities tiny in comparison with the irregular patchwork of fields stretching from coast to coast. Seventy per cent of the nation consists of farmland – so if we're not going to grow food in it any more, what exactly are we going to do with it? One answer, according to the Curry Report, is to make it somewhere nice for city-dwellers to spend their weekends:

> In a small island, a rich and varied countryside is a precious resource for us all – including those who are not privileged to live there. An antidote to busy modern life. A place for Sunday walks; a chance to 'recharge the batteries' surrounded by nature.[71]

All well and good – except that, after years of being adapted to produce large quantities of food as cheaply and efficiently as possible, the British countryside doesn't have a huge amount of 'nature' left in it:

> Beyond any doubt the main cause of this decay has been the rise of modern, often more intensive, farming techniques. Agriculture was once environmentally benign, and a healthy and attractive country-side was a relatively cost-free by-product. The practices that delivered this benefit for society are often not now economic. Farming practice and the familiar English landscape have diverged.[72]

The solution, concluded the report, was to stop subsidising farmers to produce food, and pay them to manage the countryside instead.

Which is where we are now. In 2005, the government 'decoupled' farming subsidies from food production. From now on, instead of being paid to grow food, farmers would be paid to prettify the countryside and encourage wildlife. They would be given a flat rate according to the size of their farm, and could apply for bonus payments for providing wildlife habitats, planting woodland and hedgerows and so on. So there you have it. In modern Britain, an attractive countryside is worth paying for, but local food isn't.

Which, when you think about it, makes no sense at all. The British countryside is a working landscape, the product of countless agricultural revolutions driven by urban demand. It is a landscape made by food, and those parts of it we find pretty are mostly the accidental by-products of the way we farmed in the past. The Curry Report insists that 'the countryside is not a rural Disneyland', yet its recommendations are likely to produce just that. It is all very well – indeed highly desirable – to have a rural landscape teeming with wildlife, but without food production alongside it, such a landscape would not only be fake, it would be unsustainable. The report says it wants to reconnect food production with the countryside, but is silent on the question of how that is to be achieved, when most of the food we eat in Britain today produces anything but beauty – hell on earth, more like. If we want a rich and varied landscape on our doorstep, we are going to have to start eating as though we mean it.

One of the ironies of British attitudes towards the countryside is that arguably our most famous image of it – John Constable's *The Hay Wain*, painted in 1821 – itself depicts a rural way of life that was disappearing. A contemporary of Cobbett's, Constable could see the farming communities near his home at Dedham Vale on the Suffolk/Essex border were under threat from industrialisation, and he sought to save them by painting the landscape he loved so that others might fall in love with it too. *The Hay Wain* shows a perfect English summer's day: scudding clouds sail over a flaxen meadow, oaks rustle in the breeze, a team of carthorses cools off in a stream. The immediacy of the image comes from Constable's ability to capture the constantly changing light and mood of the British weather: 'No two days are alike,' he wrote, 'nor even two hours; neither were there ever two leaves of a tree alike since the creation of the world.' Standing in front of *The Hay Wain*, one can almost feel the breeze on one's cheek, hear the horses neigh, smell the hay. Constable makes us see the world his way, through a window as manipulative as any TV screen. But, as with all pastoralist imagery, the painting's beauty masks a desperate reality. Rural life in Britain was already on its knees, squeezed out by the economies demanded by urban markets and competition from abroad. When it comes to food, some things never change.

Today, with farmers fast disappearing from the scene, the British countryside is starting to look to a growing number of people like a large piece of valuable real estate. Many, quite understandably, are asking why, if we are not going to be farming it any more, we need to keep all that green stuff empty. With a chronic housing shortage in the south-east, the sanctity of the green belts is coming under increasing pressure. Meanwhile others are looking to turn the countryside into a business opportunity. 'Constable Country' is set to become a global brand, with the proposed Horkesley Park Heritage and Conservation Centre, a £20 million leisure complex with shops, cafés and even an 'art experience' (a genuine Constable painting) at its heart. The centre, which lists as its main content an 'interactive interpretation experience of the Life and Times of John Constable', hopes to attract 750,000 visitors a year. The proposals have caused an uproar, with English Heritage, owners of nearby Flatford Mill (the original scene of *The Hay Wain*), worried that the tiny site, which already attracts 200,000 visitors a year without any publicity at all, will be completely swamped.

Projects like Horkesley Park highlight how detached we have become from rural life in Britain. By turning our countryside into a heritage theme park and buying all our food from abroad, we might think we are getting the best of both worlds, whereas what we are actually getting is the worst. While we prettify and petrify our own back yard, our eating habits are despoiling those of others. Like the picture of Dorian Gray turning nasty in the attic, we are letting a hidden world bear the brunt of our urban lifestyles, while we pretend those consequences don't exist. Never mind pastoralism – what we are practising is Nimbyism, and on a global scale.

No Business Like Agribusiness

With its rural depopulation, land reforms and economies of scale, the English agricultural revolution paved the way for modern agribusiness. Today, rural communities all over the world are being transformed, with traditional mixed farming methods giving way to large-scale monocultural production. Peasants are a threatened species. Although there are still 700,000 small-scale farms in India, that figure is expected to drop by half in the next 20 years, and the story is the same all over Asia. As Western patterns of urbanisation are adopted worldwide, so are our far-from-perfect methods of feeding ourselves.

Technical advances in farming are nothing new. Farmers have always sought ways to increase yields by improving the seeds they sow, and at first glance, the genetic modification of crops just seems like the latest step in an age-old tradition. The development of plants to make them more resistant to disease, for example, should theoretically be an entirely benign and important use of science. But recent developments in GM have taken it in a very different direction. Cell-invasion technology, in which new DNA is 'smuggled' into a host gene, now allows engineers to interfere with the very life-force of a plant. And if that seems a little sinister, how does this sound: 'terminator technology', in which plants are bred with 'suicide genes' so that they die after just one germination? For thousands of years, farmers have saved their seeds, selectively breeding them over time to create a better crop. But if modern seed companies get their way, grain, like cars, will soon have an inbuilt obsolescence. Farmers who want to sow next season's crop will have to buy next year's model – it will be a case of germinate, and terminate. If Justus von Liebig thought he was 'sinning against the Creator', one wonders what he'd call what we're doing now.

Modern agribusiness isn't just about producing food, it is about maximising the profit to be made from it – and after a landmark ruling by the US Supreme Court in 1980 that the *patenting of life* was permissible, there has been plenty to be made from GM.[73] Ever since then, the US biotechnical company Monsanto has been doing just that, accumulating more than 11,000 patents on genetically modified seeds, giving them a 95 per cent share of the global market. As the film-maker

Deborah Koons Garcia documented in her 2004 film *The Future of Food*, the company is ruthless in asserting its rights of ownership. Farmers unlucky enough to have land neighbouring Monsanto's are frequently sued by the company for illegal possession of their seed if it is found to have accidentally blown over in the wind.

Unsurprisingly, Monsanto has attracted plenty of criticism for its bully-boy tactics, but its lobby is a powerful one. Several board members have served on the US Environmental Protection Agency, which has taken a remarkably soft line on GM testing. Now, thanks to something called TRIPS (the Trade Related Intellectual Property Rights Agreement), companies like Monsanto can claim patents on life all over the world.[74] As the Indian farming campaigner Vandana Shiva points out, that is not good news for millions of farmers in the developing world. Not only is the ancient practice of farmers saving their own seed under threat, but those who take out loans to buy expensive seed and fertiliser are finding themselves in a spiral of debt. Worse still, many of the crops they buy are failing. Designed in a laboratory somewhere in the USA, many of the crops turn out to be unsuited to the conditions in which they are actually grown. For the first time in history, Indian farmers – who are not exactly unused to hardship – are committing suicide in their tens of thousands.[75] As Shiva observes, when food production goes global, small farmers are the first to go.

Eating Oil

Whatever your agricultural persuasion, it is hard to ignore the fact that there is something very wrong with the way we're feeding ourselves now. One doesn't have to look very far for the physical evidence: deforestation, soil erosion, water depletion, poisoning and pollution – it all speaks for itself. Our food may *seem* cheap, but that is only because the price we pay for it doesn't reflect its true cost. The damage is accounted for elsewhere. One recent study by Essex University found that the annual cost of cleaning up the chemical pollution caused by British agriculture was £2.3 billion a year – almost as much as farmers themselves got back in income.[76]

Leaving aside the questions of soil, seed and pests for a minute, there is one element of farming that is often overlooked: energy. Energy, in the end, is what food is, and in order to produce it, we need the help of our greatest energy source, the sun. Photosynthesis, the process by which plants convert carbon dioxide and water into glucose and oxygen, depends on it, as does the 'fixing' of atmospheric nitrogen necessary for plant growth. Until about 1850, harnessing solar energy in edible form is basically what farmers did; and it is more or less what they have done ever since, except that from around that date, they have supplemented the process with the use of fossil fuels. From the earliest experiments with powered farm machinery and fertiliser to modern combine harvesters and food processing, fossil fuels have transformed farming from a thankless, back-breaking task (the punishment of the gods) into something really quite rewarding. Today, almost every aspect of industrial farming involves the use of oil in some way, from running machinery to making fertilisers and pesticides to the transport, processing and preservation of produce. Around four barrels of the stuff go into feeding each of us in Britain every year; nearly double that amount is used for every American.[77] We are effectively eating oil.

The problem with that, as the German economist Ernst Friedrich Schumacher pointed out as early as 1973 in his book *Small is Beautiful*, is that fossil fuels are no more than the sun's energy, captured millions of years ago and packaged in a readily available form. 'One of the most fateful errors of our age,' he wrote, 'is the belief that "the problem of production" has been solved.' The confusion arises, argued Schumacher, because we fail to distinguish between 'income' and 'capital' from the natural world: 'Every economist and businessman is familiar with the distinction, and applies it conscientiously . . . except where it really matters: namely, the irreplaceable capital which man has not made, but simply found, and about which he can do nothing.'[78]

For the past 150 years, we have been living in the 'oil age': an era of unprecedented cheap energy that has allowed us to drive cars, fly planes, wage wars and wander around our homes in winter wearing nothing but a T-shirt, munching a sausage roll that cost us next to nothing. But our gas-guzzling lifestyles are about to run out of guzzle. Opinions differ over quite when it will happen, but most agree that

'Peak Oil' – the moment when the rate of oil production from known global reserves will reach its peak – is coming sooner rather than later, with some experts predicting it within the next five years.[79]

While driving and flying are useful, neither is strictly necessary for survival. Food is a different matter. Whether we do it by growing crops, foraging for berries or hunting rabbits, we have to feed ourselves, and we must expend energy in order to do so. We face what the carbon educator Richard Heinberg calls the 'net energy principle': a nutritional version of Mr Micawber's famous dictum that human happiness rests on making sure one's income exceeds one's expenditure. Which is far from what modern agribusiness is doing at present. For every calorie of food it produces, it is burning an estimated 10 in the form of fossil fuels.[80] Modern farming might like to call itself efficient, but with outputs like that, it is a strange kind of efficiency.

A Third Way

Rome versus Germania; lord versus peasant; Young versus Cobbett – farming has always divided opinions, and things are no different now. As far as the question of how we are going to feed the world goes, the jury is out. Even those in the best position to know, professional farmers, cannot agree. While the organic movement argues passionately for an approach that harnesses natural biosystems, the industrialists insist that only modern techniques can feed the planet. The latter have some impressive statistics to back them up: according to the geographer Vaclav Smil – not himself an industrial lobbyist – were it not for the Haber-Bosch process (a method of artificially 'fixing' atmospheric nitrogen so that it can be absorbed by plants), two out of every five people in the world would not be alive today.[81] But, counter the organic lobby, commercial farming is killing the planet, and its results, which look so impressive now, won't last. Not only could we feed the world organically, it is the only sustainable option. So, what is the truth?

Polarised debates often frame the wrong questions. Rather than asking how we're going to feed ourselves in the future, we ought to be questioning the way we eat now. Food is the most devalued commodity in the industrialised West, because we have lost touch with what it means. Living in cities, we have learnt to behave as if we did not belong to the natural world; as if we were somehow distinct from 'the environment'. Rather than see ourselves as part of it, we see it as something to exploit or control from the outside, or (once we have messed it up enough) to try and save. We forget that we are animals bound to the land; that the food we eat links us directly to nature. We stuff ourselves with chicken without a second thought, but if we were locked in a room with a live hen and a sharp knife, most of us would probably starve. We have forgotten the ancient lesson of sacrifice: that life is part of a cycle, and that effort and, ultimately, death are necessary in order to renew it.

All of which brings us back, more or less, to those two very different Christmas dinners that popped up recently on British television screens. In the end, the difference between them is cost: you get the food and the countryside you pay for. Two pounds won't buy you a happy chicken or a beautiful landscape; 10 pounds might. But to express it like that – as an either/or dilemma – is to fall into the classic polar trap. There is another way. If more of us were prepared to pay just a *little* bit more for food, the operational costs of producing whatever it was – free-range chicken, organic lettuce – would start to fall. More importantly, if food were a bit more expensive, we might start to pay more attention to what is, after all, the most important thing in our lives. We might, for example, start to eat less meat, which would be no bad thing, for us, our planet or the animals we breed to eat.

Although perceptions about food in Britain *are* beginning to shift, the 'foodie revolution' remains a predominantly middle-class phenomenon; farmers' markets and organic box schemes are tiny countermovements against a general trend.[82] How to scale them up is the challenge – and that, as a quick bit of turkey-maths makes clear, is no small task. The real barrier to changing the way we eat, however, does not lie in practicalities, but in our minds. 'Third way' methods, such as the farming of salmon in large pens in the open sea, or chickens in open sheds with access to the outdoors, already exist in Britain. In the absence of a magic fix along the lines of someone inventing a miracle pill or manna descending from heaven, those sorts of responsible, middle-scale farms are probably the closest thing we are going to get to a way of feeding ourselves without destroying the planet in the process.

What would a Lorenzetti fresco look like today? It is hard to imagine how a painter could represent city and country on the same wall, let alone the effects of good or bad government on either. Feeding cities has become rather more complicated than it was in the fourteenth century. But one thing is certain: however much we look the other way, our rural hinterland will always mirror the way we live. Ancient cities were run on slave labour; so were the farms that fed them. Medieval cities thrived on trade; so did their hinterlands. Modern cities, like their industrialised hinterlands, have little respect for nature. If we don't like what's happening out there in the landscape, we had better rethink how we eat, because one will never change without the other.

Chapter 2
Supplying the City

It is no coincidence that Dickens never writes about agriculture and writes endlessly about food. He was a cockney, and London is the centre of the earth in rather the same sense that the belly is the centre of the body. It is a city of consumers . . .

George Orwell[1]

Animals were a common sight in British cities until relatively recently.

Apple Day, Brogdale, Kent

Ever since I first heard about it, I have wanted to go to Brogdale. Brogdale is the home of the National Fruit Collections, where every known variety of pear, apple and soft fruit in the land is nurtured, alongside new varieties which are being bred all the time to see if any of them has what it takes to make it in the cut-throat world of modern food production. Throughout the summer and autumn, Brogdale holds festivals in honour of its various fruit species, and I have come to the biggest daddy of them all: Apple Day on 21 October, the British fruit equivalent of the Oscars.

Apart from its all-important tree collections, Brogdale consists essentially of a group of unprepossessing sheds; but on this, its grandest day of the year, it exudes the atmosphere of a village fête. There are tractor rides, a miniature train, stalls selling home-made chutneys and jams, and last but not least, a pig roast. Resisting them all, I head straight for what will surely be the crowning glory of the day: a large barn where this year's apple harvest is on display. I am expecting this to be something extraordinary: a Busby Berkeleyesque piece of bravura along the lines of a prize-winning roundabout using apples instead of geraniums. Yet when I enter the shed, it is so dark and echoingly empty that at first I can't make out any apples at all. Then I spot them in the gloom, snaking around the walls on a low plywood plinth, each variety represented by four perfect specimens next to an identifying label. People in rustling waterproofs file past the apples, peering down at them and murmuring to each other in low, appreciative voices. 'It's a bit like a fruit version of the Crown Jewels,' I mutter to myself before realising that, actually, that is precisely what it is.

I fall in behind the queue and begin my dutiful scrutiny of the collection. As the apple trail unfolds beneath my gaze, I begin to realise its modesty is misleading. There is a staggering number of varieties here. Every few yards, they change from big to small, shiny to rough, red to yellow, green to brown and back again. I find myself becoming transfixed by them. Apple varieties are like languages, I decide. There are some 2,300 of them in Brogdale alone, each representing a tiny universe; a culture rooted in time and place, unique and irreplaceable. And just like languages, apple varieties are dying out all over the world. There is no place for them, it seems, in the global food economy. As I peer down at the distant cousins of Cox and Bramley, I marvel at each family's survival. All of them have a story, a provenance, a legacy – and a taste. Hmm, yes . . . taste: that's the one thing that's missing here. Realising that for the past half-hour I have been fighting the urge to pick up one of the apples and take a large bite out of it, I can't trust myself in here any longer. I've got to get out and find something to eat.

Back in the daylight, the harvest festival mood is in full swing. Children run about laughing and squealing, tractor rides come and go, and there is a heartening whiff of roast pork in the air. But there is a long queue for the pig, and I see there is a walking tour of the orchards just about to start. My excitement returns: perhaps now I will finally get to discover the true Brogdale. I join the group, and we set off with our anonymous guide (a compact, weatherbeaten type somewhere between a mountain explorer and a Boy Scout) in search of fruity enlightenment.

A short walk past some poplar trees and a near-miss with a tractor later, we arrive in the orchard, and for the second time today my illusions are shattered. In place of the majestic Elysium of my imagination, we are in a flat rectangular field the size of a couple of football pitches, full of shrubs no higher than my head. Is this just the nursery? I wonder. But no: it seems that modern fruit trees are all grafted on to special rootstocks so that they only grow to six foot or so, making it easier to pick the fruit.[2] Our guide, possibly sensing our disappointment, produces a worrying-looking knife and plucks one of the few remaining pears off a nearby tree, slicing it expertly into portions for us all to try. The pear is a Comice: sharp and sweet, dripping with juice and absurdly delicious. My first bite elicits an immediate flood of emotion: gratitude and pleasure, but also puzzlement. How is it possible that I can walk past a bowl of these very pears at home for days on end and never be tempted to try even one? Here, plucked straight from the tree, they are pure ambrosia. The undramatic surroundings are forgotten once again – I am a townie on a voyage of discovery, and life is good.

We weave our way up and down a few times, tasting more pears as we go (like echoes of a first love, none quite matches up to the Comice), before filing round a tall hedge and past a field of brassicas into the heart of the collection, the apple orchard. There are some 4,600 apple trees here (two for every variety), and it looks like it. Lilliputian shrubs drip with edible baubles as far as the eye can see. 'Does anyone have any apples they particularly want to visit?' asks our guide. 'Cox!' pipes up a little girl, only to be swiftly reprimanded by her mother. 'Ashmead's Kernel?' drawls a bespectacled know-all, easily trumping the little girl, and making me suspect he's been swotting up his name-tags on the way in. 'Excellent choice!' says our guide, and off we tramp.

Since our quest involves travelling to some far-flung corner of the orchard, our guide inducts us into Apple World as we go. First he gives us a Linda to try (which is light and fragrant); a Lynn's Pippin (sweet, but lacking lift); an Elstar (an in-your-face, Barbra Streisandish sort of fruit). We learn about russeting, the deliberate cultivation of rough or reddened skin to improve sweetness and richness of flavour, and why so many English varieties have failed in the face of competition from easier-cropping ones like Golden Delicious. We snub the latter when we come to it, although, to be fair, most of us are rather appled out by now. At last, after what feels like several hundred samplings, we track down Ashmead's Kernel, which turns out to be rather a fine specimen: Cox-like in colour, texture and taste, with just a hint of additional fragrance. It's a good way to end our tour. As we trudge back to the centre, I catch sight of all the apple-related products I swept past on the way in. They make me realise I'm not going to be able to eat another apple again for weeks.

Brogdale is an amazing place, but it only exists by the skin of its teeth. The original collections were set up in Chiswick by the newly formed Horticultural Society in the early 1800s, where they remained until 1921, before being moved first to Surrey, and finally to Kent in the 1950s, when they were taken over by Defra's predecessor, the Ministry of Agriculture, Fisheries and Food (MAFF). But in 1990, MAFF decided Britain didn't need National Fruit Collections any longer, and the orchards, the result of two centuries' worth of continuous research and breeding, were threatened with destruction. Prince Charles intervened, helping to broker a deal in which the site was sold to the newly formed Brogdale Horticultural Trust, with the government maintaining ownership of the trees. However, funding levels were so minimal that seven years later, the Trust decided to sell the land and lease it back, and in 2005 did another dodgy deal, this time with Tesco, who are now principal sponsors of the site. Although Defra claims it remains committed to preserving the collections, it has a strange way of showing it. Brogdale faces an uncertain future – so if you fancy a walking tour of a Very Large Orchard (and possibly a pork roast) any time between May and October, you had better hurry along while you still have the chance.

In its quirky, British, miniature-steam-trainy sort of way, Brogdale is the kind of place that gets you thinking. Why did the government think it so important to have National Fruit Collections in 1921, yet so unnecessary in 1990? How did we manage to acquire 2,300 varieties of apple in this country anyhow? And now that we've got them, what are we going to do with them? Supermarkets typically stock fewer than eight varieties, of which only two – Cox and Bramley – are indigenous, so what about the rest? The answers all come down to a question of scale. Apple varieties (and all other food varieties, for that matter) are the result of local cultures: the product of generations of farmers struggling to get the best out of the land, and the accumulated knowledge of how to do just that. It's what the French call *terroir*: a term originally used to describe the effects of local climate and geography on the quality of a particular wine – right down to the angle of the hillside where the vines are grown – and that now encompasses not just the physical terrain, but the traditional know-how that goes into producing any local food.

Local food, however, is not the sort that keeps vast, throbbing metropolises going. Modern city-dwellers demand constant supplies of cheap, predictable food, and agribusiness has evolved to produce just that. The food we eat today is driven not by local cultures, but by economies of scale, and those economies apply to every stage of the food supply chain. In order to feature in the urban diet nowadays, produce not only has to be bigger, better and breastier than ever before; it also has to be capable of withstanding the rigours of a global distribution system the aim of which is to deliver fewer and fewer products to more and more of us – that's how economies of scale work. Wheeling your trolley down a supermarket aisle, it might be tempting to think that we have never had a greater choice of things to eat. But that is not quite true. Yes, you can now eat strawberries at Christmas if you really want to; but if you want to choose the variety, forget it. Three quarters of all the strawberries sold in the UK today are of just one kind, Elsanta (which, oddly, even sounds a bit Christmassy). If you want to eat another sort, you will probably have to pick it yourself. Strawberries these days are a commodified product; the result of a food industry geared less towards the niceties of *terroir* than to the principles of car assembly pioneered by Henry Ford. Its success lies in its ability to reduce a highly complex process (food production) to an operation so streamlined that its very product (food) is now subservient to it. As Henry Ford is once supposed to have said, 'You can have your Ford any colour you like – as long as it's black.'

Some months after my visit to Brogdale, I found myself chatting to Peter Clarke, a farmer who spent most of his career in the international fruit and veg trade but found that he missed the hands-on experience of growing food himself. We're standing shivering in Sainsbury's car park on the Finchley Road, where Peter comes every Wednesday during the summer with a vanload of lettuces, cabbages, beans and broccoli (plus more types of radish and beetroot than I even knew existed) to sell at the farmers' market. His farm is just within the M25 – ideal for supplying London – and he's doing reasonably well at it, although life is one continuous slog, spent driving to different markets four days a week and farming the other three. I ask him why, with all this mind-boggling variety of vegetables in their car park, Sainsbury's have so few apple varieties on sale inside their store. I explain that I've just been to Brogdale, and can't quite get the taste of Ashmead's Kernel out of my head. 'Ah yes,' says Peter, 'that reminds me of a farmers' meeting I went to once. There was a guy there who'd come to persuade us to try growing some traditional apple varieties. People were just starting to get interested, when one old farmer got up at the back of the room and said that that was all very well, but old varieties were like old girlfriends: very exciting when you first met them again after a long time, before you remembered why you dumped them in the first place.'

It seems that we are doomed to a future of ubiquitous Golden Delicious, not because they're either golden or delicious (they're neither), but because they perform spectacularly well in all the areas that other, tastier apples don't. They're steady croppers, they can be picked early, they store easily, they travel well and – most importantly – they can be grown in both the northern and southern hemispheres, so can be made available all year round. Supermarket customers get upset, apparently, if they have to change the variety of apple they buy from season to season. Since for some reason most people don't seem to object to Golden Delicious's mushy, sugary blandness, it makes the perfect commercial apple. Granny Smiths, another commercial favourite, have similar handling and cropping properties that outweigh their cannonball-like hardness and searing acidity. No wonder two thirds of the apple orchards in Britain have been grubbed up over the past 30 years – they were producing the 'wrong' sort of apple. And what goes for apples goes for every other kind of food too.

According to Defra, 38 per cent of the food we eat in Britain is now imported. The figure includes half of all our vegetables and a staggering 95 per cent of all our fruit.[3] You might assume that this is the result of our increasingly exotic tastes – the kumquatification, as it were, of everyday life – but you would be wrong. More than half the food we import into the UK is indigenous food in season: in other words, we could have grown it ourselves.[4] The reason why we don't is simple. Foreign growers, with their year-round sunshine and low-cost labour, can deliver apples and onions to us far more cheaply and consistently than we can grow them here – until they run out of water, that is, which some already are. The region of southern Spain where most of our salad vegetables are grown (under a polytunnel so large it can be seen from space) is fast turning to desert.

After a lifetime in the fruit and veg industry, Peter Clarke is a realist. Farmers' markets are all very well, he says, but they will never be able to feed cities. Price is what consumers care about, and only the largest retailers have the scale of operation to compete on price these days. Sainsbury's are happy to have farmers' markets in their car parks because they're good for business: people come to the market to buy their novelty beetroot, and then go to the supermarket to get the bulk of their food. Within 20 years, Peter reckons, small producers in Britain will have died out altogether, apart from those who survive by selling luxury foods to people who can afford it. I leave him selling his fancy veg and head off towards Sainsbury's myself, feeling rather guilty, and secretly hoping he can't see me. I suspect he can't. It is, after all, a very large car park.

The Chain Gang

In the modern food industry, small producers, suppliers and retailers all share the same problem. They are relics of a bygone era. Cities in the past were fed by thousands of individuals – a plethora, if you like, of Peter Clarkes – who either brought produce to market themselves, or sold it on to suppliers to take it for them. The food supply was so vitally important to cities that most had laws in place to prevent anyone from gaining a monopoly in the trade, either by getting too large a share in the market for any one food, or by operating in more than one stage of the food chain. Bakers in pre-revolutionary Paris were prevented from milling their own grain, and millers prevented from baking bread, for that very reason.

Nothing could be further from the way cities are fed today. Most of the food we eat now is produced and distributed by vast conglomerates, described by the American social scientist Bill Heffernan as 'food clusters', 'firms that control the food system all the way from gene to supermarket shelf'.[5] Modern food companies don't just deal in one aspect of the supply; they spread their operations up and down the food chain, using mergers and acquisitions to achieve so-called 'vertical integration' within the supply system (the very thing the eighteenth-century Parisian laws were put in place to prevent). You might not have heard of 'food clusters' before, but you will certainly be aware of their end product: supermarkets. Supermarkets were invented in the early twentieth century by American food processing companies looking for ways to sell their high-volume, long-life products as cost-effectively as possible. Supermarkets haven't evolved much in their 80-year history: the first ones were boxy sheds built on the edges of towns – so the supply trucks could reach them easily – filled with rows of branded produce and surrounded by capacious car parks. Then, as now, their primary aim was not to charm people, it was to transfer industrial food as efficiently as possible from factory to consumer. They proved to be more successful at it than even their inventors could have dreamed.

Supermarket dominance of the grocery trade in Britain first made front-page news in 2004 when Tesco's profits hit the £2 billion mark, but really it shouldn't have come as such a shock. Supermarkets, and the industrial food systems that supply them, have been making themselves indispensable to us for almost a century – it is only now that they have achieved their aim that we are starting to worry about the consequences. In 2006, an all-party parliamentary committee report entitled *High Street Britain 2015* stated: 'There is widespread belief . . . that many small shops across the UK will have ceased trading by 2015, with few independent businesses taking their place. Their loss, largely the result of a heavily unbalanced trading environment, will damage the UK socially, economically and environmentally.'[6] The report went on to recommend 'a moratorium on further mergers and takeovers until the government has brought forward proposals to secure the diversity and vitality of the retail sector'. It might just as well have said 'Lock the stable door and start looking for the horse.'

The disappearance of independent food shops in Britain has finally brought the state of the grocery trade to public attention, but it is just the visible tip of a very large iceberg. We might not like the corporate takeover of our high streets, but we absolutely love being able to buy fresh salmon or ready-made lasagne from a Tesco Metro or a

Sainsbury's Local at eleven o'clock at night, seven days a week. It suits our modern lifestyles. The processes that make it possible – that can conjure up a salmon from a Scottish loch, gut it, package it, and dispatch it so that it arrives in perfect condition at the same time as a lasagne with a totally different provenance – are little short of miraculous. The ability to do it, cheaply and reliably, week in, week out, in the middle of the night and out of season, is what sets super-markets apart. Their real power lies not in their takeover of the high street, but in their control of the food supply chain. That particular horse bolted long ago.

We're so wedded to the year-round availability of just about everything – what the food journalist Joanna Blythman calls 'perma-nent global summertime' – that we tend to forget the phenomenal effort that it takes to bring it to us.[7] The logistics would be daunting enough were we just talking about tennis balls. Given that it's food, they become positively mind-boggling. Food isn't something one would naturally choose to transport very far. It is organic in the old-fashioned sense of the word, which means it goes off rather quickly unless subjected to some sort of preservation process such as drying, salting, smoking, canning, bottling, freezing, gassing or irradiating. Such processes do have their uses – champagne, cheese, bacon and kippers being some of the tastier ones – but in an ideal world, one would not salt food or blast it with gas simply in order to preserve it. One would harvest or butcher it, cook it as necessary and put it in one's mouth – which, give or take a custom or two, is how rural communities have eaten for centuries. But getting food into cities is quite another matter. Apart from its tendency to go off, food is seasonal, squashable, bruiseable, unpredictable, irregular – the list goes on. The success of the modern food industry lies in its ability not just to provide us with hitherto unimaginable quantities of food, but to deliver it in good, or at least edible, condition. Most of it doesn't taste as nice as it might have done straight out of the ground, but since most of us rarely eat really fresh food, we've forgotten what it's supposed to taste like anyway.

One of the ways in which supermarkets manage to keep us supplied with fresh food is by stretching the concept of what counts as 'fresh'.

New Zealand lamb, for instance, used to be shipped to Britain frozen, but is now shipped 'chilled', sealed in containers at minus one degree Centigrade filled with a 'gas flush' (an inert gas such as argon) to kill the bacteria. In this way the lamb can be kept 'fresh' for 90 days after slaughter, although it loses its 'freshness' pretty quickly once the containers are opened. The need to keep the lamb at a precise temperature creates a so-called 'chill chain', which in turn is changing the way our food is transported. Old-style bulk-carrying refrigerated ships, or reefers, are being replaced by vessels fitted with 'plug-ins': individual docking bays into which the containers are slotted, like so many patients in an intensive care unit, each with a chart to log its journey and a record of its temperature on the voyage. Any variation in the latter means that the whole cargo has to be destroyed. Once the ships reach port (which in the case of food destined for Britain is usually Rotterdam), the containers are plugged into dockside bays to await transfer across the Channel by ferry. Most food entering the UK will make several more trips before it ends up at its final destination. A recent report by Defra reckoned that British food transport accounted for 30 billion vehicle kilometres in 2002 – 10 times further than a decade earlier and the equivalent of circumnavigating the globe 750,000 times.[8]

To get some idea of what these international food dodgems actually look like, I can heartily recommend a journey up or down the M1, turning off at Junction 18 and ignoring the signs to Crick. I have nothing against Crick: it is a dear little town with a neat high street, a couple of decent pubs and a resolutely old-fashioned Spar. But the real attraction of Junction 18 lies on the other side of the road. Here, just a couple of roundabouts away from the cosiness of Crick, is the landscape of modern food supply – and a very bizarre landscape it is. The 'other' Crick consists of what can only be described as a series of thumping great sheds: vast boxes clad in off-white crinkly tin, so featureless that only the dozens of lorries crowding their loading bays, like piglets at the belly of some monstrous sow, give any hint of their true scale. These buildings could cheerfully swallow jumbo jets; but what they are actually handling at Crick is the cereal, eggs and milk that you and I are going to eat tomorrow for breakfast, plus some 20,000 different product lines besides, in a minutely timed international distribution operation about as sophisticated as the sheds are bland to look at.

Crick is a national food hub: one of about 70 similar sites up and down the country that between them manage the vast bulk of our food supplies. The airport-scale sheds are regional distribution centres (RDCs): vast warehouses that operate 24 hours a day, receiving thousands of pallets of food and other goods from 'upstream' supplier lorries, and sorting them into batches to be taken by 'downstream' ones to supermarkets. The pallets are manoeuvred by teams of forklift trucks and 'pickers' (men with electric barrows) in a constant race against the clock. Fresh food supply lorries are scheduled to arrive within half-hour time slots, with the aim of 'cross-docking' their goods directly into a delivery vehicle. Increasingly, food travels via specialist 'consolidation centres' in order to streamline the process. The entire mechanism is triggered every time you or I buy something from a supermarket, since the item's bar code passing through the checkout sends an automatic order through to the RDC to ensure its replacement arrives just in time for the shelves to be restocked the following day. The bar codes also allow supermarkets to keep tabs on their goods, telling them when and where they are bought, and, if customers use loyalty cards, by whom.

Since supermarkets have no on-site storage, the burden of keeping their shelves fully stocked is passed up the food chain to their suppliers – no easy task, according to Fred Duncan, director of Grampian Foods, one of the largest meat producers in the country. 'A customer can order a hundred or a thousand cases of fresh meat,' he says, 'and then they can phone up on Monday morning and say they want the order doubled that afternoon. We're frantically trying to meet that, and they penalise us like hell if we don't.'[9] The entire operation is run on a knife-edge, so any disruption to it, such as the Hemel Hempstead fuel depot fire in 2005, causes instant chaos. That fire affected only one M&S dry goods depot, but, according to Duncan, it could have been a lot worse: 'If one depot goes down you have a complete logistical nightmare. If a Tesco's depot went down, they're so huge, I can't imagine the consequences.' Moving food around Britain is hard enough, but when you factor in the food we import from abroad every year, you have a very complex operation indeed. 'Global trading is the future,' says Duncan, 'and understanding logistics is it. The timing and processing of the order – you can't get it wrong. It's in different languages too: you're working in Thailand; it's a Chinese boat; you've got Dutch legislation; I don't know how it works! You wouldn't want to think about it for too long – you'd go crazy.'

As the name of its own research body, the Institute of Grocery Distribution (IGD), indicates, the British food retail industry is obsessed with logistics. To read the IGD's annual report, *Retail Logistics*, is to wallow in the code language of a rapidly evolving industry. According to the report, 94.7 per cent of British supermarket groceries are now handled by depots like the one at Crick, an increasing number run by specialist 'third-party logistics' (3PL) companies, set up to cope with the complexities of international haulage. Third-party logistics is a fast-growing business: a 2005 merger between two of its major players, Exel and Deutsche Post, created a company with half a million employees and an annual turnover of £38 billion. Other hot distribution trends for 2007 included RRP (retail-ready packaging), packaging that can protect food in transit yet be displayed directly on supermarket shelves; CPFR (collaborative planning, forecasting and replenishment), an industry resolution to talk to itself more; and RFID (radio-frequency identification), computer chips embedded in packaging that will eventually allow supermarkets to trace food all the way from its source and into our homes. But for now, the supermarkets' chief goal remains on-shelf availability (OSA). Apparently the one thing that can actually lose them customers is a failure to supply us with our favourite brand of cupcake or tea bag.

However many gizmos they employ, there is no doubt that super-markets have got the business of food supply down to a fine art. Advanced preservation techniques and transport technology have combined to create the illusion that feeding cities is easy. It isn't. Yet the better the food industry gets at what it does, the more we forget how much we depend on it. The reality is that supermarkets have a stranglehold over not just the grocery sector, but the entire infrastructure that supplies our food. Without them, we would struggle to feed ourselves; and that makes their position close to unassailable.

This Little Piggy . . .

One of the reasons it can be hard to appreciate the effort it takes to feed a modern city is the sheer invisibility of the process. Not many of us make casual trips to food hubs like Crick. Even if we wanted to, visitors are about as welcome there as they would be at a top-secret military installation. The food industry is a highly secretive operation. We live in ignorance of the 24-hour effort that keeps our lasagnes coming, and that suits the industry just fine.

Before the railways, it was a very different story. Transporting food was often harder than growing it in the first place – no more so than for grain, every city's staple food. Grain was too heavy and bulky to carry more than a few miles overland: a 100-mile journey by cart in Roman times is estimated to have cost half the value of the load.[10] Transport by water was easier, but the grain was then exposed to the risk of rotting. Grain was also difficult and dangerous to store, prone to weevil attack and explosive if its temperature rose too high. One solution was to convert the grain to flour before it reached the city, but this added a further logistical problem, since mills ran on wind or water power, and were often inconveniently located in order to make best use of the elements. Several famines that hit Paris during the seventeenth and eighteenth centuries were caused not by failed harvests but by severe winters that froze the Seine and prevented the city's watermills from operating.

In terms of transport, meat had one great advantage over grain. Cattle could walk themselves to market, which made it possible to raise them far from the city. Many of the sheep that fed ancient Rome were pastured 500 miles away in Apulia, while the cattle that fed the cities of medieval Germany and north Italy came from as far afield as Poland, Hungary and the Balkans, travelling westwards in herds up to 20,000 strong. The landscape all over Europe was criss-crossed by networks of drovers' roads that ran separately from those carrying human traffic, along which sheep, geese and cattle were driven by highly skilled (and highly paid) men. Sir Walter Scott described the task of driving cattle from Scotland to London in the early nineteenth century:

> They are required to know perfectly the drove-roads, which lie over the wildest parts of the country, and to avoid as much as possible the highways, which destroy the feet of the bullocks, and the turnpikes, which annoy the spirit of the drover; whereas in the broad green or gray track which lies across the pathless moor, the herd not only move at ease and without taxation, but if they mind their business may pick up a mouthful of food by the way. At night the drovers usually sleep along with their cattle, let the weather be what it will, and many of these hardy men do not once rest under a roof during the journey on foot from Lochaber to Lincolnshire.[11]

After their three-week cross-country marathon (or biathlon, in the case of cattle from Skye, since they had to swim the first leg of their journey), animals bound for London could lose up to 100lb in weight, and had to be fattened up again before slaughter. Fattening was a specialist occupation in the suburbs, and breweries had a nice sideline in feeding cattle on spent grain. Many counties close to London combined fattening with dairy farming, and Islington, conveniently placed on the route south to Smithfield, specialised in both. But the most troublesome stage of the cattle's journey was the last. In order to avoid the meat going bad, the animals had to be slaughtered as close to the markets as possible. That meant driving them through the middle of the city, which could cause chaos at busy times, and occasionally led to the trampling of a passer-by (several fatalities were reported at Smithfield in the nineteenth century). The animals were then slaughtered in the open, or in makeshift cellars beneath butchers' shops. The sights, sounds and smells of death were some of the least charming aspects of life in the pre-industrial city.

Fresh fish was the other main source of protein for many cities, especially during the winter when there was little fresh meat to be had. The problem was to find a means of keeping the catch edible before bringing it ashore. The range of London's fishing fleet at Barking, for instance, was limited by the distance it had to sail up the Thames, which made the discovery in 1837 of a sole spawning ground just off the Norfolk coast particularly vexing, since it lay just out of reach. It took a Barking fisherman by the name of Samuel Hewett to come up with a solution. Ever since Roman times, winter ice had been collected from low-lying fields and stored in thick-walled ice houses for use during the summer. Hewett's idea was to station a fleet of trawlers out at sea for weeks on end catching the fish, and use another fleet of high-speed cutters to bring it back to Billingsgate packed in ice. The business was so successful that in 1862 Hewett moved his fleet to Gorleston on the Norfolk coast; a move that signalled the end of Barking's dominance in the supply of London's fish.[12]

Fruit and vegetables did not figure greatly in the diets of most pre-industrial city-dwellers, largely because they were so expensive to produce. Even the humblest pea, carrot or bean was considered a high-maintenance crop, needing careful tending, plenty of manure, and gentle handling. Fruit and vegetables were grown as close to cities as possible, in order to benefit from the manure and 'nightsoil' (human waste) that the town could provide, as well as to minimise the bruising journey to market. That meant paying high land rents, which had to be offset by high profits, the pursuit of which led to the production of speciality crops, such as 'forced' vegetables, made to ripen weeks before their natural season by being grown under glass in 'hot beds' – pits filled with manure.[13] City-dwellers then, as now, were prepared to pay absurd prices for out-of-season produce; and then, as now, they were often disappointed with what they got. Today the complaint is that the food tastes of nothing; 300 years ago, it was that it tasted of the dung it had been grown in. Nevertheless, market gardens always thrived on the edges of cities, catering to the luxury urban market. 'Oh! The incredible profit by digging of ground,' as the London gardener Thomas Fuller exclaimed in 1662, unconsciously echoing the Roman agronomist Varro's enthusiasm for specialist suburban farming, *pastio villatica*, 2,000 years earlier.[14]

Perhaps the food that best illustrates how hard it was to feed a city the size of London before the age of steam is milk. Although its nutritional qualities were well recognised, the speed with which milk went off meant that it had to be produced more or less on the spot, either in insalubrious inner-city cowsheds (an estimated 8,500 cows were kept in late eighteenth-century London) or in suburban dairies. The suburban herd, which was 20,000 strong at its peak, was milked at 3 a.m. each day by milkmaids, who carried the liquid into the city in open pails to 'milk cellars', basement rooms where it was left to stand in order to separate out the cream, after which the remainder was sold (often watered down) as milk. As Tobias Smollett's description in *Humphry Clinker* suggests, on every stage of its journey the milk was exposed to some peril or other. Even if it was free from disease, it was often adulterated, going sour, or both:

> But the milk itself should not pass unanalysed, the produce of faded cabbage-leaves and sour draff, lowered with hot water, frothed with bruised snails, carried through the streets in open pails, exposed to foul rinsings, discharged from doors and windows, spittle, snot and tobacco quids from foot-passengers, overflowings from mud-carts . . . dirt and trash chucked into it by roguish boys for the joke's sake . . . and finally, the vermin that drops from the rags of the nasty drab that vends this precious mixture, under the respectable denomination of milk-maid.[15]

Even allowing for Smollettian hyperbole, there is little doubt that London milk in the eighteenth century was far from the fresh 'pinta' we pour over our cornflakes today. No wonder the majority of Londoners never touched the stuff.

Small is Beautiful

Given the physical difficulties of getting food into town, it is hardly surprising that most pre-industrial cities were compact by modern standards. A day's journey by cart, a distance of around 20 miles, was the practical limit for bringing in grain overland, which limited the width of the city's arable belt. The simple laws of geometry meant that the larger a city grew, the smaller the relative size of its rural hinterland became, until the latter could no longer feed the former. Of course cities on rivers could bring in grain from a greater distance, but even then the grain still had to be carried to the river first.

Little surprise, then, that few cities reached a population greater than 100,000 in the pre-industrial world, and most were considerably smaller than that. Even a city as powerful as fifteenth-century Bologna peaked at 72,000, before plague reduced its numbers again to around 50,000. Had plague not intervened, the city might well have struggled to feed itself. As early as 1305, the council recognised the strategic importance of being able to supply itself with food 'from its own possessions', something larger cities were unable to do.[16] With a population of 90,000, fourteenth-century Florence was already having to import much of its grain from Sicily; no mean task, given that the city was 60 miles from the coast up the River Arno.

The transport of food in the pre-industrial world also determined the way in which cities' rural hinterlands were arranged, a phenomenon first analysed by the German landowner and geographer Johann Heinrich von Thünen, in his work of 1826, *The Isolated State*. The eponymous 'state' consisted of a 'very large town' in the middle of a featureless, fertile plain, the latter inhabited only by rational, profit-seeking farmers.[17] Under such conditions, postulated von Thünen, the farm belt around a city would organise itself into a series of concentric rings, like ripples from a pebble chucked in a pond. The innermost one would consist of market gardens and dairies, whose profits would be high enough to pay the rent and whose activities would most benefit from the city's manure. Beyond this would be a ring of coppices for firewood; and beyond that, arable land where the city's grain would be grown, close enough to the city to make its transport feasible. Beyond that, there would be grazing for livestock, and finally, wilderness: land so far from the city that it wasn't worth exploiting. (The question of where the inhabitants of the *Isolated State* might want to spend their weekends did not arise.) If the city was on a river, von Thünen argued, the low cost of water transport would distort its rural hinterland, stretching it along the river's banks in a series of linear strips.

Despite its disregard of politics, culture and most forms of geography, von Thünen's land-use model mirrored the pre-industrial world rather well. Of course it was essentially a mathematical rationalisation of the way most cities had been fed up until his day – cities, that is, without recourse to the most important influence on food supplies in the pre-industrial world: the sea.

The First Food Miles

> Those who use the metaphors of war when they talk about food
> are often more accurate than they would care to admit.
>
> Derek Cooper[18]

It can be tempting to hark back to a golden age when all food was produced and consumed locally, with no more than a short trip 'from field to fork'. But of course no such age ever existed. Although small cities in the pre-industrial world were able to feed themselves locally, 'food miles' featured in the feeding of larger ones from the start.[19] Before the railways, sea transport was the only way cities could transcend geography, and although not every great European city was a maritime power, those that were not – Paris, Florence and Madrid among them – all eventually faced the same fate. The larger they grew, the harder they found it to feed themselves, while their maritime rivals flourished.

Athens began importing grain from the Black Sea as early as the seventh century BC, since the local soil (a light, sandy loam) was unsuited to growing it. The city managed to turn its weakness into a strength, developing a powerful fleet that would later become a decisive weapon of war. Indeed, war and food were never far removed in the ancient world: many of Athens' political allegiances, such as those made with Cyprus and Egypt against Persia in the fifth century BC, served the dual purpose of increasing the city's political security while giving it access to those countries' grain reserves. Critical supply routes were also heavily protected: the Hellespont, the narrow stretch of the Bosporus through which all Black Sea shipping must pass, was protected in times of war with a special army. Even in times of peace, such as that following the Persian defeat in 480 BC, Athens made sure it maintained superior naval power in the eastern Mediterranean in order to secure its grain supplies.

Poor local soil was not the only reason for cities to import their food. Rome, London, Antwerp and Venice all had fertile hinterlands, yet all imported food from overseas. One reason was that imported food – as is the case today – was often cheaper than local. Sea transport cost next to nothing relative to land transport in the ancient world: one estimate puts the ratio at 1:42.[20] Even had Rome been capable of feeding itself from its own backyard, it would still have made economic sense for the city to import its grain from North Africa. As it was, cheap sea transport became so critical to the capital's survival that Emperor Diocletian issued an edict to keep Mediterranean shipping costs artificially low, just as aviation fuel remains untaxed today by international agreement.[21]

By the third century BC Rome already relied on grain from Sicily and Sardinia, and as the capital expanded, its conquest of new territory became paramount in order to secure fresh supplies. Feeding itself was fast becoming a vicious circle from which the city could not escape: its need for grain, not political gain, often drove its empire onward. Two military conquests, over Carthage in 146 BC and Egypt in 30 BC, were crucial victories, securing access to coastal North Africa, territory as vital to Rome's survival as the American Midwest would be to London's almost 2,000 years later. Rome lost no time in turning its new colonies into efficient bread-making machines, occupying them not just with officials and soldiers, but with farmers, 6,000 of whom were given generous portions of land in North Africa on which to grow grain for the capital.

Rome may not have been the first city to import food by sea, but the scale of its trade made it the true pioneer of food miles. By the first century AD, the capital was a metropolis of a million or so citizens: a quite staggering number for the time, and one that no Western city would match until London in the nineteenth century.[22] Life in contemporary London seems unthinkable without Brazilian coffee and New Zealand lamb; 2,000 years ago, the same was true in Rome of Spanish oil and Gallic ham. The entire Mediterranean sent food to the city: wine and oil came from Spain and Tunisia, pork from Gaul, honey from Greece, and last but not least came Spanish *liquamen,* a fermented fish sauce without which no Roman's life was apparently worth living. When the Greek orator Aristides arrived in Rome in AD 143, he marvelled at the deluge of food flowing into the city:

> . . . whatever is grown and made among each people cannot fail to be here at all times and in abundance . . . the city appears a kind of common emporium of the world . . . arrivals and departures by sea never cease, so that the wonder is, not that the harbour has insufficient space for merchant vessels, but that even the sea has enough, if it really does.[23]

The physical and administrative effort required to bring all this fodder into the capital was truly immense. Sea transport in the ancient

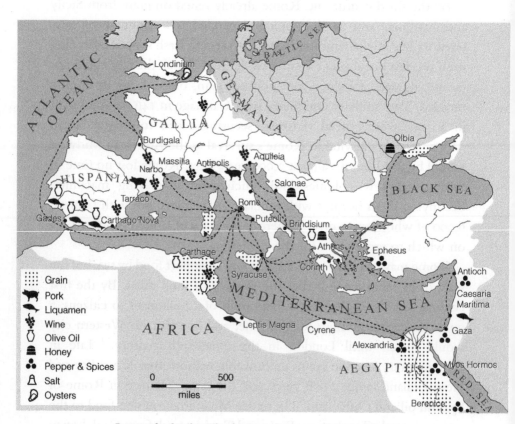

Roman food miles. The food supply routes of Ancient Rome.

74

world might have been cheap, but it was far from straightforward. Unprotected grain could easily be spoiled in open, wooden-built ships, and winter storms often made the sea voyage too treacherous to attempt, so that grain had to be held at Alexandria, waiting for conditions to improve. Even if the ships did make a safe landfall, that was far from the end of it. The Roman port of Ostia was too small to take large Alexandrian grain ships (the supertankers of their day), so that many had to dock at Puteoli in the Bay of Naples, transferring their cargoes to smaller vessels for the trip to Rome. When food finally got to Ostia, it still had to be lugged 20 miles upstream along the narrow, swift-flowing Tiber. This final leg of the journey was the most arduous of all. It took teams of men and oxen three days to tow barges of food upriver – often longer than it had taken to complete the sea voyage from Africa.[24] The effort could never let up, even for a day – Rome gobbled up stocks of grain like sand pouring through an hourglass, and the city rarely had a comfortable safety margin to play with. When Claudius came to power, there were reckoned to be just eight days' worth of grain left in the city.

The scale of the effort can still be felt in the ancient ruins of Ostia. The Rotterdam of its day, Ostia was a thriving city of some 30,000 souls, and its theatres, temples, villas and baths are all remarkably well preserved – as are its streets, with their shops and four-storey apartment buildings above. It requires only the feeblest effort to imagine what life must once have been like here: one ancient *taberna* is so uncannily like a modern Italian bar that you have to restrain yourself from walking up and ordering a glass of wine. In the city centre, a large piazza lined with shops was once the city's commercial hub, with merchants' insignia – ships, dolphins, fish and the Pharos, the great Alexandria lighthouse – still visible in its mosaic pavement. But perhaps the most spectacular reminder of the scale of the capital's appetite is the port itself: Trajan's massive hexagonal dock, built by the emperor in AD 98 to solve the harbour's perennial problem of silting up. The 350-metre-long quaysides can still be made out under a tangle of brambles, and the ground crunches underfoot with shards of the amphorae that once brought oil and wine to feed the greatest city on earth.

The Politics of Supply

> You who control the transportation of food supplies are in charge,
> so to speak, of the city's lifeline, of its very throat.
>
> Cassiodorus[25]

It was rare for any city in the pre-industrial world to leave its food
supplies to chance – they were far too important for that. From the days
of the earliest city-states, managing the food supply was a matter for
civic authorities, a responsibility they took very seriously indeed. In
the ancient cities of Egypt and Mesopotamia, temples were the food
hubs of their day, combining the symbolic function of feeding the gods
with the less exalted, yet equally necessary one of feeding the people.

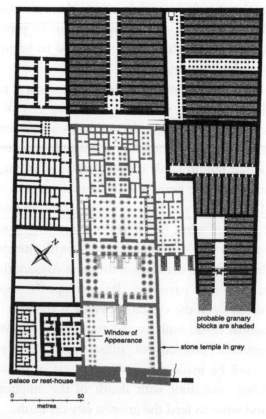

The Ramesseum at Thebes, showing the public granaries around the temple.

Temples received taxes from landowners, organised the harvest, managed stocks of grain and doled them out – the latter task usually involving offering food to the gods first, before distributing what they did not take.[26] Grain was more than just food in the ancient city, it was wealth; and maintaining adequate stocks was crucial. The Ramesseum at Thebes could hold enough grain to support 3,400 families: the population of a medium-sized city. As the Egyptologist Barry Kemp remarked, such temples were not just ceremonial centres or public granaries, they were 'the reserve banks of the time'.[27] Since Egyptian labourers were paid directly in grain and beer, the pharaohs knew by the size of the harvest just how much work could be carried out the following year.

Temples might have been capable of controlling food distribution in the city-states of the ancient Near East, but supplying a city the size of Rome was an entirely different matter. Not only was the population vast, but the average Roman lived in hellish conditions, in cramped *insulae* (tenements) six or seven storeys high, separated by narrow alleyways just a few feet across and with no drainage or running water.[28] Most were as cut off from the countryside as we are in modern cities, and were utterly dependent on the state to feed them. From early Republican times, the Senate provided citizens with a subsidised monthly grain ration, the *annona*, both to keep them fed and to keep them quiet: the populace lived close to boiling point, and nothing got it bubbling faster than a threat to the food supply.

Although not all Romans received the *annona* (it was limited to a privileged group of free adult males, the *plebs frumentia*), the cost of maintaining it was considerable. When the tribune Clodius had the idea in 58 BC of securing his popularity by making the rations free, Cicero reckoned it cost Rome a fifth of all its revenue.[29] Successive emperors tried to reduce the numbers eligible, but were met with immediate rioting, and were usually forced to back down. Julius Caesar's attempt to curb the *annona* caused bloody civil unrest that lasted until his own assassination in 44 BC.[30] The lesson wasn't lost on Augustus. Political animal that he was, he realised soon after taking office that, however irksome the task, feeding 320,000 citizens would prove a safer bet than trying to fiddle the numbers. It was one of his smartest moves according to Tacitus: the historian later wrote that Augustus had 'won over the people with bread'.[31]

Nobody close to the elite in Rome could be in any doubt that food and political power were closely linked, or that failing to feed the people was the surest path to political ruin. Seventy years after Clodius' gift to the plebs, Tiberius acknowledged his need to uphold the pledge: 'This duty, senators, devolves upon the emperor; if it is neglected, the utter ruin of the state will follow.'[32] But even the might of Rome could not control the food supply fully. A particularly bad spate of piracy in the 70s BC sent grain prices rocketing, causing unrest in the city during which an angry mob attacked some consuls in the Forum. Realising the urgent need for action, the Senate nevertheless rejected an offer by the prominent general Pompey to clear the sea of pirates on the grounds that his success would give him unrivalled political power. They were soon proved right. When the people got wind of Pompey's offer, they stormed the Senate, demanding a reversal of the decision and forcing the senators to cave in. Within weeks, Pompey had cleared the sea of pirates, causing an immediate fall in grain prices and securing him the unassailable power the senators had known it would.[33]

The Baltic Bonanza

As urban civilisation spread further north in Europe, so did its sources of supply. By medieval times, the Baltic was the new Mediterranean, and in place of the military smash-and-grab raids that characterised food supplies in the ancient world came a new, highly lucrative commercial trade.

Before the days of canning and freezing, salted herring was the unloved mainstay of many a city-dweller's diet, particularly since the Church forbade the eating of meat on Fridays and holy days, which could amount to over 100 days a year. The demand for salted fish was such that the discovery in the Baltic of an almost unlimited supply of herring led to the formation of one of the most powerful trading cartels in history, the Hanseatic League. A treaty with Denmark had given the German city of Lübeck rights to the spawning grounds off the Swedish Scania coast, and together with nearby Hamburg and its local salt mines, the city saw a way of turning the fish into cash. In 1241 the two cities formed a trading partnership that by the fourteenth century was exporting 300,000 barrels of salted fish all over Europe, with such impressive profits that other cities in the region such as Bruges, Riga and Danzig (Gdansk) were keen to get in on the act. The resulting Hanseatic League (from the Old High German *Hansa*, 'group') enjoyed a monopoly on Baltic trade until well into the fifteenth century, when a series of blows – not least the sudden migration of herring to the North Sea – began to weaken its grasp. The League's collapse signalled the start of Dutch influence on trade in the region that can still be felt today – one based not just on herring, but on the most vital urban food of them all: grain.

Long before the American Midwest was inhabited by farmers, the plains of Poland, Lithuania, Hungary and Russia fed European cities, which, by medieval times, were getting very hungry indeed. Despite an extensive fertile agricultural belt, fourteenth-century Venice had a navy of more than 3,000 ships, and kept 44 dockside warehouses stocked with Baltic and Black Sea grain; reserves that saved it when it was besieged by the Genoese in 1372. Sixteenth-century Constantinople was no one-horse town either: capital of the rapidly expanding Ottoman Empire, it had an estimated 700,000 mouths to feed, and needed, in the words of the historian Fernand Braudel, 'every available flock of sheep from the Balkans to support it; rice, beans and corn from Egypt; corn and wood from the Black Sea; and oxen, camels and horses from Asia Minor'.[34]

Although medieval and early modern cities bought their grain with gold rather than by military conquest, the sea was still the only means of carrying it very far. Just as the Nile had once carried grain through Egypt to Alexandria, the Vistula now conveyed it from the Polish interior to Danzig on the Baltic Sea, whence it could be shipped all over Europe. The journey, which often took many months, culminated in the spring, when the snows melted and hundreds of flat-bottomed craft floated downriver on the resulting floods. Once they reached Danzig, the rafts were broken up and sold for firewood, while their owners, having sold their corn to shipping merchants, faced a weary trudge back home. This annual migration, known as the *frujor*, was a major cultural event in Poland, widely celebrated in poetry and prose. As the historian Norman Davies has pointed out, it was the only time, other than in times of war, that many Poles came into contact with the wider world; the one thing that connected them with the 'strange foreign world of ships and the sea'.[35]

That division would prove decisive, not just to Poland's fortunes, but to the nation best placed to benefit from it – the Dutch. Like the ancient Athenians before them, lack of agricultural land had forced the Dutch to start importing grain earlier than most, so that by the sixteenth century when others started to catch up, they already had a sizeable merchant fleet with a strong presence in Danzig. By 1650 they had virtual control of the Polish grain trade, not least because of a bizarre law of 1496 forbidding Polish merchants to travel overseas. Dozens of Dutch merchants had permanent bases in Danzig, and the 'Amsterdam Fleet', consisting of around 2,000 ships, carried grain to France, England, Portugal and even as far as Venice. The Dutch merchants' power was reflected in the commonest type of contract between them and their Polish suppliers: the *Lieferantzkauf*, which would seem depressingly familiar to many modern producers. The quantity, price and date of delivery were all set a year in advance, and made entirely at the growers' risk and expense.

There has always been plenty of money to be made from feeding cities. The trick, as the Dutch knew very well, is to make sure you have control of the supply. Despite branching further afield with the Dutch East India Company in 1602, Baltic grain remained the backbone of Netherlanders' 'Golden Age', the business they always referred to as the 'Mother Trade'.

Paris – Bread and Violence

> One would have trouble imagining that there are sources capable
> of meeting the needs of this vast pit.
>
> N.T.L. Des Essarts[36]

No matter how much grain came out of the Baltic, it was no good to cities that could not get their hands on it. By 1750, Paris was one of the largest cities in Europe, with around 650,000 mouths to feed. Dubbed 'New Rome' because of its size, the city (unlike Constantinople, the actual 'New Rome') had to rely on its local hinterland to feed it. Although it sits on a river, Paris is 170 miles from the sea – too far to make the large-scale importing of foreign grain practicable. The result, as the historian Stephen Kaplan described in *Provisioning Paris*, was that the Parisian grain trade both dominated and stifled the rural economy of northern France.[37] A series of 'provisioning crowns' were declared around the capital; the first consisting of a zone 20 miles deep in which only grain for the city could be grown. With a good harvest, this 'first crown' could just about cope, but in bad years (which could come as often as once in every three) the capital asserted its right, by force if necessary, to acquire its grain from further afield. The 'second crown', including Picardy and Champagne, then came into play; and if that wasn't enough, the third, or 'crisis', crown was invoked, essentially consisting of most of the rest of France, from its Atlantic to its Mediterranean coasts.

The capital's habit of putting 'a knife to the throat of the people', as one local put it, didn't go down too well in the countryside.[38] When the harvests failed, rural folk needed their grain just as much as city-dwellers did, but since they posed rather less of a threat than their urban counterparts, they generally didn't get to keep it. Citizens of Paris were as dependent on the authorities to feed them as those of Rome had been, and they were equally bellicose – as well as fussy. They insisted on eating a pure white loaf known as the *bis-blanc*; a bread so fine that, as one writer observed in 1709, 'the small artisan eats a more beautiful loaf than the best bourgeois of the provinces'.[39]

The Parisian authorities recognised, just as those of Rome had done, that feeding the people was a political necessity. In the words of the minister Jacques Necker, it was 'the most essential object that must occupy the administration'.[40] But without easy access to foreign grain, the authorities' options were limited, and they responded by throwing as much legislation at the problem as they could. The administration was dominated – one might say crippled – by its grain police, an unwieldy hierarchy of hundreds of officials, headed by no less a figure than the king himself, the 'baker of last resort'. The police oversaw every aspect

Paris's main grain port in the seventeenth century. Merchants and suppliers were obliged
to trade on muddy quays or on barges tied up alongside.

of the grain trade, sending spies out into the countryside to gather information on current market conditions, the state of the crops, weather, local gossip and so on, and receiving reports back at weekly meetings. In an attempt to control the trade as fully as possible, every part of it was supposed to be transparent. All transactions were meant to take place in the open so that they could be monitored, and only licensed grain merchants were allowed to function within 20 miles of the city. The hoarding of grain was forbidden, and millers, bakers and merchants were all prevented from engaging in one another's business.

That was the theory, anyway. In practice, a huge amount of trade went on illegally, via an extensive black market that included a network of illegal 'corn exchanges' held in taverns, farms and even out on the open road. Institutions licensed to hold stocks of grain for their own use, such as convents and hospitals, acted as illegal granaries, allowing dealers to store grain there in exchange for a cut of the profits.

Meanwhile merchants, millers and bakers engaged in a struggle to wrest control of the supply: first millers began to deal in grain, accumulating vast wealth in the process; then bakers began milling their own flour, taking away the millers' business. The grain police were well aware of these illegal practices, but they were powerless to stop them. As the officers themselves recognised, the black market – one might call it the free market – had an essential role to play in feeding the city. The police were in an invidious position, forced to turn a blind eye to the very practices they were supposed to prevent. The result was the worst of all possible worlds: a policy of complete control over a trade that was inherently uncontrollable.

Even the most casual of historians knows that bread played some part in the French Revolution. Rather than seeing food shortages as a privation to be mutually endured, the people saw them as a failure of the authorities – and ultimately of the king himself. Signs of things to come were already evident in 1665, when Louis XIV tried to switch army pension rations from wheat to rye, only to be met with the instant threat of mutiny. Again, when Louis XV tried to avert famine by importing grain from Barbary in 1725, he was accused of 'forcing the people to eat rotten wheat', a notion that was widespread during the Revolution.[41] The inevitable crisis came with a string of poor harvests during the 1780s, culminating in two disastrous ones in 1788 and 1789. As the population turned to riot, the 'baker of last resort' tried to flee Paris, but was apprehended and brought back to the city. Louis XVI had in fact stopped to change horses, but was popularly portrayed as having paused to eat a meal: the ultimate gesture of a monarch too greedy to save his own skin, let alone those of his people.[42]

London – Feeding the Wen

Of all cities, none deserved the honorary title 'New Rome' more than London. Just 20 years after its founding in AD 43, Londinium was described by Tacitus as a 'celebrated centre of commerce', and much of that was based on the old Roman obsession with foreign food.[43] Olive oil, wine, pine nuts, raisins, pepper, ginger and cinnamon – not forgetting copious quantities of the all-important *liquamen* – were all shipped in from the Mediterranean to make life bearable for expat Romans shivering in the frozen north.[44]

Blessed by its position on the tidal, navigable Thames, London always had plenty of options when it came to feeding itself. The river not only gave the city easy access to foreign foods, it also provided the channels by which produce from the rich farmland of south-east England could reach the city. The supply of grain to the capital already dominated the local economy by the thirteenth century, with market towns such as Ware on the River Lea, Henley-on-Thames, and Faversham, Maidstone and Rochester on the north Kent coast already well established by 1200. Henley grew so rich supplying Midlands grain to London that many of the capital's cornmongers established granaries as well as second homes there.[45] Yet despite its abundance of local supplies, London never lost the habit of importing food from abroad. Records from the tenth century onwards show the medieval city regularly supplementing its grain supplies from the Baltic.

With so much food at its disposal, London always had a uniquely hands-off approach to feeding itself. English monarchs never took responsibility for feeding their citizens; on the contrary, royal inter-ference in London trade was seen as more of a hindrance than a help. London merchants traded independently of Westminster, and dues from the city's two main river ports, Billingsgate and Queenhithe, went to City and Crown respectively, making the question of which did the better trade a matter of great concern to the permanently cash-strapped monarchy. Being upstream of London Bridge, Queenhithe was the less well placed of the two, a disadvantage that successive monarchs tried to overcome by issuing edicts such as that of Edward IV in 1463, cited by John Stow:

> . . . it was ordained, that all manner of vessels, ships, or boats, great
> or small, resorting to the city with victual, should be sold by retail,
> and that if there came but one vessel at a time, were it salt, wheat, rye,
> or other corn from beyond the seas, or other grains, garlic, onions,
> herrings, sprats, eels, whiting, place, cod, mackerel &c, then that one
> vessel should come to Queene Hithe, and there to make sale: but if

two vessels came, the one should come to Queene Hithe, the other
to Billingsgate: if three, two of them should come to Queene Hithe,
the third to Billingsgate &c. always the more to Queene Hithe.[46]

Whichever port it came to, there was certainly no shortage of food
arriving in London, which perhaps explains why the English were so
slow when it came to exploring global trade. It was only when
Christopher Columbus accidentally bumped into America while
attempting to find a sea passage to Asia in 1492 that the English finally
woke up and – as it were – smelt the coffee.[47] It didn't take them long
to realise their mistake: just three years later, Henry VII engaged the
Venetian explorers John Cabot and son, giving them 'full and free
authority' to 'conquer, occupy and possess whatsoever such towns,
castles, cities and islands' they could find anywhere in world.[48] It was to
be the start of four centuries of exploration and trade – or exploitation
and piracy – that would turn England from a relative backwater into a
global superpower.

The English might have entered the global trade race in search of
gold, but what they found was a substance that would turn out to be
even more valuable – sugar. When Admiral William Penn seized
Jamaica on behalf of the Crown in 1655, he could hardly have
imagined the wealth that would soon pour out of the new colony.
Sugar was to prove a food so irresistible that within the space of a
century it would transform not just Britain's economic fortunes, but
the very fabric of its society. During the seventeenth century, demand
for it grew so rapidly that plantations were soon established all over
the Caribbean, run like factories on African slave labour, the shameful
'false commodity' on which so much colonial wealth was based.[49] To
begin with, England exported half its sugar to the rest of Europe, but
by 1750, home consumption had outstripped supply to such an extent
that all exports had virtually ceased. Yet, as the governor of the East
India Company Sir Josiah Child pointed out, England didn't need to
export its sugar – it could manage very nicely just trading with its own
foreign colonies.[50]

Thanks largely to trade in the new 'white gold', eighteenth-century
London was a boom town. A tenth of the population was living in the

capital, a quarter of them engaged in port trades, dealing with goods flowing in from every part of the world. Walking through the burgeoning dockyards, Samuel Johnson marvelled at their contents:

> He that contemplates the extent of this wonderful city, finds it difficult to conceive, by what method plenty is maintained in our markets, and how the inhabitants are regularly supplied with the necessities of life; but when he examines the shops and warehouses, sees the immense stores of every kind of merchandise piled up for sale . . . he will be inclined to conclude that such quantities cannot easily be exhausted . . .[51]

London was becoming rich; and, as Daniel Defoe noted, the city was getting increasingly frivolous with it. 'It will hardly be believed in ages to come,' he wrote, 'that a pastry cook's shop, which twenty pounds would effectively furnish at one time with all needful things for sale, yet that fitting up one of these shops should cost upwards of £300, Anno Domini 1710: let the year be recorded!'[52] Defoe might have been outraged at his contemporaries' extravagances, but he could also see their benefits to the nation. Londoners might have been high on sugar, but they also needed their bread and butter, which, as Defoe noted in his *Tour Through the Whole Island of Great Britain* in 1720, was good for everyone:

> It is not the kingdom which makes London rich, but London makes the rest of the kingdom rich. The country corresponds with London, but London corresponds with the world. The country supplies London with corn and cattle; and if there were not such a metropolis, what would become of the farmers? . . . The country send up their corn, their malt, their cattle, their fowls, their coals, their fish, all to London, and London sends back spice, sugar, wine, drugs, cotton, linen, tobacco, and all foreign necessaries to the country . . . London consumes all, circulates all, exports all, and at last pays for all; and this is trade.[53]

The craving for sugar was turning London – and Britain – into the world's first consumer society. Mixed with the bitter trio of coffee, tea and cocoa, it was creating an intoxicating desire; a blurring of the boundaries between luxury and need. As one of the first to witness the phenomenon, Defoe could see that the world about him was changing, yet it would take another 50 years before the events he described were acknowledged as a whole new economic order; the start of a hunger that could never be satisfied.

The Case for Free Trade

By the early eighteenth century, the contrasting fortunes of Paris and London were stark. With a population of 675,000, London had just surpassed Paris as the largest city in Europe; yet while the French capital became increasingly obsessed with its food supply, Londoners were so busy making money that the authorities barely gave a second thought to how their citizens were to be fed.

One man for whom the contrast did not go unnoticed was Adam Smith, Scottish son of a customs officer, professor of moral philosophy at Glasgow University, and author of one of the most influential economic tracts ever written, *An Enquiry into the Nature and Causes of the Wealth of Nations*, published in 1776. In this famous work, Smith set out many of the principles of modern capitalism; in particular the idea that a market based on free trade is the best way to generate wealth. The fact that his idea seems so obvious today is testimony to its power, but back in Smith's day it was far from obvious. Smith argued that although agriculture formed the basis of a nation's wealth, cities played a vital role in driving it forward:

> The great commerce of every civilised society, is that carried on between the inhabitants of the town and those of the country . . . The country supplies the town with the means of subsistence, and the materials of manufacture. The town repays this by sending back a part of the manufactured produce to the inhabitants of the country. The town, in which there neither is nor can be any reproduction of substances, may very properly be said to gain its whole wealth and subsistence from the country. We must not, however upon this

account, imagine that the gain of the town is the loss of the country. The gains of both are mutual and reciprocal . . .[54]

Together city and country created a mutually beneficial market – one that required no regulation, since it operated entirely through the competing self-interest of many individuals. The 'hidden hand' of commerce therefore regulated itself.

Having established the concept of free trade, Smith went on to consider how to maximise its benefits, concluding that the best way was to expand the market by investing in transport:

> Good roads, canals, and navigable rivers, by diminishing the expense of carriage, put the remote parts of the country more nearly upon a level with those in the neighbourhood of a town. They are upon that account the greatest of all improvements . . . They are advantageous to the town, by breaking down the monopoly of the country in its neighbourhood.[55]

No farmer himself, Smith was able to view the relationship between city and country with a dispassionate eye. However, he did acknowledge the unpleasant truth that William Cobbett would spend his life railing against: namely that the free operation of capitalism would create inevitable human casualties:

> The inhabitants of a city, it is true, must always ultimately derive their subsistence, and the whole materials and means of their industry, from the country. But those of a city, situated near either the sea-coast or the banks of a navigable river, are not necessarily confined to derive them from the country in their neighbourhood. They have a much wider range, and they may draw them from the most remote corners of the world . . . A city might in this manner grow to great wealth and splendour, while not only the country in its neighbourhood, but all those to which it traded were in poverty and wretchedness.[56]

A mighty city on a navigable river: there could be no better description of eighteenth-century London. Although Smith did not mention it by name, London demonstrated the power of what he called 'perfect competition': the forces of supply and demand left to their own devices. Smith's model predicted human wretchedness, but also economic gain – a formulation that would prove mightily enduring.

'Nobody Does It'

Eighty years after *Wealth of Nations*, the social chronicler George Dodd published what he called a 'sketch' of London, describing 'the chief varieties, sources of supply, probable quantities, modes of arrival, process of manufacture, suspected adulteration, and machinery of distribution of the food for a community of two millions and a half'.[57] The resulting tome, *The Food of London*, is an exhaustive record of everything to do with the Victorian capital's food supply. You want to know how many tons of potatoes were sold at Covent Garden in 1853? Ask George Dodd: 72,000. The number of livestock imported into the capital in that same year? Two point two million. How many ships docked each day at the city's ports? One hundred and twenty-one, of which all but 15 were British built, and 52 came from the colonies, bringing, among other things, an annual 86 million pounds of tea from India and China. Dodd's researches were exhaustive, but when he tried to explain how all this produce was reaching London, he had to admit that he was stumped:

> It is useless to ask by what central authority, or under what controlling system, is such a city as London supplied with its daily food. 'Nobody does it.' No-one for instance, took care that a sufficient quantity of food should reach London in 1855, for the supply of two millions and a half of human beings during fifty-two weeks. And yet such a supply *did* reach London.[58]

By George Dodd's day, the 'hidden hand' that fed London was in full swing, and its methods had barely changed for centuries. Cattle were still herded down St John Street to the livestock market at Smithfield, geese still waddled in from Essex, tea clippers still sailed up

The Great Western Railway in 1840, carrying animals bound for the city.

the Thames. Yet things were on the verge of change. In 1835, the first railway line into London was completed (connecting London Bridge to Greenwich), and two years later, the rather more impressive London to Birmingham line was constructed, terminating at Euston Station. As Dodd recognised, the railways were set to revolutionise the way cities were fed. 'It is scarcely possible,' he wrote, 'to exaggerate the value of quick and easy transmission of food to so enormous a city as London; the variety of the commodities, and the prices at which they can be sold, are so intimately dependent thereon, that it becomes almost a matter of life and death to the inhabitants.'[59]

The most obvious and vital effect of the railways, at least to the hungry citizens of London, Liverpool and Manchester, was to allow food to be transported in bulk, so saving them from the fate that had engulfed Paris 50 years previously. What was less apparent was that in solving the greatest and oldest problem to afflict cities, the railways were creating another, ultimately greater problem. Up until the nineteenth century, food, and the natural geography that provided it, had determined where cities were built, and how large they could grow. But railways made it possible to build cities just about anywhere, and just about any size. They broke the one constraint that had always held back urban sprawl, and as geography was swept aside (along with

von Thünen's land-use theories), the urban carpet began to roll out in earnest. Cities sprouted suburbs, and suburbs merged to form conurbations, whose new inhabitants expected to be fed, and began to succumb to the sort of consumerism previously limited to maritime cities like London.

There was plenty of money to be made from feeding the expanding cities, but the biggest profits were no longer in basic commodities such as grain, rather in added-value consumables such as milk, the first food to benefit not just from the railways' carrying capacity, but from their speed. To Victorian Londoners, 'railway milk' was a revelation. No longer the product of unsanitary inner-city cowsheds, fresh milk from wholesome counties such as Devon, Dorset and Somerset could now be loaded on to trains at 6 a.m., arriving in London in time for breakfast. Although the system wasn't perfect (in hot summers the milk often went off in transit, arriving not only sour, but churned solid by the motion of the train), railway milk was soon regarded as a highly desirable, and profitable, commodity. Together with American cereal and Danish bacon and eggs, it helped forge a new gastronomic institution, the Great British Breakfast, making those supplying it (among them a London grocer by the name of John Sainsbury) very rich indeed.

Then, as now, Sainsbury's emphasised the cleanliness and freshness of its food. The original shop in Drury Lane, opened in 1869, was immaculately scrubbed, and allowed customers to fill up their milk jugs from shining churns set on a marble counter. Despite coming from a lot further away, railway milk seemed – and probably was – fresher than milk bought straight from the cow in the dung-strewn cowshed a few doors along, and carried with it the welcome breath of the countryside. The milk was soon so popular that Sainsbury's made it available to customers out of hours via a 'mechanical cow': a coin-operated pump that could be operated standing in the street. Sainsbury's was inventing the modern grocery trade as it went along, and within a few years it began opening new branches in London, supplying them from a central depot with a 'distribution fleet' of horse-drawn vans. The vans might have run on hay, but modern retail logistics had effectively arrived.

Other aspects of the London food supply were modernising too. Due to its rapid increase in population, London was struggling to feed itself for the first time in its history, and the government felt it had little choice but to extend the principle on which the city had always depended – the 'hidden hand' of commerce – as far as it could. By the century's end, the nation was the world's biggest importer not only of grain, but of processed and preserved foods too. While the urban poor dined on American wheat, middle-class Britons discovered the delights of tinned prunes, apricots and peaches from California and condensed milk from Switzerland. When the first shipload of frozen Australian meat arrived in London in 1880, still in perfect condition after many weeks at sea, the future pattern of British consumption was set.[60]

The Milk Combine

By the end of the nineteenth century, there was no shortage of food in London, but not all Londoners could afford to eat it. When Queen Victoria died in 1901, two thirds of the wealth in her realm was in the hands of just 2.5 per cent of her subjects, and as the social reformer Charles Booth revealed in his exhaustive 1903 survey *Life and Labour of the People in London*, many of the remaining 97.5 per cent lived in conditions as grim as those of ancient Rome (or worse: at least some Romans had received free bread).[61] Booth's survey, which ran to 17 volumes, made shocking reading. Many Londoners were living in slum conditions, 30 per cent of them under the breadline. Booth castigated his contemporaries for their lack of empathy towards their fellow men:

> The words 'Give us this day our daily bread' have not much meaning to us; do we ever think what they mean to the poor? I am constantly impressed with the different aspect of our life compared to that of those who live on daily wages, from day to day, from hand to mouth. Some of my friends will say 'You mean the difference between the thrifty and the unthrifty' but I do not think I do.[62]

What was becoming clear was that leaving the food supply solely to the 'hidden hand' of commerce had its downside. While the nascent food industries were very good at producing and transporting food, feeding the urban poor wasn't their goal. Left to their own devices, they naturally sought to maximise profits, which meant targeting those who could afford to pay. While poorer city-dwellers disappeared off the food-supply radar, food companies competed for the lucrative end of the market by doing what every urban authority in history had sought to prevent them from doing: they consolidated.

By the start of the First World War, greater awareness of the nutritional benefits of milk had elevated it from a novelty drink into what the government called 'a most necessary food'. Public access to 'good, clean milk' was now seen as a more urgent priority than bread; yet London's milk was supplied by just five major wholesalers, two of which merged in 1915 to form United Dairies, gaining control of half the capital's supply. While the House of Commons debated whether or not this constituted a dangerous monopoly, the new 'milk combine' answered the question itself, hoicking up its prices to such an extent that the government was forced to act. In 1918, it nationalised milk production under a new Milk Control Board; but the new regime was to prove short-lived. After a year spent wrangling with milk producers and retailers, the Board was unable to fix a fair price for milk, and it collapsed soon after. The 'milk combine' was then referred to the Standing Committee on Trusts, a forerunner of the Monopolies and Mergers Commission, and about as toothless.[63]

By the end of the war, the government's failure to wrest control of

London's milk supply was clear. United Dairies' share of the trade had increased to 80 per cent, and in 1920 it augmented its business with the acquisition of 470 retail outlets in the capital. As a memo from the Ministry of Food noted, 'if the State stands aside, this growth will continue unchecked, placing the consumer at the mercy of a powerful monopoly controlling an essential food'.[64] But it was already too late. From then on, it would be the food industry, and not government, that would be calling the shots.

Biggest is Best

Things have moved on somewhat since London was first menaced by its 'milk combine'. As Adam Smith foresaw – but on a scale that he could not have imagined – better transport links between city and country have indeed opened up urban markets to greater competition. But the global scale of those markets changes everything. The world's industrialised nations now effectively represent one enormous city; the rest of the world their rural hinterland. In the new global village, we all eat the same food, supplied by the same companies, available in the same shops, and the laws of competition envisioned by Smith no longer apply. Throughout the twentieth century, consolidation within the food industry went virtually unchecked. Today, just 30 companies handle 30 per cent of all global trade in food; a neatly symmetrical statistic that gives some idea of the unprecedented power that major conglomerates now have over the food supply.[65] Similarly awesome statistics are the annual sales figures of the three biggest: Nestlé, Philip Morris Co. Inc. (Kraft) and ConAgra Foods sold food worth $61 billion, $34 billion and $14 billion respectively in 2005. Never in the field of human consumption has so much been fed to so many by so few.

With food producers like that to deal with, no wonder retailers like Tesco are keen to expand: they need all the buying power they can get. Tesco might loom large on the British retail scene, but in global terms it is still a relative minnow. Its sales revenues of £38 billion in 2006 paled beside those of Wal-Mart, whose staggering sales of $312 billion (£167 billion) that year confirmed its status as top global grocery dog.

Wal-Mart's annual report, *Building Smiles*, announced a 9.5 per cent sales increase that year, with an additional 537 stores and 50,000 employees (or 'associates', in Wal-Mart speak), making a global total of 6,100 stores and a workforce of 1.8 million.[66] Reading statistics about Wal-Mart is rather like reading about outer space: the numbers are so huge they don't really sink in. In 2000, the UN reckoned that the company's sales were bigger than the gross domestic product of three quarters of the world's economies. Six years later, those figures had all but doubled. The biggest smiles, one imagines, are on the faces of Wal-Mart's shareholders.

Feeding cities these days is very big business indeed, but as seventeenth-century Polish grain producers discovered, you have to be at the right end of the food chain in order to profit. Power in the modern food industry has shifted more than ever away from farmers, to those who control the food supply chain. In 1996 the food policy expert Marion Nestle reckoned that a mere 20 per cent of US food expenditure went to producers; the rest went on added value, 'labour, packaging, transportation, advertising and profits'.[67] In the modern food industry, major conglomerates are a powerful tail wagging a very small dog.

Grain in the seventeenth century was a sufficiently valuable commodity to command a reasonable price, but as the food policy experts Tim Lang and Michael Heasman argued in their book *Food Wars*, in modern agribusiness, farming itself is 'becoming irrelevant'.[68] Basic foodstuffs such as grain and potatoes have become 'commodified', their intrinsic market value so low that farmers are often paid less than cost in order to produce them. Prices are set by retailers, whose decisions bear little or no relation to the products they are selling, often with devastating results. For instance, Wal-Mart's decision in 2002 to slash the cost of its bananas by a third (a pure sales gimmick, since bananas are known to sell in equal quantities whatever their shelf price) created an immediate worldwide slump in banana prices. Other retailers were forced to follow suit, putting a squeeze on suppliers, who passed on their losses to their Caribbean and Costa Rican growers, who ended up being paid less than the legal minimum to produce the fruit.[69] It is not just farmers in the developing world who are going to the wall either. When we pay 70–80p for a litre of milk in Britain, most of us assume that farmers are getting more than the 18p many are in fact paid – representing a *loss* of 3p per litre for the average farmer.[70] When you consider that an extra 3–4p per litre would keep British dairy farmers in business, it makes no sense at all.

Food manufacturers are affected too. Another Wal-Mart sales gimmick described by Charles Fishman in his book *The Wal-Mart Effect* involved the selling of gallon (yes, *gallon*) jars of pickles for the absurdly low price of $2.97.[71] The bargain was so compelling that despite the fact that very few ordinary people have much use for a gallon of vinegary cucumbers (which, once the jar is opened, quickly go mouldy), the jars were soon flying off the shelves at the rate of 200,000 a week. The gimmick nearly sent Wal-Mart's pickle supplier, Vlasic, to the wall. For two and a half years, despite sales volumes beyond their wildest dreams, the company was forced to expand, while making virtually no profit. As Fishman pointed out, the entire pickles market was a phantom, benefiting neither customer nor producer. The phenomenal scale of modern food conglomerates gives them the power to create their own reality.

The Revolving Door

> Our competitors are our friends. Our customers are the enemy.
> James Randall, former president of grain
> company Archer Daniels Midland[72]

The modern food industry has provided us with what our ancestors always craved: cheap and plentiful food. Now that we've got it, few of us worry about how it gets to us. But the companies who supply our food have an extraordinary hold over us; one that should have us very worried indeed. Farming may be 'becoming irrelevant', but we still need to eat. So when it turns out, for instance, that 81 per cent of all American beef is in the hands of just four giant processing companies, who between them raise half the cattle in the USA, where does that leave the American burger-eater?[73] Consolidation within the food industry isn't limited to the US either: 85 per cent of the global tea market is controlled by just three companies, and a mere five control 90 per cent of global trade in grain.[74] Adam Smith must be turning in his grave.

At a global level, there is no such thing as free trade in food. Instead, an ever more powerful oligopoly of companies are slicing up the cake between them. Anti-competitive practice is endemic in the food industry: a recent report by Action Aid found that 85 per cent of all fines imposed for price-fixing were paid by agrifood companies. But fining transnational corporations for fixing cartels is about as effective as fining footballers for swearing. Paying fines is just one of the hazards of doing business. Wal-Mart's recent track record with the judiciary reads like a serial offender bent on collecting ASBOs: the company has a varied portfolio of lawsuits that includes the biggest in history, concerning the underpayment of 1.6 million female staff.[75] Companies like Wal-Mart behave as though they were above the law, and as long as their profits exceed their fines as comfortably as they do now, they might as well be.

In Britain and America, the supply of food has effectively passed beyond government control. Transnational corporations are relied upon to carry out this most vital of roles. In 2002, George Bush caused outrage when he announced that the US Senate would be paying a whopping $174 billion in subsidies to US farmers over the next 10 years, most of whom are not exactly the sort of folksy homesteaders of *Little House on the Prairie*. In truth, US agribusiness has a powerful role in government, and in shaping global food policy too. When Dan Amstutz, a former vice-president of Cargill, did a stint at the US Trade Office, he is credited with having helped draft the proposal that was subsequently adopted as the World Trade Organization's Agreement on Agriculture.[76] No wonder US agribusiness is consistently blamed for the failure to reach international trade agreements on food and farming. It is basically operating in a system of its own making.

The 'revolving door' between government and the food industry is less obvious in Britain, because we no longer have a powerful farming lobby in this country. However, that doesn't mean that those links don't exist. In his book *Captive State*, the journalist George Monbiot listed the policy decisions that the British Retail Consortium (BRC) has helped shape in the past few years, including the decision not to tax supermarkets for out-of-town car-parking; permission to use 41-tonne lorries on British roads; and amendments to the Competition Bill that allowed, in his words, ' "vertical agreements" of the kind that super-stores strike with their suppliers'.[77] In 1998, the Director General of the BRC, Ann Robinson, confirmed the cosy nature of the relationship, commenting that 'BRC is no longer an organisation that simply reacts to Government proposed legislation or White Papers, but sets out to help shape them . . . the intention is to work in a non-confrontational way so we are involved at the beginning of any legislative process'.[78] It seems farming isn't the only dog the tail is wagging.

No great surprise, then, that the biggest EU farm subsidies in Britain, far from going to the small producers who most need the help, go instead to the sorts of food manufacturers that one might have thought could fend for themselves. In 2005, the food journalist Felicity Lawrence revealed that the sugar company Tate & Lyle had received £227 million in export subsidies the previous year, while Nestlé was paid to export milk – presumably their $60 billion food sales were in need of a boost.[79] The result of such export subsidies is that world commodity markets are undermined. A recent report by Oxfam estimated that EU sugar 'dumping' had lowered world prices by 17 per cent, preventing countries such as Mozambique, where sugar produc-tion is the largest source of employment, from developing their own industry.[80] The same goes for milk: according to the United Nations Food and Agriculture Organisation (FAO), subsidised powdered milk from the EU in 2002, exported at 60 per cent of the international price, put the Jamaican dairy industry out of business.[81] In a bizarre twist of logic, it seems that milk and sugar – two of the most profitable urban foodstuffs in history – are now being used against the very people who could most benefit from supplying them.

Western countries are constantly accused of sabotaging world trade talks in order to protect outdated farming policies. But whatever agreements are reached at such talks (or not, as the case may be), the real powerbrokers in the negotiations are not governments, but agrifood corporations. That's not to say that national governments have no power – far from it. It is just that most choose not to use it. As long as the food industry carries on delivering plenty of cheap food, it suits the British government to let it be. Like the eighteenth-century Parisian grain police, the government *pretends* to control the food supply, while all it really does is provide a legal veneer for the abusive market practices that keep food nice and cheap.

Food Security

It might seem alarmist, even tasteless, to mention food security in the West when we appear to be enjoying the greatest era of abundance in history. Food security is something we tend to associate with the developing world, and considering how many people worldwide face starvation every day, worrying about our own food supply seems almost obscene. Yet the two phenomena are directly connected. Both are the products of a global food system gone mad, that no longer bears any relation to the people it evolved to serve. The modern food industry is a law unto itself: a transnational cartel with its own rules of engagement, more political clout than governments, and bank accounts to match. In the end, control of food is power, and over the past hundred years or so, it has been passing steadily out of the hands of nation states (to say nothing of cities, farmers and consumers) and into the paws of an elite group of global corporations.

On the face of it, the modern food industry seems to have solved the problem of food supply. Far from waiting anxiously at the quayside to see whether our ship will come in, there is now so much food swilling about in Western cities that most of us are more likely to die of obesity than hunger. Supermarkets ply us with BOGOF (buy one get one free) offers, and when we get our food home, it never seems to go off. What could possibly go wrong?

The short answer is: just about everything. The 'quick and easy transmission of food' may not *seem* like a matter of life and death today, but it still is, arguably more than ever. The cities we live in were shaped by modern food distribution systems; without them, our cities wouldn't even exist. We are as dependent on food conglomerates as ancient city-dwellers were on their king or emperor (or, in the case of London, a myriad of small suppliers), yet unlike them, we have no direct relationship with those who feed us – apart, that is, from when we hand over our cash at the till. Supermarkets supply us with 80 per cent of our food in Britain, but theirs is a business prerogative, not a political one. They take no responsibility for feeding us: if we can't pay, they aren't interested.

Contrary to appearances, we live as much on a knife-edge now as did the inhabitants of ancient Rome or *Ancien Régime* Paris. Cities in the past did their best to keep stocks of grain in reserve in case of sudden attack; yet the efficiencies of modern food distribution mean that we keep very little in reserve. Much of the food you and I will be eating next week hasn't even arrived in the country yet. Our food is delivered 'just in time' from all over the world: hardly the sort of system designed to withstand a sudden crisis. The fuel tax protest led by British lorry drivers in 2000 showed how quickly the slick, split-second operation that delivers our food can break down – and how quickly our sophisticated, take-it-or-leave-it attitude to food can break down with it. On that occasion, panic buying of food began within hours.

Perhaps surprisingly for an island nation, we have never been overly worried about food security in Britain – apart from when German U-boats showed us how vulnerable we were. After the Second World War, the government vowed never to be reliant on food imports again, but 'never' can be a short time in politics. Britain produced just 62 per cent of its own food in 2005, with the figure falling steadily.[82] Yet in the same year, the Minister for the Environment, Elliot Morley, was quoted as saying that 'in an increasingly globalised world, the pursuit of self-sufficiency for its own sake is no longer necessary or desirable'.[83] So that's fine, apparently.

Of course the *economic* logic for abandoning local food production in Britain is obvious, so long as international freight costs remain artificially low. Quite what will happen when the oil starts to run out is anyone's guess, but one thing is certain: the way our food is produced and delivered will change beyond recognition. Even George Bush Jr recently recognised that oil and food weren't quite the inexhaustible commodities Americans like to imagine them to be. In a speech delivered in April 2006, he announced a new initiative to increase US production of the biofuel ethanol from corn. But in the same speech, he also acknowledged that the new fuel wouldn't provide any easy answers: 'Ethanol is good for the whole country,' he said, 'but you've got to recognise there's a limit to how much corn we can use for oil. After all, we've got to eat some; and animals have got to eat.'[84]

Deficiencies of Scale

Even forgetting politics for a moment (never easy to do when talking about food), the scale of modern food production has security implications that affect us all. In the name of 'efficiency', we are streamlining nature itself, reducing the variety of foods worldwide to dangerous levels. Never mind Ashmead's Kernel; what about bananas? Almost all commercial bananas in the world today are of just one variety, Cavendish, yet 50 years ago, the variety didn't exist. It had to be bred specially when worldwide stocks of the previous commercial banana, Gros Michel, were wiped out by the Black Sigatoka fungus, the banana equivalent of Dutch elm disease. Luckily, a wild banana resistant to the disease (Cavendish's ancestor) was found in a remote forest in India; but should a similar pandemic occur today, we could be in serious trouble. In 2006, the FAO expressed alarm at the rate at which wild banana species – which are chiefly found in India – were being lost through the destruction of natural habitat.[85] The FAO urged a worldwide exploration of small-scale producers who still grow non-commercial species, in order to gather the remaining gene pool before it is lost. The future of commercial banana production may well depend on peasant farmers who have never heard of the five companies (Chiquita, Del Monte and the rest) who between them control 80 per cent of global trade.[86]

The loss of genetic variety is not just occurring in the exotic plants and animals of the rainforest either; it is also occurring in those we breed to eat. Over 90 per cent of milk in America now comes from a single breed of cattle, and over 90 per cent of commercial eggs from a single strain of hen. According to the FAO, 30 per cent of 4,500 livestock species worldwide are at a high risk of extinction.[87] In terms of food security, whichever way you look at it, that is not a very sensible approach. It's the genetic equivalent of putting all our eggs in one basket. As the meat-producer Fred Duncan put it: 'We're dependent on very few varieties of grain that are effectively our store of food. Most beef and dairy cows are fed on grain; all pigs and chickens are fed on grain. If there were a disease, there could be a massive problem. That's a doom-watch scenario.'[88]

The scale of modern food supply systems creates other vulnerabilities too. In his farewell speech in 2004, the US Health Secretary Tommy Thompson admitted that 'I, for the life of me, cannot understand why the terrorists have not attacked our food supply, because it is so easy to do.'[89] After 11th September 2001, the US government is taking the threat very seriously indeed, setting up a federal bio- and agro-defence facility to deal with the problem. There is little doubt that the physical concentration of the American food chain makes it uniquely vulnerable to attack. Research carried out at Stanford University suggested that contamination with botulinum toxin of one of the 50,000-gallon milk silos that feed American consumers could kill 250,000 before the contamination was even discovered.[90] Another possible target could be the state of Kansas, where 80 per cent of US beef is reared in vast feed lots that contain tens of thousands of cattle at a time. Farmers there are so worried about the threat to their herds that they have formed an 'Agro Guard', a kind of neighbourhood watch for farmers, to protect them.[91]

In the pre-industrial world, the surest way to attack a city was to lay siege to it: to surround it and wait for the food to run out. In the post-industrial world, the situation is reversed. As cities become increasingly amorphous, their sources of food are becoming more concentrated. It is a tendency with far-reaching consequences, not just for those who supply our food, but for the very future of urban dwelling.

The irony of the modern food industry is that it has made the very thing it promised to make easier – the feeding of cities – infinitely more complex. We depend just as much on our gas-guzzling, chilled plug-in, 'just-in-time' food deliveries as ancient Romans did on foreign conquests, shipping and slaves – and our food system is no more secure, ethical or sustainable than Rome's was. In both cases, the problem is one of scale. Rome was the monster of its day, stretching ancient food supply systems to breaking point. The same is true of the way we live now. Industrial supply chains are what sustain us as urban beings, yet we behave as though they were no big deal. Which no doubt suits those who supply our food just fine.

Chapter 3
Market and Supermarket

The shopping centre which can do more than fulfil practical shopping needs, the one that will afford an opportunity for cultural, social, civic and recreational activities will reap the greatest benefits.

Victor Gruen[1]

The *Palazzo della Ragione*, Padua. Town hall and market together at the heart of the city.

Borough Market, London

Friday lunchtime, on a cold, wet day in February. Opposite Southwark Cathedral, an assortment of white vans, cardboard boxes and debris shelters under a dripping railway viaduct. Trains rumble overhead, sending shock waves through the brickwork, pigeons peck distractedly at the ground. This is London at its gloomiest, but not all here is gloom. Stretched between two iron columns is a green banner that reads *Borough Food Market – Knowledge, Service, Traceability – Handy for all your food shopping.* Beneath it, a clutch of food stalls, awnings aglow with fairy lights, burst with an improbable range of produce: organic pork and wild rabbit, stuffed olives and 'urban honey', rustic bread and round yellow cheeses the size of car tyres. The place is heaving. Herds of tourists in rainproof jackets jostle with City types in pinstriped suits and cashmere overcoats. 'Let the Feasting Begin!' roars one of the latter to his two companions, who, to judge from their startled looks, are new to this latest form of urban grazing. 'Just Wander and Eat, Wander and Eat Some More!' adds Gargantua, before plunging off into the fray.

Following him through a maze of brick arches, I find myself in the main market hall, where, beneath a decaying iron canopy, there is a seething, hissing, sizzling city of food. Alleyways lined with stalls and kitchens stretch out in all directions, their narrow passages stuffed with guzzling humanity. Everywhere I look, groups of people stand huddled against the cold, tucking into great fistfuls of food. Most of them look slightly furtive, as people eating on the hoof often do, but the relish with which they eat is unmistakable. The air is filled with the smell of garlic and sausages, as frenzied cooks fry and shout, trying to keep up with demand. Above their heads, cows and sheep gaze meditatively down from painted rural idylls, proclaiming the pedigree of the produce on offer. Fatty steam rises up through the pastoral troposphere, lending a dreamy quality to the already struggling light.

Back at ground level, there is a sense of barely suppressed excitement, as if everyone has stumbled on the same great secret, and can't quite believe their luck. One pair of smartly dressed young lads dash from one stall to another, in an apparent attempt to taste everything on offer before returning to their desks. 'Are you in the falafel line?' asks a breathless American voice behind me. I am not, as it happens, but she can be forgiven for her mistake. The place is so hectic that it feels more like the old Stock Exchange during a crash than the superannuated wholesale fruit and veg market that, until around 10 years ago, it was. Pushing on through the throng, I come across one couple transfixed by a dazzling cheese display. 'This is just like France!' exclaims the man, as I try to squeeze past. It couldn't be much less like France, I think, but I know what he means. Heady encounters with food are rare in Britain, while in France they remain relatively commonplace.

Returning to another cheese stall I saw earlier, I commit the unspoken sin of asking for a piece of cheese without trying some first. 'Have you tasted it?' asks the stallholder, with a look of real concern. 'It's got a bit of a funny taste, that one. I remember the day I made it last October. The cows had just gone on to some new silage, and I remember thinking there was something *meadowy* about it.' Thrilled to be getting all this unsolicited information, I ask the stallholder to tell me more about himself. He is Tom Bourne, whose family have been making Cheshire cheese for over 200 years. Most of it is sold anonymously these days under supermarkets' own labels, although some gets sold under his own name at the delicatessen counters of larger stores. The supermarkets have been good to him, he says, although he has heard plenty of horror stories from other farmers supplying the 'Big Four'.[2] Asked why he chooses to come in person to Borough Market, he says it's the fact that nobody seems to understand Cheshire cheese any more. The taste is so dependent on its freshness, on how it is made, stored and sold, that he feels compelled to show people what it can be like at its best. I agree that his cheese (which is sharp, tangy and, yes, *meadowy*) is unlike any Cheshire I've tasted before. At this point some other customers arrive and I ask Mr Bourne if we can meet up later, but he says he is going for an organ lesson in Southwark Cathedral. That's the sort of place Borough Market is. The yellow cheeses the size of car tyres I spotted on the way in turn out to be Comté, a rich, nutty cheese from the Jura mountains. They have been personally imported by a stand-up comic with a philosophy degree who is using them to finance his first novel.

There is something odd about Borough. It is a food market, but not, as Captain Kirk might have said, as we know them. At first glance it appears to be a farmers' market, but don't go there expecting to buy cheap lettuces covered in earth. The food at Borough Market is expensive, some of it phenomenally so. Of course high cost is the price one pays for real food, made in traditional ways – it is a real cost, as opposed to the artificially low prices we have got used to paying for industrial food. Yet despite what the banner says, Borough is a food-lover's playground, not somewhere to go and buy your daily groceries. The reason it feels so unlike French markets is that in France, people still go to market as a matter of routine, not just on the occasional whim or as a special treat. On one recent visit to Paris, I counted no fewer than 20 people queuing at a market stall (most of them equipped with decidedly unglamorous wheeled shopping baskets) in order to buy high-quality vegetables at a good price. This was no flea market either: this was Marché Monge, in the well-heeled *cinquième*, where some of the stalls are every bit as rarefied as those at Borough. One handful of black tomatoes I bought there nearly bankrupted me. The point is that Marché Monge caters to every kind of customer, not just to people looking for a foodie thrill.

Borough feels odd because it exists in a country that has lost touch with its food culture – where the vast majority of us do most of our shopping in supermarkets. What Borough offers is an experience; an echo, for those who can afford it, of the excitement that food markets once brought to cities. Borough is not really about *buying* food at all, it is about celebrating it. Nothing new in that – food has always been celebrated in cities, especially in cosmopolitan ones like London. But that has generally meant attending magnificent feasts or dining in fancy restaurants, not gobbling something down while standing up in one's overcoat. At Borough, food has become an end in itself. It has become fetishised, as if it were invested with some cathartic power to transform lives. The people who come here, although plainly enjoying themselves, seem to be searching for something more: for roots, for meaning, for salvation, even.

Borough is neither a farmers' market nor a neighbourhood one, so what is it exactly? It certainly doesn't lack tradition: there has been a market here or hereabouts since pre-Roman times. Thanks to its prime position next to London Bridge – London's only river crossing until the surprisingly late date of 1729 – the market enjoyed a virtual monopoly on produce coming into the capital from the south, remaining integral to London's wholesale fruit and vegetable trade until the early 1970s, when the opening of New Covent Garden robbed it of much of its business. The market limped through the 1980s, steadfastly refusing all overtures from developers who were then converting much of the area into a mirror image of the City on the opposite bank. This remarkable resistance to the forces of Mammon was due to the market's 1754 charter, which put it in the hands of a local board of trustees with the proviso that it was to be run solely for the benefit of the local parishioners, the basis on which it is still run today.

It was a lucky escape. Many famous food markets in the West were swept away during the 1970s and 80s, once their role in feeding cities was at an end. In 1971, London's Covent Garden came within days of demolition to make way for one of the Greater London Council's most lamentable (thankfully unrealised) projects, a precast concrete office precinct replete with those essential accoutrements of seventies urbanism, pedestrian podiums and flying walkways.[3] To London's eternal benefit, the GLC was foiled by a determined band of local residents and traders in a landmark public enquiry, and the market went on to become the thriving mixed-use neighbourhood it is today.[4] Thirty years on, it seems extraordinary that anyone could have thought demolishing Covent Garden was a good idea, but planning history is full of such lapses. The citizens of Paris, for instance, have had over three decades to lament the loss of Les Halles, the beauty of which put even Covent Garden in the shade. Its fabled glass and iron halls were demolished to make room for an underground shopping centre whose chief contribution to the urban landscape is a series of giant plastic tubes descending into a gaping pit: a desolate, crime-ridden wasteland in the heart of the city.

By the mid-1990s, with planning's Brave New World phase safely over, Borough Market found itself in a part of town that was suddenly trendy. The reconstructed Globe Theatre was just down the road, and the Tate Modern and Jubilee Line were nearing completion. Some food retailers had already moved into the area, among them Randolph Hodgson, co-founder of Neal's Yard Dairy and a veteran of Covent Garden's renaissance. Hodgson was convinced that something similar could be achieved at Borough, and in 1998 he approached the trustees with the idea of setting up a farmers' market there, receiving a far warmer welcome than any developer ever had. The market invited Henrietta Green, pioneering champion of small British producers, to mount a Food Lovers' Fair there for a trial weekend. It was a huge success, attracting more than 30,000 visitors over three days, and Borough has never looked back. It is now a firm fixture on London's gastronomic map, even finding a new home for some ironwork reclaimed from Covent Garden's Floral Hall, demolished during the refurbishment of the Royal Opera House.

The use of food to foster urban renewal is a relatively new phenomenon, one that can be traced back to Boston's Faneuil Hall Marketplace, one of America's most successful tourist attractions.[5] These days, 18 million people flock to Faneuil Hall every year, but back in the early 1970s, the market's future looked bleak. It had been empty and derelict since ceasing trading in the mid-1960s, and nobody could think what to do with its elegant colonial buildings – a failure of imagination that seems incredible now, given that one of them, the eponymous Faneuil Hall, is none other than the famed 'Cradle of Liberty' where Bostonians first demanded 'no taxation without representation'. Cradle or not, the Hall was facing the chop when it received a last-minute reprieve in the shape of Edward J. Logue, newly appointed head of the Boston Redevelopment Authority and a man determined to make the market a 'purveyor of honest beef' once more. The question was, how?

The answer came from the unlikeliest of sources: the shopping mall. Ever since the 1950s, malls had been springing up all over America, and developer Jim Rouse had unparalleled knowledge of them, having built more than 50. But Rouse was starting to have his doubts about malls, and the inner-city decay they helped to create. When Edward Logue approached him to develop the Boston waterfront, it occurred to him that if he could package the market like a mall, with lots of shops and restaurants, people might want to come to spend time there, just as they did at the out-of-town version. It was an untried concept, but since nobody had any better ideas, they went with it.

Faneuil Hall Marketplace was the result, and it was an immediate success, thanks to all the factors that should have been obvious from the start: its buildings were stunning and packed with history, they were on Boston's 'Freedom Trail', and there were thousands of tourists mooing around with nowhere else to go. The derelict market was transformed into a lively leisure complex full of shops, theatres, restaurants and cafés, its cobbled streets thronging with performance artists, street vendors and tourists eating ice-cream. For Rouse, it was a revelation. He never built another mall, ploughing his considerable fortune instead into a number of charitable projects focused on urban renewal. Faneuil Hall became his prototype 'festival marketplace', a concept he took all over the world. The formula, which in essence is food tourism, should be familiar to anyone who has visited New York's South Street Seaport, Baltimore's Harbor Place or London's Covent Garden: Rouse developed the first two and advised on the latter.

Although in some respects 'festival marketplaces' are fake, the life they engender is very real. By inhabiting buildings and spaces made by food, they acquire an authentic quality that transcends the inevitable shop and restaurant chains that form the backbone of their commercial operations. Borough Market goes one better, bringing genuine artisanal food back to the heart of the city. Sometimes it tries too hard: one cider-seller there looks like an extra from *Tess of the D'Urbervilles*, complete with pastiche rustic hut and thatched roof. But if the cider he sells is excellent, why should we complain? Buying cider from him is still better than getting some tasteless brew off a supermarket shelf. For one thing – if you can get past the straw wig – it involves human contact. For another, it helps preserve what remains of quality local food in Britain.

Wherever food markets survive, they bring a quality to urban life that is all too rare in the West: a sense of belonging, engagement, character. They connect us to an ancient sort of public life. People have always come to markets in order to socialise as well as to buy food, and the need for such spaces in which to mingle is as great now as it has ever been – arguably greater, since so few such opportunities exist in modern life. The success of markets like Borough suggests that we have not lost the appetite for such encounters in Britain, yet ordinary street markets are dying out all over the country. This seeming paradox is explained by the fact that food is not embedded in our culture. We only lavish time and money on it when we are 'treating ourselves', not as part of daily routine. That is why we respond so well to food tourism, why we love to shop in markets when we go abroad, why the man at Borough said it felt 'like France'. Borough is a manifestation of our overwhelming disconnection with food in Britain, not the opposite.

Bring on the Clones

Twenty years ago, if you needed to buy a few basic items – say, a loaf of bread, a pint of milk and half a dozen eggs – you would probably have nipped down to your local shop to get them. Today the chances are you would buy them from a supermarket. Independent food shops in Britain are currently closing at a rate of more than 2,000 a year, and the total number has fallen by half in just over a decade. One recent study predicted that by 2050 there won't be any left at all.[6] But you don't have to read industry research to know what is happening in the British grocery trade: just glance at your monthly bank statements. Unless you live in some remote part of the country supermarkets haven't yet reached (or you are one of those rare beasts who has the time, means and inclination to source your food elsewhere), the likelihood is that one name – that of your nearest supermarket – will recur with monotonous regularity.

Shopping for food is when most of us become aware of the industrial supply chain for the first time – the moment it impacts directly on our lives. With their miles of stocked-up shelving and serried ranks of tills, supermarkets are the means by which the global food superhighway enters our cities and is transferred down to our individual scale – a daily feat equivalent to converting a raging torrent into millions of glasses of water. As far as supermarkets are concerned, this last stage of food delivery is the trickiest one of all – the operation they are least well suited to. The human scale is not what supermarkets have ever been about; nor are the idiosyncratic layouts of traditional city centres. Both mess up the economies of scale on which their profits rely.

Supermarkets aren't really compatible with cities; at least not with the dense, higgledy-piggledy sort you get in the Old World. The first ones in the USA barely ventured into cities at all: they just sat on the outskirts of towns and waited for customers to drive to them. Eighty years on, out-of-town retailing remains the ideal for supermarkets, because it allows them to stick to what they do best – source food cheaply and move it around in bulk – and leaves customers to do the rest. Given that the public role of historic city centres was chiefly the buying and selling of food, supermarkets are at odds not just with local high streets, but with the very concept of what a city is.

I still remember my first encounter with the problem. It was on a day trip with some friends to Somerset in the early 1980s, and we had stopped in a small market town to get a newspaper, some coffee and some aspirin. It was a lovely Saturday morning and the town had a beautiful high street, but there were very few people about, which I remember seemed a little odd at the time. After wandering up and down the street for a few minutes, we were unable to find a café, chemist, or newsagent, although had we wanted to buy property in the area we could have chosen from any one of at least six estate agents. Perplexed and starting to get just a little grumpy, we finally asked a passer-by for some help. He looked at us as if we were a bit slow, and pointed down the road, where a few hundred yards out of town (how could we have missed it?) was the sprawling red-tiled roof of a Tesco superstore. It was one of the new breed of 'village centre' types – all fake-vernacular detailing with a cartoon clock tower – and none of us had ever seen such a thing before. Within a few minutes, we had our aspirin and newspaper, but the cup of coffee still eluded us. Although the store had a café, it was so full of what seemed like the entire population of the town stuffing itself with burgers and chips at 11 a.m. that we decided we couldn't face the queue.

Nobody would make the same mistake today. In the intervening 25 years, supermarkets have transformed the British urban landscape. Although the first out-of-town superstore was built as early as 1970 (guess which: a Tesco), the great era of superstore expansion in Britain took place in the 1980s and 90s, during two decades of rampant development that, unlike anywhere else in Europe, went virtually unchecked by planning constraints. By the time the Tory government woke up to the damage out-of-town stores were causing, it was too late. By the mid 90s there were more than 1,000 in Britain, and the lingering death of the British high street had already begun. A study carried out by the Department of the Environment, Transport and the Regions (DETR) in 1998 found that a new superstore built on the edge of a town could reduce market share for city-centre food shops by as much as 75 per cent.[7] A subsequent report by the New Economics Foundation (nef) entitled *Ghost Town Britain* showed how even a small reduction in business in the high street was enough to start killing shops off, eventually reaching a 'tipping point' when the old town centre was no longer viable: 'Once the downtown starts to shut down, people who preferred to shop there have no choice but to switch to the supermarket. What begins as a seemingly harmless ripple becomes a powerful and destructive wave.'[8]

A decade after the superstore tsunami devastated British town centres, the supermarkets realised that the resultant void represented a new business opportunity. Once again, Tesco led the way, opening its first 'Metro' stores in 1998 – corporate replicas of the local shops it had just helped to destroy. At first Tesco moved cautiously, not sure how well the new 'convenience' format would perform, but it need not have worried. It was soon clear there was an enormous untapped demand for inner-city food shops, and the battle was then on to claim as many prime high-street sites as possible before their rivals. In 2002, Tesco bought T&S, an existing convenience chain with 450 stores, converting them at the rate of four to five a week. Although the land grab raised some City eyebrows (one analyst reckoned it would have taken Tesco 15 years to expand its business that quickly without the takeover), it was approved by the Competition Commission on the basis that convenience food shopping is a different market to that of 'one-stop' shopping at supermarkets.[9]

The logic was absurd, but it has stuck. For many independent food retailers, this 'second wave' of supermarket expansion was even more devastating than the first, since it meant that for the first time, they were competing directly for the same business. By 2006, supermarkets had gained a 12 per cent share of the convenience sector and the figure was rising fast.[10] My local food shop duly got Tesco'd in 2005. It was a sad day for me. Although no gastronomic Aladdin's cave, the old shop had a certain quirky charm to it, and stocked a great range of pickles. Living in central London, I do not have to shop at Tesco if I don't want to – it just means walking a bit further. But not everyone in Britain is that lucky. Residents of Bicester in Oxfordshire, for instance, a town of just 32,000, had no fewer than six Tesco stores by 2005, and very little else. One resident interviewed by the BBC was so desperate for a change that she was prepared to drive 'as a special treat' to Sainsbury's in Banbury, a round trip of some 40 miles.[11]

Eviscerated City

Supermarkets are now so much part of our everyday lives that it can be hard to remember what cities were like before they came along. To anyone born after 1980, butchers, bakers and candlestick makers must seem about as remote as the days before mobile phones and computers (which, come to think of it, seem pretty remote even to me). Yet just a generation ago, high streets were the social hubs of urban neighbourhoods, and shopping for food was a time to swap news and gossip. Supermarkets today are impersonal filling stations: pit stops designed to service the flow of life. They support individual lifestyles, not sociability; a characteristic they share with iPods and computers. The internet may be a great communicative tool, but it can't replace the connection we feel when we meet people in the flesh. That is where food is so powerful. It brings us together in physical space, forging bonds other media can't reach.

In her seminal 1960s study *The Death and Life of Great American Cities*, Jane Jacobs described the 'ballet of Hudson Street': daily life in the Greenwich Village neighbourhood where she lived in New York. With its mixture of houses, shops and small businesses, the street was animated at various times by people going about their daily routines: the cafés were crowded at midday with factory workers eating lunch; the shops were busy in the mornings and evenings when the locals did their shopping. Jacobs argued that the myriad of personal exchanges that took place every day in the street created a strong sense of local identity; a sense of communal ownership that encouraged people to look after the street, and by extension, one another. She recalled one incident, when she witnessed a pavement struggle between a man and a little girl:

> As I watched from our second-floor window, making up my mind how to intervene if it seemed advisable, I saw it was not going to be necessary. From the butcher's shop beneath the tenement had emerged the woman who, with her husband, runs the shop; she was standing within earshot of the man, her arms folded and a look of determination on her face. Joe Cornacchia, who with his sons-in law keeps the delicatessen, emerged about the same moment and stood solidly on the other side . . . that man did not know it, but he was surrounded.[12]

The struggle turned out to be a false alarm (the man was the girl's father), but the point was that on Hudson Street, anything out of the ordinary was immediately noticed; potential crimes were a matter of communal concern. Local shopkeepers acted like neighbourhood policemen: they knew everyone, and made it their business to know what was going on. As the title of her book suggests, Jacobs was a passionate critic of the monolithic, monocultural, 'zoned' approach to city-building that was then taking over in America. Her book was a paean to traditional mixed neighbourhoods, and their capacity to foster a sense of belonging.

Jacobs didn't emphasise the role of food in forging social bonds, but without it, her beloved Hudson Street would have been a far emptier place. She took food's role in urban life as a given – something too obvious to mention. Yet 40 years later, that role is not only under threat in America and Britain, but routinely undervalued or ignored. Unlike, say, the demolition of a beloved landmark, food's disappearance from cities often leaves the urban fabric virtually untouched – as it did in the neighbourhood of my childhood. Growing up in central London in the 1960s, we had a small row of shops – a butcher, fishmonger, baker and greengrocer – at the end of our street. Every day, my mother took me and my brother there to do our daily shop. The shopkeepers knew us very well, and would offer us kids toys and sweets. Sometimes my mother would send us back to fetch something she had forgotten – her trust in her local shopkeepers was as implicit as their trust in her to pay them the following day. Today, that row of food shops is a series of antiques showrooms of the kind that displays just one item of furniture in the window, and it would be unthinkable for a six-year-old to be sent out shopping alone. To look at a map of that part of London now, you would hardly notice the difference – the buildings all look the same – yet the experience of living there has changed fundamentally. Forty years ago, it was the centre of a busy urban village. Now it has about as much life to it as an empty motorway.

Street life isn't the only casualty of food's disappearance from cities. Another seemingly trivial loss, but one that contributes a great deal to a city's character, is smell. Our sense of smell is our most underrated faculty – something we have learnt to disdain. Yet nothing links us more powerfully to our emotions and memories. London was once a city of smells, and I can map my life there through them. Every morning on my way to school in Hammersmith, I had to run the gauntlet of the Lyons factory on Brook Green, with its heavenly aroma of chocolate sponge – something to which I was (indeed still am) very partial. Although the factory condemned me to arrive at school most days hopelessly salivating, it was an exquisite pain I bore quite happily. Other memorable odours included the stink of hops in Chiswick and Fulham from the breweries along the river, and the fishy whiff of Billingsgate, which lingered long after the market closed in 1982. Around that time I was living above a bean-sprout factory in Wapping, where the Chinese workers slept in hammocks over the bean-sprout tanks. The stench every week when the tanks were cleaned out was indescribable (actually, it was perfectly describable, but you probably don't want to know what it smelt like).[13] In any case, the air outside our front door was pungent enough to stop us from hanging about. I must have had a knack for smells, because my next move was to Bermondsey, close to the Sarson's Vinegar factory on Tanner Road (which, as the name suggests, had once smelled even worse). When the wind blew in the right direction, you didn't need to put vinegar on your chips; the air did it for you. Somehow the ubiquitous tang was rather comforting. You could always find your way home in the dark.

Most of London's homely (and less homely) smells are now gone; expelled to factory complexes well outside the city. London is off the olfactory map – and a good thing too, you might think. Who wants to open their front door to the stench of rotten bean sprouts? The thing is, so many other things have disappeared along with those smells. Without anything to compare them with, it can be hard to realise quite how dead British cities have become – until you go abroad, that is. On a recent trip to India, it took me days to get used to the teeming life in the streets: to the cows and elephants, the goats and chickens, the beggars and sellers, the hooting, shouting and bellowing. To my health-and-safety-conscious eyes, everything seemed like an accident waiting to happen, catching my attention like pencils rolling off a desk: tottering lorries piled high with sugar cane, a pregnant woman crossing a six-lane highway between slamming buses and lorries, a cyclist wobbling in the wrong direction through the same metallic onslaught. Underpinning all this frenetic activity there was food: people cooking on pavements, smearing sweetmeats on the walls of holy shrines, buying snacks from carts and stands, carrying baskets of vegetables on their heads. Everywhere there were smells, too: delicious spicy ones, mingled with petrol, mud and excrement. India assaults your senses, but you soon get used to it. After India, it is Europe that is the real shock. The streets seem positively deserted; the cars and buses impossibly large and shiny; the spaces between buildings huge and empty. Everywhere you look, there seems to be an absence of something: of people, animals, vegetables, smell, noise, ritual, necessity, death. The juxtapositions of human life have been designed out of our cities, leaving us to live in an empty shell.

The Carved City

Look at the plan of any city built before the railways, and there you will be able to trace the influence of food. It is etched into the anatomy of every pre-industrial urban plan: all have markets at their heart, with roads leading to them like so many arteries carrying in the city's lifeblood. London is no exception. The first measured survey of the capital, John Ogilby's *Large and Accurate Map of the City of London* of 1676, shows just how closely the city mirrored the landscape that fed it. The plan is essentially that of the modern City: its Roman walls roughly semicircular in shape on the north bank of the Thames, with St Paul's just west of centre and the Tower pinning down its south-east corner.

Detail of Ogilby's map, shaded to show food markets and supply routes.

Running through the middle is a single broad street, joining Newgate in the west to Aldgate in the east. The various names along this street – Cheapside, Poultry and Cornhill – confirm that this was London's central food market ('cheap' is from the Old English *ceap*, to barter). At Cornhill it crosses another broad street running from north to south: the City's other main axis leading over London Bridge.

A closer reading of the map reveals how food once reached the city. London's sheep and cattle, many of them from Scotland, Wales and Ireland, approached from the north and west, streaming down the country lanes to Newgate, where the ancient city's livestock market was held. During the ninth century, the market expanded to a 'smooth field' (Smithfield) just outside the city gate, where a meat market remains to this day. In its heyday, Smithfield dominated the neighbourhood, as George Dodd's description of the 'Great Day', held annually in the week before Christmas, attests:

> What a day was this! . . . On that day, 30,000 of the finest animals in the world were concentrated within an area of four or five acres. They had been pouring in from ten o'clock on the Sunday evening, insomuch that by daylight on the Monday they presented one dense animated mass, an agitated sea of brute life. All around the market, the animals encroached on space rightfully belonging to shop-keeping traffic; Giltspur Street, Duke Street, Long Lane, St John's Street, King Street, Hosier Lane – all were invaded; for the cauldron of steaming animalism overflowed from very fullness.[14]

Animals may no longer walk to Smithfield, but their memory lingers in its physical fabric. The names of local streets – Cowcross Street, Chick Lane, Cock Lane – recall a time when the area was full of living beasts, and St John's Street, the chief route into the market from the north, is a broad, curving thoroughfare that still has something of the air of a country lane, its sweeping contours carved by the 'sea of brute life' that once flowed down it like a river.

Since London's turkeys and geese came mainly from Suffolk and Norfolk (as many still do), they entered the city through Aldgate, having made the journey with specially protected cloth-wrapped feet.

Poultry, to the east of the city, is where they were bought and sold. Fruit and vegetables from Kent and Surrey were either sold at Borough Market or along Gracechurch Street, the road leading up from London Bridge to Leadenhall at the city's main crossroads. Leadenhall was London's first enclosed market, and still stands today on its historic site, near to the site of the ancient Roman forum. Such physical longevity is typical of markets everywhere – once established, they very rarely move. The river ports of Billingsgate and Queenhithe (originally owned, as we saw in the last chapter, by City and Crown) doubled as London's main markets for fish and grain, as well as imported food. The streets leading up from the ports to Cheapside also became markets in their own right, as their names – Bread, Garlick and Fish Street – attest.

At first glance, London's medieval plan may seem irrational, with its crooked streets, crowded spaces and lack of geometrical clarity. But seen through food, it makes perfect sense. Food shaped London, as it did every pre-industrial city, and as a way of engendering life and urban order, few things work half as well.

Necessary Chaos

The presence of food in cities once caused chaos, but it was necessary chaos, as much a part of life as sleeping and breathing. Food was bought and sold openly in the streets, mainly so that authorities (such as the Parisian grain police) could keep an eye on proceedings. The principle of visibility meant that selling food indoors was prohibited in most medieval cities, which in turn meant that food shops as we know them now did not exist. Although houses facing on to markets were allowed to sell food, they had to do so over open boards, while their customers remained standing in the street. Most food was sold in the market, either from packs or barrels on the ground, or from portable trestles, set up and dismantled each day and stored in nearby houses. Market traders were granted pitches allowing them to sell certain foods in specific places and at set times, and were forbidden to wander about or sell their produce in any other way. Because of this, pitches were jealously guarded, and disputes over territory were common. In fifteenth-century Padua, one quarrel between the city's fruiterers and vegetable-sellers was only settled when the mayor himself intervened, marking a line on the ground with his own hand.

The space in which food could be sold in cities also had to be controlled in order to stop it from taking over the streets entirely, as this thirteenth-century London edict suggests:

> All manner of victuals that are sold by persons in Chepe [Cheapside], upon Cornhill and elsewhere in the city, such as bread, cheese, poultry, fruit, hides and skins, onions and garlic, and all other small victuals, for sale as well by denizens as by strangers, shall stand midway between the kennels [gutters] of the streets, so as to be a nuisance to no-one, under pain of forfeiture of the article.[15]

Since markets were often the only large public spaces in cities, most had to double as ceremonial spaces too. One contemporary sketch of Cheapside shows the market transformed to receive Marie de Medici .[16] A series of grandstands decked out with striped awnings and banners line the space, with rows of feather-hatted noblemen watching a seemingly endless procession of horse-drawn carriages, flanked by pike-bearing soldiers and drummers. The market's half-timbered buildings serve as the peanut gallery, their windows crammed with faces, one to each leaded windowpane. The sketch demonstrates what a naturally theatrical space Cheapside was. Swap the ducks and geese for a few royal props, and hey presto: the market metamorphoses into a royal reception room. It is a pity (but typical) that no similar sketch exists of Cheapside in its ordinary, everyday use. Nobody ever thinks the mundane routines of their own day are worth recording.

Markets often represented cities on formal occasions, but at other times they were the place where the countryside came to town. Rome's Piazza Montanara was one of the city's liveliest markets until it was destroyed by Mussolini during his imperial makeover of the city in the 1930s. The piazza, which was on the site of the ancient city's vegetable market, the Forum Holitorium, was the Sunday meeting place for *contadini*, country folk who walked through the night to sell produce there, exchange labour, or use the services of the barbers, scribes and tooth-extractors who came each week to attend to their needs. At festival times, such rural invasions could take over the city completely. Many urban festivals were derived from country traditions in any case; and local peasants often chose to come to the city to celebrate them, giving the latter a changed, bucolic flavour. A group of English visitors to Prato in Tuscany for the Feast of Our Lady in 1605 remarked on the curious appearance of the large crowd gathered in the main piazza, 'whereof we judged one half to have hats of straw and one fourth part to be bare-legged'.[17]

The Political Market

The pivotal role played by markets in urban life made them inherently political. Two of the most famous public spaces in the world, the Roman Forum and the Athenian Agora, were both originally food markets, that gradually made the transition from commercial to political use as the cities they served grew in size. The pattern was to be repeated all over Europe: one only has to think of the number of town halls on market squares to understand the power of the relationship. Such urban set pieces were both highly practical and gave a clear symbolic expression of the civic order.

The thirteenth-century Palazzo della Ragione in Padua – affectionately known locally as *il Salone* – is one such arrangement. The building's nickname refers to its council chamber, a vast first-floor hall with the largest vaulted wooden roof of its day, set over a series of arcades and shops. The vertical arrangement was necessary because the *Salone* was built right in the middle of the city's market square, whose two halves thus had to be reunited beneath its belly. For centuries, representatives of the Paduan Commune gathered here to discuss matters of state, while the bustle of market life carried on below. Hall and market were a perfect reflection of the urban hierarchy: politics supported by commerce, and the mutual dependence of one upon the other. The *Salone* has dominated visual representations of Padua since it was built, looming out of prints like some benign whale beached in the midst of the city. The architect Aldo Rossi called it an 'urban artifact', a civic monument so powerful that it held its meaning for the city long after its original use had ceased:

> In particular, one is struck by the multiplicity of functions that a building of this type can contain over time and how these functions are entirely independent of the form. At the same time, it is precisely the form that impresses us; we live it and experience it, and in turn it structures the city.[18]

What Rossi didn't say is that much of the *Salone*'s power comes from its relationship with the market. Food is always getting overlooked in this way, not least by architects trained to think of space as something defined by bricks and mortar rather than by human actions. But space is also created by habit: the pitching of stalls in the same place day after day, multiple lifetimes of deals and nods, conversations and exchanges. Surviving records from the Paduan market suggest its space was delineated just as precisely as that of the *Salone*. One document from the fourteenth century lists the exact locations where one would go to buy wild game, birds and fish; piglets and cooked trotters; hay and horse fodder (horses need to eat too).[19] Another map from the eighteenth century shows how the positions of stalls for sea fish would change from summer to winter, a reminder that the use of the space, like the food it sold, changed with the seasons. Such spaces may be ephemeral, but they are no less powerful for that. They remind us that it is often the way in which spaces are inhabited that matters most, not just the physical boundaries that appear to define them.

A perfect example of this is the ancient Athenian Agora, arguably the most complex and radical public space the world has ever known, yet you wouldn't have guessed so by looking at it. A large, irregular space, roughly diamond-shaped in plan and fringed on three sides by *stoas* (long, low buildings with open colonnades facing inwards) it contained numerous archaic monuments and shrines, and was cut in two by a road leading up to the city's sacred compound, the Acropolis. The ground was made of packed earth, and there were clumps of plane trees here and there to provide shade. Food and other goods were sold from trestles in the open air, and each type of produce had its own section, so that locals might say, 'I went off to the wine, the olive oil, the pots'; or 'I went around to the garlic and the onions and the incense, and straight on to the perfume.'[20]

The Agora was generally held to be full of rascals, with fishmongers giving customers what the historian R.E. Wycherley called the 'Greek equivalent of the Billingsgate', a colourful stream of oath and invective designed to befuddle customers and disguise the fact that they were being sold rotten fish.[21] The Agora was also famous for its oratory. Socrates was a regular speaker, gathering large crowds to his favourite spot near the food-sellers and money-lenders, where he would hold forth on the topics of the day. There was always something going on in the Agora, and men and women often went there for an evening stroll, to visit the stalls and wine shops, listen to speakers, or just hang out. The word *agora* comes from the Greek verb *ageiro*, meaning 'to gather', and *agorazein* meant variously 'to frequent the Agora', 'to buy in the marketplace', or (best of all) 'to haunt the Agora'. As its lexical complexity suggests, the Agora was much more than just a food market. It was a sacred precinct, a law court, a social space – as well as the seat of Athenian democracy. It was here, among the discarded grape pips and rotten fish heads, that Athenian citizens gathered to debate matters of state, making political decisions on the basis of on-the-spot public votes.[22]

The heady mix of food, politics and philosophy made the Agora a favourite target of comic poets – the satirical comedians of their day. This extract from Euboulos is typical:

> Everything will be for sale together in the same place at Athens: figs, summoners, bunches of grapes, turnips, pears, apples, witnesses, roses, medlars, haggis, honeycombs, chickpeas, lawsuits, bee-stings-pudding, myrtle berries, allotment machines, irises, lambs, water clocks, laws, indictments.[23]

For Aristotle, the fact that political life was carried out in such a melee was degrading to the lofty ideals of the polis.[24] He pleaded for a separate food market to be built in Athens – an arrangement already adopted in some other Greek cities – but his pleas fell on deaf ears. It seems that most Athenians liked the Agora just the way it was.[25]

Today it seems both strange and wonderful that Athenian politics were conducted in such a marketplace, yet for a society in which political life was tantamount to a philosophical calling, nothing could have been more appropriate.[26] Where better to debate the human condition than in its very midst? The ancient Greeks had no use for ivory towers: for them, privacy was the realm of *idion*, the isolated world of idiocy.[27] The true calling of civilised man was *praxis*, public action, and the Agora was its perfect stage. It was where the idealised conditions of Greek theatre – tragic, satyric and comic – could come to life. Whether Aristotle liked it or not, the Agora was as critical to the functioning of Athenian democracy as the food it sold was to the people it fed. It was *negotiated* space – somewhere the drama of human existence could be played out, in all its chaos, triumph and frailty.

The Comic Market

The Agora was unique in its range of uses and meanings, but something it shared with all marketplaces was its potential for comedy. As well as being naturally political, markets are naturally comedic spaces: pageants and parody, oaths and wisecracks are as essential to them as speeches and tedium are to parliaments. Markets in the past acted as the safety valves of cities, places to let one's hair down and forget one's sorrows. In Christian cities, that role was never more explicit than during Carnival, a time of Rabelaisian excess common all over Europe in the weeks leading up to Lent, when every bodily pleasure was given one last fling before the annual prohibition. Nothing was taboo during Carnival: kings and beggars wandered around disguised as fools and bishops; people borrowed one another's clothes, dressed in drag and wore grotesque masks – often with suggestively long noses. Behaving badly was de rigueur: people entered strangers' houses, insulted one another, or ran about hitting each other with inflated pigs' bladders or sticks, throwing flour, sugar plums and eggs.[28] As the festival's name suggests (from the Latin *carnis*, meat + *levare*, to put away), meat was central to Carnival, and the final feast on Shrove Tuesday was described by one seventeenth-century English observer as

> a time of such boiling and broiling, such roasting and toasting, such stewing and brewing, such baking, frying, mincing, cutting, carving, devouring, and gorbellied gourmandising, that a man would think people did take in two months' provision at once into their paunches, or that they did ballast their bellies with meat for a voyage to Constantinople, or the West Indies.[29]

Butchers' guilds often played a key role in proceedings, organising competitions and games, and putting on displays such as the Koenigsberg procession of 1583, in which 90 butchers carried a giant sausage weighing 440 pounds through the town. The sausage, like the pigs' bladders, embodied the many sides of *carnis* at once: carnivorousness, carnal desire, and carnage. Food, sex and violence shared centre stage during Carnival: all the pleasures – and dangers – of the flesh mingled together. It was a popular time to hold weddings, as well as less exalted ceremonies, such as the German custom of harnessing up unmarried women for a highly suggestive public 'ploughing' in the market square.[30]

In his book *Rabelais and His World*, the social historian Mikhail Bakhtin described Carnival as embodying ritual laughter: the archaic tradition in which, as he put it, 'the serious and the comic aspects of the world and of the deity were equally sacred, equally "official"'.[31] Carnival, in other words, was a celebration of 'otherness' – all the things that ordinary life suppressed. Urbane respectability was stripped away to reveal its grotesque underbelly, and the depredations of the flesh were celebrated as part of human mortality:

> . . . copulation, pregnancy, birth, growth, old age, disintegration, dismemberment. All these in their direct material aspect are the main elements in the system of the grotesque image. They are contrary to the classic images of the finished, completed man, cleansed, as it were, from all the scoriae of birth and development.[32]

Detail from Pieter Bruegel's *The Fight Between Carnival and Lent*, 1559.

In Pieter Bruegel's painting of 1559, *The Fight between Carnival and Lent*, we see the festival at its culmination. It shows a busy market square in which people are going about their daily business: a woman in a white cap sells fish from a basket; another makes pancakes over an open fire; a man hurries along carrying firewood; two children play with spinning tops. All are apparently oblivious to the harlequin in their midst, wandering around carrying a lit torch, even though it is broad daylight. But these figures are all in the background. The main event is in front: a joust between a fat man sitting on a barrel with a pie on his head, and a wizened old 'woman' (in fact a man) dressed in a nun's habit. Both are holding weapons: a sucking pig on a spit for the man; a wooden fish pallet for the woman. Contemporary viewers would immediately have recognised the figures as Carnival and Lent, fighting for the spirit of the marketplace. They would also have known that Carnival would lose the battle, and that his defeat would presage his mock trial, sentencing and public 'execution'. The ritual was a convulsive moment in the rhythm of urban life, when fleshliness confronted religious abstention head-on – and lost. But by Bruegel's day, the ritual itself was under threat from Protestant reformers, who found its pagan violence and licentiousness distasteful. From the mid sixteenth century onwards, the excesses of Carnival (which were, after all, its whole point) were gradually suppressed in northern Europe. People afterwards had to look elsewhere for their fun – had to find new outlets for their ritual laughter.

In London, the comic role was taken up – entirely against its creators' intentions – by Covent Garden Piazza. Designed in 1631 by Inigo Jones, the piazza was inspired, as its name suggests, by the Italian Renaissance, and with elegant arcaded terraces and the temple-like portico of St Paul's Church at its western end, it certainly looked the part. Jones and his employer, the 4th Earl of Bedford, were hoping to emulate the success of the Place Royale (now Place des Vosges) in Paris, a speculative development by King Henri IV which had, through his patronage, become the most fashionable square in the city, counting Cardinal Richelieu among its residents.[33] To begin with, all went well for the London piazza: the newly completed houses to the north were soon sold off to noble residents. But the scheme had a fatal flaw. Unlike the Place Royale, with its fashionable parades and royal patron, there was nothing much going on in the space. While the Earl was away during the Civil War, fruit- and vegetable-sellers took to gathering there to profit from London's increasing demand for garden produce; and before long the market was well established – along with its attendant mess. Just 10 years after Covent Garden's noble residents moved in, they began to move out again, complaining about all the noise and rubbish.

One could see the story of Covent Garden Piazza as a cautionary tale to architects. Inigo Jones should have seen it coming: in his day, open spaces in cities became unofficial markets in a flash – it happened every time the Thames froze over, for example. Jones failed to anticipate the way his piazza would be inhabited, but he did at least produce a magnificent void into which all of London's life could pour; and pour it did, once the food-sellers had lowered the tone to a suitable level. The piazza was soon popular for football matches, puppet shows and firework displays, and the area filled up with taverns, 'hummums' (Turkish steam baths that were essentially glorified brothels) and coffee houses, the latter becoming the focus of London's cultural and intellectual life, as well as its bawdier, seedier side. Tom King's Coffee Shop, perched underneath the portico of St Paul's, was the notorious haunt of London's rakes and roués. In William Hogarth's engraving *Morning*, a group of well-heeled revellers, much the worse for wear, are shown emerging from its doorway at dawn, blearily oblivious to the pickpockets depriving them of their remaining cash.

By the nineteenth century, even Covent Garden's vegetables had achieved comic status. The market buildings in the centre of the piazza (built by the architect Charles Fowler for the 6th Duke in 1830) failed to contain what was by then the largest fruit and vegetable market in the world. As *Punch* noted, keeping the streets clear was proving well beyond the authorities' control:

> Mud-salad market, like its own vegetables, has now sprouted out in all directions. You may start from cabbage-leaf corner, near the site of Temple Bar, on a market-morning, and may go as far as turnip-top square in Bloomsbury, or cauliflower-place at Charing Cross, and it is all mud-salad market. Houses are barricaded with mountainous carts of green-stuff, cabs lose themselves in vain attempts to drive through the maze of vegetables . . . while the roads are blocked with waggons, carts, donkey-trucks, and porters struggling under the weight of huge baskets. Carrots, turnips, vegetable-marrows, potatoes, lettuces and onions are masters of the situation.[34]

Carrots and turnips remained masters of the situation until 1971, by which time the 4,000 or so lorries coming to the market each morning caused a semi-permanent gridlock throughout the whole of central London. The fact that Covent Garden stayed put for as long as it did is testimony to the staying power of markets. Nothing is ever quite the same when they are gone – but if their fabric is preserved, something of their spirit remains. Covent Garden still celebrates its comic past with 'Punch's birthday', held annually on 9 May, the day in 1662 when Samuel Pepys first saw the Italian puppet Pulcinella

(Punch's ancestor) in the piazza. With his big nose, baton, lack of respect for authority, and violent tendencies, Punch is clearly Carnivalesque. He now plays mainly to children at the seaside, but his annual sermon in St Paul's Church is an echo of the very adult 'otherness' he once brought to the city.[35]

The Tragic Market

The same qualities that lent markets so well to comedy also lent themselves to the opposite. Protests, riots and executions often took place in markets, with the theatricality of the arena lending the events heightened significance. The culmination of the 1381 Peasants' Revolt was a case in point. An army of angry countrymen led by Wat Tyler had marched on London demanding an end to a crippling new poll tax. After several days of inconclusive rampaging around the city, Tyler finally came to Smithfield to confront the 14-year-old Richard II and the Lord Mayor, Sir William Walworth. After a public stand-off, the Mayor stabbed Tyler and strung him up outside the church of St Bartholomew, bringing the revolt to a decisive end. It was a major event in English history, but just one of a long litany of hangings, burnings and executions in Smithfield's violent past.

The thin line between comedy and carnage was often demonstrated by Carnival itself, when its ritualised violence could spill over into the real thing. Carrying weapons during the festival was often banned for that reason; yet, as some civic authorities recognised, controlled rumbustiousness could also have its uses. One such occasion was Carnival in Palermo in 1648, held during a period of simmering tension in the city after a failed harvest. The Spanish viceroy came under pressure from his nobles to cancel the festival for fear that it would spark riots, but the viceroy was cleverer than that. Rather than cancel the festivities, he arranged for them to be celebrated on a more lavish scale than usual. The ruse worked. After several weeks of boisterous revelry, all the tension in the city was dissipated, and order restored.[36] Public disorder can be threatening, but it can also have its uses. The trick is in knowing how to deal with it.

Popular unrest was never far from the surface in pre-industrial cities, often due to the unpredictability of the food supply, and markets were naturally the focus of such disturbances, not least because of their connection with food. In Paris the situation was made worse by the fact that the capital was fed almost entirely from a single central market, Les Halles. Whereas London markets were scattered all over the city and specialised in certain foods, Les Halles reflected Paris's rationalised, centralised food supply. It was split into various quarters selling different kinds of produce, each presided over by its own dynastic clan, who married amongst themselves and kept a mafia-like grip on their respective trades. Dubbed *Le Ventre de Paris* (the belly of Paris) by Émile Zola, the market was a city within the city, with its own population, customs, rules, taverns – even its own clocks that showed the seasons as well as the time of day. As the *encyclopédiste* Denis Diderot noted, it also had its own opinions: 'Listen to a blasphemy. La Bruyère and La Rochefoucauld are very ordinary and pedestrian books when one compares them to the wiles, the wit, the politics and the profound reasonings that are practised in a single market day at the Halle.'[37]

Market traders, like taxi-drivers, have never been shy of expressing their views, and their closeness to food has always given them a ready audience. In *Ancien Régime* Paris, the frequent food shortages made Les Halles a hotbed of political ferment. It even had its own group of ringleaders, the *forts*, strongmen who acted as the market's beasts of burden, doing the work of the official porters for a fraction of their wages. The *forts* were born fighters (many were part-time soldiers), and they delighted in stirring up trouble, spreading rumours of food shortages from the market into the surrounding streets. In the weeks leading up to the Revolution, they became natural leaders of the mob. The *forts* were beyond the control of the police, and, as with so many other aspects of the Parisian food supply, it was a problem of the latter's own making. By concentrating all the city's food in one place, they created a powerhouse strong enough to defy them.

Even in times of peace, food is never far removed from violence. Both are part of our animal natures, and when live beasts are present in the city, the relationship becomes explicit. The slaughter of animals in London remained unregulated until the surprisingly late date of 1848,

'An agitated sea of brute life'. Smithfield Market, around 1830.

by which time there were over 100 slaughterhouses in the Smithfield area alone, many of them in the ordinary basements of houses and butcher's shops. The so-called 'shambles' were horrific places by all accounts, where the cattle were 'killed and flayed in dark, confined and filthy cellars'.[38] The streets above were little better, to judge from one contemporary account: 'Through the filthy lanes and alleys no one could pass without being butted with the dripping end of a quarter of beef, or smeared by the greasy carcasse of a newly-slain sheep. In many of the narrow lanes there was hardly room for two persons to pass abreast.'[39]

By Victorian times, such grotesque scenes were no longer accept-able. A growing distaste for animal cruelty led to a clamour for the market to be closed down – a move made possible for the first time by the arrival of the railways. The livestock market was shifted to specially built facilities in Islington in 1885, and Smithfield became the meat market it remains today. The moment the sight of animal slaughter became too much to bear, the railways came along and saved the day

– or perhaps it was the other way around. It is human nature to deal only with what we really have to.

Nobody could argue with the need to close Smithfield down; by the end it was overcrowded, cruel and unsanitary. But its removal cost London something too. For all their mess, noise and nuisance, markets bring something vital to a city: an awareness of what it takes to sustain life. They are what the French sociologist Michel Foucault called 'heterotopias': places that embrace every aspect of human existence simultaneously, that are capable of juxtaposing in a single space several aspects of life that are 'in themselves incompatible'.[40] Markets are contradictory spaces, but that is the point. They are spaces made by food, and nothing embodies life quite like food does.

The Grocers' Tale

Well into the nineteenth century, markets remained the primary source of fresh food in cities all over Europe. However, London proved something of an exception. The authorities' refusal to grant further market licences during the city's rapid expansion in the seventeenth century (for fear of losing control) led to food shops springing up illegally. Before long, there were so many in the capital that their presence was tacitly accepted, and the city's streetscape was duly transformed. Bowed shop windows began to appear, in Cheapside and elsewhere, along with large heavy shop signs, some of them so cumbersome that they were deemed a public danger and banned.[41] Many shops still served their customers through an open window, but as Georgian estates spread into the West End, new kinds of food stores opened in order to serve them. The age of the high street had arrived.

With the arrival of the railways, high streets began to replace markets as urban food hubs all over Britain. As cities spread, authorities had no choice but to relinquish the control they had once exercised over food trades. The industrialisation of the food supply made such controls appear unnecessary in any case. Butchers, bakers and grocers began to open in new suburban neighbourhoods, catering to their mainly middle-class residents. The new shops marked a radical shift in the way food was bought and sold in cities. For the first time, significant numbers of the relatively well-off – the burgeoning middle-classes – were buying their own food. No less significantly, trade in food began to move from the public to the private realm.

The grocery trade did not get off to a very auspicious start. The new shops were the antithesis of the old adage that food should be sold transparently. Their interiors were cramped and dark, and most of the produce was stored in sacks or drawers under the counter. There was little advertising and items were not priced, so customers were forced to haggle for goods, something many were not used to. To make matters worse, there was little competition, so customers often had no choice of where to shop (modern occupants of Tescotowns will sympathise). Unsurprisingly, many grocers took advantage of the situation. Deliberate adulteration was rife, with traders mixing fine earth with cocoa powder to make it go further, alum with flour to make it whiter, or displaying fresh butter on the counter while serving customers from rancid stock below. As the opening verses of G.K. Chesterton's 'Song Against Grocers' suggests, such practices became endemic to the grocery trade.

> God made the wicked grocer
> For a mystery and a sign,
> That men might shun the awful shops
> And go to inns to dine;
> Where the bacon's on the rafter
> And the wine is in the wood,
> And God that made good laughter
> Has seen that they are good.
>
> He sells us sands of Araby
> As sugar for cash down;
> He sweeps his shop and sells the dust
> The purest salt in town,
> He crams with cans of poisoned meat
> Poor subjects of the King,
> And when they die by thousands
> Why he laughs like anything.[42]

Perhaps it was no bad thing that the poor, who represented at least half the urban population of the time, did not frequent these early shops at all. Most still bought their food at weekly markets that specialised in selling cheap cuts and leftovers from regular markets, and were usually held in community halls on Saturday nights, when most workers' pay packets came in.

In 1844, a group of Lancashire weavers decided that honest labourers deserved a better deal. Calling themselves the Equitable Pioneers of Rochdale, they banded together to form the world's first retail co-operative, buying a limited range of goods (flour, butter, sugar and oatmeal) in bulk in order to get them cheaply, and selling them on to their fellow workers at fixed prices, splitting the profits at the end of the year as dividends. The shops were unlike any that had gone before. Every expense was spared in their decor: they had stark interiors bare of any furnishings, with food simply displayed on planks set on barrels or on the floor. But they were well lit, and the produce was clearly priced, much as it is in a modern supermarket. Since the shops were run by people who themselves worked during the day, they were only open in the evenings, but that didn't stop them from becoming an overnight success. By the First World War, the co-operative movement had three million members in Britain, and a 15 per cent share of all food sales.[43]

The idea of buying and selling in bulk was soon copied by shop-keepers with rather less socialist intentions. Among them was Thomas Lipton, who had spent much of his youth in America, and returned to his native Glasgow with a concept completely new to British food retail: advertising. When Lipton began selling eggs, bacon, butter and cheese to an unsuspecting public in 1871, he launched his shop with newspaper adverts and posters and a flurry of showmanlike stunts. He imported 'the World's Largest Cheese' for Christmas, hauling it through the streets to the cheers of the crowd, and issued customers with the 'Lipton £1', for which they could buy £1 worth of goods in his shop for only 15 shillings.[44] The latter wheeze landed Lipton in court, but it was worth it. The additional custom it brought boosted his turnover to such an extent that he was able to undercut his rivals – the first step in his inexorable rise to building the world's first global food empire. By 1900, Lipton had an international distribution network serving hundreds of retail outlets, his own tea plantations in Ceylon, and 10,000 employees worldwide. Lipton's Tea, which was sold far more cheaply than any before it, cornered the growing working-class market, and remains Lipton's most visible legacy. However, it was his pioneering approach to retail, with his dedicated supply chain, own-brand products, loss-leading sales pitches and advertising campaigns, that made him the true pioneer of the modern grocery trade.

Shopping in Sheds

One innovation that eluded Lipton – one that was about to turn shops like his into supermarkets – was the concept of self-service. That was the contribution of Clarence Saunders, a flamboyant Memphis grocer who realised that one of his biggest overheads was the time spent by staff dealing with customers. At the start of the twentieth century, most Americans bought their food from homely 'mom-and-pop' stores, all-purpose family grocers that often acted as unofficial social centres for the local community. Saunders realised that if he could cut out the sociability of food shopping, he could reduce his prices to unbeatable levels. His self-service Piggly Wiggly store, opened in 1916, was the result. The Piggly Wiggly was essentially the world's first supermarket, and, considering how many of its features were radically new, its resemblance to the modern version was remarkable. Customers entered through turnstiles, picked up wire baskets to carry round as they shopped, took food off shelves themselves, and queued up to pay for it at checkouts.[45] Today we take such behaviour for granted, but back in 1916 it was startlingly different. The store opened to a chorus of cynicism from Saunders' competitors, but that soon changed to a stampede to copy his ideas when it became clear that, if food was cheap enough, customers couldn't care less whether they had a cosy chat over the counter as they bought it. Saunders, who had seen this coming, had the foresight to patent his invention, and now made his fortune franchising it to his rivals. Soon, self-service stores were popping up all over America, not just on high streets, but on the edge-of-town sites that were their natural home.

When supermarkets first appeared on the suburban horizon in America, they were viewed with suspicion. Everything about them seemed alien – not least their soulless anonymity. But once word got out about how cheap their prices were, public caution melted away. Taking a leaf out of Thomas Lipton's book, the new stores offered huge discounts for bulk purchases, and since most customers drove to them, they could load up with as many bargains as they liked. Motorised punters were the last piece of the food retail puzzle – the missing link that signalled the true arrival of supermarket shopping. From now on, the mom-and-pops wouldn't stand a chance.

By the mid 1950s, the daily food shop was a distant memory for most Americans. Postwar affluence and unlimited space had combined to create a new suburban landscape in which middle-class wage-earners and their baby-boom families lived out the American dream. Throughout the fifties, a million new 'Homes for Heroes' were built each year, most of them on plots large enough to require no boundary fences and with plenty of parking space for the essential family fleet of cars. The low-density lifestyle suited supermarkets perfectly. From now on, no suburban neighbourhood would be without one; no American home complete without its automobiles and 'ice-box'. In the four years after the war, Americans bought 21 million of the former and 20 million of the latter, and while they certainly appreciated their fridges, they positively adored their cars. People shopped in them, ate in them, watched movies in them, made love in them. Even to die spectacularly in them, as James Dean did, was seen as somehow glamorous.

Quite what all this driving around meant for cities was an open question – and it took a European to see that what it demanded was a whole new urban typology. That man was Victor Gruen, a 'short, stout and unstoppable' Viennese architect, who escaped to America just before the Second World War with, in his own words, 'an architect's degree, eight dollars, and no English'.[46] Gruen was soon making a name for himself designing eye-catching shop-fronts for fashionable New York boutiques, but his ambitions demanded a bigger stage, and when the department store Daytons approached him to design a new shopping complex in Minnesota, his chance came. Gruen seized the opportunity to address something he felt to be lacking in his adopted country. It was clear to him that old 'downtowns' were dying, and that nothing much was coming in to replace them. American-style suburbia, he felt, had none of the 'heart, brain and soul' of traditional European cities.[47] He decided it was time to give it some: to create a new kind of city centre for the motor age.

Southdale Shopping Centre, completed in 1956, was the result. The world's first enclosed shopping mall, its basic idea was simple: take the European high street, and recreate it, under controlled conditions, indoors. It was a brilliant commercial response to Americans' increasing reluctance to get out of their cars. A vast, introverted, featureless box built in the middle of nowhere, the mall contained enough goodies on the inside – tropical birdcages, luscious planting, fountains and piped music – to become a 'destination' in its own right; a fantasy world where people went for a special treat, just as they had gone to department stores in the nineteenth century. Shoppers happily drove there without noticing that once inside, they were actually required to walk. With the benefit of air-conditioning, the extremes of Minnesotan weather – typically a choice between blast furnace or blizzard, depending on the season – were effectively neutralised, creating a 'year-round climate of eternal spring', which, according to Gruen, lulled people into walking ten times further than they would have done in a crowded, rainy street.[48] In fact, people behaved much as they might have done on a lovely spring day on a traditional high street, spending several hours browsing the shops, stopping for a bite to eat, and then shopping some more. 'The shopping centre consciously pampers the shopper,' explained Gruen, 'who reacts gratefully by arriving from longer distances, visiting the centre more frequently, staying longer, and in consequence contributing to higher sales figures.'[49] Southdale opened to euphoric popular acclaim, and shopping would never be the same again.

Within a few years, malls were being built all over America, many of them designed by Gruen himself (and built, as we saw earlier, by Jim Rouse). The malls' effect on nearby city centres was immediate and striking: they sucked all the commercial life straight out of them. Gruen knew this perfectly well, but, urbanite though he professed to be, his view of 'downtowns' was remarkably unsentimental: he believed they

Southdale Shopping Centre in 1956.

were past saving. Malls might spell the death-knell of American cities, but in their place would rise up newer, better ones, designed by – Victor Gruen. For Gruen, malls *were* cities, creating a new urban order that would provide everything that traditional cities had done, only better. He predicted that malls would become 'not only a meeting ground but also, in evening hours, the place for the most important urban events'.[50] His words have turned out to be horribly prophetic. With Southdale, Gruen created a blueprint whose power turned out to be more potent than even he could have imagined. Like some Tolkienesque ring in the wrong hands, its influence has spread all over the world, destroying the cherished city centres that were once its inspiration.

Supermarket Cities

By the early 1950s, America was in love with supermarkets, and Britain was in love with America. Despite the lack of space and even greater lack of fridges (fewer than 8 per cent of British households had one in 1950), the American suburban lifestyle was irresistible to postwar Britain.[51] Suburbia, after all, was a British invention; now Britons yearned for the latest American version, with its forecourts, drive-ins and malls.

Supermarkets had been around in Britain since the 1920s – high-street branches of Tesco and Sainsbury slotted in between the butchers, bakers and the rest. But it was American-style superstores that the British now hankered after, and as soon as levels of car and fridge ownership rose high enough to make 'one-stop' shopping possible, Britons took to them like eager ducks to water. Superstore development in Britain, as we saw earlier, went virtually unregulated during the 1970s and 80s, the first hint of planning restraint coming in 1988, with the guidance note PPG6 requiring local authorities to 'take into account' the effect of new superstores on local town centres before reaching their planning decisions. To judge from the rate at which superstores carried on getting approval (the number more than doubled over the next 10 years), most authorities thought their effect was entirely beneficial. But research published by the Department of the Environment, Transport and the Regions (DETR) in 1994 suggested otherwise. It found that only 3 per cent of traditional market towns considered themselves 'vibrant', and as many as 15 per cent were in decline.[52]

Things developed very differently in mainland Europe, where laws were put in place to protect traditional town centres as soon as the threat from supermarkets became clear. An Italian law of 1971 required special permits for shops larger than 1,500 square metres, favouring local shopkeepers who wanted to enlarge their stores over any proposals for new development.[53] The French *Loi Royer* of 1973 required local government approval for stores larger than 1,000 square metres, and that of central government for stores larger than 10,000. Although plenty of hypermarkets were built in France, at first they sold mainly non-food items, leaving traditional shopping streets intact. In West Germany, where postwar reconstruction focused on rebuilding town centres destroyed by bombing (even to the extent of faithfully recreating market squares from old photographs), the last thing the government wanted was for those centres to lose their trade. A law was passed in 1980 restricting the size of suburban retail units to 1,500 square metres.[54]

Britain had to wait until 1996 for any planning legislation with real teeth: a revision to PPG6 requiring local authorities to adopt a 'sequential approach' when selecting sites for new superstores. Town-centre and city-edge sites had to be considered first, and only if these were unsuitable would out-of-town sites be permitted. The so-called 'Gummer effect' (after the Tory minister John Gummer, who introduced the legislation) was to cause an immediate, if undramatic, slowing down of superstore development. But the new law had other effects too. Deprived of their favourite greenfield sites, supermarkets became inventive about other ways to expand. Their move into the convenience sector dates from this period, but small-scale shopping was never what supermarkets were about. What they really wanted was to build big again. As Joanna Blythman described in her book *Shopped*, 'space-sweating' was the solution they came up with: ways of increasing the size of existing stores, either by building extensions in car parks, or constructing internal mezzanines that, thanks to a loophole in PPG6, required no planning permission.[55] In 2003, Asda Wal-Mart used such a move to add a cool 3,300 square metres to its Sheffield store (more than twice the size of an average 'one-stop' supermarket), announcing plans to add mezzanines to a further 40 stores. But space-sweating, although useful in the short term, was never going to satisfy the supermarkets. Even as the government moved to close the planning loophole, they had found a much better way to get around the planning system: buying land.

By 2005, the 'Big Four' had acquired a land bank of 302 undeveloped sites between them, with options on a further 149 should planning permission become available.[56] Tesco had by far the largest share, with 185 sites and enough land to increase its market share from 30 to 45 per cent should it all be developed.[57] A 2006 report by Friends of the Earth, *Calling the Shots*, described how supermarkets were using their land to hold local authorities to ransom. Tactics included leaving key sites vacant while lobbying councils to change their minds over permission, putting restrictive covenants on sites to prevent rivals from developing them, and offering councils sweeteners in the form of Section 106 agreements – legal bribes otherwise known as 'planning gain' – that might involve anything from providing some additional landscaping to building community facilities or affordable housing. The report listed more than 200 recent planning applications that had gone the supermarkets' way due to such tactics; among them a Tesco development in Streatham whose 'inadequate design quality' had apparently become 'adequate' once the supermarket agreed to build some local leisure facilities, and another in Coventry for a 13,000-square-metre superstore (the largest in Britain) granted on the basis of a new football stadium being thrown into the deal.[58] Joanna Blythman quoted one Tesco spokesperson who summed up the rules of the grocery space race thus: 'Sometimes the value of the land is enough to push the deal; sometimes you have to build the stadium.'[59]

With the connivance of local authorities, supermarkets in Britain are now full-blown urban developers. In 2004, Asda Wal-Mart completed a new 5,400-square-metre superstore in Poole, Dorset, part of a £30 million development that included 96 waterside apartments, 64 non-waterside (i.e. affordable) ones, a 600-space car park, offices, a shopping arcade and a public green space. Spot the planning gain. The scheme featured prominently on the council's website as a key part of its urban regeneration strategy. Poole is far from unique: building chunks of city is now a favourite gambit of supermarkets. With enough 'planning gain' in the mix, not only can they build new superstores more or less wherever they like, but they create ready-made captive markets to go with them; all in the name of 'urban regeneration'. As Tesco's corporate affairs manager put it in 2005, 'We're now thinking a lot more like a developer and not just like a retailer.'[60]

In 2005, Tesco turned its rivals green when it announced plans for a £100 million 'sustainable community' in Tolworth, south-west London. The scheme, described by its architects Building Design Partnership (BDP) as a 'vibrant mixed use development suited to the 21st century', included a new 5,500-square-metre superstore, 835 flats, 700 square metres of other retail and community facilities, new public open spaces, and a 'green bridge' over the A3 linking the site to the existing town centre. The scheme's 'sustainable' label derived from a raft of 'green' measures including solar panels, a combined heat and power (CHP) system run on bio-gas, and rainwater recycling. The architects described the scheme on their website:

> The development is being led by a strong sustainability agenda, and proposes to exploit the synergy between a Tesco store and residential apartments above which has the potential to make Tolworth an exemplary sustainability project that will be a benchmark for future developments in the UK, Europe and the world.[61]

With its Tolworth project, Tesco is bidding to make the transition from 'destroyer of town centres' to 'creator of sustainable communities' in one go. Great. The problem is, the 'sustainability' of the scheme's central element – its superstore – is, to put it mildly, questionable. It depends how you define sustainability. Or what it is you're trying to sustain. In this case, the thing most likely to be sustained by Tolworth is Tesco's profit margins. As for local shops and businesses, the existing community, or the planet, its likely effect is rather the reverse.

Supermarket urbanism got a significant boost in 2005, when the oft-adjusted PPG6 was finally scrapped in favour of Planning Policy Statement PPS6. Although the new law professed to be aimed at 'promoting sustainable and inclusive patterns of development, including the creation of vital and viable town centres', it contained a loophole you could drive a truck through, namely that 'larger stores may deliver benefits for consumers, and local planning authorities should seek to make provision for them in this context'. PPS6 signalled the green light for 'supermarket cities', and planning policy now looks set to be relaxed even further after a 2007 Planning White Paper proposed replacing the PPS6 'need test' (requiring superstores to demonstrate a need) with a new test that 'promotes competition and consumer choice and does not unduly or disproportionately constrain the market'.[62] Quite what the position will be in a few years' time is anyone's guess, but one thing is for sure. Supermarket power is not set to diminish any time soon.

Supermarket expansion is now a global game, with larger companies like Tesco concentrating their efforts on finding new markets abroad. Accession states to the EU such as Poland, Hungary and Slovakia have made gloriously easy pickings for the company, with few planning restrictions, and citizens who find a new Tesco on their doorstep as thrilling as Britons did 30 years ago. By 2003, Tesco already had more than 150 stores in Eastern Europe, but even that level of expansion wasn't enough to keep the chain happy. In 2005 it did a deal with the French giant Carrefour, agreeing to swap some of its Asian holdings in exchange for some of Carrefour's European ones, and in 2007 it embarked on its most daring venture yet, opening its first 'Fresh and Easy' store in the supermarket motherland, the USA. Wherever it chooses to go next, it is likely to find willing customers. When it comes to food retail these days, it is a truth universally acknowledged that a town in possession of a good fortune must be in want of a supermarket.

Malls Without Walls

Fifty years after tropical birds first chirruped at Southdale, Victor Gruen's dream has become reality. Markets were once the nuclei of cities; now we're building supermarkets in the middle of nowhere, putting houses round them, and calling them towns. Perhaps this should come as no surprise – food has always shaped cities; why should it be any different now? But there is a difference. Food was once the most highly regulated commodity in existence; now it is over-whelmingly in corporate hands. Supermarkets enjoy the same monopoly over food that markets once did, but unlike markets, they have no civic role to play. They are businesses with one thing on their minds: making money (remember the words of Victor Gruen). Because we need to eat, supermarkets have got us over a barrel. Wherever they build their stores, we must follow. Control of food gives control over space and people – something our forebears knew very well, but we seem to have forgotten.

The endgame of this trend is the death of public space itself. In 1994 the New Jersey Supreme Court ruled that 'shopping malls have replaced the parks and squares that were traditionally the home of free speech'.[63] The finding came after a group of political activists were forcibly ejected from a shopping mall for handing out leaflets, some-thing they defended their right to do on the grounds that the mall was the only place there was anyone to give them to – the traditional downtown was almost deserted. The New Jersey court agreed, con-cluding that 'a mall constitutes a modern-day Main Street'.[64] But as the recent ban on hoodies at Bluewater confirmed, malls are *not* Main Streets. Unlike real public spaces, they don't accommodate 'otherness'. Wear the wrong clothes, hand out leaflets, or try taking a photograph, and you are likely to get yourself thrown out. Markets are public spaces; malls are private ones.

Supermarkets might bring welcome cash to struggling local authorities, but the 'urban regeneration' they offer is really urban destruction. Supermarkets are changing the social and physical texture of cities, and with it the very nature of urbanity. Traditional city centres support a dense patina of individual shops, trades and businesses: the sort of mixed-use grain described by Jane Jacobs and plagiarised by Victor Gruen. Streets are the building blocks of cities, providing some-thing that supermarkets can never provide: a common space with which people identify, in which they have a stake. Above all, streets are *shared* spaces: in both their use and ownership, they form the basis of the urban public realm. It is no accident that 'street life' is synonymous with the social buzz of a busy city, and that no equivalent term exists for suburbia. The suburban ideal has always been one of autonomy: private ownership of your house and garden, garage and car. Now supermarkets are extending that notion to urban dwelling as a whole.

For a snapshot of the urban future, fast-forward to Santana Row, a district just south of San Jose in California first occupied in 2002 and already home to 30,000 people. Described by developers Federal Realty as 'a real urban neighborhood', Santana Row consists of a radiating series of luxury apartment blocks on six-lane boulevards arranged around a vast 'Europe-inspired' mall replete with open-air shopping arcades, restaurants, gardens, fountains, and even a reconstructed nineteenth-century chapel shipped over from France. The sales blurb makes life in Santana Row sound like one long holiday. 'Every city relies on vibrant neighbourhoods,' it purrs. 'For most, this means a place to relax, shop, or meet a friend for coffee and a stroll along a sunny, tree-lined street.' Whether or not one buys into this description of a 'vibrant neighbourhood' ('vibrant' is every urban developer's favourite adjective), Santana Row has certainly been successful enough to suck all the 'vibrancy' out of neighbouring San Jose. As for being a 'real urban neighbourhood', pull the other one. Santana Row is a mall without walls: an exclusive, private club masquerading as a piece of city, with its own management systems, security guards, and hidden sets of rules (pets are forbidden). Nothing can be allowed to disturb its smooth commercial operation: when local artist Emmanuel Flipo poured salt on to the street outside his gallery in 2003 to form the words 'no blood for oil' – an act for which he had gained permission – it got cleaned up by security within the hour.[65]

Santana Row is so obviously fake that its claims to full-blooded urbanity barely warrant discussion. However, the phenomenon it represents is very real. Ten years ago, the British town of Hampton, near Peterborough, was a 2,500-acre brownfield site, but by 2015 it is destined to become the largest private development in Europe, home to 18,000 people, with its own commercial district, schools and leisure facilities. Its residential quarters consist of the usual mix of mock-Georgian and faux-Victorian dwellings typical of developer-led housing projects in Britain, but there is nothing faux (apart from the name) about its so-called 'Township Centre' – a socking great 26,000-square-metre mall that includes the second-largest Tesco Extra in the country. Even when supermarkets aren't building cities, they are replacing what would once have been at their core – lusty, messy, negotiated public space – with the very opposite: controlled, security-sensitive private property.

Supermarket cities might provide places to shop, work and live, but to call them 'vibrant urban communities' is very wide of the mark. They are what the French anthropologist Marc Augé calls 'non-places': ersatz, branded versions of the real world with little sense of local identity.[66] Augé contrasts such places (for example, shopping malls and airports) with what he calls 'anthropological places', spaces that carry memories and associations, that express embedded history. Vibrancy can only exist in such places, where public life in all its forms is allowed: not just what is safe, familiar and comfortable, but also what is unexpected, strange, even dangerous. Public life, with all its contradictions – its 'otherness' – is the essence of urbanity. Take that away and put it in a corporate box, and you destroy the whole point of urban existence. As Jane Jacobs noted 40 years ago, 'In city areas that lack a natural and casual public life, it is common for residents to isolate themselves from each other to a fantastic degree.'[67] You might as well live in a mall.

Food Deserts

If supermarket cities are the future, where does that leave those of us living in cities (or anywhere else, for that matter) made by the finer-textured food systems of old? The answer, for some at least, is in a 'food desert'. As local shops close down, entire tracts of inhabited land (especially in low-income areas unappealing to supermarkets) are being stranded without any source of fresh food. A 2000 study undertaken by the University of Warwick found that many residents in the West Midlands town of Sandwell had no fresh food within 500 metres of their homes – the distance a fit person is considered to be able to walk in 10–15 minutes.[68] That might not sound very far, but when you consider that not everyone is fit, that many people have to work, look after children, or have other calls on their time, plus the fact that any walk to the shops inevitably involves walking in the opposite direction laden with shopping, you start to see the problem. The study found that Sandwell residents either had to use public or private transport to get to the shops, or survive on what was available locally: predominantly 'high fat, high salt, cheap, easily storable foods'. The situation is similar all over Britain, not least in its capital. A hundred years after Charles Booth's survey of the lives of the London poor, the statistics are, if anything, even more shocking. According to the London Development Agency, 53 per cent of inner-London children live below the poverty line, and according to the same survey, 13 wards across three inner-London boroughs contain sizeable tracts of food desert.[69]

Urban sprawl has made food distribution within cities as much of an issue as getting food to them once was. Back in the days when residential streets had corner shops and neighbourhoods local markets, food reached every part of the city through a fine-grained distribution network, supported by the wholesale trade. But those supply systems are long gone. Wholesale markets in Britain today are the food-supply equivalent of oxbow lakes, remnants of the days when food's journey through the city was very different. Just 20 per cent of London's fresh food is now dealt with wholesale, and all but two of its markets (Smithfield and Borough) have moved to the periphery. The wholesale trade now concentrates on the public service sector (schools, prisons and hospitals), the catering industry, and the few independent local shops still trading. The rest of the city's food supply is mostly controlled by supermarkets.

As ever in matters food-related, Paris's approach is different to that of London. All wholesale trade in the French capital is concentrated at Rungis Market, which does good business supplying a wide range of foods to the city's shops and restaurants. Rungis offers traders the equivalent of a one-stop shop, making it more convenient to use than London's scattered approach. Following a joint review carried out by Defra and the Corporation of London in 2002, plans are now underway to try something similar in London, closing all but three markets – New Covent Garden, New Spitalfields and Western International – and expanding those remaining in order to offer a wider range of produce and more user-friendly service.[70] The success or failure of the project could determine the future of independent food retail in London.

In 2006, the London Mayor, Ken Livingstone, launched a Food Strategy that attempted to address some of the issues facing the capital. Acknowledging that the current system was neither doing a very good job, nor very eco-friendly, the strategy set out its vision to 'deliver a food system that is consistent with the Mayor's objective that London should be a world-class sustainable city'.[71] Specific objectives included reducing London's ecological footprint, supporting a 'vibrant food economy' and improving the city's food security. Among the proposed actions were the expansion of direct selling between producers and consumers, the use of the planning system 'to protect the diversity of food retail provision where viable and appropriate', and the setting up of 'food hubs' to provide an alternative food supply network within the capital.[72] The trouble was, the strategy was put together without any co-operation from the supermarkets. As the document itself recognised, this presented something of a difficulty:

> The Strategy has already noted that just four major supermarkets account for 70 per cent of grocery sales in the UK. The scope for these retailers to achieve positive change is huge. Equally, if their involvement is not secured, the potential of the Strategy to make real improvements throughout the food chain will be severely constrained.[73]

Well, quite. The non-involvement of supermarkets, coupled with the traditional lack of support from central government, meant that the chances of London's Food Strategy achieving much more than a cosmetic sound bite or two were negligible even before its launch. For all its noble aims, London's Food Strategy cannot tackle the real forces shaping the city's food systems. The Mayor can approve or disapprove high-rise tower blocks, give the nod to swathes of housing developments, and win Olympic bids. What he or she cannot do is control the capital's food supply. As far as that is concerned, civic aims and corporate power simply co-exist in Britain. When their aims and goals conflict, there can be only one outcome.

Food Oases

One group of people who *can* make a difference to the way food shapes cities is ordinary customers – you and me. Our cash is what drives the food system, and our decisions about what food we buy, and from whom, have a greater influence than we might think. In 1998, the east Suffolk town of Saxmundham demonstrated the fact by saying no to Tesco, with a vigorous campaign organised by a local resident, Lady Caroline Cranbrook, supported by her MP, none other than John Gummer, he of PPG6 fame. As part of her campaign, Lady Cranbrook spoke to every trader in the town, as well as many local producers, in an effort to map the devastating impact the superstore would have on local businesses. Her work proved decisive, and six years after the council decision went in her favour, she revisited the same traders to see how they were faring. What she found was extraordinary: not only was every one of the town's 81 local shops still intact, but several more were opening up, and the number of local producers had risen from 300 to 370 – an unheard-of state of affairs, given the general trend in Britain.[74] Saxmundham was, in Cranbrook's words, 'on the verge of becoming a food destination'. It is true that the social demographic of Saxmundham is such that most residents can afford to pay a bit more for their food, but then so could a lot more of us. It is just a question of priorities. You don't have to be rich to eat well in Britain, and if more of us realised that, good food would soon get cheaper. Tipping points can work in both directions.

Despite the general decline of food markets in Britain, many still flourish, and not just those that sell cut-price food or rely on food tourism either. Some of the most successful are those serving the nation's ethnic communities, whose inhabitants still shop for traditional raw ingredients to cook at home. With its diverse population, London has many such markets, such as that in Brixton where, in the narrow arcades and leftover spaces beside the railway viaduct, one can buy anything from shark and salt fish, goat and plantain to okra, breadfruit and yams, all to the throb of reggae. Apart from the weather, one could almost be in the Caribbean. Likewise in Southall High Street, a huge variety of South Asian vegetables spill out on to the pavements, most of them air-freighted in via Heathrow. No worries about the death of the high street here: you can hardly make your way along the pavement for the crowds, and not a tourist in sight. When food takes centre stage like this, even unpromising spaces become animated, and show themselves capable of engendering human warmth.

The passion such markets inspire only becomes obvious when they come under threat. Queen's Market in Upton Park is London's most ethnically diverse, with 80 stalls and 60 local shops serving the local African, Afro-Caribbean and Asian communities. But in 2005 Newham Council proposed demolishing it to make way for an Asda Wal-Mart superstore, a mall, and 220 flats. Although the market was to be retained in reduced form, the locals were having none of it, organising a petition with 12,000 signatories against the proposals. In 2006, Asda Wal-Mart pulled out of the deal, but by then the council had signed a management lease with the developer St Modwen, admitting that 'the Council and the Developer's income will depend on the success of the new shopping centre'.[75] In other words, no supermarket, no deal: the familiar cry.

Thirty years on from Covent Garden, it seems London councils still haven't learnt their lesson. However, the Parisians appear to have learnt theirs. In 2005, Mayor Bertrand Delanoe announced his determination to prevent what he called '*La Londonisation*' (the corporate takeover of retail) from happening in Paris. Delanoe placed restrictions on half of the city's 70,000 independent shops to protect their use, so that, for instance, local butchers and bakers cannot be taken over by mobile phone companies.[76] Delanoe's approach did not meet with universal approval: some commentators accused him of trying to preserve Paris in aspic for tourists. Some of the loudest criticism came from Mayor Livingstone, whose spokesman dismissed Delanoe's approach as backward-looking: 'Paris's choice will increase London's competitive edge in a globalised and modern economy – in reality trying to buck the trend of a modern, globalised city won't work.'[77] Quite how being a 'modern, globalised city' squares with the Mayor's ambition to make London a 'world-class sustainable' one remains to be seen. However, since London seems, as ever, to be putting its trust in the forces of commerce, you can place your bets now.

As usual with polarised debates, there is a third way – in this case represented by the city of Barcelona. The Catalan capital proves that cities don't have to be folksy or old-fashioned to sustain authentic neighbourhood life. Barcelona manages it perfectly well, and the city has a gridded block structure about as rational as it gets. Tough government legislation prevented supermarkets from gaining a foothold in Spain the way they did in Britain; and although there are plenty in Barcelona, they are prohibited by law from selling fresh food at street level, so cannot compete with the city's food markets. Barcelona has 43 of the latter, including the famous Mercat de la Boquería off the equally famous street Las Ramblas. Recently twinned with Borough Market, La Boquería is a world-renowned food emporium, but it is not just urban showstoppers like these that preserve Barcelona's street life; rather the fact that people there still take their food very seriously indeed, and support local food shops and markets as a matter of course. Nobody could accuse Barcelonans of being backward-looking: their bold transformation of their city for the 1992 Olympics stunned the architectural world. Yet after more than a decade of urban renewal, Barcelona has managed to maintain a balance between commercial development and traditional ways. It can be done.

The battle over food is not just about what we eat; it is about society itself. Public life is the social glue of cities; public space its physical expression. Without them, urban society – civilisation itself – is fatally weakened. The role of food in forging both is immense. There is no question that supermarkets have a role to play in our lives, but it is up to us to decide what that role should be. They are businesses doing a job; in some cases, doing it very well. Supermarkets fit in with our crazy, hectic lifestyles. But do we really want them to design where we live? Is cheap food really that important? In the end it comes down to whether or not you agree with Margaret Thatcher's infamous dictum that 'there is no such thing as society'.[78] If all we want is a comfortable suburban lifestyle for ourselves, then supermarket cities – for those who can afford them – are the future. But if we believe civilisation should deliver more than that, we are going to have to fight for it.

Chapter 4
The Kitchen

My definition of man is, 'a cooking animal'.

James Boswell[1]

A sixteenth–century London cookshop caters for a wedding feast.

A Tale of Two Kitchens

The kitchen at the Savoy Hotel is about the closest you can get to a culinary holy grail in London. Created at the turn of the century by the legendary French chef Auguste Escoffier, it is the spiritual home of haute cuisine in Britain. Here the author of the 1903 *Guide culinaire* (an essential chef's bible even today) constructed banquets for kings and queens, created peach Melba for the eponymous soprano Dame Nellie while La Melba was performing at nearby Covent Garden, and raspberries Pavlova for the prima ballerina Anna Pavlova while La P was doing likewise. Waiting in the plush River Restaurant for my guide, Rebecca Todd, I am anticipating a grand theatre of cookery, a worthy counterpart to the velvety art deco luxury of the Savoy's public rooms.[2] But, as Rebecca arrives and leads me behind a discreet wooden screen, I am rapidly disabused. Down a sloping passage, its worn lino patched with masking tape and its walls covered with messy rotas, we arrive in the main kitchen, which, far from the imposing chamber of my imagination, is a cramped, sweaty inferno: a long, low, hellishly hot room in which the only thing more startling than the temperature is the noise. The food of the gods, it seems, comes from the other place.

Immediately in front of us, a group of black-clad waiters are standing at the pass (the long steel counter where orders are dispatched), gazing at the white-hatted chefs beyond, who work with concentrated precision, apparently oblivious to the waiters' eyes trained on them. The *chef de cuisine* is also at the pass, barking out orders to his 'brigade', who shout back without once looking up from their work. The military terminology is not misplaced. A professional kitchen at full throttle resembles nothing so much as an army unit under siege. Flames burst forth like mortar shells, faces are grim and determined, and tasks are carried out with soldier-like focus and urgency. Teamwork and discipline are vital in a kitchen such as this, since it is split into different sections (*parties*), each of which performs a different culinary function – hors d'oeuvres, sauces, roasting, grilling and so on – so that a miracle of co-ordination is required to assemble each dish at precisely the right moment. Cooking, like comedy, is all in the timing. The division of the kitchen into *parties* was Escoffier's idea: a way of streamlining the professional cooking process. Watching the Savoy chefs turn out their lunch service, I find myself wondering how much here has changed since Escoffier's day. The equipment might be modern, but its purpose is ancient. No technology will ever remove the stress, heat and noise of proper cooking.

After a while, Rebecca leads me back to the entry passage and a winding, almost domestic staircase down to the floor below. The stairs smell faintly of icing sugar as we descend, and sure enough, resting somewhat incongruously on a lower step is a tray of miniature cakes: puff-pastry castles with piped cream battlements, sitting in tidy rows. We have arrived in the pastry kitchen, a tranquil oasis a world apart from the raging bedlam above, where the products seem more like philosophical musings than food. On a counter to our right, several trayfuls of gravity-defying concoctions in millefeuille, chocolate and cantilevered biscuit wait to make their impact on some well-heeled diner's waistline. But it seems that not even this fairy-tale world is immune from stress. When a couple of waiters arrive to take the cakes off to a distant banqueting room, it seems there is a crisis underway, and the manoeuvre is accompanied by a volley of Ramsayan expletives. Time for us to beat a retreat back upstairs.

This far into our tour, it is becoming clear that the Savoy kitchen is a culinary rabbit warren: a series of burrow-like rooms in the bowels of the hotel connected by numerous narrow staircases and passageways. This impression is confirmed as we proceed to the rooms beyond the main kitchen, each of which can only be reached through the one before. First in the sequence is the sandwich room, where two chefs are cutting the crusts off dozens of loaves with long, narrow knives. They have clearly been at it for some time, since the pile of offcuts is already the size of a small bonfire. I ask one of the chefs what happens to all the crusts, and with an apologetic smile he indicates the bin. Such wastefulness is endemic in top-flight professional cookery: part of the price we pay for 'perfect' food, such as the razor-edged sarnies Savoy guests get with their tea.

Our next stop takes us to a far less tidy world: the butchery, now being scrubbed down for the day. In the middle of an otherwise unremarkable room is the largest wooden chopping board I have ever seen. At least eight inches deep at the edges, it could easily accommodate an entire cow. The board is clearly old: years of slicing sirloin and fillet have reduced its depth by several inches in places, so that its contours resemble a scale model of the Scottish Highlands, from where much of its meat must have come. There is something powerful about this hunk of wood — something of the sacrificial slab about it. Even when empty, it feels like this is the kitchen's epicentre — the place where the seriousness of cooking can be most keenly felt.

Down yet another sloping passageway is the last space in the culinary enfilade: the fish room. A small, dim space facing on to a glazed brick light well, it feels more like a cave than a kitchen, a melancholy chamber filled with damp, clammy air and the sound of running water. A lone chef stands at an enamel sink shucking oysters, sliding his knife swiftly round the encrusted shells to reveal their pearly insides. The tiled floor is lethally slippery, so that we skate, rather than walk, across it to the cold store, a cabinet of cold secrets rather like a bank vault. Inside, behind a heavy door, are stacks of wooden boxes packed with every kind of fish: gleaming salmon, turbot and bream, striped prawns and shining mussels, all packed on beds of ice. There are also live lobsters, dopey in the cold, pincers tied to prevent any last-minute bid for freedom. The chef picks up one of them to show us: a jet-black female with clusters of bright orange eggs on her underbelly. The sight inspires a sense of horror in me, but also one of pity. Kitchens can do the strangest things to you.

Back out in the fish room, I spot a yellow wooden notice on the far wall, with the words *NO BANGING OF SALMON CARPACCIO AFTER 7.30 – THE THEATRE REQUIRES SILENCE* painted on in red. It turns out that the stage of the D'Oyly Carte Theatre is just the other side of the wall, and that not even the thumping strains of Gilbert and Sullivan can drown out the sound of high-impact haute cuisine. It takes me a while to adjust to the idea that just a few bricks away from this fishy cave, there is all the opulent splendour of Edwardian theatre. It is a reminder that however celebrated chefs may be, theirs will always be a backstage art.

The Savoy kitchen is a one-off, producing food of the sort that few of us will eat more than once or twice in our lives. Yet in many respects, it is like any other professional kitchen. Its heat and noise, stress and swearing are all typical; as is its hiddenness. Professional cookery is essentially a cabalistic pursuit, steeped in traditions developed behind closed doors. As Grimod de la Reynière, the world's first professional gourmand, put it, 'With food, as with the law, to find it good, you must not see it being made.'[3] The thrill of visiting a restaurant kitchen is rather like discovering how a magic trick is performed: it feels somehow transgressive. Yet plenty of people these days are prepared to pay for the privilege: a meal at the chef's table at the Savoy will set you back something in the region of £600, and there is no shortage of takers. Despite various exposés of the restaurant trade from chefs such as Gordon Ramsay and Anthony Bourdain, our fascination continues to grow. As the titles of Ramsay's TV programmes suggest (*Boiling Point*, *Ramsay's Kitchen Nightmares*, *Hell's Kitchen*), his media career rests largely on playing with the taboos of cookery; in showing us things we are not supposed to see.

Few of us have enough cash to dine regularly at the Savoy, but as a nation we are eating more restaurant-style food than ever before. The reason for that is ready meals, which over the past 20 years have made Dame Nellies of us all. Back in the 1980s, Marks & Spencer's chilled meals still seemed bizarre enough for the comic Ben Elton to devote an entire stand-up routine to them. One wonders how many he and his audience have consumed since. In the 10 years to 2004, the convenience-food sector in Britain grew by 70 per cent, and continues to grow at 6 per cent a year. We eat ready meals on average at least twice a week, spending £1.6 billion on them in 2006 – almost as much as the rest of Europe put together.[4] Ready meals have become, as Tony Blair might have put it, the food of the people; not haute cuisine, perhaps, but fancier food than any previous generation ever dreamed of eating regularly – let alone in the comfort of their own homes.

The scale of this latest culinary revolution becomes palpable once you see the factories where the food is cooked. Pennine Foods is a ready-meal producer near Sheffield that employs 1,000 people and supplies all the major supermarkets. Its main kitchen – or, to be more correct, its cookhouse – feels like the engine room of a large ocean liner. Three storeys high and 50 metres long, it is, like the Savoy kitchen, decked out in stainless steel and extremely noisy, but unlike the Savoy, it is also full of pungent steam that tastes of soy sauce (Pennine specialises in Chinese cuisine). The cookhouse workers are also clad in white, although instead of chef's aprons and jackets, they sport lab coats and wellies, and in place of chef's hats, those plastic hairnets that make caterers' uniforms the least sexy on the planet.

But the most obvious difference between the Savoy kitchen and this one is their scale. Professional cooking equipment is all big, but 'big' hardly does the machinery at Pennine justice. The food mixers, for instance, consist of a row of kettledrums six feet wide, each fitted with a hinged lid and an oar-sized rotor blade. Accessed from a raised steel gantry, these drums are where the sauces for your stir-fry prawns and Shanghai chicken are blended, made up from recipe cards no different to those you would use at home, apart from their gargantuan quantities. Next to them are the factory's ovens and steamers: three stainless-steel boxes, each the size of a decent lock-up garage, into which trolley-loads of marinated pork, duck and chicken (or 'protein', as they are collectively called) are wheeled, to be roasted or 'steam-thermed', a process that bakes and steams at the same time.

On a whiteboard by the door is the day's schedule, which tells workers what quantities of food they are each to make. *STEAM-THERM*, it reads, *PILAU YELLOW x 52; PILAU WHITE x 13; COU PAELLA x 2.5; GASTRO PAELLA x 5*. The list confirms what the factory manager Kevin Hand has already told me: cooked rice is Pennine's biggest-selling product, coming out of the factory at the rate of 700 kg per hour. *COU* means Count On Us, the Marks & Spencer diet range, and there is plenty of that on the rota too: *COU STICKY x 1.5; COU CAJUN x 11; COU SHANGHAI x 4; COU CAJUN TOM x 13*. Clearly Pennine's customers are eating a lot of exotic food and trying to lose weight at the same time. Sounds familiar. The bewildering list goes on and on. According to Kevin, the factory produces 120 lines in all, requiring up to 600 recipe 'components' to be cooked on site each day. We watch one of them, a steel wheelie bin full of freshly made pasta, being tipped by an electric hoist into a vast cauldron of boiling water, causing a loud hiss and an instant local thickening of the savoury mist. Scaling up the cooking process is one of the great challenges of ready-meal production, and at the far end of the cookhouse we pause to admire Kevin's pride and joy: an induction wok unique to Pennine that uses a very high current passed through coiled wire to heat up a steel plate to 300°C, whereupon prawns and suchlike can be cooked in seconds as they are 'tumbled' across it using a set of flippers, rather like a giant game of table football.

In order to see what happens to the prawns after they have been cooked, we now have to perform an elaborate ritual. So far we have been in the 'low-risk' part of the factory – so called because it deals with raw food, any contamination of which is likely to be blasted out of existence by the cooking process (not many pathogens can withstand a 300°C game of table football). But once cooked, the food passes into a 'high-care' zone that we can only enter after purging ourselves of our outer clothing, walking though a bath of disinfectant, scrubbing our hands at an enamel trough and disinfecting them with alcohol, much as we did when we first entered the factory. We come to a changing room that has a stainless-steel bench running down the middle, with hundreds of pairs of green 'low-risk' wellies on one side, and a similar number of white 'high-care' ones on the other. As we sit on the bench and swing our legs over in an attempt to get our stockinged feet into our wellies without touching the wet floor, I remark on the extraordinary precautions we are having to take. 'I used to work in a nuclear power station,' says Kevin, 'and it was just like this.' I can't decide whether or not I find this reassuring.

Suitably clad, shod, dunked and scrubbed, we emerge in a large fluorescent-lit space in which hundreds of workers operate rows of Heath Robinsonesque production lines full of machines that process, assemble and package different sorts of food. My favourite is the spring-roll machine, which sucks up yellow pastry mix from a black tray and smears it on to a heated steel drum that cooks the pastry as it rotates. The sheets peel off automatically on to a conveyor belt that runs beneath a series of syringes, which dollop blobs of 'spring' on to them as they go past. Finally, the sheets come to a series of tiny interlocking rollers that wrap them up deftly and tuck in their ends. It's not quite as good as watching an Italian mamma making pasta, but it's pretty mesmerising nonetheless. Before these spring rolls leave the factory, they will have to undergo a visual quality check, random tastings by line operators and quality-control staff, an X-ray machine, a metal-detector, a high-accuracy weight sensor and an RFID (radio frequency identification) scan that will automatically log their provenance and sell-by date. If they make it out of here, they will be some of the most rigorously monitored food in history.

Pennine produces between 310,000 and 740,000 'units' of food a week, consisting of ready meals, packets of spring rolls and so on. Not only is that a staggering amount of food, but the variation from day to day is also startling. Kevin tells me that the factory's output is not just determined by traditional peaks such as Christmas (which he starts planning for as soon as the last one is over) but by something as unpredictable as the British weather. 'If it starts to rain,' he says, 'our orders shoot up. They can swing by as much as 400,000 pounds' worth on a single day.' Asked what rain has to do with it, Kevin says it is about customers' moods. If it starts to drizzle, many of us apparently try to cheer ourselves up with a ready meal, but when it rains more heavily, we tend to stay at home and raid the fridge instead. Given that Pennine uses only fresh ingredients and only has enough stocks on site to last a single day, meeting such demands is, to put it mildly, something of a challenge. How, I ask Kevin, do Pennine's suppliers cope with all these fluctuations? 'They have to be very responsive,' he says in level tones.

I am starting to realise there is more to the convenience-food business than meets the eye. As if cooking hundreds of thousands of ready meals every week were not difficult enough, it seems that the customers who eat them – you and me – are as hard to please as any operatic diva. We may not have dishes named after us, but our gastro-nomic whims are catered for just as assiduously. Take duck à l'orange, for instance. This hangover from the *bon vivant* 1970s still has a considerable fan base in Britain, most of whom like it just the way they remember it back then. Kevin tells me ruefully that Pennine found a fantastic way of cooking and packaging the duck so that its skin remained perfectly crisp, creating a delicious textural contrast with the sauce. The dish bombed. What true duck à l'orange aficionados really want, it seems – and what, thanks to their intransigence, they now get – is a ducky, orangey gloop. Every dish that Pennine cooks has some interest group to please: savoury vegetable rice is bought mostly by pensioners who like their vegetables very well cooked, while the thirty-somethings who buy the stir-fry Thai range like theirs somewhere between al dente and raw.

From tales of the cookshop, one soon starts to build an intriguing portrait of British eating habits. Whether we like our vegetables crunchy or boiled to death, it seems that we have a broad-based predilection for spicy, sticky meat. Post-modern fusion is creating a whole new British cuisine: dishes such as battered sweet and sour chicken (the bastard child of Chinese chow and fish and chips) and sticky chilli chicken, a sort of alternative spare rib with an Asian twist that recently gave Pennine their most successful ever launch. Although the company's development team makes regular trips to China, nobody in the factory is Chinese, because we British don't like Chinese food cooked the Chinese way; we like it deep-fried, sweet and fatty. Because we know it is bad for us, we tend to buy it as a special treat at weekends – and when we've decided we want a blowout, we really mean it. When Pennine launched a low-fat batter that tasted almost as good as the real thing, nobody went near it. We may never meet those who cook our food these days, but they still know all our guilty secrets.

Spaghetti on Trees

No matter whether they produce naughty treats like Pennine or posh nosh like the Savoy, in one sense all professional kitchens represent the democratisation of food. Meals as luxurious as those at the Savoy were once the privilege of nobility, and only the well-to-do had kitchens capable of producing elaborate meals until well into the nineteenth century. Now the vast majority of us can afford to eat exotic, professionally cooked food at home whenever we choose. Marvellous, isn't it?

Well, yes – and no. The problem is not with ready meals as such – the best ones are very tasty, using only fresh ingredients – but with what they prevent us from doing. With ready meals, supermarkets have found a way of extending their influence over us just that little bit further – a critical bit further, as it happens, since by keeping us out of the kitchen, they reduce our ability to influence the way our food is produced. When we buy food raw, we can prod it, test it, squeeze it and smell it, look it in the eye, compare it to other specimens. We can, in other words, make sure we are getting what we pay for. If we have regular suppliers, we can go one better, building up a relationship with them, asking their advice, ordering something special. We become what the Slow Food Movement calls 'co-producers': discerning buyers who have a reciprocal, rather than passive, relationship with those who produce our food.[5] But the less we cook, the less we care about how our food is produced. High-quality supermarkets such as M&S and Waitrose have discovered that even customers who are prepared to pay a bit more for fresh chicken from higher-welfare breeding programmes are unwilling to pay extra for the anonymous protein in their ready meals. As a result, even top-quality lines use intensively reared meat, increasingly sourced from abroad.[6]

Then there is the problem of scale. At the enormous volumes we are consuming, ready meals are distorting the entire food chain. However fastidious the on-site operations of factories like Pennine, they could never source their ingredients from small-scale producers such as those who still supply the independent restaurant trade. Just think about that rainy (but not too rainy) Friday evening, as thousands of us decide on a whim to stuff ourselves with sticky chilli chicken. Only supermarkets and their suppliers have the scale of operation to deal with such a surge of demand. It is, after all, one they have themselves created.

Our fondness for ready meals in Britain is symptomatic, like so much else in our gastronomic culture, of our lack of real connection with food. More than any other European nation, we have embraced industrialised food production, warts and all. The health implications of this are well rehearsed – hydrogenated fat, palm oil and bucketfuls of salt are just some of the horrors we have been unwittingly consuming for years.[7] But our convenience-food habit is affecting more than just our health. It is distancing us not just from food, but from everything that goes with it, with implications that extend well beyond the kitchen.

Although few city-dwellers before the twentieth century cooked for themselves, the intricacies of the food supply network meant that people had much closer contact with those who produced their food. Middle- and upper-class mistresses discussed menus with their cooks, often dealing directly with suppliers, or approving the produce they delivered. The urban working classes also had direct access to suppliers, of whom there were a lot more than there are today: food deserts are a modern phenomenon. Even the 'added value' in cooked food was real in the nineteenth century: when Victorian workers bought a baked potato from a street hawker, most were paying for something they could not produce themselves. Yet now that we all have kitchens, we are still prepared to pay other people to cook our food – which might make sense for those who can afford to do it occasionally, but for the less well off it makes no sense at all. The great paradox of convenience food is that the 'added value' in it is all in the part (the cooking) we could easily do ourselves. The part most of us could *not* provide (the raw ingredients) is the one we seem most reluctant to pay for. Strange, isn't it?

Cooking is about much more than chopping up a few vegetables and throwing them in a pan, or putting a ready-made pizza in the microwave. Because cooks control not just what goes out of a kitchen, but what comes into it, they are a vital link in the food chain – the guardians of our gastronomic know-how. Only cooks know how to source raw food, tell its quality, make it taste delicious, manage and store it, make use of leftovers. Few skills have a greater collective impact on our quality of life. People who don't cook don't use local food shops, invite their friends around for dinner, know where food comes from, realise what they're putting into their bodies, understand the impact of their diet on the planet – or educate their children in any of the above.

As it happens, both my parents know how to cook. My mother and father can draw you an approximate anatomical section through a cow or pig (both are medically trained, which probably helps). They can tell you which cuts are tough or tender and why (it depends what the animal used them for), which bits are cheap or expensive; which are good for roasting, frying or stewing. They know when vegetables are in season, what to do with giblets, how to tell whether fruit is ripe, whether meat is safe to eat. This knowledge, as my parents constantly reminded me and my brother when we were growing up, was forged during the Second World War, a time of general deprivation when common awareness of food had never been greater. My generation is lucky never to have known such hardship, but even as postwar babies, we learnt some of the lessons of wartime. Like many people my age, I find my parents' horror of waste has rubbed off on me. Growing up in the 1960s, I also picked up some basic knowledge of seasonality. I can still remember my childhood pangs of disappointment (motivated by sheer greed) when the summer absence of old King Edwards meant I would have to forgo my mother's peerless roast potatoes, known among family and friends as 'crunchies' in tribute to their crackingly crisp exteriors, achieved, needless to say, through liberal basting with dripping left over from the previous Sunday.[8]

Today, unless you choose to make a career of it, picking up that sort of culinary knowledge is close to impossible. Go to a supermarket and try to find someone there to ask for advice, and good luck. Try to work out which bit of animal you are about to cook, and ditto. Of course supermarkets deliberately obscure the origins of meat, knowing that if most of us recognise a bit of animal in the packet, we won't buy it. As for vegetables, trying to pick out local, seasonal varieties amid the profusion of 'eternal global summertime' can be hard work – or impossible. So much for gathering food. As for cooking it, there is a big difference between reading a saturated-fat statistic on the back of a ready-meal packet, and cutting off a lump of butter and sticking it into a pan – an act that never fails to afford me pleasure, even though I shudder at what it must be doing to my arteries. There is no better way to learn about food than by cooking it; yet few of us today are shown how.

Back in 1957, the BBC screened one of the most famous April Fools of all time: an episode of *Panorama* in which the highly respected broadcaster Richard Dimbleby reported, with complete seriousness, on the unusually good spaghetti harvest that year in Switzerland, due to the mild winter. His report included footage of Swiss farm-workers in a mountain orchard picking spaghetti off trees.[9] Since few in the audience had ever cooked spaghetti, most believed the report to be true. Fifty years on, not many of us would be taken in by such a programme: spaghetti is one of the few foods that we bother to cook. But 20 years from now, who knows? As Jamie Oliver discovered during his recent TV school-dinners campaign, food knowledge among modern British schoolchildren is shockingly low.[10] Most of the kids in Oliver's class stared in puzzlement at the leeks, onions and potatoes he showed them as if they were creatures from another planet (the vegetables, that is, not the kids; although both could arguably apply). If we continue as we are, the prospect of the next generation being totally ignorant not just of foreign foods, but of basic British staples, is scarily plausible.

The Hidden Art

Although cooking is a vital human skill, its position in society has always been ambivalent. Considered taboo by many ancient cultures, it was commonly viewed as an unclean act, and of lowly status. No doubt some of this prejudice came from the fact that cooking involves serving others, but a more powerful reason was probably the mess and brutality inherent to it. An essential part of a cook's work is knowing how to gather and produce food, something which in the past generally meant knowing how to raise and slaughter animals. Domestic cookbooks published before the twentieth century invariably contained advice on the latter, and even today certain foods – notably various kinds of seafood such as lobsters, crayfish and eels – are routinely killed in the kitchen. In addition to killing, cooks through history have been expected to skin, pluck, bone and gut animals – skills that even a generation ago were common among ordinary housewives. One 1965 recipe in *Elle* magazine took for granted that its readers would be capable of skinning a rabbit; a task that would make most *Elle* readers today run screaming from their kitchens, assuming they were there in the first place.[11] Cooking is brutal and dirty work, but its product, the meal, is of immeasurable cultural significance. Cooks kill and nurture, give pleasure or poison. They are servants who hold power over those who employ them. Their knowledge is vital, yet they work in secret. Cooking is full of such contradictions – no wonder we are so confused about it.

Although the traditions of cookery fall into two distinct camps – professional and amateur – the distinction between the two is not synonymous with public and private. Since only wealthy households had separate kitchens until the early nineteenth century, they were invariably run by professional cooks. What we think of today as domestic cookery – that is, amateur – was largely confined to the countryside, where people had access to raw ingredients, and houses often had large open fires or brick ovens. Many early rural dwellings were simply kitchens in which people lived (Finnish smoke saunas being one example), and such buildings remain emblematic of the ancient marriage between hearth and home. Although early town houses also had open fires, as cities grew larger the fires got smaller, and the nearest most city-dwellers came to cooking for themselves was to sling a pot over the living-room grate and make some sort of stew. For the most part, urban populations subsisted on a diet of bread, cheese, salted fish or meat, plus the occasional hot meal bought from a public cookshop; which is why the latter had a vital role to play in cities right from the start.

Public cookshops date back to the city states of the ancient Near East. As well as acting as urban food hubs, Egyptian and Mesopotamian temples often had public bakeries too. When Sir Leonard Woolley excavated the great ziggurat at Ur, he found several such bakeries in the temple compound – his comment was that the building was more like a kitchen than a temple.[12] Woolley also discovered less exalted cookshops in the city. One on a side street appeared to be an ancestor of the modern kebab shop, with a solid brick range, a charcoal tray with brackets for carrying braziers of meat, and a wide brick counter on to the street for displaying cooked dishes to customers. Similar establishments have been found all over the ancient world. Roman citizens could choose from a large variety: *thermopolia* sold hot snacks and drinks over the counter, *popinae* specialised in cheap meat left over from temple sacrifices, and *tabernae* served hot meals that one could sit down to eat.[13] Another common practice in the past was the taking of raw food to the baker to be cooked. Romans did it with their free grain, and working-class Britons took their Sunday joint to the baker's to be roasted until well into the twentieth century.

Medieval fast-food joints were open all hours, just like their modern counterparts. One of the earliest descriptions of such an establishment is that of a London *publica coquina*, written by the Canterbury monk William Fitzstephen in 1174:

> There is in London upon the river's bank, a public space of cookery
> . . . There every day ye may call for any dish of meat, roast, fried or
> boiled; fish both small and great; ordinary flesh for the poorer sort,
> and more dainty for the rich, as venison or fowl. If friends come upon

Londoners collecting Christmas dinner from the baker's in 1848.

a sudden, wearied with travel, to a citizen's house, and they be loth to wait for curious preparations and dressings of fresh meat, let the servants give them water to wash and bread to stay their stomachs; and in the meantime they run to the waterside, where all things that can be desired are at hand.[14]

William had nothing but praise for cookshops, which he found 'very convenient to the city, and a distinguishing mark of civilisation'. But they have often met with a far less rosy press. Juvenal spoke with distaste of the 'smell of tripe in some hot and crowded cookshop', and in 1698 Ned Ward described leaving a cookshop at Pie Corner in Smithfield because the cook operating the spit 'rubbed his ears, breast, neck and arm-pits with the same wet cloth which he applied to his pigs'.[15] No doubt many public kitchens in the past were dodgy, as no doubt many still are (stories like Sweeney Todd don't come from nowhere). Yet however grim they were, the kitchens of the past have gone largely unrecorded, the taboos of cookery have seen to that. One of the earliest descriptions of life in a professional kitchen came as late as 1933, when George Orwell dished the dirt on a Parisian hotel in *Down and Out in Paris and London*:

> It was amusing to look round the filthy little scullery and think that only a double door was between us and the dining room. There sat the customers in all their splendour – spotless table cloths, bowls of flowers, mirrors and gilt cornices and painted cherubim; and here, just a few feet away, we in our disgusting filth. For it really was disgusting filth. There was no time to sweep the floor till evening, and we slithered about in a compound of soapy water, lettuce-leaves, torn paper and trampled food.[16]

As Orwell's account suggests, there can be many reasons to hide a kitchen. The first and most obvious is that cooking is dirty, noisy and smelly – especially when carried out on a large scale. On that score, the separation of cooking and eating is simply a matter of decorum. The tradition of haute cuisine extended the principle, insisting that even a well-ordered kitchen should remain invisible, lest its secrets be revealed to diners, so ruining the 'magic' of the food. The third, less exalted, yet most common reason for hiding a kitchen is simply that if people could see how their food was being cooked, they would refuse to eat it. In kitchens, the contradictions of cookery find physical form. In many ways, kitchens are as political spaces as markets: the functions they perform and the issues they raise at least give them claim to such status. But unlike markets, kitchens hide their politics behind closed doors.

Women's Work

The division between professional and amateur cookery might have been blurred through history, but in one respect it is clear. Professional cooks predominantly have been male; amateur ones overwhelmingly female.[17] When we think of home cooking, we invariably think of food 'like mother used to make', which in the USA means 'Mom's apple pie'; in Italy '*pasta di Mamma*', in Britain 'Mother's Yorkshire pudding' and so on. What these dishes all have in common is that they are essentially rural in nature: the sort of wholesome, hearty food that country housewives cooked for their families, long before many city-dwellers even had kitchens. The apple pies and Yorkshire puds of yesteryear may not have tasted quite as good as we like to imagine; but that is not the point. It is the fact that our mothers (and grandmothers) cooked them at all that makes them so special.

As far as the history of home cooking is concerned, the twentieth century was an aberration. Before then, few urban households had kitchens capable of producing dishes 'like Mother used to make', and if they did, those dishes would not have been cooked by Mother, but by servants.[18] If the mother of the house *had* cooked the meal, she was almost certainly working class, in which case she would not have sat down to eat with her family, but would have remained standing in order to serve her husband at table. Except on special occasions, working-class men usually ate alone, watched by their wives and children, who had to wait to see what would be left over for their own supper.[19] Family meals as we think of them today (not only cooked by

Mother, but shared by her at table) were a purely twentieth-century phenomenon; the product of the servantless nuclear family brought about by two world wars. Fixed in the minds of the postwar generation in Britain by the Bisto adverts, the family meal was in many ways as ephemeral as the ads that celebrated it. Even as it reached its apogee, the phenomenon was in decline, as the social conditions that brought it about disintegrated once more.[20]

No matter who did the cooking, the fact that domestic kitchens have always been associated with women has had a profound influence over house design. Through kitchens, the female associations of nurturing, hiddenness and taboo have been carried into the physical fabric of the home.[21] Even today, in our neutralised, microwaved cooking culture, domestic gender boundaries are palpable. In the ancient world, kitchens in houses large enough to have them were typically arranged in or around open courtyards. This was the family domain – a world of women, children, cooking and servants, segregated as far as possible from the public parts of the house. Entrances from the street were either fitted with screens or designed with bends in them to prevent passers-by from seeing in – an arrangement that remains common in traditional Arabic households today.

In ancient Athens, the gender association of public and private parts of the house was explicit.[22] The private areas – the courtyard and, in larger houses, the upper floors – were the realm of *idion*, a hidden world whose associations (mystery, uncleanliness, otherness) mirrored those of the female body.[23] The most important space in the house was the *andron* – literally, the 'man's room' – where male guests were entertained at a *symposion*, a ritualised dinner followed by entertainments and debate, to which the women of the house were forbidden entry.[24] Although such dinners were considered supremely important in Athenian society, the cooking of them was not. Plato, whose philosophical works all took the form of sympotic dialogues, had little time for cooking, declaring it to be 'not an art at all'. Philosophers at his academy were reported to have smashed a casserole to the floor, complaining that it was 'too fancy'.[25] In Athens, where public life was exclusively male, cooking belonged firmly to the lesser, female realm. Much the same was true of Rome, where dining remained an important networking tool. Although Roman women were allowed to dine with their men, no high-ranking mistress would have dreamt of doing the cooking herself – kitchens in wealthy houses were the domain of slaves. The fact that women and men dined together meant that the Roman dining room (*triclinium*) was more central to the house than was the Greek one, often placed next to the semi-public *atrium*, with the family quarters and kitchen arranged around a private courtyard beyond.[26]

Domestic cooking arrangements evolved rather differently in northern Europe, largely due to the chillier climate. Rather than trying to expel the warmth of cooking from the home, traditional longhouses, with their great halls and central hearths, embraced it as a convivial centrepiece. Longhouses were an architectural response both to the weather and to the prevailing hunting culture of the north, in which the roasting of the day's spoils was a celebratory act, very different to the 'boiling' cuisines of southern Europe that would eventually lead to the sauces of haute cuisine.[27] The arrangement of a central hearth persisted in northern medieval town houses, which were essentially urban versions of their rural counterparts. When such houses began to be built with separate kitchens during the fourteenth century, it was a sign that urbanism was taking hold, and that cities were starting to lose their close ties with the countryside.

Haute Cuisine Comes Home

The rise of the bourgeoisie in medieval France and Italy marked a resurgence of professional domestic cookery in Europe. Increased urbanisation meant there was a growing demand for cooks from the twelfth century onwards, although they were required to display little culinary skill. When the bourgeois entertained, they did their best to imitate courtly feasts, which at that time meant one thing above all else: abundance. In order to impress one's guests, all one had to do was to offer them more food than they could possibly eat. But even as bourgeois tables heaved with superfluity, courtly cuisine was moving in an altogether different direction. Partly to distinguish their food from lowly imitators, courtly chefs were developing a radical new cuisine, in which quality, rather than quantity, was paramount. The new cookery required supreme skill, and for the first time in history, chefs began to express their individuality in what they did.

By the mid fifteenth century, courtly cuisine in Italy was a highly complex art form, practised by well-regarded yet still anonymous chefs. The cabalism of the kitchen ensured that the secrets of the new cookery remained inaccessible to all but a few, but demand for culinary knowledge was growing steadily, and with the arrival of printed books, the means of satisfying it finally came within reach. Cookery books were among the world's first bestsellers, with Maestro Martino's *Libro de Arte Coquinaria* top of the list. Published in 1475 by the semi-anonymous papal chef, Martino's treatise is often cited as the first modern cookbook. It was revolutionary in that it emphasised the flavour of food, rather than just its physical appearance, and although some of the recipes clearly belong to another age (one for 'Flying Pie' details how to bake the classic 'four and twenty blackbirds' dish, with live birds inside), others anticipate the techniques of haute cuisine, dealing with refined fruit sauces, wine reductions and so on.[28] Martino's recipes were widely copied, not least because they revealed for the first time the secrets of courtly cuisine. Martino became the first celebrity chef; not yet in the full-blown sense (little is known of his personal life), but famous enough to be identified with his own style of cookery.

By the seventeenth century, the flaming baton of culinary invention had moved from Italy to France. Cookbooks such as La Varenne's 1651 *Le Cuisinier François*, in which the author gave the first recipes for classic techniques such as making bouillon and roux, were essential manuals among the French bourgeoisie, and serving one's guests *cuisine à la mode* a ruinously expensive necessity. The pressure to entertain in the correct fashion was exacerbated in 1682 when Louis XIV gathered his court at Versailles, creating a focus of custom and manners that the whole of polite society felt obliged to follow. However, the same period in England saw things moving in the opposite direction. The 1688 over-throw of James II by the 'Glorious Revolution' brought an end to culinary opulence at court, signalling a more sober approach to cookery reflecting the rural lifestyles of the English gentry. Good plain country cooking (the pies, roasts and puddings we now think of as quintessentially British) took centre stage, even in the houses of the wealthy. The prophets of the 'low' cuisine were mostly women, who treated cookery as a branch of household management, proclaiming their preference for an 'honest' approach, partly in riposte to the extravagances then being perpetrated across the Channel. 'If Gentlemen will have French Cooks,' sniffed Hannah Glasse in her aptly named 1747 *The Art of Cookery Made Plain and Easy*, 'they must pay for *French* tricks.'[29]

The stage was set for a clash of culinary cultures that rumbles on even today. When the Revolution relieved courtly chefs in France of their posts in 1798, many came to Britain, bringing their 'French tricks' with them. A battle of 'high' and 'low' cuisines ensued in the dining rooms of middle Britain, at the very moment when the habit of giving dinner parties (long established in France) was taking root. A raft of books on the subject of entertaining was published, unanimous in their view that haute cuisine was to be preferred for dinner parties – it had, after all, a 200-year head start on its rival as a vehicle for impressing guests. Out went the no-nonsense approach of Hannah Glasse and her sisters, and in came a new bastardised form of Anglo-French cuisine. Although it was still acceptable – even necessary – to serve one's guests a roast, it now had to be accompanied by a profusion of other dishes – hors d'oeuvres, *entremets*, *relevés*, entrées – either served all at once *à la française*, or (even more fashionably) brought to table one after the other *à la russe*.[30] Either way, the bourgeois dinner party had arrived in Britain, and it required a small army to deliver it.

Knowing how to give a good dinner party was not just a question of being hospitable in Victorian society; it was a matter of social survival. 'Dining is the privilege of civilisation,' declared Isabella Beeton, high priestess of the new culinary religion and author of its bible, the *Book of Household Management*, published in 1861.[31] But that privilege came at a cost. The pressure to entertain was so great that families who could barely afford it still felt obliged to find a way. A further swathe of manuals aimed at these poor unfortunates was published, such as the evocatively titled *From Kitchen to Garret* of 1888, which advised families with only one maid how they could save up all year in order to give that one crucial dinner party.[32] Even if a hostess could afford to entertain, getting the details wrong could still banish her to social oblivion. As one manners book put it, 'there is no better or surer passport to good society than having a reputation for giving good dinners'.[33] What was left unsaid – but was perfectly understood – was that the obverse was equally true.

Fear of Food

The use of food as a means of shaping social identity in Victorian Britain could not have come at a worse time. Attitudes towards food were shifting as fast as society, and not just because the menus were written in French. The irony of a rich nation – the capital of an Empire, no less – in which three quarters of the population could barely afford to eat should have been troubling enough, but that was not the main source of anxiety among those who could. Other aspects of material existence were beginning to trouble the Victorian conscience, raising awkward questions about man's place in the natural order of things.

First and foremost was the question of meat. The British had long been notorious for tucking into their beef bloody and raw with a gusto that, as far as the French were concerned, betrayed a want of manners. As the chef Châtillon-Plessis put it, 'Compare what I would call the *bleeding dish nations* with the *sauce nations*, and see whether the character of the latter is not more civilised.'[34] But now the cheerful carnivorism of *les rosbifs* was beginning to melt away. The case for vegetarianism was not new: it had been an enduring theme of the Enlightenment in both Britain and France. Philosophers of the stature of Newton and Rousseau had argued its case on the basis of compassion for animals, but few had gone so far as to say that the killing of any beast in order to eat it was wrong. Now that view began to take hold. An increasingly vocal lobby argued that the eating of any meat was barbarous; a view formalised in Britain in 1847 with the founding of the Vegetarian Society.[35] Although take-up of membership was slow (the society only attracted 5,000 members in its first 50 years), the mere existence of such a body helped to fuel a sense of guilt, and corresponding squeamishness, among the vast majority who continued to eat meat.[36] A new repugnance at the killing of animals was taking root; one that found expression not, as might have been logical, in the gradual abandonment of meat-eating, but in greater efforts to hide the evidence. Like a bunch of guilty murderers trying to stash the corpse, Victorians repressed their doubts and set about arranging the world so that its less savoury aspects disappeared from view. Faced with the inconvenient divergence of their preferred diet and their sensibilities, they plumped for denial – an approach we have been following ever since.

Just as slaughterhouses were disappearing from cities, cooks now began to alter the appearance of food in order to disguise its origins. Piglets, rabbits and geese that would once have been presented at table in all their lifelike glory – snout, fur, feathers and all – now either arrived with all their distinguishing features removed, or were served *à la russe*: carved out of sight of diners and brought to the table on individual plates. The new sensibility echoed the remarks of the humanist William Hazlitt: 'Animals that are made use of as food should either be so small as to be imperceptible,' he wrote, 'or else we should . . . not leave the form standing to reproach us with our gluttony and cruelty.'[37] Ritual carving at table, once a way of celebrating the life of the creature about to be eaten, was now replaced by ruses to obscure the fact that it had ever lived.

Victorian levels of carnivorous guilt were heightened in 1859 with the publication of Charles Darwin's *Origin of Species*, in which the author raised the awful possibility that, far from being distinct from all other animals, man might actually be related to some of them. Although Darwin's theory was highly controversial at the time, the possibility that man might be consuming the flesh of his own distant relatives lent a new potency to the meat debate. Food, which had always occupied a place in the human psyche somewhere between desire and fear, now took a decided lurch towards the latter. The materiality of meat became a source of repugnance; the sight of a bloody lump of steak too close to human flesh for comfort. The British, once mocked by the French for eating their beef barbarously underdone, now took to blasting it to oblivion, much as we still have a tendency to do.

The Divided House

While Victorians struggled to come to terms with their bodies, the physical space they inhabited was changing too. Until the eighteenth century, people of all classes had mingled together in cities, often living next to one another in the same streets. Georgian estates were the first to break with this tradition: exclusively middle and upper class, they presaged modern gated communities, with private security guards and barriers that were locked at night. Such estates marked the beginnings of social segregation in Britain, but it was the railways that firmly established single-class enclaves – social monocultures – as the dominant residential pattern. From the mid nineteenth century on, those who could afford to do so began to abandon cities for suburban neighbour-hoods such as Bedford Park in west London, completed in 1881 by the architect Richard Norman Shaw. With its redbrick gabled houses and winding, leafy lanes, Bedford Park was essentially an idealised rural hamlet; the prototypical British garden suburb.

The flight of the well-to-do from the city was not just because of the desire to escape overcrowding. Cities had always been known to be filthy places full of plague and pestilence, but since the cause of such infections had never been understood, the risk of disease was accepted as one of the hazards of urban life. Then in 1854 the London physician John Snow made a discovery that put a new perspective on things. During a particularly virulent outbreak of cholera in Soho, Snow managed to trace the source back to a single contaminated water pump. He recommended that the pump be dismantled, which (after some argument) it was, causing an immediate drop in the number of cases, just as he had predicted. The incident showed for the first time that infectious diseases were carried not by some form of bad air, or 'miasma', but by the spread of germs in a physical medium – in this case, water. The discovery of so-called 'germ theory' was both a crucial step in the history of microbiology, and the start of a psychological shift in people's attitudes towards their fellow humans. All of a sudden, rubbing up against one's neighbours didn't seem quite so appealing. Germ theory heralded a new era, not just of social segregation, but of mental segregation too.

By mid-century, there was a powerful sense of 'them and us' both outside and inside the home. The semi-detached villas that proliferated around cities increasingly took on the aspect of refuges. John Ruskin hailed the family home as a 'temple', calling it 'the place of peace; the shelter, not only from all injury, but from all terror, doubt and division'.[38] But few mistresses of their oak-lined, heavy-curtained 'temples' felt quite as sheltered by them as they would have liked. Left isolated while their husbands commuted to the city, women spent their days paying morning calls on one another, maintaining the illusion of competence in front of the servants, and planning the next – dreaded – dinner party.

It was against this background of unease that Victorian houses evolved. Dinner parties were full-blown theatrical productions, and middle-class houses vehicles for staging them. No matter how much blood, sweat and toil were required to produce the meals (and it was a lot), they depended for their success on the illusion of effortlessness. Until the late eighteenth century, meals even in affluent homes had often been taken informally, sitting at foldaway tables in the family living room. Now such an arrangement was seen as far too casual. Separate dining rooms were de rigueur, as were complex service quarters arranged so that, as one architect put it, 'what passes on either side of the boundary shall be both invisible and inaudible on the other'.[39] The 'upstairs–downstairs' segregation of the Victorian house-hold was taking shape, and with it a new desire to hide the inner workings of the home. The design of kitchens became an urgent preoccupation; not in order to make them easier to cook in (a plenitude of servants could overcome any degree of inconvenience on that score), but in order to suppress their very existence. The architect J.J. Stevenson stated the problem in 1880:

> . . . unless the kitchen itself is ventilated so that all smells and vapours
> pass immediately away, they are sure to get into the house, greeting

us with their sickly odour in the halls and passages, and finding their way to the topmost bedroom, notwithstanding all contrivances of swing doors and crooked passages.[40]

Stevenson's description of cooking smells as 'sickly' rather than 'appetising' tells its own story. An unwelcome reminder of baser bodily realities, cooking in the Victorian household was seen as a source of embarrassment. However, as the architect Robert Kerr conceded in 1865, for a society hell-bent on lavish entertaining, this was something of a self-defeating attitude:

> The means of communication, or *Dinner-route*, ought to be primarily as direct, as straight, and as easy as can be contrived, and as free as possible from interfering traffic. At the same time it is even more essential still that the *transmission of kitchen smells* to the Family Apartments shall be guarded against; not merely by the unavailing interposition of a Passage-door, but by such expedients as an elongated and perhaps circuitous route, an interposed current of outer air, and so on – expedients obviously depending for their success upon those very qualities which obstruct the service and cool the dishes.[41]

The Victorian kitchen was required to produce meals on an unprecedented scale, and to do so invisibly, inaudibly and odourlessly. In social and spatial terms, it represented a fundamental contradiction – one that we have yet to resolve. Victorian society is long gone, but as far as food is concerned, many of its attitudes still linger. Squeamishness, faddishness, suppressed and unacknowledged guilt – all took root then in the British psyche, and despite all we have been through since, they are still with us.

Home and the Range

One of the reasons that fear of food took such a powerful hold over our Victorian forebears is that so few of them knew how to cook. Mass migration to the cities had separated many people from their traditional links with food, and few city-dwellers cooked much for themselves. It was beneath the dignity of the middle classes to do so, and the poor lacked the wherewithal. Living conditions for the urban working classes were deteriorating rapidly, with many previously decent neighbourhoods becoming overcrowded 'rookeries' where entire families lived in a single room. New housing built for industrial workers was often little better: the notorious 'back-to-back' terraces common in northern cities consisted of doubled-up rows of houses with no rear windows; containing just two single-aspect rooms one above the other. The houses had no running water, and were generally arranged around courtyards with a communal stand pump in the middle.[42]

From the 1830s onwards, better housing for skilled workers began to appear in cities: 'two-up, two-downs', which, as the name suggests, had two rooms to each floor, and usually backed on to alleyways. Most had sculleries at the rear giving on to a small yard, and it was in these rooms – originally intended as washrooms and storerooms – that the cooking, such as it was, was usually done, as well as the eating. All family life, in other words, took place in the scullery, while the parlour at the front was 'kept for best': it was barely used. These modest terraced houses, together with the more elaborate versions that followed, would form the dominant blueprint for Victorian domestic architecture. Blocks of flats never took off in Britain as they did elsewhere in Europe, but those that were built, whether model workers' housing built by philan-thropists such as George Peabody, or serviced mansion flats for the middle classes, continued to treat kitchens as repressed service spaces. Many of us still live in these flats and houses, and whether we like it or not, they help to preserve the Victorian mindset about the place of cooking in the home.

Gradually domestic sculleries in terraced houses morphed into what we would now recognise as kitchens. The transformation was largely due to a single piece of equipment: the closed kitchen range, invented by the Anglo-American thermodynamic physicist Sir Benjamin Thompson (Count Rumford) in the 1790s, primarily as a means of saving fuel. In place of an open fire, from which most of the heat escaped straight up the chimney, Rumford proposed enclosing the fire in an iron box, beneath a hot plate on which pots could be placed, so making much better use of the heat. The Rumford range could also produce hot water for the house, and later models featured an iron compartment with a hinged door beside the firebox – the first commercially produced domestic oven. Although kitchen ranges remained essentially middle-class accessories until the early twentieth century due to their cost, their gradual adoption made home cooking, with its familiar processes of boiling, roasting and baking, possible in much humbler households than ever before. With the arrival of the kitchen range, the class distinctions of domestic cookery began to dissolve. The question among the aspirant classes was no longer whether or not one had one's own kitchen, but whether or not one employed a cook to do all the work. Despite all the advances in kitchen technology, cooking for oneself at the turn of the century remained the social anathema it had always been, but the First World War was about to sweep away any such scruples.

The Ideal Housewife

By decimating the working population, the First World War brought a more emphatic end to *fin de siècle* society in Europe than any protest movement could have done. The so-called 'servant problem' made the running of houses along Victorian 'upstairs–downstairs' lines close to impossible. In the same way that plagues had once raised the fortunes of peasant farmers, the devastation of war now changed those of domestic servants for the better. From now on, mistresses lucky enough to employ them would have to treat them properly. As for everyone else, they would just have to learn to fend – and cook – for themselves.[43] For the first time in history, genteel European women were forced to enter their own kitchens, and few of them liked what they saw. Considering their importance, kitchens had been astonishingly neglected spaces. In the days when servants had done all the cooking, nobody had cared much what their kitchens looked like, so long as they did their job adequately. But now that mistresses were going to be putting on aprons, what did that make kitchens? Could they still be considered mere service spaces, or did the status of their new occupants elevate them to centre stage in all matters domestic?

A century on, the question remains unanswered. Years of debate have failed to clarify the role of cooking in the modern home. The subject goes to the heart of so many twentieth-century preoccupations: questions of identity, family values, feminism. For the past 100 years, domestic kitchens have been political battlegrounds; stages upon which the ongoing struggle for social prestige and meaning have been played out. Everything about them has been a matter of debate: their function, their design, their materiality, their image, their visibility. There could be no more eloquent symbol of our conflicted attitudes towards cooking than our lack of consensus about any of these questions.

Although the design of kitchens in 'servantless homes' became a major preoccupation for European architects and designers after the First World War, they were far from the first to address the issue. Due to an earlier 'servant problem' across the Atlantic, Americans had had an 80-year head start in facing up to the problem. First to the task was Catherine Beecher, leading light of the American women's movement and author of the groundbreaking 1842 *Treatise on Domestic Economy*, in which she sought to dignify the role of the housewife. 'It may be urged,' she wrote, 'that it is impossible for a woman who cooks, washes and sweeps, to appear in the dress, or acquire the habits and manners, of a lady; that the drudgery of the kitchen is dirty work, and that no one can appear delicate and refined, while engaged in it.'[44] However, that view, argued Beecher, belonged to the past: 'As society gradually shakes off the remnants of barbarism, and the intellectual and moral interests of man rise in estimation above the merely sensual, a truer estimate is formed of women's duties, and of the measure of intellect requisite of the proper discharge of them.'[45]

Having made the case for housework to be held in higher regard, Beecher came to the crux of the matter: how it was to be carried out. The immediate problem that struck her was one of efficiency. Now that housewives were having to cook for themselves, their labour-intensive kitchens were hopelessly inadequate. Beecher's solution was simple: to restore the kitchen to the centre of the home. That way, a housewife could do everything she needed, while keeping an eye on her children and her other housework. Beecher may have restored the ancient marriage of hearth and home, but her view of the relationship was far from romantic. Her ideal house plans had more in common with Jeremy Bentham's *Panopticon* (a circular ideal prison plan that allowed all the cells to be surveyed from a single central guardroom) than with John Ruskin's temple.[46] This was no misty-eyed vision of the sacred housewife; women were simply placed at the centre of the domain they were expected to control. Cooking, along with other womanly duties, was a job that had to be done. As for the kitchen itself, it needed to be radically simplified: in later writings, Beecher compared it to a ship's galley.

Beecher's many followers included Ellen Richards, whose degree in chemistry from MIT was the first in science ever awarded to a woman. Whereas Beecher had sought to give housewives social dignity, Richards wanted to turn them into scientists like her; ones with urgent duties to perform at that. In 1861, the 'germ theory' posited by John Snow had received clinical proof from the French chemist Louis Pasteur, whose laboratory experiments confirmed that micro-organisms in nutrient broth were the result of external contamination.[47] Richards was among the first to understand the implications of these findings: they made kitchens far more dangerous places than anyone had realised. With the connivance of her long-suffering husband, she turned her home into an experimental laboratory, investigating every possible application of science to cookery and housework. Meanwhile, she urged for chemistry to be taught to women so that they could fight food adulteration and contamination for themselves. In 1876, Richards finally got permission to set up a Women's Laboratory at MIT. Here she instructed women in the 'advanced study of chemical analysis, mineralogy, and chemistry related to vegetable and animal physiology and to the industrial arts', the basis of the new discipline she was to call 'domestic science'. Richards was a visionary, but sadly her dream of a new generation of chemically aware housewives inspired by 'the zest of intelligent experiment' never came to pass.[48] Instead, increasing aware-ness of 'germ theory' caused widespread panic about dirt in all its forms. The mood at the turn of the century was summed up by Mrs H. M. Plunkett, author of *Women, Plumbers and Doctors, or Household Sanitation*, in 1897. A housewife's failure to prevent disease, she said, was 'akin to murder'; her neglect of proper cleaning 'tantamount to child abuse'.[49]

It would rest with a pupil of Richards, Christine Frederick, to come up with some practical advice that housewives could actually follow. Through her husband's work as a factory inspector, Frederick had become aware of a revolution then taking place in factories: the streamlining of production methods that would become known as 'Taylorism'. In 1899, a mechanical engineer named Frederick Taylor had been asked to analyse the working practices of a group of pig-iron workers to see if he could increase their productivity. Taylor performed the world's first time-and-motion study on the workers, plotting their various tasks and the sequence in which they were carried out. He concluded that many of the workers' movements were unnecessary, and proposed a new 'production line' approach to streamline their actions and maximise efficiency. The principles of Taylorism are widely familiar today, but when Christine Frederick first heard about them, they were revelatory. She came up with the idea of applying them to kitchens; for, as she put it with unarguable logic, 'Why walk eight feet to a kitchen table and eight feet back again for the bread-knife which is always needed near the bread box kept on the cabinet across the room?' In her 1915 book *Efficient Housekeeping, or Household Engineering*, Frederick contrasted two different kitchen layouts, one 'efficiently grouped' and the other 'badly grouped', to explain how each responded to the cooking process: 'This principle of arranging and grouping equipment to meet the actual order of work is the basis of kitchen efficiency. In other words, we cannot leave the placing of the sink, stove, doors and cupboards entirely to the architect.'[50]

The result of her analysis was the 'labor-saving kitchen': the first kitchen designed entirely around the ergonomics of cooking. It featured cabinets with pull-out worktops, built-in hoppers for flour and sugar, and 'workshop-style' wall-mounted storage racks for utensils. The kitchen, said Frederick, should be full of light and air, avoiding the 'ugly green or hideous blue colourings' of former times. Work surfaces should be 'covered with non-absorbent, easily cleaned materials' to make them germ-free and easy to maintain.[51] As for the actual work to be done, housewives were to adopt an 'efficiency attitude', making lists

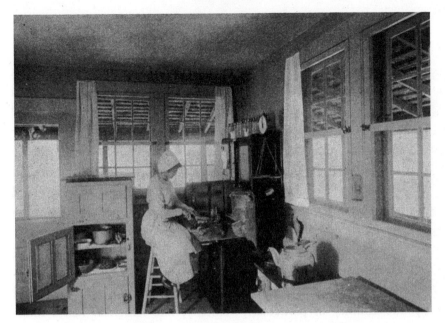

The ideal housewife at work. Illustration from *Household Engineering*.

of tasks to be achieved each day and ticking them off as they went along – even timing themselves to monitor their own performance. There was no room for slackers in Frederick's engineered household. In a tone that makes even the late Fanny Cradock seem conciliatory, she continued: 'There is no excuse for "Oh, I forgot to order more sugar", for making four trips upstairs which could have been taken in one, or for finding that there isn't another egg in the house.'[52]

Frederick believed that her methods were 'a route from drudgery to efficiency and personal happiness', and strangely, her readers seemed to agree. More textbook than cookbook, *Household Engineering* ended each chapter with a series of questions for readers to answer, like an exam. Yet far from having nightmares about being back at school, women wrote to her in their thousands, begging for more information about her methods. Whether they managed to live up to her exemplary standards was another matter.

Home-maker, intellectual, scientist, engineer: American housewives had been through a few paradigm shifts by the start of the First World War – as had their kitchens, from hearth to galley, laboratory and factory. By the time European architects faced the task of postwar reconstruction, the 'engineered' kitchen was a ready-made prototype that would fit right into their new way of thinking. The mood in Europe after the war was evangelical: designers, philosophers and politicians alike felt the need to build a new world that would liberate mankind not just from the horrors of war, but from the social iniquities that preceded it. For that, they needed not just new sorts of buildings, but a whole new approach to living in them.

The role of women in creating this new world was recognised by one country in particular. Germany, like America, had a long-established women's movement, whose members had since the 1880s been addressing issues of household efficiency, the teaching of domestic economy in schools and so on. The value of their work was recognised by architects such as Bruno Taut, who in 1924 summed up his view of the ideal architect–client relationship with the motto '*Der Architekt denkt, die Hausfrau lenkt*' (the architect thinks, the housewife guides).[53] When Christine Frederick's book was translated into German after the war, it found an eager readership, among them the Austrian-born female architect Grete Lihotzky, creator of one of the most influential designs of the twentieth century, the 'Frankfurt kitchen'. Partly inspired by a railway carriage galley, the Frankfurt kitchen was essentially a scaled-down version of its American predecessor. Designed to be cheap and compact, it had a number of space-saving devices, such as a fold-down ironing board and a series of pull-out metal hoppers (à la Frederick) for basic ingredients such as rice, sugar and flour. It was the first kitchen ever to be mass-produced – more than 10,000 were installed in Frankfurt's social housing programme during the 1920s – and it was the prototype for the modern fitted kitchen in ubiquitous use today.

Despite its ingenious design and commercial success, the Frankfurt kitchen was not universally loved. Designed around the body movements of a housewife performing her daily tasks, it effectively cut women off from the rest of the home – and from their own families. The kitchen was found to be inflexible: too small for two people to cook in at once; impossible for children to play in (the pull-out hoppers were temptingly within toddler range); and certainly too small to eat in. All this was deliberate on the part of Lihotzky: by the 1920s, the idea of cooking and eating in the same space was considered unhygienic. For Lihotzky, cooking was a chore, and must be separated from its object, the meal. As she herself put it, 'What is life today actually made of? Firstly, it consists of *work*, secondly of *relaxing, company, pleasure*.'[54] Liked or not, the Frankfurt kitchen's success ensured that the no-nonsense – and no-pleasure – approach to cooking pioneered by American feminists would have a lasting impact in the West. Once again, cooking was banished to the invisible parts of the house; only this time, the mistress of the house was banished with it. Far from releasing housewives from drudgery as intended, the Frankfurt kitchen – and the millions of galley kitchens that followed in its wake – would ensure that cooking would remain the isolated, thankless task that polite society had always believed it to be.

The Frankfurt kitchen exposed a fatal flaw within early modernist thinking that has plagued approaches to architecture ever since. With the best of intentions – the building of a better society – modernism tried to create a world so perfect it would liberate men and women from their own imperfections. Household engineering became social engineering: the creation of rational buildings that demanded rational people to live in them. Of course the whole thing was an illusion – a sleight of hand that owed most of its power to the undeniable beauty of much modernist design. Yet the image was powerful enough to stick. Even today, the idea that society's salvation might come through design alone seems, at least to some, perfectly plausible.

The man chiefly responsible for promulgating this vision of a brave new world was the Swiss-born architect Le Corbusier. For him, the cluttered interiors of *fin de siècle* Europe reflected the 'crushing bourgeois values' of 'an intolerable period which could not last'.[55] Nothing short of a complete physical and moral purge was required, and in a series of caustic essays, including his groundbreaking manifesto of 1923, *Vers une Architecture*, Le Corbusier showed his readers the way. 'Demand bare walls in your bedroom, your living room and your dining room,' he commanded. 'Once you have put ripolin [whitewash] on your walls you will be *master of yourself*. And you will want to be precise, to be accurate, to think clearly.'[56] As the architect Mark Wigley has observed, Le Corbusier used the colour white as a sort of architectural hygiene, much as men in the eighteenth century might have put on a white shirt instead of washing.[57] Le Corbusier believed that by living in a pure environment, modern man would be purged of his imperfections both physically and morally: 'His home is clean. There are no more dark, dirty corners. *Everything is shown as it is*. There comes inner cleanness . . .'[58]

The stripped, white building was to become the leitmotif of modernism, an image fixed by the Stuttgart Weissenhofsiedlung of 1927, an international exhibition of model housing designed by a who's who of twentieth-century architects, including Peter Behrens, Le Corbusier, Walter Gropius, Mies van der Rohe, Hans Scharoun and Bruno Taut. The Weissenhof housing – clean, pure and white to a fault – had enormous impact, as did the series of modernist tomes that followed in its wake, such as F.R.S. Yorke's seminal survey of 1934, *The Modern House*. But as Yorke's book illustrates, the socialist intentions of early modernism hid an underlying paradox. 'We do not need large houses, for we have neither large families to fill them nor domestics to look after them,' he wrote, yet the iconic villas in his book suggested otherwise.[59] All but a few had separate kitchens linked to substantial servants' quarters.[60] Even Le Corbusier's supposedly proletarian Maison Citrohan, the prototypical 'machine for living in', had a separate kitchen and service entrance with a maid's room off it.[61] Despite Le Corbusier's pronouncement that everything was 'shown as it is', not quite everything was. Modernism glossed over the problem of cooking by putting all its mess behind a wall. As Reyner Banham observed in his book *Theory and Design in the First Machine Age*, the defining works of the modern movement focused on the pure image of the buildings, rather than on the biological needs of their inhabitants.[62]

Contrary to appearances, the immaculate world of modernism involved as much denial as did the era it sought to replace; arguably,

even more. At least Victorian house-builders had agonised openly
about how to hide the bowels of their buildings; modernists simply
edited them out of the frame. Although bodily needs were central to
modernist rhetoric, the references were all of the 'pure' variety: the
need for exercise, light and air. 'Other' bodily needs were suppressed.
At the Villa Stein-de Monzie, structured by Le Corbusier around a
series of outdoor terraces upon which the owners were invited to
cavort half-naked, the kitchen was as hidden as that of any Victorian
house. Yet official photographs show it to be an immaculate space full
of light, its gleaming worktops barely hinting at the use to which they
might be put. A carefully arranged raw fish and coffee pot are the only
allusions to the room's real purpose. Designed to be hidden from the
owners of the house, the kitchen is nevertheless allowed to appeal
directly to the anonymous eye of aesthetic judgement. Whiter and
shinier-than-thou even in its dirty bits, the Villa Stein-de Monzie was
an icon of wipe-clean architecture: fetishised, purified space that could
only be spoiled by the mess of human inhabitation.

In his 1933 essay *In Praise of Shadows*, the Japanese author Jun'ichiro

The kitchen at Villa Stein-de Monzie in 1926.

Tanizaki remarked on this growing tendency in the West to shun the 'other' side of human nature – the dark, the dirty, the old, the worn out – in favour of sanitised perfection. 'Westerners attempt to expose every speck of grime and eradicate it,' he wrote, 'while we Orientals carefully preserve and even idealise it.'[63] And in this newly polarised Western view of the human condition, cooking somehow ended up on the 'wrong' side: that of filth rather than health, work rather than pleasure, solitude rather than sociability.

Can't Cook, Won't Cook

Despite the best efforts of early feminists to raise the status of cooking, they failed to address one essential fact: their contemporaries had no more desire to cook than their ancestors had. Hygiene and efficiency were all very well, but they weren't much fun – and the fact that every household guru from Catherine Beecher to Grete Lihotzky had denied there was any pleasure to be had from cooking hardly helped. To have admitted that cooking for its own sake might actually be *enjoyable* would have risked undermining one of the central props of feminism. Better to insist on it as a science or profession; at least that way, one could pretend that it was not the thankless drudgery that, deep down, everyone really believed it to be. With so much subterfuge surrounding their early development, it is hardly surprising that modern domestic kitchens evolved into such ambiguous spaces. By the 1920s they had become highly sophisticated machines for cooking in. The trouble was, no one wanted to cook in them.

American women had another reason to be reluctant to cook. The Depression meant that increasing numbers were having to go out to work, and for those who remained at home, economic hardship removed any vestiges of pretension about lab-coated housewives, reviving instead the much older tradition of the hardy homesteader's wife, with her make-do indomitable spirit. The new role was epitomised by *American Gothic*, a 1930 painting by Grant Wood in which a plainly dressed couple (she with gaze averted, he clutching a pitchfork) stand resolute outside their clapboard Iowan farmhouse. The portrait captured the pioneer spirit of small-town America, but increasing numbers of women no longer lived there. They lived in cities and worked for a living, and were still expected to conjure up wholesome meals for their husbands every night. The stage was set for the creation of one of the twentieth century's greatest fictions, the domestic goddess – the product not of painterly imagination, but of something even more potent: advertising.

To nascent American food-processing companies, a nation of overworked, guilty housewives presented the perfect market for their new convenience foods. All the industry needed to do was to press home the message that cooking delicious meals was a housewife's sacred duty. The bakery giant General Mills was one of the first to get in on the act, creating in 1926 the first official domestic goddess, 'Betty Crocker', a fictional character with her own radio show, in which she interviewed celebrity guests and dispensed domestic advice and recipes. Betty's message was simple: a happy home was one filled with the smell of fresh baking. 'Good things baked in the kitchen,' she said, 'will keep romance far longer than bright lipstick.' The programme attracted a huge following: 40 home economists had to be employed to answer all its correspondence, amounting to hundreds of thousands of letters every year.[64] Rival food companies soon set up their own propaganda machines, with several starting their own women's magazines filled with cookery tips laced with the same subliminal message. 'Hitler threatens Europe,' ran one advert in *The American Home*, 'but Betty Haven's boss is coming to dinner and that's what *really* counts.'[65]

Having set the entry level to domestic deity impossibly high, food companies offered mere mortals a short cut to achieving it – by using their products. Magazines brimmed with improbable recipes involving processed foods, such as one, cited by the historian Harvey Levenstein in his book *Paradox of Plenty*, that suggested mixing Campbell's split pea soup with Ancora green turtle soup, adding sherry to the result and topping it with whipped cream.[66] Extraordinary though this concoction sounds now, it was far from unique for the time. For a couple of decades at least, the novelty of processed foods seemed to have persuaded the entire American nation to simply switch off its taste buds. The public fascination with opening cans of soup was marvellous for food-processing companies while it lasted, but by the end of the Second World War, new convenience foods were needed to satisfy increasingly sophisticated customers. Betty Crocker cake mixtures, launched by General Mills in the late 1940s, were the result. The initial products only required water to be added to achieve a delicious 'home-baked' result, but the company soon realised that if housewives were asked to add an egg as well, they really felt they were baking. The egg was a ruse; a way of deceiving women into believing they were cooking properly.

By encouraging housewives to cheat, food-processing companies achieved the double whammy of raising the status of cooking, while preventing people from actually doing it. Rather than getting the satisfaction of baking a cake (which, after all, takes hardly any more effort than adding an egg and some water to a mixture of flour and cocoa powder), women were lured into paying for the privilege of pretending they had. Throughout the 1940s, the amount Americans spent on food rose steadily – the opposite of the normal trend in an era of prosperity. People were spending more on food, not because they were buying better quality, but because they were paying for the 'added value' of convenience. Food industry profits soared, thanks mainly to middle-class women – most of whom would have been perfectly capable – being persuaded they couldn't cook.

By 1953, *Fortune* magazine was noting America's 'relentless pursuit of convenience', in which one could 'buy an entire turkey dinner: frozen, apportioned, packaged. Just heat and serve.'[67] Ready meals had arrived, just as family lifestyles were relaxing, allowing food processors to move out of the 'pretend-you-cooked-it-yourself' strand into a new leisure market. TV dinners became the new height of sophistication, eaten, for maximum effect, off specially designed plastic lap-trays. For the first time in history, food was fun, even trendy, all of which made domestic kitchens seem suddenly very out of date. In their influential 1945 book *Tomorrow's House*, the architects George Nelson and Henry Wright argued that the galley kitchen was no longer appropriate to modern life:

Servants, as a group, are disappearing. World War One took women out of domestic occupations and put them into offices. World War

Two took a vastly greater number and put them into factories. The middle-class families and the rich, thrown more and more on their own resources, have been casting a jaundiced eye on the minimum kitchen.[68]

The answer, argued the authors, was to merge kitchen and living room, replacing the 'hospital operating-room atmosphere' of galley kitchens with a space that was 'pleasant to live in as well as work in . . . thanks to the incorporation of natural wood surfaces, bright colour, and fabrics'.[69] It was a radical vision. Never before had kitchens been admitted to polite society; now they were to become part of the furniture. Open-plan kitchens were the new must-have accessories of cutting-edge 'contemporary' homes: trophy cabinets brimming with gadgetry to show off to one's friends. The 'dream kitchen' even became a weapon of the Cold War, when Richard Nixon tried to persuade Nikita Khrushchev of the merits of the West by showing off a mocked-up version at the 1959 Moscow Trade Fair.

With the open-plan kitchen, the humblest room in the house finally had its moment in the sun; but even in this, the kitchen's finest hour, there were rumbles of dissent among its intended users. Most American housewives already resented having to cook. Now they were expected to do so without burning the roast, dropping peelings on the floor, looking resentful, or (worst of all) being allowed to cheat. Cooking might have come out of the closet, but as far as most women were concerned, it could go straight back in there. Before long, separate kitchens were making a comeback – this time not in order to hide the fact that people were cooking in them, but in order to hide the fact that they weren't.

By the late 1960s, instead of burning the roast, many women had taken to burning their bras. The new politics of feminism saw cooking as the oppression of the housewife; something to 'shackle her time, keeping her from more stimulating endeavors'.[70] It was a return to the rhetoric of a century earlier, and to the women's movement pioneers who saw cooking as a tedious chore. After a century of rebellion and invention, women were back where they had started. In many ways, the rejection of cooking by women's lib was more of a reaction to the fake domestic goddess invented by food companies than it was to anything real; yet their attitude opened up new opportunities for those very companies. Refusing to cook became a badge of honour among feminists. From now on, serving up frozen pizza was not only socially acceptable; it was a positive political statement.

Postwar British housewives were just as keen as their American counterparts to cast off the shackles of culinary oppression, and the 'relentless pursuit of convenience' soon crossed the Atlantic. Birds Eye fish fingers and frozen peas were the first such foods to become national treasures in the 1960s, followed by Vesta curry and Cadbury's Smash in the 1970s, M&S chilled ready meals in the 1980s, and their many imitators ever since.[71] Just as they had done on the other side of the pond, convenience foods became the national panacea, first for house-wives, then for householders at large: salvation from the curse of having to cook. By 2003, the British convenience-food sector was worth £17 billion; by 2011 it is predicted to reach £33.9 billion.[72] As the ex-head of the M&S food division Clinton Silver put it, 'Feminism owes an enormous amount to Marks & Spencer, and vice versa.'[73]

One could argue that we Anglo-Saxons have been ill served by the food industry: cheated out of the more positive view of cooking that we might otherwise have developed. But if that is the case, how come other European countries have survived with their culinary traditions intact? A recent survey of European eating habits found that in Germany, the home of the Frankfurt kitchen, seven out of ten women 'love to cook'.[74] The same was true of Spanish and Italian women, while 41 per cent of French adults were described as 'traditional cooks who enjoy cooking'.[75] Of course there are many reasons for these cultural differences. Rural traditions have remained stronger in many parts of continental Europe than in Britain, so helping to preserve local culinary cultures: food 'like Mother used to make'. In most parts of the Mediterranean, traditional family structures (the *sine qua non* of family meals) also survive relatively intact. Last but not least, the postwar 'special relationship' between Britain and America has ensured that, for better or worse, our culinary as well as our political fortunes have been inextricably linked.

For now at least, home cooking in most European countries has a healthy base, but for how much longer? The French are sufficiently concerned about the loss of food knowledge among schoolchildren to have instituted *La semaine du goût*: compulsory tasting classes in primary schools. Even in Italy, bastion of motherly home cooking, there is no room for complacency. Twenty years ago, the arrival of McDonald's in Rome's Piazza di Spagna prompted a group of protesters to serve up dishes of home-made pasta to bemused passers-by. Today that protest has grown into the Slow Food Movement – an international organisation with over 80,000 members, whose 2006 Turin conference, the Terra Madre, was opened by the Italian president himself.[76] In countries like Italy and France, the question of whether or not people cook is not left to chance. It is seen as a matter of national importance; as a critical part of the jigsaw that keeps not just gastronomic culture, but society itself alive.

The Shrinking Kitchen

Today in Britain, those who cook regularly from scratch are a vanishing and ageing minority, and food knowledge among the young is patchy to say the least. Fifty per cent of those under the age of 24 questioned in a 2007 survey admitted to having 'no skills' in the kitchen.[77] No wonder the industry analysts Mintel reckon that ready meals are about the safest bet in British commercial food: 'Future growth is assured. The economic parameters are highly favourable and the social and cultural trends which are re-shaping UK eating habits are well-entrenched and non-reversible. For better or worse, the convenience habit is here to stay.'[78]

A hundred and fifty years ago, architects strove to perfect the invisible, silent, odourless kitchen. Today ready meals have gone one better, ridding houses of cooking altogether. As a result of our 'convenience habit', private kitchens, those hardest-won of domestic spaces, are in danger of redundancy. Many of the trendy loft apartments that sprang up in British cities during the 1980s and 90s barely contained them at all – just tiny cupboards large enough to house a freezer, microwave and sink. Admittedly, the occupants of such flats are often young professionals living on their own, as almost a third of us in Britain now do. They were always likely to survive on ready meals, takeaways and eating out. But to the despair of nutritionists, our national disinclination to cook is not limited to singleton yuppies. Families on low incomes, who could most benefit from cooking from scratch, are increasingly spending what little money they have on convenience foods and takeaways. The urban poor are the real victims of our confused attitudes towards cooking. Despite food costing a fraction of what it did a century ago, their diets have barely improved: they have simply swapped one kind of malnutrition for another.[79] Only among ethnic communities in Britain do the majority regularly cook for themselves, spending their food budgets on just that: food.

Even if more of us in Britain wanted to cook, the homes we live in are hardly conducive. Urban lofts are not the only homes with inadequate kitchens: many of us live in ageing housing stock with kitchens crammed at the back, badly converted versions of the same, or social housing with minute galley kitchens à la Frankfurt. Then there is our new housing stock. For some reason, the dominant new-build dwelling in Britain is a mock-Georgian or Victorian villa with a cramped, boxy kitchen (often with a lousy view) whose only virtue is that it allows its owners to fantasise that someone else is doing the cooking (which, thanks to microwaves and ready meals, they often are).

Worse still, British domestic space standards are shrinking. Even new-build family homes often have kitchens too small to accommodate basic equipment such as fridges and washing machines, let alone a dining table.[80] Average figures compiled across 10 London boroughs showed that the recommended minimum size of kitchen for a three-bedroom dwelling was just 6.5 square metres.[81] Try having a family meal in that. British space standards are some of the smallest in Europe, unregulated by central government since the mid 1980s on the basis that the size of dwellings is a 'matter for the marketing judgement of developers, in the light of their assessment of their customers' requirements'.[82] So the good old forces of commerce are supposed to look after us as usual. Except, of course, they're not. A 2003 report by the

Popular Housing Group found widespread dissatisfaction with space standards in all types of housing, including the common complaint that kitchens were too small.[83]

With residential space at such a premium, kitchens are more than ever under threat in Britain – and our ambiguous attitude towards them doesn't help. Despite evidence that most people regard them as 'the heart of the house', there is no consensus as to what this actually means.[84] According to the Mayor of London's *Housing Space Standards* report, confusion reigns even among house-builders:

> . . . there is continuing uncertainty over whether the kitchen space needs to be maintained, can be reduced (are meals only ever cooked in a microwave or are cookers and food preparation space still needed?), or (with households using more appliances) needs to be larger.[85]

In the absence of any clear notion of what a kitchen is supposed to be – and no concerted effort to find out – the housing industry's default position is to stay rooted in the past, building homes with ever tinier kitchens. The result is that we are no longer building what the Rowntree Foundation calls 'Lifetime Homes': dwellings capable of providing for the long-term needs of their occupants.[86] By assuming that people will not cook for themselves in the future, we are cutting off our options. Most of us barely cook now, and the more our kitchens shrink, the less likely we are ever to try.

What's Your Poison?

Without the basic knowledge that our grandparents took for granted, cooking can be a daunting prospect. A growing number of people find the very idea terrifying. Fear of getting it wrong – at an extreme, of poisoning oneself – is enough to put off many from even having a go, and, as Joanna Blythman pointed out in her recent book *Bad Food Britain*, that attitude is now being drummed into British schoolchildren as young as seven. The government Food Hygiene Mission Control programme, an interactive resource issued by the Food Standards Agency, seeks to educate children in the dangers of food by inviting them to help 'exterminate Pathogens [with a capital P] and save the human race from food poisoning'.[87] Hardly the kind of thing designed to lure a new generation of chefs into the kitchen.

The food industry has even come up with a way of persuading those of us on the verge of cooking not to bother. 'Ready-to-cook' ranges such as M&S Cook! and Waitrose Easy consist of some raw ingredients assembled inside a transparent packet that allows us to see, say, a whole chicken breast sitting next to a sprig of thyme and a sachet of sauce. First launched in 2004, the ranges are flying off the shelves, not least because they quell people's fears about what is inside the packet. However, whatever they say on the front, ready-to-cook ranges have nothing to do with cooking. The Waitrose website tacitly admits as much: 'Our ready meals are, of course, designed to make your life easy. But we're also passionate about making them every bit as good as the food you'd prepare for yourself – if you had the time.'[88]

Supermarkets love to persuade us that we don't have time to cook. But of course that's nonsense. We have never had more leisure time than we do now; we just prefer to spend it doing something else. True, few households now have full-time housewives to run them – but even working mothers today have more time than those of a generation ago. A quick bit of maths also tells you that these stripped-down not-quite-ready meals are supermarket nirvana: 'added value' taken to the ultimate degree of preposterousness. Paying someone else to cook our food is one thing, but paying them to place a chicken breast next to a sprig of thyme? That is just plain barmy. We're back to Betty Crocker all over again.

The consequences of not cooking are far more serious now than they were even a generation ago. In our industrialised, urbanised society, cooking is the one chance most of us have of taking some control over what we eat, and all that means. Cooking is not just about what goes on in the kitchen; it is the pivotal point in the food chain: the one that, arguably, affects everything else in it.

Strangely, the one thing most likely to drive us back into our kitchens is the ready-meal revolution itself. Now that we no longer *have* to cook for ourselves, cooking has, for the first time in history, become cool. It is fast becoming a popular leisure pursuit among affluent urbanites in Britain, even – and this really is a historic first – among men. The number of us who consider ourselves 'foodies' is steadily rising, which is good news for artisanal producers. In 1990 there were fewer than 10 farmers' markets in Britain; today there are more than 500, and hand-crafted food production is booming. Patricia Michelson, one of Britain's foremost artisanal cheese retailers, says the number of producers in Britain was in freefall a decade ago, but has expanded so rapidly since that British cheese is now 'firmly on the map'.[89]

Yet despite the recently converted foodies in Britain, we are still a long way from having a 'vertical' food culture in this country – one that permeates every stratum of society. In order to achieve that, we need to take radical action: something along the lines of, say, introducing compulsory classes about food and cooking (rather than merely poisoning) into primary schools. Few parents today have much interest in cooking, so to expect them to teach their offspring is a forlorn hope. If the British government was really interested in improving the nation's health, it would use primary schools to teach kids not just how to cook, but also about the far-reaching influences of food.[90] Getting young children to grow their own food and cook their own lunches would be a great way of overcoming their fear of food, as well as introducing them to a whole range of food-related issues, such as understanding ethnic diversity, the environment, and obesity. In fact it is hard to think of an important subject that could not be well taught in a kitchen.

Cooking, like talking and writing, requires education – and like those other essential skills, it comes easily once you know how. Practised regularly, it is so instinctive that it can be done half-consciously, while chatting to friends, looking after children, listening to the radio, or thinking up the next sentence of your book. That is when cooking becomes both useful and a pleasure; when it need not take inordinate amounts of time. At the start of the twenty-first century, there is a growing perception among a limited group of mostly affluent middle-class Britons that cooking is both important and a pleasure. The real trick would be to find a way of spreading that perception. The result of such a shift in attitudes would be profound – revolutionary, even. It could make a vital difference to all our lives in the coming century. No generation in history has ever thought cooking was cool. Maybe, with our help, the saving grace of the next one will be that they are the first who do.

Chapter 5
At Table

The fate of nations depends on the way they eat . . .

Jean Anthelme Brillat-Savarin[1]

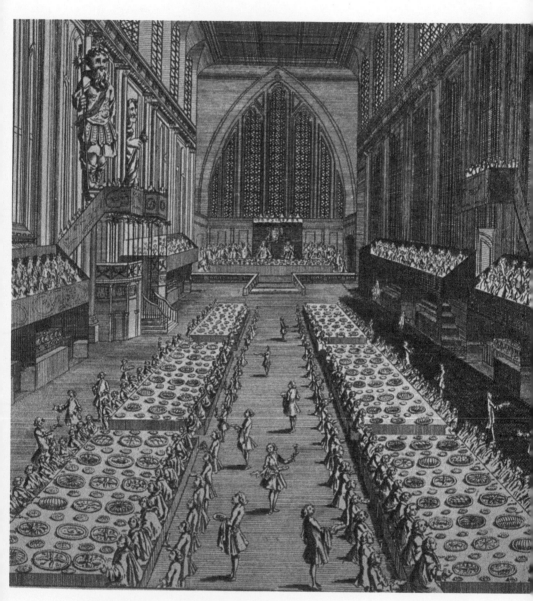

The Lord Mayor's Banquet in 1761. The annual feast at the Guildhall remains an important political event.

Middle Temple Hall

Middle Temple Hall is not your average sort of dining room. An imposing Tudor chamber with a dramatic double hammer-beam roof that soars 47 feet above its broad-planked floor, it has been the heart of Middle Temple Inn, one of London's four Inns of Court, since Elizabethan times. Its oak-panelled walls, lovingly restored after heavy damage during the Second World War, provide a suitably sober back-drop to the brightly coloured coats of arms of its many distinguished alumni. At the far end of the hall is the Bench Table, raised on a dais and fashioned out of four 29-foot planks of oak cut from a single tree in Windsor Forest and floated down the Thames on a barge. Reputedly the gift of Elizabeth I, the table is where the Benchers sit; members of the Inn's elected parliament, most of them 'silks' at the very top of the legal profession.[2] Behind the Benchers hang a series of royal portraits, above the centremost of which – a rather lugubrious rendition of Charles I on a horse – is the Inn's heraldic emblem, the Lamb and Flag. In front of the Bench Table stands the Cupboard, a ceremonial desk given to the Inn by one of its more colourful members, Sir Francis Drake, made out of a hatch cover from his ship, the *Golden Hind*. Next to the Cupboard is the Ancients' Table, where the eight most senior barristers in Hall have dined since 1595. Just about the only objects in the room unworthy of historical footnotes are the oak refectory tables where ordinary members of the Inn sit.

With its royal connections, majestic roof, and heraldic imagery (not to mention the odd chunk of pirate ship), Middle Temple Hall has undeniable pedigree. For over four centuries it has witnessed the social, practical and ceremonial life of one of London's greatest institutions. To misbehave within its hallowed walls, under the beady eye of the law, would be unthinkable – which was what made my first meal there something of a trial. The reason for my dining at the Inn was my friend Nick, who, after a successful career in our mutual profession of architecture, had decided to become a barrister. This, as you might expect, involved him in a lot of hard work, but it also involved something rather less expected: his attendance at no fewer than 18 formal dinners in Hall. When Nick asked me to join him at one of these compulsory feasts, at first I thought it sounded like a jolly night out, but I soon realised my mistake when he warned me to dress soberly, and to expect some elaborate (yet unspecified) rituals. It was thus with some trepidation that I met Nick on the front steps, and we proceeded into Hall – he in knee-length black gown, me in my funeral kit – along with 200 similarly clad individuals already taking their places at table. As we scrambled to two of the last remaining seats, the head porter banged his staff on the floor and bade us all rise to face the room, whereupon the Benchers, resplendent in silken robes, proceeded in stately procession to their table, grace was said in Latin, and we all sat down.

Nick and I found ourselves opposite a young female lawyer and a much older male one; the latter, to my relief, immediately began engaging us in conversation. Since he seemed to be the only one of us remotely at his ease, we happily let him take the lead, and when the first course arrived – a homogeneous green soup – it seemed only natural that he was the first to be served and to take up his spoon. This pattern continued all evening, and at some point it dawned on me that the entire procedure was somehow codified: there could have been no other explanation for the curious combination of elaborate manners and indifferent food of which the meal consisted. While our host continued to behave as if he were leading some sort of panel discussion, the food got steadily worse: after the tasteless soup, we were regaled with grey lamb served with waterlogged vegetables and industrial mint sauce, followed by chemical-tasting fruit trifle with artificial cream – not the sort of food you normally get dressed up for.[3]

Apart from the bottle of Bordeaux Nick bought for us to wash it down with, the meal felt a bit like being back at school, which, as I later discovered, was more or less exactly what it was. Had I not been so overawed by my surroundings, I probably would have noticed earlier that the table at which we were sitting was laid up in groups of four, with the side plates on alternate sides so that they formed a series of natural barriers. These sets of four, known as 'messes', are one's designated company for dinner at the Inn, and it is forbidden to talk to anyone in an adjacent mess, apart from asking for the salt. The most senior barrister in each mess, who sits nearest the Bench Table facing the room, is designated 'mess captain' for the evening, and it is his or her duty to make the juniors feel welcome, to steer the conversation towards interesting topics, and to encourage everyone to express their opinions. In short, for the duration of the meal, they are expected to act as host, mentor and teacher.

The system is as old as the legal profession itself, dating back to the fourteenth century, when the Inns of Court replaced the clergy as arbiters of English law. The Inns were originally run like universities, and with their inner courts, lockable gates, chapels, libraries and dining halls, they resemble Oxford and Cambridge colleges, those other great educational inheritors of medieval monasticism. In the case of Middle Temple, the monastic inheritance is explicit: the site once belonged to the Knights Templar, whose title, Lamb and Flag emblem and ancient chapel were all adopted by the Inn.[4] Even the Inn's social structure derives from the warrior monks: the Knights' habit of living and dining together in pairs, for both companionship and discipline, is the origin of the chambers system and the messes in which barristers still dine.[5]

From the outset, dining was integral to life at the Inn. Students were expected to 'keep terms' (live on site) and attend regular meals in Hall, where a specially appointed barrister, the Reader, read out articles of law, or presided over mock trials in which students could test their skills. However, the arrival of printed books in the sixteenth century marked a decline in formal training, and by the seventeenth century it had died out altogether. Students resorted to dining in Hall simply in order to try to learn something from their elders, and in 1798 the arrangement was formally ratified with the introduction of compulsory dining – a move that did little for the Inns' reputation, since it gave the (essentially correct) impression that 'gentlemen could eat their way to the Bar'.[6] Formal lectures were reintroduced in 1852, but by then, obligatory dining was considered too valuable to lose.

Although modern Bar students receive rather more training than their seventeenth-century counterparts, their attendance at dinner is still taken very seriously indeed. Tickets must be handed in to the head porter on arrival, and once the Benchers have arrived in Hall, nobody may leave without written permission from 'Master Treasurer' until after Second Grace (people of a nervous disposition thinking of entering the legal profession might like to think again). As an extract from the current Middle Temple rule book suggests, breaches of etiquette are taken equally seriously:

> . . . if any irregularity has been detected in either Grace, it is the custom for the senior Ancient to send a note, preferably in Latin, in to Master Treasurer, while the Benchers are taking dessert, 'humbly' drawing attention to the omission and requesting a 'solatium' [recompense]. This usually takes the form of a bottle of port presented thereupon by the offender to the Ancients.[7]

Reproofs in Latin and 40 per cent proof apologies notwithstanding, dining rituals at the Inns of Court serve a practical purpose. Successful barristers need to be quick-witted, confident, persuasive and courteous – skills that no textbook can teach them. With their moots, debates and challenges, dinners in Hall give students a chance to test their mettle against whatever life in court will throw at them, as well as keeping senior members of the Inn on their toes. Even the seemingly draconian rule forbidding communication between messes serves a purpose, forcing students to learn how to get on with whomsoever they happen to find themselves sitting next to. Above all, the legal profession is a social network, and, as the Inns have recognised for centuries, there is no better way of socialising – or networking – than by sharing meals regularly with other people.

An Ancient Feast

Needless to say, most meals in Britain today are far removed from the sort of rarefied dining practised by the Inns of Court. More than half the meals we eat are eaten alone; the majority of those consumed on the hoof, in front of the telly, or sitting at a desk.[8] Our lifestyles are increasingly fuelled by food, not structured around it; not least because of the enormous social changes that have taken place over the past century or so. In 1871, there were six children in the average British household; by the 1930s that figure had shrunk to two; by 2003 it was less than one.[9] Thirty-six per cent of households now consist of couples and 27 per cent people living on their own. Our splintering domestic arrangements mean that we are relying increasingly on restaurants for our social dining. Over a third of the food we consume in Britain is now eaten outside the home; a figure that by 2025 is expected to rise to half, close to the current level in the USA.[10] The trend has even got the supermarkets worried: with a 'share of stomach' worth £34.5 billion in 2003 and rising fast, the catering industry is closing the gap on their dominance of the convenience-foods market.[11] The supermarkets have responded by stocking takeaway brands such as *Pizza Express* in their stores, and ready meals claiming to be 'restaurant-quality food to eat at home'.

Whether we eat out or in, there is no doubt that formal dining in Britain is on the wane. A quarter of households no longer even have a dining table large enough for everyone to sit around.[12] But although most of our meals (or 'meal occasions', as the food industry insists on calling them) consist either of fast food or ready meals ('meal solutions'), there is one kind of occasion for which only one sort of meal will do. Whenever we have a really significant event to celebrate, a feast is still overwhelmingly the way we choose to do it. Tables may be shrinking and lifestyles speeding up, but nothing has yet replaced feasting as a celebratory mechanism. Dinner parties may no longer be quite the make-or-break social events of a century ago, but even they retain a certain potency. Being asked to dine at someone's house remains something of an honour, and an unmistakable token of friendship.

A couple of years ago, my friend Karen invited me to join her for Seder, a meal traditionally eaten by Jewish families on Passover eve. With origins stretching back more than 3,000 years to the original night of Passover, Seder is a ritual devoted to the retelling of the Haggadah, the story of the Israelites' delivery from slavery in Egypt.[13] Traditionally narrated by the male head of the household, the story is accompanied by prayers, blessings, songs – and food; although as I took my place beside Karen at her mother Susan's table, all I could see of the latter was a puzzling array of dishes, including large flat matzo biscuits, sprigs of parsley, some grated horseradish, a burnt egg, a greyish-brown paste which I later discovered was called *charoset*, and, strangest of all, some sort of animal bone. Even the edible offerings looked decidedly unappetising, which, as I soon found out, they were supposed to be.

Bracing myself for a voyage into the gustatory unknown, my main concern was to avoid offending anyone at table by doing something wrong. However, I need not have worried. As well as a sacred ritual, Seder is a sort of edible history lesson aimed at children; and as I listened to Karen's Uncle Harold reciting the Haggadah (in Hebrew, with whispered translations from his niece), I was gently guided through the meal and its various meanings. Parsley, I discovered, is dipped in salt-water at Seder to represent the tears of the Israelites, matzo symbolises their hurried departure from Egypt without time to raise dough to make bread, horseradish is eaten to represent the bitterness of slavery, and the burnt egg is a symbol of mourning and of new life. But the food that appealed to me most was *charoset*: made of finely chopped apples, walnuts and sweet wine, it is supposed to represent the mortar with which Jewish slaves were forced to construct the buildings of their Egyptian oppressors.

As I tasted each of these foods in turn, the Haggadah came alive for me – increasingly so as the evening advanced, since by the time we came to the bitter herbs a second time, I was getting mightily hungry. That, of course, was the whole point: unlike most celebratory meals, Seder is not simply about filling oneself up in the pleasantest way possible. The food has a symbolic, rather than a nutritional purpose; indeed the most significant 'food' on the table – the animal bone, which turned out to be a lamb shank – is not even edible. It is there to recall a defining moment in Jewish history: the night when God told the Israelites to sacrifice a lamb so that they would be spared the planned slaughter of the firstborn. This sacrifice (Pesach) is what gives Passover its Hebrew name, and its annual celebration provides a link back to a time when all major feasts were preceded by ritual slaughter: when the giving of life in order to receive it was fundamental to the order of the meal. Today that sacrifice is celebrated only in memory, but I am happy to report that the other part of Seder – the feast that follows the ceremony – is still very much alive, and that Karen's mother Susan is a very fine cook.

The Sacrificial Meal

The pleasure of eating requires, if not hunger, at least appetite . . .
Jean Anthelme Brillat-Savarin[14]

Meals like Seder remind us of the ancient origins of table rituals. Whenever we sit down together to eat, we repeat the actions of our distant ancestors, whose beliefs and customs structured civilisation itself. Our forebears had no choice but to follow the rhythm of the seasons, but their festivals did more than merely echo the natural world; they attempted to reconcile the everyday rhythm of human life with the divine. Sacrifice was used to appease the deities, while fasting and feasting – the two extremes of ritualised eating – responded to the eternal seasonal cycle of want and plenty.

The Muslim festival of Eid-al-Adha gives some idea of the transformational power that harvest festivals must once have had in ancient cities. The feast (whose Arabic name means 'festival of sacrifice') is a joyous celebration of spiritual renewal that comes at the end of the Hajj, the ritual pilgrimage of Muslims to Mecca. The meal itself is usually a large family lunch at which special foods are eaten, mainly dishes of meat, traditionally from an animal ritually slaughtered by the male head of the household. In Cairo, the sense of anticipation intensifies with the arrival of the many sheep and goats brought in from the countryside for the festival. Crammed into every available space, such as makeshift pens, balconies and rooftops, the animals fill the air with their plaintive bleating as they await the knife. The scale of the bucolic invasion ensures that Eid affects more than just its celebrants. On the day of slaughter itself, the city is transformed into a spontaneous outdoor slaughterhouse, with animals running amok in the streets and gutters coursing with blood. To those of us brought up in the sanitised West, such scenes can be shocking, but there is no denying their power to bring the dilemmas of human existence to the very heart of the city.[15]

Although ritual slaughter is not practised by Christians, the idea that sacrifice is both necessary and redemptive remains embedded in the religion. Christ's ultimate sacrifice is remembered through the Eucharist, a re-enactment of the Last Supper, when Christ bade his disciples eat bread and wine as symbols of his body and blood. Of course, the sacrifice is also celebrated at Easter, a feast preceded by the ritual fasting of Lent. Although modern observance of Lent often consists of only modest acts of self-denial (such as the giving up of chocolate or alcohol), Easter nevertheless derives much of its spiritual power from the period of abstinence that precedes it.

Although Easter is the most spiritually significant festival in the Christian calendar, the feast itself has long been outstripped in secular popularity by its rumbustious counterpart, Christmas. A joyous feast that embraces the pagan spirit of the winter solstice, Christmas has always been an excuse for a jolly good knees-up: the sort of revelling and abandon capable of banishing the dark and cold of a deep, black winter's night. Although early Church fathers called for fasting during Advent, the practice was less rigorously observed than during Lent, and was never common in the Protestant north, where the natural privations of winter ensured Christmas would have plenty of festive impact. Those of us for whom those privations no longer exist can find the obligation to make merry during the 'festive season' something of a trial, even oppressive. Christmas for many in modern Britain has dissolved into a non-stop noshathon devoid of spiritual significance – and, as many of us discover each year, roast turkey with all the trimmings rather loses its appeal when one has spent the previous month stuffing oneself with sausage rolls and devils-on-horseback at various Christmas parties. Even in the secular world, abstinence has a part to play in the enjoyment of a feast.

As Jean Anthelme Brillat-Savarin observed almost two centuries ago, if one is not properly hungry, one can't properly eat. Yet hunger, even of the mildest sort, is something most of us rarely experience in the

West. The nearest many of us come to fasting is when we go on a diet; an act that, whatever it might do for our waistlines, does little for our positive mental outlook. Nothing is more calculated to reduce us to a state of miserable, food-obsessed isolation: very different to the cathartic experience of ritualised communal fasting.[16] For most people in history, fasting has been a spiritual act; not a desperate attempt to rectify overindulgence. The preciousness of food made eating a highly conscious process; every meal an occasion to give thanks. Yet few of the meals we eat today recognise the provenance of our food, let alone its importance. Most of the time we eat distractedly, even grumpily; either while doing something else, or wishing that we were. We graze, we nibble, we bolt our food – even when it does manage to claim our attention, few of us are truly grateful for what we are about to receive. The only time most of us think before we eat is when we find ourselves confronted by table rituals derived from the past; from a time when famine reigned more often than plenty.

Life, death, sacrifice, rebirth – the eternal subjects of every religion – lie at the heart of all ritual feasting, and whether or not we believe in a god or gods, they are implicit in every meal we eat. Every culture has its own table rituals, yet their great diversity pales in comparison with their far more striking affinity. The rituals of food transcend doctrine, myth or belief: they carry deeper messages, about life itself. Nothing could speak more eloquently of our basic commonality: of what it means, in the end, to be human.

Companionship

There is no preparation so sweet to me, no sauce so appetising, as that which is derived from society . . .

Montaigne[17]

We are omnivores, which means that the ritual sharing of food goes deep into our past. Our hunter-gatherer forebears had to find ways of distributing the spoils of the hunt equably among themselves, and the fellowship of those far-distant meals resonates with us still. Although modern lifestyles have made solitary meals increasingly common, we generally prefer to eat in company.

Few acts are more expressive of companionship than the shared meal. As the Latin derivation of 'companion' indicates (from *cum* 'together' + *panis* 'bread'), someone with whom we share food is likely to be our friend, or well on the way to becoming one. Eating among friends instils a powerful sense of well-being in us, arousing primitive emotions of which we are barely aware. In the final scene of Charles Dickens's *A Christmas Carol*, Bob Cratchit and family sit poised to tuck into an enormous turkey, sent round unexpectedly by Bob's miserly, but now repentant, employer Scrooge. As we contemplate this heart-warming scene, we cannot help but feel the future happiness of the Cratchits is assured, and that, by extension, all is well with the world. Splendid dinners such as this, fictional or otherwise, exert a powerful influence over us, creating a paradigm against which all other meals are judged.

Sharing food with those to whom we are closest is a primal act, but as people who grew up in a large family can testify, the rules of engagement still have to be learnt. Restraint at table is a cultural, not a natural skill, and when we are young, we can be tempted to deprive our siblings of the juiciest slice of beef, the largest piece of cake. Watch a pride of lions eat, and you get some idea of what table manners are covering up. The default state of wild animals is hunger; the satisfaction of that hunger a basic instinct. When hunting animals share a kill, they eat warily but fast, with the more powerful animals getting the 'lion's share'. That is not to say that animals do not have elaborate strategies for sharing food (they do), or that animal parents do not regularly deprive themselves of food in order to feed their young (ditto). But in the animal world, the right to eat, like the right to mate, usually depends on the display of individual power. While good for speeding up the effects of Darwinian evolution, this approach to food-sharing could scarcely be called civilised. Yet its principles lie under the surface whenever people share food too.

In his 1910 essay 'Sociology of the Meal', the sociologist Georg Simmel touched on the primitive underpinnings of shared meals.[18] Hunger, he argued, brings people together by necessity at certain times and in certain configurations, making the common meal the most potent ordering device in society. Inclusion or exclusion at such gatherings is socially defining; yet the civility of the table is just a veneer to mask the real motive of the meal: the satisfaction of individual selfishness. Whether or not one signs up to Simmel's somewhat misanthropic view, there is no doubt that in human society, power and status have a large part to play in determining what, when, how much and with whom one gets to eat. Merely to sit at table confers a certain status: in order to eat, someone has to cook; in order to be seated at table, somebody must serve. All meals, however humble, have an implicit hierarchy, in which diners enjoy a higher status than those who cook and serve their food. Since cooking and eating occupy complementary positions in the social order, that means that the social and gender divisions of the kitchen translate – in reverse – to the table. Everyone has to eat; but the history of dining has been dominated, like society itself, by men, and powerful ones at that.

Long before Brillat-Savarin made his most famous observation – that you are what you eat – the essential tribalism of the table was well understood.[19] We are hard-wired to feel close to those with whom we share food, and to define as alien those who eat differently from us. The tribal nature of food is clear from the frequency with which it has been used by one nation as a term of abuse for another, as in 'Frog', 'Kraut', 'Rosbif' and 'Limey'. The latter reference, from the British practice of carrying lime juice aboard ship to avoid scurvy, is pertinent. Food rituals have always been integral to life at sea, as a way both of boosting morale, and of ordering the social and fighting hierarchy of warships. Nineteenth-century gun crews ate together at tables slung between their weapons, taking turns to serve each other from the ship's galley. The natural camaraderie of the table was thus transferred directly to the fighting effectiveness of the ship: men who ate their meals together worked better as a team and would more readily die together.

The power of shared meals to forge human bonds makes their context particularly significant. Beyond the table, a series of questions arises. Does the meal have a 'purpose' other than the mere feeding of those present? Who is allowed to attend? Whose table is it anyway? The answers to these questions, and to others like them, hold the key to food's influence in society. In ancient Greece, Zeus himself was the god of hospitality, and no crime was considered more heinous than the betrayal of trust at table. Participation in a *xenia*, a friendship meal, bound host and guest together in a bond of loyalty close to that of kinship – even the diners' descendants were forbidden to fight one another in battle.[20] All of which would have made Homer's description of Agamemnon's return from the Trojan Wars doubly horrific to the audience of his day. The hero was murdered at his own table, slain by his wife's cowardly lover Aegisthus, who had plotted to murder his superior opponent by laying on a feast for him and attacking him as he ate.[21]

Above all else, the shared meal is a social tool; open to manipulation, use and abuse, gestures of friendship or betrayal. Paradoxically, some of the easiest meals to 'read' in these terms can be elaborate feasts such as those held at the Inns of Court. However arcane their rituals, one at least knows what the main purpose of such meals is: to reinforce the prestige, traditions and fellowship of the Inn. The message is clear. But the social dynamics of private hospitality can be far more ambiguous, as the etymology of the words 'host' and 'guest' suggest. Both derive from the Indo-European *ghostis* (stranger), from which the Latin *hostis* (stranger, enemy) comes: the root of our word 'hostile'.[22] That the words host and hostile should share a common root may seem odd until one considers that it is the act of hospitality itself that binds people together; that can turn strangers – and potential enemies – into friends.

Table Talk

After a good dinner one can forgive anybody, even one's own relatives.

Oscar Wilde[23]

Good table manners may be unnecessary for survival, but they can be critical to social acceptance, which comes close to the same thing. Nothing short of blasphemy is more guaranteed to give offence than rudeness at table, and gestures that can seem innocent enough to us can cause mortal offence to others, especially when we share food with those from another culture. You would be unlikely to seal a business deal in Japan, for instance, if you tried to pass someone food with your chopsticks – always assuming you had the skill to commit such a transgression in the first place. The way we touch food at table is a matter of convention and varies greatly from one culture to another. In India, for instance, it is polite to eat food with one's fingers, whereas in our own culture it is considered the height of bad manners. The social historian Margaret Visser cites the case of one American businessman whose career took a nosedive when his son attended a formal dinner and proceeded to eat spaghetti by scooping it up with his hands.[24] Such catastrophic misdemeanours are not merely comic; they can be offensive, even threatening. As Visser points out, part of the function of table manners is to ensure mutual conformity, to reassure one's fellow diners that one is not about to perform some transgressive act – like Agamemnon's murderer – when they are at their most vulnerable.[25] Eating is a serious business; table rituals a cultural expression of the fact.

Manners have always been more than a question of 'the way you hold your knife', as Ira Gershwin once put it. Above all, the table is a social space, and learning to behave there is as much an exercise in communication as anything else. It is not only lawyers who can benefit from being lucid, companionable, and good at listening – these are skills we could all benefit from, and it seems that the table is where we learn them best. Several recent studies have linked many of the social ills of modern British youth – short attention spans, inability to listen, fidgetiness, depression – to the fact that children no longer eat regularly with their elders. A 2001 survey found that three quarters of British families have abandoned regular meals, and that one in five never sit down together to eat.[26] No wonder, then, that a recent study of preteens eating in restaurants found that 20 per cent were using their fingers more than the cutlery – ambitious parents of spaghetti-eating progeny beware.[27] But the likelihood of British youths blighting their futures, or those of their parents, by manhandling pasta is as nothing compared to the handicap their lack of social skills is likely to cause. With children spending increasing amounts of time plugged into iPods, MySpace and other personalised universes, many are failing to acquire even basic social skills, such as how to listen, communicate and share.

The process is starting ever earlier too: one recent report found that parents were turning increasingly to 'electronic babysitters' (children's television programmes) during mealtimes, so that even toddlers are being left to eat on their own. Forget learning how to hold a knife – at this rate, the next generation will be struggling to hold a conversation.

But perhaps the most crucial outcome of learning to eat properly is that of developing a healthy relationship with food itself. Long before the age of the nuclear family, mealtimes formed an essential part of a child's upbringing. Children were rarely if ever given a choice of menu, so they were faced either with eating what was put in front of them, or going hungry – a process that over time accustomed them to accepting their given diet. British children today have a greater choice of food than ever before, yet perversely many refuse to eat most of it, sticking to just a few dishes – often highly processed 'kiddie' foods – they have grown used to. This apparent paradox is explained by the fact that children need to be *taught* how to eat. Unless they are encouraged to try different foods from an early age – a process that can take up to 14 attempts – they can develop food aversions and a resistance to new tastes that will last into adulthood. Seen in this light, the British habit of feeding children special foods – often blander or sweeter than their adult counterparts – is at best unwise, at worst downright harmful. In failing to educate our children's taste buds, we are breeding a generation with little or no sense of their own food culture – and few defences against a food industry keen to sell its products to them.

The idea that you have to feed children special food is unheard of beyond the Anglo-Saxon world. The Indian food writer Madhur Jaffrey has talked of her love as a nine-year-old child for hot mango pickle, while children in most parts of Europe are expected to eat adult food from an early age, both at home and at school.[28] Three quarters of French families still eat regular meals together at table, and French school meals commonly consist of four courses – including one of cheese – that children sit down to eat together.[29] Children in France and Italy are also encouraged to drink a little diluted wine with their meal from an early age. Feeding young children hot pickle and alcohol might seem like irresponsible parenting to the British mindset, but in reality it is the reverse. Early exposure to adult foods teaches youngsters healthy eating habits that will stay with them all their lives. A childhood taste for spices is arguably preferable to the Anglo-Saxon lust for salt, sugar and fat; while the habit of drinking a little wine with food from an early age is generally acknowledged as the best defence against a later addiction to alcohol. The fact that drinking in order to get drunk is almost unheard of in Italy – despite the fact that wine there is often cheaper than water – is a constant source of puzzlement to the British, yet it is the direct result of Italian food culture.

Manners Maketh Man

Let us not drink and eat everything merely to satisfy our belly, like the persons whom we name parasites or flatterers.

Athenaeus[30]

Some aspects of table manners, such as not licking shared utensils, being greedy, or coughing up one's food, are simple common sense. One does not want to disgust one's fellows, deprive them of food, or threaten their meal with contamination. However, other matters of etiquette (the correct use of a grapefruit spoon, how to dispose of an artichoke) are rather more complex. In the same way that dinner invitations can be used as social weapons, table manners can be used as a second line of defence by the powerful against those they wish to exclude. As one Victorian etiquette manual put it, manners are 'the barrier which society draws around itself; a shield against the intrusion of the impertinent, the improper, and the vulgar'.[31]

Whenever dining has been socially important (and there have been few periods in history when it hasn't), knowing how to eat properly has been an essential social skill. In ancient Athens, for example, meals generally consisted, as they do in modern Greece, of individual pieces of bread (*sitos*), dipped into shared dishes known collectively as *opson*: the taramasalata and hummus of our day. Then, as now, the success of the meal depended on everyone taking their fair share and no more: *opsophagia* (guzzling *opson*) was considered a major sin. Socrates was so outraged by one man's greed that he called on his neighbours to watch him 'to see whether he treats the *sitos* as *opson*, or the *opson* as *sitos*'.[32] In ancient Athens, greed at table could bring you more than dirty looks: it was seen as a clear sign of moral corruption, and to be branded an *opsophagos* was enough to ruin a political career.[33]

In times of great social mobility, manners have also taken on huge significance. For the bourgeoisie of the Italian Renaissance, knowing how to throw a dinner party was matched only in importance by knowing how to behave at one – and the undisputed guide was *Il Libro del Cortegiano*, written by Baldassare Castiglione in 1528. In describing the life of a courtier, Castiglione penned the ultimate manual for the socially aspirant, listing the various accomplishments – urbanity, swordsmanship, conversational skills and, of course, exquisite table manners – essential to courtliness. But the defining feature of courtliness, according to Castiglione, was an effortless grace unique to those of proper breeding, and a *sprezzatura* (contempt) for those without it. Ostensibly aimed at courtiers, the book was naturally avidly devoured by just about everyone else in the hope that its wisdom would gain them access to the highest social circles; a vain hope, since the very effort it took them to get there would automatically exclude them.

A significant counterblast to this elitist approach came from the Dutch humanist Desiderius Erasmus, whose 1530 *De civilitate morum puerilium* (*On the moral civilising of boys*) argued that *all* boys, not just those of the nobility, should be trained to eat properly at table. For Erasmus, table manners were fundamental to the civilising process; valuable in that they recommended morality 'to the eyes of men'.[34] Good manners should be accessible to all, for 'no one can choose his own parents or nationality, but each man can mould his own talents and character for himself'.[35] In Erasmus' hands, table manners became a passport to self-betterment, and the openness of his approach ensured that *De civilitate* enjoyed widespread popularity, remaining a standard school textbook all over Europe until well into the nineteenth century.

That table manners should have aroused such passions in the class-bound societies of the past is perhaps understandable, yet they have by no means been limited to such social milieux. Even in the supposedly meritocratic democracy of 1920s America, the debutante Emily Post

A daunting sight for any *parvenu*. A formal table setting from Emily Post's
Etiquette in Society, 1922.

made a career out of terrorising her fellow Americans over such
questions as whether to serve their guests soup in two-handled cups or
bowls (the latter was 'never' done at luncheon, apparently) or whether
it was polite to pass food to one's fellow guests at table (it wasn't).[36] As
well as instructing readers on how to give immaculate dinner parties,
Post taught them how to recognise when their hosts were failing to
come up to the mark. 'To eat extra entrées,' she wrote, 'Roman Punch,
or hot dessert is unknown except at a public dinner or in the dining
room of a *parvenu*.'[37] Yet despite her fondness for faultless manners, Post
was an Erasmusite at heart, believing that they could – and should – be
acquired by everyone: 'Manners are made up of trivialities of
deportment which can be easily learned if one does not happen to
know them; manner is personality – the outward manifestation of one's
innate character and attitude toward life.'[38]

Even in eat-off-your-lap Britain, manners retain significance. 'Having dinner with the Queen' was the dream–nightmare scenario with which my generation was shamed by our parents into behaving properly at table, and despite British dining habits since having largely followed the path of increasing entropy, such an honour remains a real, if distant, possibility for the highest achievers among us. At the very top of the social tree (and despite the revelation that Her Majesty's breakfast table is graced with Tupperware), the distinctions of table manners in Britain remain terrifyingly intact.

Political Dining

Read the historians, from Herodotus down to our own day, and you will see that there has never been a great event, not even excepting conspiracies, which was not conceived, worked out, and organised over a meal.

Jean Anthelme Brillat-Savarin[39]

The table is where the politics of food are at their most explicit. Apart from the problem of getting oneself invited to the right meals, there is always the hierarchy of the table itself. For the lawmaker Solon, the symbolism of the table made it a natural tool with which to shape Athenian democracy, and he bade the standing committee dine regularly together in public to express their equality. In 465 BC a special dining chamber, the Tholos, was built in the Agora for the purpose. It was the only round building there: a deliberate sign that the committee was sharing a humble meal together, not engaging in the privileged couched dining of the *symposion*. From King Arthur and his knights to the parliamentary chambers of contemporary democracy, the political symbolism of the round table is familiar to us: the gathered circle implies equality and friendship. But not all political dinners in history have been that equitable.

Roman dinners were ruthless exercises in one-upmanship. Guests were arranged strictly according to rank, with the most important placed next to the host on his right, and the rest taking their places accordingly. The food served was often hierarchical too: the equable sharing inherited from the Greeks was swept away in imperial times by the need to entertain on a lavish scale, which, for those who struggled to afford it, led to serving inferior dishes to lower-ranked guests as a compromise. The practice disgusted Pliny the Younger, who wrote, 'I serve the same to everyone, for when I invite guests it is for a meal, not to make class distinctions.'[40] However, Pliny was in the minority: for the majority of Romans, making class distinctions was precisely what dinner was about.

As famous fictional dinners go, Petronius' account in his *Satyricon* of dinner with Trimalchio is up there with the Mad Hatter's tea party. Long considered a gross parody of the truth, the account is now thought to be somewhere close to reality. Trimalchio, a notorious social climber, is trying to impress his guests with a feast that lasts all night and includes, among other things, a wooden hen that lays pastry 'eggs' with tiny birds inside, a hare dressed up to look like Pegasus with wings attached, and a wild boar with date 'acorns' dangling from its tusks, surrounded by cake 'piglets'.[41] Each dish is presented as a *coup de théâtre*: the boar, for instance, arrives with a fanfare, and a pack of hounds is set loose to run around the room while the beast is carved by a 'huntsman' slave. Throughout the meal, guests are regaled with a running commentary by their monstrous host, who even manages to spoil the effect of his own dinner by admitting that the boar had been offered to guests the night before and refused. The evening descends into debauchery, with diners peeing freely into vases, farting, and having sex with anything that moves.

Whatever the accuracy of the *Satyricon*, historic descriptions of Roman civic feasts (*convivia publica*) make Trimalchio's excesses seem pardonably modest. One banquet given by the emperor Vitellius is described by Suetonius as 'the most notorious feast', involving 'two thousand magnificent fish and seven thousand game birds', plus a dish dedicated to the goddess Minerva that 'called for pike-livers, pheasant brains, peacock brains, flamingo-tongues, and lamprey-milt; the ingredients collected in every corner of the Empire'.[42] As Roman palates became increasingly jaded – and the Empire depleted – the city's feasting became more and more theatrical. Guests seated at imperial banquets far enough away from the emperor could even find themselves being served fake food, reducing them to mere props in the display. As produce poured into Rome's great maw, respect for food was replaced by a hunger for novelty and excess unmatched even in the post-industrial West. Although individuals battled with their consciences, conspicuous consumption in public became mandatory.[43] The fact that many ordinary Romans lived in fear of starvation simply added to the drama of excess. When food loses its social value, it also loses the ability to bring people together – and to civilise.

Conspicuous consumption in the ancient world was by no means limited to Rome. King Solomon slaughtered 22,000 oxen at the dedication of his temple, while the ninth-century BC king Assurnassipal of Assyria dedicated his palace with a 10-day feast for 69,000 guests.[44] Such epoch-making blowouts served the dual purpose of emphasising the importance of the rulers who gave them, while currying the favour of their subjects – a principle that extended to the catering of royal households until medieval times. In fourteenth-century England, Richard II kept a staff of 300 to feed the thousand or so who ate at his table. Communal dining was also typical of noble households of the period, when lord and family, guests, servants and pets would all gather together in the great hall for the sort of chuck-the-bones-to-the-dogs feasts beloved of early Hollywood. However, by mid century, it was becoming more common for noblemen to eat separately from their retinues, a development lamented by William Langland in *Piers Plowman*:

> Wretched is the hall . . . each day in the week
> There the lord and lady liketh not to sit.
> Now have the rich a rule to eat by themselves
> In a privy parlour . . . for poor men's sake,
> Or in a chamber with a chimney, and leave the chief hall
> That was made for meals, for men to eat in.[45]

The new division soon spread to civic feasting, so that instead of sharing food with their subjects, rulers took to eating in front of them. Much as gods in the ancient cities were fed sacrificial food, the public feeding of monarchs – who increasingly claimed divinity – came to represent their subjects' well-being by proxy. The Habsburg kings dined in public four times a year from 1548; Henry VIII dined from time to time in a 'presence chamber'; and although his daughter Elizabeth I never dined in public, the ceremony was performed every day as if she did, with the Queen's place being laid at table 'with the utmost veneration' and her food served as if she were present.[46] Yet as the historian Roy Strong described in his book *Feast*, even this dumb show was as nothing compared to what was going on in France. At the death of Francis I in 1547, a meal was served to the king's coffin, while a wax effigy (complete with moving parts) was set up in a *salle d'honneur*, where it was ritually fed until the king was buried.[47] The public feeding of French kings, both alive and dead, went on until the Revolution. Louis XIV's meals at Versailles, whether taken in public (*au grand couvert*) or in private, took on ever greater ceremonial complexity: for instance no fewer than 15 high-ranking officers were required to serve the king's meat.

After the storming of the Bastille, the need to express '*liberté, égalité, fraternité*' revived a more equable form of public feasting. Consciously evoking the democratic dining of ancient Athens, the Marquis Charles de la Villette proposed that all Parisians should dine together in the streets, for at such a feast, he declared, 'the capital, from one end to the other, would be one immense family and you would see a million people all seated at the same table'.[48] The immediate result was the Fête de la Fédération, a two-week-long rolling banquet at the Champ de Mars, at which thousands of Parisians supped to the accompaniment of music, dancing and plays. Impromptu 'fraternal feasts' continued to be held in the streets of Paris for several years after the Revolution, to which all residents were invited to bring their own tables, chairs and food. However, by all accounts the feasts were fraught affairs. Those who made too modest a contribution to the meal were often accused of unfraternal selfishness, while those who were overly generous risked being branded bourgeois. But the worst sin of all was to miss the banquet altogether: absentees were considered traitors to the cause. What began as a spontaneous popular celebration soon became a political nightmare, and when fraternal banquets died out due to natural causes during the 1790s, one imagines it was to private sighs of relief all round.

Meat and Drink

Even the briefest glance through the history of dining makes one thing clear: food lends itself naturally to ritual complexity. Yet the vast majority of meals we consume have no hidden agenda: they are simply eaten because it is 'lunchtime' or 'teatime', or, less often, because we are actually hungry. Food can never be completely free of messages, but for the most part, those messages are buried by habit or necessity. It is ordinary meals, not politically charged feasts, that have exerted the greatest influence over cities. Unburdened by the heavy symbolism of their 'higher' relatives, ordinary meals make their presence felt through iterative, cumulative effect, building up the social and spatial structures of everyday life.

The diurnal rhythm of breakfast, lunch and dinner – or something very like it – is common to cities everywhere. Whether or not we eat regular 'proper' meals ourselves, the cities we inhabit are geared to them, their streets, cafés, restaurants and bars filling and emptying to their rhythm as surely as the sea turns with the tide. We are usually too busy queuing for a sandwich at lunchtime or a drink after work to notice how animated cities get at mealtimes. However, when we travel abroad, the effect is obvious. Many an Englishman out in the midday sun has been puzzled by the complete shutdown of Mediterranean cities for the post-prandial siesta; similarly, many have felt ready for bed just as the rejuvenated locals come out for their evening stroll, such as the Italian passeggiata, followed by dinner. Cities eat according to their climates, and during the summer months in the Mediterranean it is far more comfortable to eat out of doors and after dark than at any other place or time. The fact that young children share in such meals can seem strange to northern visitors, for whom night life is an adult-only pursuit mainly based around alcohol, not food. Such differences are fundamental not just to the way we socialise, but to the way we inhabit the public spaces of cities.

Our own mealtimes seem so immutable that it can be a surprise to discover that they have shifted considerably over time. In the twelfth century, the main meal of the day in Britain was eaten as early as 10 a.m., and it has been gradually moving later ever since. By Georgian times it had reached between 2 and 4 p.m.; today it is usually eaten around 8 p.m.[49] The shift towards evening was due to the nineteenth-century arrival of artificial lighting, which lengthened the day and made room for a more substantial midday meal. Lunch, or luncheon, was the result, derived from 'nuntions', a light snack eaten in Tudor times to stave off hunger between what were then the two main meals of the day – breakfast and supper.[50]

All meals in the past carried a social code in Britain: the times they were eaten, the names they were given, what was consumed all connoted class. Breakfast for the gentry in the eighteenth century was usually taken after exercise around 10 a.m., and consisted of rolls and coffee; a very different meal, except in name, to that of the working classes, who typically set off for work four to five hours earlier on a breakfast of bread, meat or cheese and ale. By 1936, the first comprehensive survey of British eating habits found that all classes were now eating breakfast before they went to work, but what they ate had effectively reversed. The upper classes were now eating a high-protein breakfast of bacon and eggs, while the poorer made do with porridge or cereal.[51] The same survey found that the midday meal – 'dinner' to all but the richest group, who called it 'luncheon'– was mostly eaten at home, with 50 to 60 per cent of husbands returning from work in order to eat it. For all but the upper classes, this was the main meal of the day, consisting of meat, potatoes and greens followed by pudding for the relatively well-off, and stews, pies or sausages for the less so. Only the wealthy ate 'dinner' in the evening: a five-course meal taken around 7–8 p.m. and consisting of soup, fish, meat or poultry, pudding, cheese and fruit. The rest of the population ate a light 'supper' of bread and butter, biscuits, cheese and cake between 9 and 10 p.m.; similar to the northern working-class 'tea', eaten between 5 and 6 p.m.

Although such rigid class distinctions were blurred by the Second World War, the basic patterns of British meals were still discernible in 1972, when the social anthropologist Mary Douglas – more used to focusing on the dietary habits of African tribespeople – turned her anthropological attentions on herself.[52] In her essay 'Deciphering a Meal', Douglas analysed what she ate over the course of a year, attempting to classify the results. She found that her unvarying daily routine consisted of breakfast, lunch and dinner, which fitted into a weekly rhythm starting on Monday and running through to Sunday lunch, the main meal of the week. The meals themselves also fell into distinct patterns, with 'proper' breakfast consisting of fruit juice, cereal and eggs (in that order), and 'proper' dinner a starter, main course and pudding. 'Higher' meals such as Christmas dinner, wedding feasts and so on were superimposed on to this everyday rhythm. Together, suggested Douglas, the meals formed a continuous hierarchy, in which the rituals of the 'higher' ones were echoed by those of the 'lower', investing even simple snacks with significance. They combined to form a 'grammar of food' that could be read as a social code. Douglas's analysis, carried out from a middle-class perspective and before the demise of the nuclear family, would require some revision today. However, her basic premise still holds true. Even our least ritualised meals – burgers stuffed down on a station platform, drunken late-night kebabs – register against an underlying social code, and are mostly found wanting.

London – the Business Lunch

Although the great majority of meals in the past were eaten at home, dining out has always been a feature of urban life. In pre-industrial cities, public eateries were classless, and rich and poor often shared the same table, just as they lived together in the same street. Sixteenth-century Londoners ate in taverns offering 'ordinaries', fixed-price meals consisting of several dishes all brought to the table at once. As some satirical advice to a 'young gallant' in 1609 suggests, eating such meals required particular skill. The youth is advised to arrive

> . . . some half hour after eleven, for then you shall find most of your
> fashionmongers planted in the room waiting for meat. When you are
> set down to dinner, you must eat as impudently as can be (for that's
> most gentlemanlike). When your knight is upon his stewed mutton,
> be you presently (though you be but a captain) in the bosome of your
> goose; and when your justice of peace is knuckle-deep in goose, you

may, without disparagement to your blood, though you have a lady
to your mother, fall very manfully on your woodcocks.[53]

Taverns varied greatly in size, from single-room establishments to
premises with as many as 30 rooms. The historian Hazel Forsyth
describes the typical arrangement as a bar entered directly off the street,
fitted with tables, benches, stools and a fireplace; then a taproom, cellar
and kitchen, plus various rooms for hire. The latter varied greatly in
price, but the most expensive provided a high degree of comfort, with
wall-hangings, upholstered chairs, paintings, a mirror, clock and
privy.[54] Larger premises were arranged around courtyards, with
outhouses and gardens at the back. A survey by Ralph Treswell of some
of London's most famous cookshops and taverns in 1611 (those at 'Pye
Corner' frequented by, among others, that most notorious English
epicure Sir John Falstaff) gives some idea of their physicality.[55] The
buildings are so tightly packed that many rooms either lack windows,
or face on to narrow courtyards. The premises are long and narrow,
with street frontages no more than 14 feet across, and corridors and
stairs two and a half feet wide at the most; the latter winding steeply up
like corkscrews. Heated by open fires and lit by candlelight, the rooms
must have built up some serious fug, to say nothing of the massive
ovens, some of them as large as rooms themselves. Londoners clearly
spent a lot of time in cramped, airless, smelly spaces, but to judge from
the literary evidence, that did little to dampen their appetites.

Taverns operated rather like clubs, with credit extended to regular
clients and small favours carried out. Like many of his class, Samuel
Pepys used them a great deal, often preferring the convenience of the
tavern to dining at home, and treating the former as an extension of the
latter. In August 1630, Pepys records having bought a lobster in Fish
Street and bumping into some friends carrying a sturgeon, whereupon
the group repaired to the Sun Tavern in order to get their fish cooked
and enjoy it together.[56] The sociability of taverns made them natural
places to do business, and Pepys often entertained colleagues there, and
was frequently schmoozed himself.

Taverns ruled supreme in London's social and business life for several
centuries, but during the 1650s their supremacy was threatened by the

arrival of an 'outlandish' new drink, coffee. Treated at first with suspicion (as new foods generally are), coffee soon gained in popularity, thanks largely to its relative cheapness compared to the wine that brought the taverns most of their profits.[57] For the price of a dish of coffee, anyone was free to sit for as long as they liked – anyone male, that is: although coffee-house proprietors were frequently women, the clients were all men. In appearance, coffee rooms were generally well lit and plainly furnished, with large communal tables and benches and a coffee booth from which the proprietor dispensed drinks. They usually had a large open fire, with a copper boiler over it and an iron for roasting the beans. Within 11 years of the first one opening in 1652 (the exotically named Pasqua Rosee in Cornhill), there were more than 80 coffee houses in the City, but the aftermath of the Great Fire of 1666 was when business really took off.[58] While the Royal Exchange was being rebuilt, coffee houses became de facto trading houses, incidentally giving birth to one of the City's oldest institutions, Lloyd's of London, first formed in Edward Lloyd's coffee house nearby.

Coffee houses soon became the favourite haunt of newsmen, for whom their open debate made them ideal places to pick up the latest gossip – although, as one contemporary ballad noted, its veracity might be doubtful:

> You that delight in wit and mirth,
> And love to hear such news
> That come from all parts of the earth,
> Turks, Dutch and Danes and Jews;
> I'll send you to the rendezvous,
> Where it is smoking new;
> Go hear it at the coffee house
> It cannot but be true.[59]

By the end of the century, coffee houses were well established in the City; they also dominated political and intellectual life in London. As we saw earlier, Covent Garden drew coffee houses like a magnet, and there was intense rivalry between various establishments as to which was the most 'happening' place in town. Will's in Russell Street boasted

Chewing the fat in a seventeenth-century London coffee house.

the patronage of Dryden for 40 years: he could be found in winter occupying a large chair by the fire, or in summer on the balcony, dispensing witty remarks to a captivated audience. Meanwhile, up the street was Button's, established in 1712 by Joseph Addison, founder-editor of the *Spectator*, who played host there to a gallery of influential politicians and writers including Richard Steele, Alexander Pope and Jonathan Swift. Anyone was welcome to join in the debate: the front door even had a letter box shaped like a lion's head, through which passers-by could post contributions to the paper.

With their shared intimacy, free speech and political leanings, coffee houses created a completely new sort of urban social space. They represented the arrival of what the sociologist Jürgen Habermas called the 'bourgeois public sphere': a domain in which people from all walks of life could meet and converse as equals; where, for the first time, 'public opinion' could form.[60] During the eighteenth century, the sphere would expand into the salons and academies of Paris and 'table societies' of Germany; during the nineteenth, it would include London clubs and Parisian cafés. But in the days of London's first coffee rush, that was still a long way off. While Londoners sat around and dished the dirt, Parisians remained mired in the *Ancien Régime*: a milieu that was to give rise to a radically different kind of eatery – one that would eventually challenge the very sociability of public dining.

Paris – Rise of the Restaurant

Paris before the Revolution had no equivalent to London's taverns and coffee shops, nor to the intellectual life they fostered. The nearest to the former were *traiteurs*, eating-houses that enjoyed a state monopoly over the sale of cooked meats, and served table d'hôte meals to loyal groups of regulars. However, as fashionable society in the eighteenth century responded to the Romantic rediscovery of nature, a dissatisfaction grew with the *traiteurs'* heavy fare, and various figures, Rousseau prominent among them, began to call for an altogether lighter, more natural diet. In 1767, a *traiteur* by the name of Minet responded, opening an establishment in Paris with the following advertisement: 'Those who suffer from weak and delicate chests, and whose diets therefore do not usually include an evening meal, will be delighted to find a public place where they can go and have a consommé without offending their sense of delicacy . . .'[61] The consommé in question was a restorative meat bouillon known as a *restaurant*, kept on the boil all day long so that clients could pop in for a cup of it any time they liked. More medicine than food, the *restaurant* – and the establishments to which it gave its name – was destined to change the face of public dining for ever. The new restaurateurs were soon dishing up other 'healthy' foods such as semolina, rice-creams, fruit in season, eggs and white cheeses; the very foods, as Rebecca Spang pointed out in her book *The Invention of the Restaurant*, that were eaten by Rousseau's rustic heroines.

Restaurants presented an entirely new way of eating out. Anyone, including women, could go there at any time of day, sit at their own table, order what they liked off a menu, and pay for it separately. Individual, independent, anonymous; restaurants were about as far from the enforced camaraderie of *traiteurs* as one could get; which, as the latter soon realised, made them hugely attractive. Soon *traiteurs* began opening their own *salles du restaurateur*, many of them staffed by ex-courtly chefs relieved of their posts by the Revolution. Richly decorated with boudoir-like interiors complete with mirrors, chandeliers and painted nature scenes, restaurants were unlike any previous public eating-house, and tourists flocked to Paris to be shocked by their louche decors and even loucher clients, whose behaviour they found utterly perplexing. This account by Antoine Rosny, who visited Paris in 1801, is typical:

> On arriving in the dining room, I remarked with astonishment numerous tables placed one beside another, which made me think that we were waiting for a large group, or were perhaps going to dine at a table d'hôte. But my surprise was at its greatest when I saw people enter without greeting each other and without seeming to know each other, seat themselves without looking at each other, and eat separately without speaking to each other, or even offering to share their food.[62]

It would take another hundred years for restaurants to catch on outside Paris, but what Rosny was witnessing was nothing short of a social revolution. By giving clients a choice of what to eat, restaurants were dismantling the ancient laws of the table, replacing its companionship with theatrical individualism. From now on, dining out would focus not on the camaraderie of diners, but on the gastronomic genius of the chefs who cooked for them.

Restaurants required a whole new kind of diner to appreciate them fully, and Grimod de la Reynière, maverick nobleman and gastronomic guru, was the self-appointed man. In 1803, Grimod went on a series of 'nutritive strolls' through Paris, publishing the results in his *Almanach des Gourmands*, the world's first restaurant guide. It was an instant hit. Where the bourgeois had once fallen over themselves to learn how to give the perfect dinner party, they now clamoured to be told where to go out and eat. The *Almanach* became an annual publication, acquiring the sort of holy status reserved today for the *Guide Michelin*, with the power to make or break the restaurants it reviewed. Professional gourmandism was soon flourishing in Paris, along with the idea that fine food could only be enjoyed by refined aristocratic palates. The latter notion appealed to restaurateurs themselves, many of whom were used to pleasing noble employers. The bouillon-serving simplicity of early restaurants soon disappeared under a cuisine of towering complexity. Menu comprehension replaced effortless grace as the new social test, as arriviste diners struggled to decipher florid descriptions of dishes and the processes that went into producing them.

Given their obfuscation and snobbery, it is perhaps unsurprising that restaurants took a while to catch on outside Paris. However, their influence eventually spread, thanks to the diaspora of chefs who travelled first to the royal courts of Europe, then to the world at large. Men like Antonin Carême and Alexis Soyer became the first true celebrity chefs, cooking for royalty (Tsar Nicholas I and Queen Victoria respectively), and popularising the art of haute cuisine. Carême, generally held to be one of the greatest geniuses ever to wield a wooden spoon, used the Rumford range to refine the art of sauce-making, while in the 1830s Soyer created a kitchen at the Reform Club so radical that people paid to go on guided tours of it.[63] Slowly but surely, French influence spread through the clubs and hotels of London, bringing with it, as the author of the *Epicure's Year Book and Table Companion* William Jerrold announced in 1868, a new culinary sensibility: 'If the princely kitchens have decayed, the number of people who know how to eat has vastly increased. Clubs have spread among men of modest fortune a knowledge of refined cookery.'[64]

This 'refined cookery' was, of course, French. By the turn of the century, haute cuisine was synonymous with culinary excellence in Britain, in both public and private dining rooms. 'Mixed dining' was soon all the rage, as fashionable men and women began eating out together for pleasure, in a way we would recognise today. By the early twentieth century, restaurants were the new focus of social life in the West, and through them, French cuisine gained a grip on the gastronomic high ground it is yet to relinquish.

Chain Eating

Restaurants are now so much part of the urban landscape that it can seem strange to think of them as relatively new to the scene; yet their proliferation into the range of eateries we know today took place mainly during the twentieth century. The arrival of the railways was what first gave rise to a need for new sorts of public eating-houses, as large numbers of people began commuting to cities each day and needed somewhere to have lunch. While factories generally had their own works canteens, clerical and city workers resorted to dining rooms and chophouses, often clustered around railway stations or in business districts. Although the new establishments served similar food to the old taverns, they were on a much larger scale, and had smaller tables in individual booths. As restaurant-style service spread to chophouses, the anonymity of public dining that so shocked visitors to Paris the century before became commonplace. Restaurants were morphing into the diners, bistros and fast-food joints of the modern city.

While the new breed of restaurants served a useful purpose, they also posed a problem. Although city-dwellers in the past had treated public cookshops with suspicion, they had generally visited so few of them that they had come to know and trust the proprietors personally. But dining out in the industrial city was an entirely different matter. The new eateries were large and anonymous, and fears over hygiene made their unseen kitchens deeply threatening. Added to that was distrust about the way the food itself was being produced. Upton Sinclair's 1906 book *The Jungle*, in which the author exposed the grotesque and unsanitary conditions prevalent in the Chicago meat trade, led to public revulsion on both sides of the Atlantic at the idea of factory meat. Since cheap industrial meat formed the basis of every working man's diet, something had to be done, and that something was the creation of a new kind of restaurant – one that would reassure customers about eating in public.

The answer was restaurant chains, and the idea behind them was simple. Just as food manufacturers had used brands to reassure people about their products, restaurants now used them to persuade diners there was nothing nasty lurking in the kitchen. By adopting a recognisable format repeated at every outlet – such as Howard

Johnson's orange-tiled roofs – restaurant chains could build up a sense of brand recognition and trust among customers. Cleanliness and openness were the new watchwords, an approach that White Castle, a Kansas company founded in 1921, took to an extreme. America's first hamburger chain, White Castle relied on selling customers the very food that *The Jungle* had put them off: cheap ground meat. As the chain's co-founder Edgar Ingram recognised, this presented something of a challenge. Somehow, he needed to find a way to 'break down a deep-seated prejudice against chopped beef'.[65] His solution was to create an image of such purity (down to the use of the word 'White' in the chain's title) that customers would feel reassured about the safety and wholesomeness of the food. The resulting restaurants had sparkling white-tiled exteriors, stainless-steel interiors, and, most radically of all, open kitchens fully visible to the dining room, so that diners could watch their meals being cooked. The company's promotional brochure of 1932 reinforced the subliminal safety message:

> When you sit at a White Castle, remember that you are one of several thousands; you are sitting on the same kind of stool; you are being served on the same kind of counter; the coffee you drink is made in accordance with a certain formula; the hamburger you eat is prepared in exactly the same way over a gas flame of the same intensity; the cups you drink from are identical with thousands of cups that thousands of other people are using at the same moment; the same standard of cleanliness protects your food.[66]

Cleanliness, simplicity, visibility, predictability – if White Castle's formula sounds familiar, it is because it was copied by one of the greatest business brains in modern catering: Ray Kroc, the genius behind McDonald's. Edgar Ingram came up with the formula for modern fast food, but it was Kroc who could see its global potential. His secret weapon was spatial demographics. At the start of the 1950s, hamburgers were sold mainly to working-class men on inner-city sites, but Kroc believed that if they were pitched right, they could be sold to just about anyone. Having discovered that 75 per cent of family meals were eaten where the children wanted – and this in the midst of the baby-boom era – that meant, as Kroc put it, 'going after the kids'.[67]

Kroc's first move in 1954 was to buy the franchising rights to an innovative conveyor-belt burger-grilling system he came across while working as a drinks-machine salesman in the California diner of two Scottish brothers, the eponymous McDonalds. Having secured the McDonald's franchise, Kroc immediately began building family-friendly restaurants in affluent neighbourhoods, run with military efficiency by teams of highly trained teenage boys. The restaurants were far cosier than their 'white' predecessors, with warm brick interiors and cheerful furnishings, but they retained one essential feature: open-plan tiled kitchens, in which the entire hamburger assembly process (now reassuringly automated) took place in full view of diners. A cleanliness freak, Kroc extended his immaculate hygiene standards to the outside of

A White Castle in Cincinnati in 1927, its gleaming walls a contrast to the grimy streetscape.

his restaurants, often spending his weekends scraping chewing gum off the forecourts. He kept his target customers happy with special kiddie meals, take-home presents and their own 'fun' figure, the spooky Ronald McDonald, who by 1970 was recognised by 96 per cent of American children, second only to Santa Claus. It was all a stunning success, but Kroc was yet to display his greatest business gift: flexibility. When the nuclear family began to disintegrate during the 1970s, he simply moved back to the inner cities, flying around in helicopters to locate the best sites (usually road intersections) to attract his new target customers, identified as 'roaming impulse eaters' with little brand loyalty.[68]

With 30,000 restaurants worldwide, 50 million daily customers and a 'Hamburger University' with 275,000 graduates to its name, the global success of McDonald's is all too familiar. Despite a millennial wobble caused by a series of exposés, including Eric Schlosser's 2001 *Fast Food Nation*, Morgan Spurlock's 2004 *Supersize Me*, and Cesar Barber's 'fat suit' (in which the latter sued McDonald's for giving him a heart attack), the Golden Arches have bounced back.[69] Accused of making the world fat and giving it coronaries, the company showed it had lost none of Kroc's adaptability, introducing new 'healthy' options, such as spring water and prepared salads, although some of the latter turned out to contain more fat than a standard cheeseburger.[70] In early 2007, McDonald's announced some of its best sales increases ever; not, as you might expect, in the fast-growing cities of Asia, but in Europe.[71] One could hardly wish for a better demonstration of the power of image to control the way we think about food.

Food and Identity

One of the great ironies of American fast food is that it is the product of one of the biggest and richest gastronomic inheritances on earth: the ethnic melting pot created by European migration to the USA. So how come such a rich cultural mix resulted in one of the blandest foods in history? The answer, as Harvey Levenstein argued in his book *Paradox of Plenty*, was that the very richness of the mix led to a national crisis of food identity.[72] As successive waves of Irish, Italians, Germans, Hungarians and

Poles landed on American shores from the 1880s onwards, a desperate search began for a common food acceptable to all. Many felt obliged to 'Americanise' their native cookery by taking out all the interesting bits – Italian garlic, German blood sausage, Hungarian paprika – that might offend others. The result was lowest-common-denominator cuisine, devoid of character or flavour, whose only saving grace was the vast quantities of fresh meat it contained; something few immigrants had enjoyed back home. As people began to eat larger portions, they also began to add more of the only flavour enhancers – salt, sugar and fat – offensive to no one. The formula ought to sound familiar, because it gave rise to the planet's blandest, yet most popular, food.

With its vast feed lots, processing plants and fast-food joints, the American food industry by the 1950s was a species apart – and the hamburger was its ultimate product. By extending the economies of scale of modern agribusiness through to the table, it achieved an astonishing feat: the intrusion of corporate branding into the very heart of food culture, the meal itself. For a mixed society desperate to ditch any vestige of individual food identity, its one-size-fits-all approach fitted the bill perfectly. But in order to succeed outside America, fast-food companies had to find markets where the food culture was already weak – where, effectively, it was already industrialised. Britain, for example. British food culture unravelled earlier than most, for the simple reason that Britain industrialised earlier than any other nation. Native cooks such as Hannah Glasse might have muttered about 'French tricks', but it was the Industrial Revolution that dealt the fatal blow to British gastronomy, by making the majority of the population reliant on imported processed food. It created the world's first industrialised palate; one that, as George Orwell noted in his withering analysis of the British working classes during the 1930s, *The Road to Wigan Pier*, had utterly corrupted the nation's taste buds:

> ... the English palate, especially the working-class palate, now rejects good food almost automatically. The number of people who prefer tinned peas and tinned fish to real peas and real fish must be increasing every year, and plenty of people who could afford real milk in their tea would much sooner have tinned milk – even that dreadful tinned

milk which is made of sugar and cornflour and has UNFIT FOR
BABIES on the tin in huge letters.[73]

What with the working classes craving processed food and the upper
classes craving French, British gastronomy in the mid twentieth century
was in a sorry state indeed. While haute cuisine can hardly be blamed
for the loss of British food culture, its colonisation of the gastronomic
high ground hardly helped, since it perpetuated the notion that the best
food was foreign, and that in order to eat it, one had to be posh.[74] In
his tragicomic survey of British restaurants in 1967, the *Bad Food Guide*,
Derek Cooper wrote:

> There is, alas, no reason for optimism on the eating front. For the
> minority prepared to pay for the privilege there will always be a small
> number of good restaurants. The majority of us will continue to put
> up uncomplainingly, perhaps even with a sort of masochistic
> pleasure, with the kind of bad food and bad service described in the
> following fourteen chapters.[75]

No wonder American fast food was such an instant hit in Britain. It met
little resistance from a national gastronomy in disarray; and, of course,
it appealed directly to the postwar British obsession with America. As
far as McDonald's, Kentucky Fried Chicken and the rest were
concerned, Britain was a rollover; which is more than can be said for
the rest of Europe. In France and Italy, American fast food was seen as
nothing short of 'gastronomic imperialism'. The first McDonald's in
France was physically attacked, and as we saw in the previous chapter,
the Golden Arches' arrival in Rome caused such outrage that it sparked
the birth of the Slow Food Movement.

It is instructive to look at the passions aroused by fast food in Italy
and France. Although neither nation has been closed to foreign culinary
influence (the tomato, now considered essential to Italian cuisine, was
imported from Peru as an ornamental plant in 1650, and only entered
mainstream cookery in the nineteenth century), neither underwent the
mass urbanisation that severed British cooking from its roots. Crucially,
this has allowed both nations to maintain 'vertical' cuisines, in which

different levels of cookery (rustic, regional, amateur, professional) continue to inform one another. For the majority in France and Italy, food remains a way of life. When it comes under threat, it is considered worth fighting for.

The new frontier for American fast food is Asia, where rapid urbanisation is having a similarly disruptive affect on local food cultures as it once did in Britain. Although Asian cuisines remain some of the most distinctive in the world, the fact that American fast food has a place in Asia at all is symptomatic of the power of industrial food to appeal to those uprooted from their rural lifestyles. When it comes to global food cultures, it seems we have a choice. As Britain and America have demonstrated, ethnic diversity and mass migration can forge food cultures of sorts; highly adaptable ones at that. Yet many of those fusions come at a cost. When 'anything goes' in the gastronomic mix, food loses one of its greatest gifts – its cultural identity.

Global Grub

For those of us addicted to the choice of whether to eat Italian, Greek, Chinese, French or Indian every night, the loss of our own food culture in Britain may seem like a blessing. Over the past 20 years, our cities have been transformed by an eruption of restaurants offering everything from Malay, Thai, Mexican and Spanish, to Japanese, Ethiopian, Afghan – even British food. London in particular has become a fantasy playground for the dedicated gourmet; yet, as the parlous state of our culinary knowledge in Britain indicates, it is entirely possible to have a thriving restaurant trade and a bankrupt food culture at one and the same time.

The role played by restaurants in any national gastronomy is a complex one. Where food cultures remain strong, professional and domestic cookery can co-exist in a mutually beneficial relationship. However, in weak food cultures like our own, restaurants can become a substitute for cooking. At their best, restaurants can be fun, entertaining or romantic, allowing us to see friends on neutral territory, and occasionally (if we are lucky) to eat sublime food we would be incapable of cooking ourselves. At worst, they stop us engaging with food, charging us vast amounts for bad dishes we could easily cook better for ourselves at home. In her 1989 book *Dining Out*, the American sociologist Joanne Finkelstein attacked American restaurants for creating 'dioramas of desire' in which artificial ambience took precedence over everything else, including the food.[76] For Finkelstein, the American predilection for eating in restaurants was 'fundamentally uncivilising', since it replaced the authentic experience of the shared meal with something that was ultimately fake.

Fake or not, there is no denying the capacity of restaurants to animate public space. London's recent 'restaurant revolution' has transformed previously empty swathes of the capital – notably the embarrassingly lifeless South Bank – into vast throbbing outdoor eateries. In the case of the Brunswick Centre (another modernist project previously inhabited only in the architect's imagination), the change has been even more dramatic. A godforsaken pedestrian precinct over an underused car park since the 1970s, 'The Brunswick', as it now styles itself, resounds with the excited chatter of cappuccino-drinkers and pizza-guzzlers from dawn to dusk. Thanks to a major makeover with all the usual branded shops and cafés – plus central London's largest Waitrose – it has been transformed overnight into that most hallowed of commercial phenomena, a mall.[77] In short, it has become what it always wanted to be, but never dared dream of becoming. The Brunswick's commercial success is obvious, but it is having the predictable effect on local businesses. One patisserie renowned for its coffee and home-made baguettes saw its trade cut by half the moment The Brunswick opened. Compared to the choice of Yo! Sushi, Giraffe, Carluccio's and, of course, Starbucks just up the road, its charm seemed to evaporate like the morning dew.

One Bloomsbury coffee shop closes, another opens: so what has changed? Those in the vicinity of Bloomsbury can still purchase coffee if they want to. Their coffee-drinking rights are not affected. But to reduce coffee, or any other foodstuff, to a commodity is to miss the point. It is food *culture*, not just food, we need to be worrying about preserving, and that means everything that surrounds food, not just food itself. If we lose sight of that, we might just as well get all our nourishment in tablet form and have done with it. Of course restaurant chains are perfectly aware of our innate need for 'ambience' when we eat – that, after all, is what they chiefly sell. But however cosy the feel of a Starbucks, with its comfy sofas, soft lighting, jazzy music and second-hand books – all the essential trappings of the Seattle coffee scene popularised by *Frasier* – it has about as much to do with local food culture as a Peppermint Frappuccino® does with coffee.[78] Starbucks outlets are stage sets, designed by marketing executives thousands of miles away to appeal to our fantasy metro-chic lifestyles. Add a mouse with big ears, and you might just as well be drinking in Disneyland.

'So what?' you might ask. If the coffee is good and the sofas soft, who cares whether Starbucks is 'authentic' or not? Once again, it is a question of scale. Going for a fantasy coffee in a pretend Seattle coffee shop might be jolly once in a while. But when that is the only choice one has, it starts to mess with one's identity. The problem with chain restaurants is not the fact that they exist, but what they prevent from existing. In her book *No Logo*, the American journalist Naomi Klein described how large chains target entire urban districts – even towns – and use their economies of scale to 'brand-bomb', putting local rivals out of business.[79] The strategy is exemplified by Starbucks' policy of 'clustering' several outlets in a single neighbourhood – specifically targeting those with thriving café cultures – in order to saturate the local coffee trade. Starbucks drop their prices sufficiently to force their rivals to quit, then move in and take over their abandoned positions. The process can involve what Starbucks calls 'cannibalisation', in which the company's own outlets fight one another to destruction in the coffee battle's bitter endgame. Whatever the name of the tactic, its effect on indigenous café cultures is similar to the one rabbits have had on local wildlife in the Australian outback.

In 2007, Starbucks announced their intention to open another 100 branches in Britain in 2008 – and one in London every fortnight for the next decade – saying the British market had proved 'way bigger' than they had expected. So if you have a nice local café in your neighbourhood, watch out for a bit of cluster-bombing coming your way soon. Unless you live in Primrose Hill, that is. In 2002, the residents of the London neighbourhood (admittedly an unrepresentative bunch consisting mainly of the sorts of people – actors, politicians, literati – who frequented coffee houses the first time round) refused to allow Starbucks to cannibalise their beloved high street, with its long-established, family-owned cafés. Their high-profile campaign, which attracted several thousand glittering signatories, was enough to persuade the company to cut its losses and try its luck elsewhere. In Primrose Hill, at least, a spark of indignation ignited the British soul at the very idea of having its food identity stolen.

The Cornucopia Complex

> Obesity is never found either among the savages, or in those classes
> of society in which men work to eat, and eat only to live.
>
> Jean Anthelme Brillat-Savarin[80]

Most of us in Britain neither know about food, nor care about it much, yet our indifference, coupled with our 'special relationship' with the nation that first brought conspicuous consumption to the masses, is affecting more than our cities. It is going straight to our middles.

We may not farm, shop or cook for ourselves any more, but we all have to eat. One way or another, we should all be experts at eating – but are we? Our environment is evolving faster than our bodies can adjust: most of us lead sedentary lives in superheated buildings, yet our appetites seem to be keeping pace with whatever the food industry can throw at us. Several recent studies have confirmed that our ancient survival instincts are still intact, urging us to carry on eating whatever is put in front of us, whether or not we are hungry. As a result, the more food we are presented with, the more we tend to eat.[81] 'Supersize' and 'BOGOF' deals, in other words, appeal to those parts of our brains that haven't evolved since we were living in the frozen wastes and hunting the woolly mammoth.

All of which would be bad enough if woolly mammoth was what we were eating. But of course it isn't. For the past 30 years, we have been consuming increasing quantities of industrialised food, which has been putting some very strange things into our bodies. In his 2003 book *Fat*

Land, the journalist Greg Critser described how, once again, the process began in America, as the food industry began to experiment with a range of new 'Frankenfoods' in the 1970s: foods geared not so much towards nutritional value as their ability to 'perform' according to the dictates of modern food production. First on the list was palm oil, colloquially known as 'tree lard': a vegetable oil that remains solid at room temperature, so giving products a good 'mouthfeel' and imbuing them with such a long shelf life that, as one insider gushed, they seemed to 'last for ever'.[82] With credentials like that, no manufacturer was going to quibble over whether it was ethical to sell customers products containing 'vegetable oil' with saturated-fat levels higher than beef tallow. Another major discovery was high-fructose corn syrup (HFCS), first developed by Japanese scientists in 1971. Six times sweeter than cane sugar, HFCS is also far cheaper to produce and remains fresh-tasting for longer: qualities that make the fact that it bypasses the body's normal digestive processes, arriving 'almost completely intact' in the liver, easier to overlook. Certainly neither Coca-Cola nor Pepsi seemed overly concerned when they switched their products over to the new sweetener in 1984.

Armed with its new range of Frankenfoods, all the food industry had to do was persuade people to eat more of them. During the 1980s, American fast-food chains took over where the labs had left off, offering 'supersize' and 'value meal' promotions to customers. Although the deals seemed a good bargain, all they were really doing was sneaking high-profit (and high-calorie) items such as Coke and fries in under the radar. Nevertheless, the strategy brought immediate results: Taco Bell, the first chain to adopt value meals in 1988, more than doubled its sales within eight years, forcing other companies such as McDonald's to follow suit. By 1996, a quarter of the $97 billion spent on fast food in America went on food sold on the basis of larger sizes or extra portions. By that time, a McMeal, which had originally contained 590 calories, had ballooned to a whopping 1,550.[83]

Bigger, faster, cheaper, pizzazzier: American fast food turned the old rules of the table on their head. 'Eating big' had always been a sign of high status; now, for the first time, an entire nation was doing it. Between 1970 and 1994, the number of calories available in the

American food supply rose from 3,300 to 3,800 per person per day – an increase of 15 per cent.[84] But, as any ancient ruler could have told you, there is a limit to how much any one person, however great, can eat. So where were all the extra calories going? By the century's end the answer was all too obvious. Several decades of porking out had taken a terrible toll on American bodies. Soaring levels of obesity, Type-2 diabetes and Type-B malnutrition – surely the most ironic of all urban diseases – meant that eating had overtaken smoking as America's most injurious activity.[85] As if that were not bad enough, researchers found that Americans were also the world's most anxious eaters, associating food more with health concerns than pleasure. As one researcher put it, Americans now believed that 'food is as much a poison as it is a nutrient, and that eating is almost as dangerous as not eating'.[86] So much for happy meals.

Fat Cities

Viewed as a way of life, American food culture could hardly be called successful. Disastrous would be closer to the mark. If the sight of citizens of Houston, Texas (regular claimant to the title of 'fattest city on earth'), driving along the pavement in their fat-buggies were not enough, the rash of exposés and lawsuits that hit the fast-food industry at the turn of the millennium ought to have been enough to ensure that its gaff was well and truly blown. So why do we in Britain, and increasingly other nations, persist in eating the American way? Although it is true that many of the fast-food industry's tactics – use of social demographics, economies of scale, aggressive marketing – are mightily effective, that does not explain why the product is so universally appealing. The real answer lies not just in the nature of the food, but in the way it has altered our whole relationship with eating.

Fast-food chains work because they offer safety in numbers – they make us feel we are not alone when we eat. In the anonymity of the post-industrial city, they appeal to the oldest human instinct of all: the sense of belonging and safety that comes from sharing food with others. When we eat fast food, our primary relationship is with the food itself, not with anyone we might be sharing it with. Fast food is the first food in the world that is *meant* to be eaten alone – that wants to be your friend. It is the food of substitution: food that comes in helpings so all-encompassing, so laden with goodies and additives that it seems to offer the world in every mouthful. Yet despite its liberal doses of salt, sugar and fat (the classic obesity triad), much fast food remains strangely unsatisfying. Layering blandness on blandness does not lead to satisfaction, any more than eating a bowl of fries brings consolation. The most tragic aspect of the cornucopia complex is that it is a search for fulfilment that will never come.

Fast food is popular precisely because of what it does *not* provide: satiety, companionship, well-being. Like the cigarette whose heady buzz wears off after the first lungful of smoke, it promises everything and delivers little, trapping 'heavy users' in a cycle of dependency that keeps them coming back for more. In essence – as Cesar Barber's lawyer John Banzhaf argued in the McDonald's 'fat suit' – fast food is addictive.[87] By its very nature, it leads us into temptation, not just because of its salty, fatty sugar-rush, but because it is an autonomous 'fix' we can get any time we want. Greed has been frowned upon by every society in history, yet we can now indulge in it with impunity, because the social mechanisms that once controlled it (table manners, ethics, respect for food) are no longer in place. Because it exists independently of any social constraints, fast food removes the last check on our tendency to behave like Labradors given half the chance. No wonder dieting in America has become a religion. After decades fighting the flab with low-fat and low-carb, Slimfast and Slimslow, F-plan and Dr Atkins, would-be American slimmers have finally turned to God. Divine Health, founded by Pastor Don Colbert MD, is the latest diet craze in the USA. With the slogan 'Lose weight, eat what Jesus ate', worshippers pray to be delivered not from the devil, but from the desire for 'food to comfort me'.

Despite increasing alarm over the obesity epidemic sweeping America and Britain, there are few signs that our Anglo-Saxon love affair with industrialised food is on the wane. Over the past 50 years, a typical British meal has morphed from meat and two veg to sticky chilli chicken, via burgers, Coke and fries. The trend is pure Americana, as is our growing predilection for eating out. Our bodies are responding too: one in four Britons is now obese, and we are fast catching up with the world's fattest nation, where the figure is now one in three. Clearly this is bad news, but threatening to deny obese patients NHS treatment or banning children from eating chips at lunchtime is to fail to recognise the nature of the problem. As one Rotherham school discovered in 2006 when it tried to introduce obligatory 'healthy meals', we British *can* become passionate about food when denied our favourite fodder. On that occasion, outraged parents simply climbed through undergrowth to feed their kids chips through the railings.[88]

Treating us like naughty schoolchildren caught with our fingers in the sweetie jar is not going to work. Obesity is not just a question of what we eat – it is an illness that goes to the heart of the way we live. It is the bodily manifestation of our disconnected, industrialised food culture – a culture in which food is not valued or understood, and is therefore open to abuse. If we are to tackle obesity, we are going to have to look at *every* aspect of our food culture, with all that implies. We are going to have to question how we dwell in cities: how we design and build them, feed and live in them.

A century ago, Americans turned their amazing ethnic inheritance into a fearful, neutered, deeply unhealthy national gastronomy. Now we need to turn things the other way. We need to reconnect with the culture of food, and remember what it means. There is always a danger, when thinking about food, of getting nostalgic for the past: for 'good old days' that probably never existed. But there is still a lot that we can learn from it. The history of the table is full of injustice, manipulation and snobbery; it is also full of pleasure, fellowship and joy. It is a reflection, in short, of society itself. To ignore its power is to deny our humanity.

The shared meal is mankind's most complex social phenomenon for a reason. It is the context in which, more than anywhere else, we define ourselves as social beings and recognise our deeper bond with land, sea and sky. We have yet to discover what a strong, local, post-industrial food culture could be like, but there has never been a better time to find out.

Chapter 6
Waste

A sewer is a cynic. It says everything.
Victor Hugo[1]

The Thames Embankment under construction in 1867.

Crossness Pumping Station, London

If Crossness Pumping Station were a dog, it would be a mongrel of very mixed breeding. A large rectangular edifice on a barren stretch of the Thames by Thamesmead, it is fashioned chiefly from pale brownish brick with a queasy yellow tinge, with details picked out in red. Style-wise, the building's round-arched windows, carved column capitals and dog-tooth string coursing all hint at the Romanesque, while its no-nonsense massing and beefy structural piers are pure Train Shed. Round the back, the architectural signals become even more confusing. In place of the expected derelict goods yard, there is a formal garden straight out of the Italian Renaissance, complete with symmetrical flower beds, gravel paths, a cedar tree, and pedimented pavilions at either end.

So far, so weird. But it is only on entering the building that one is well and truly flummoxed. Part cathedral, part machine room, the space is filled with an ethereal light, filtering down from clerestory windows through an ironwork grid two storeys above one's head. Every element of the room is decorated in some way: patterned brickwork and fancy tiles cover the walls and floor, while screens, grilles, stairs and balustrades compete with yards of elaborate ironwork, their red, yellow and green floral motifs overlapping in a visual cacophony of colour. In the centre of the room, a large octagonal opening (the cathedral crossing) punches through the ironwork grid above, each of its angled faces a writhing mass of emerald leaves from which the Metropolitan Board of Works monogram MBW peeps out in red. Perhaps because of all this ferrous foliage, it can take a while to clock the really serious pieces of ironwork in the room, but once noticed, they command all one's attention. Four looming, mostly rusting metal giants stand one to each corner, their mute power obvious even at rest. At the sight of them, all the building's visual clutter falls away, like excited chatter at a party when someone famous enters the room. Meet Victoria, Prince Consort, Alexandra and Albert Edward: the four largest rotatative beam engines in the world.[2]

A rotatative beam engine, in case you were wondering, is an engine that applies force at one end of a pivoted beam in order to do work at the other, using a flywheel to regulate the motion. It is essentially a powered seesaw, whose vertical rocking motion will be familiar to devotees of *Dallas* from the 'nodding donkeys' seen pumping oil out of the Texan desert in the series' opening credits. Sucking up large volumes of fluid from underground is what beam engines do best, and in the case of the royal quartet at Crossness, those volumes were once very large indeed. In their nineteenth-century heyday, their 43-foot, 47-ton rocking beams were each capable of lifting six tons of liquid at a single stroke, at a rate of 11 strokes per minute. However, it was not oil they were lifting, but something that once threatened to bring the world's greatest city to a stuttering, stinking standstill – its sewage.

London at the start of Queen Victoria's reign was capital of the largest, most powerful empire the world had ever seen. The city's dominion encompassed over a fifth of the world's land surface and a quarter of its population. But great global metropolis though it was, London had a serious domestic problem. The city had never adopted what might be called an integrated policy on waste, and its two and a half million inhabitants were still being served by a sewage system best described as medieval, essentially comprising the River Thames, its stinking tributaries, and around 200,000 overflowing cesspits.[3]

London's failure to deal with its ordure was far from unique. Most pre-industrial cities adopted a reactive, rather than a proactive, approach towards waste. Unlike the food supply, to which even a day's disruption caused chaos, rubbish could be allowed to pile up for years, even centuries, before it created a real nuisance. Part of the reason for this was that most waste in the pre-industrial world was organic. Although it was messy, it was also seen as a valuable resource. In what the historian Donald Reid called the 'golden age of urban ecology', very little went to waste – indeed, the more a city stank, the richer it was deemed to be.[4] Leftover food was gobbled up by pigs; human and animal faeces were collected to be used as manure; urine and fermented dung were vital to a variety of artisanal processes such as dyeing and paper-making. What little rubbish could not be used was either thrown straight into rivers, or taken to dumps on the city outskirts. That was the theory, anyway. In practice, most people simply chucked their waste out into the street – a habit that, in smaller cities at least, was not quite as antisocial as it sounds, since much of what was thrown away could be collected and put to good use.

However, as cities grew larger, their self-regulatory ecosystems began to break down. Fourteenth-century Coventry, for instance, had 10,000 inhabitants, making it the fourth-largest city in England, and to judge from the flurry of ordinances emanating from the city council, rubbish was becoming an issue. Although human and animal dung were valued for manure, the supply in larger cities often outstripped demand, leading to an insalubrious gloop that clogged the streets and blocked the drains. The council's response in Coventry was to decree that 'no person within this City shall from henceforth sweep their streets in any rain time, whereby to pester the river with filth and muck'.[5] Similar ordinances prohibited the washing of entrails and other 'filthy operations' in the market, forbade butchers to slaughter cattle in the open, and banned the throwing of fish water into the street, except after dark (quite what this did to alleviate its stench remains unclear).

If the 'filth and muck' of fourteenth-century Coventry caused a nuisance, that of London, a city 10 times the size, can be readily imagined.[6] Few houses in the capital had access to cesspits or back gardens, so the large amounts of waste thrown into the street included every sort of 'muck', from kitchen scraps to human 'night soil'. The city was forced to employ hundreds of 'muck-rakers', professional street-sweepers, to collect the stuff and cart it off, either to 'laystalls' on the city fringes, where it was matured into manure, or to special wharves, where it was loaded on to barges and taken downriver to be dumped. The authorities' battle against the rising mire was reflected, as in Coventry, by a stream of ordinances, of which the opening salvo of 1357, requiring citizens to 'remove from the streets and lanes of the town all swine and all dirt, dung and filth . . . and cause the streets and lanes to be kept clean', set the tone for the following centuries.[7]

Despite all the mayoral huffing and puffing, nothing approaching major sanitary reform was attempted in London, and slowly but surely the city simply clogged up. By 1661 things were so bad that the diarist John Evelyn was moved to write a diatribe, *Fumifugium*, in which he described the capital 'burning in stench and dark clouds of smoke like Hell'. 'The City of London,' he wrote, 'resembles the face rather of Mount Etna than an Assembly of Rational Creatures.'[8] Five years after Evelyn's outburst, his 'Etna' finally erupted, its timber houses and putrid filth helping to fuel a four-day-long funeral pyre. For Evelyn, the Great Fire was not so much a tragedy as an opportunity, and just three days after it died down, he visited Sir Christopher Wren, urging him to adopt his proposals to rebuild the smouldering city over a series of subterranean vaults that could both service its buildings and carry their waste away. But it was not to be. The urgent need to rebuild and get trading again, combined with complex patterns of land ownership in the city, put paid to any grand visions Evelyn, Wren or anyone else might have had for London. Within the space of a year, the capital had risen again from the ashes more or less as it had been, with just the occasional nod in the direction of what we would now call health and safety. Streets were a little wider, buildings made of brick rather than wood, the noxious Fleet was covered over – but as far as the city's muck was concerned, it was back to business as usual.

Over the next two centuries, London got on with what it did best: making money. Although the city was soon choking on its own effluent again, the value of night soil and animal dung was still firmly engrained in people's minds – particularly since seventeenth-century Londoners had discovered the pleasures of fruit and vegetables grown in their own manure. Indeed, demand for the latter had been so great in 1617 that the newly formed Gardeners' Company felt able to claim that it had 'cleared the city of all dung and noisomeness'; and although John Evelyn's account of the capital a few decades later rather suggests otherwise, there is no doubt that commercial market gardening provided a viable alternative to waste disposal in London.[9] The capital's most famous horticultural enterprise, Neat House Gardens in Chelsea, enjoyed a special relationship with Covent Garden for over two centuries, exporting high-quality produce to the market and receiving boatfuls of fresh dung in return. As John Strype noted in 1720, the arrangement was both efficient and highly profitable:

> A parcel of houses, most seated on the banks of the river Thames, and inhabited by Gardiners, for which it is of note, for the supplying of London and Westminster markets with asparagus, artichoaks, cauli-flowers, musmelons and the like . . . which by reason of their keeping the ground so rich by dunging it (and through the nearness to London they have the soil cheap) doth make their crops very forward, to their great profit in coming to such good markets.[10]

By the start of the nineteenth century, London's population had grown fourfold, and its market gardens, which now stretched as far as the River Lea, still received regular exports of manure from Dung Wharf, the city's main waste depot at Blackfriars. But as increasing volumes of people and goods flowed into London, the city's supplies of dung and muck began to seriously outstrip demand. Matters finally came to a head with the popular adoption of the latest must-have accessory, the flushing water-closet, first patented by Joseph Bramah in 1778.[11] At the mere pull of a lever, centuries of emptying chamber pots and ducking at the shout of 'gardy-loo' were banished to the past. But if WCs relieved an age-old domestic problem, out in the city they were creating havoc. Vastly increased volumes of waste water began to enter the sewage system, causing ancient cesspits to overflow and street drains, designed to take rainwater only, to become blocked and polluted. Most loathsomely of all, swollen underground sewers began to seep through the floorboards of houses in low-lying districts.

From the 1830s onwards, London was hit by a series of cholera epidemics, which were linked, naturally enough, to the evil miasma that hung over the city.[12] In 1842, the pioneering social reformer Edwin Chadwick published his *Inquiry into the Sanitary Conditions of the Labouring Population of Great Britain*, painting a gruesome picture of life at the start of Victoria's reign. Having reviewed the appalling conditions in which the majority lived, Chadwick concluded that

> . . . the various forms of epidemic, endemic, and other disease caused,

or aggravated, or propagated chiefly amongst the labouring classes by atmospheric impurities produced by decomposing animal and vegetable substances, by damp and filth, and close and overcrowded dwellings prevail amongst the population in every part of the kingdom . . . as they have been found to prevail in the lowest districts of the metropolis.[13]

The government responded in 1848 with the creation of the aptly named Consolidated Commission of Sewers, whose first move – encouraged by Chadwick – was to flush out every one of London's existing 369 underground drains; a well-intentioned but disastrous act, since all it succeeded in doing was to disgorge several centuries' worth of backed-up detritus into the Thames. Since many Londoners got their drinking water directly from the river, the operation, far from improving their health, actually made matters worse. Over the next few years, a series of even more destructive cholera epidemics resulted, killing up to 10,000 people a year. It was becoming clear that simply flushing out the city's existing sewers was not going to work. A more radical solution was needed.

London's crisis sparked an international debate; not just about the capital's embarrassment, but about the issue of urban waste in general. Among those taking part was Justus von Liebig, the 'father of fertiliser' whose 1836 discovery of the importance of minerals in plant nutrition convinced him that it was vital that the nutrients contained in urban sewage were returned to the soil. Without them, he reasoned, a city's hinterland would eventually be reduced to desert. Liebig drew his conclusion partly from studying that ultimate consumer city, Rome. Soon after its foundation in the sixth century BC, Rome (ever the exception to the rule) had begun constructing an elaborate series of underground drains that it continued to expand throughout its later development.[14] This extraordinary piece of foresight (arguably as vital to the capital's future as the aqueducts it began to construct three centuries later) was inherited from the neighbouring Etruscans, whose expertise in draining hills and marshland had long been applied to their own city-building.[15] Pliny declared that Rome's sewers matched the grandeur of the capital they served. Some were large enough for a wagonload of hay to be driven through, and when Marcus Agrippa had the felicitous idea of flushing out the system with overflow from the aqueducts, he was able to inspect the results of his scheme by boat.[16] But the system's crowning glory (beloved of many a Latin-studying schoolboy) was the Cloaca Maxima, a great semicircular tufa-hewn tunnel up to five metres wide that collected all the waste from the entire network and flushed its contents into the Tiber.[17]

Rome's sewers were a magnificent achievement, but to Liebig they were hardly a suitable model for London to follow; or for any other city, for that matter. To him, the Cloaca Maxima represented not an engineering marvel, but an environmental catastrophe – the means by which the greatest nutrient-squandering sump on earth had sucked up all the goodness from the soil and dumped it, never to be recovered, into the Mediterranean. Liebig wrote to the British prime minster, Robert Peel, urging him not to repeat the mistake:

> The cause of the exhaustion of the soil is sought in the customs and habits of the townspeople, i.e., in the construction of water-closets, which do not admit of a collection and preservation of the liquid and solid excrement. They do not return in Britain to the fields, but are carried by the rivers into the sea. The equilibrium in the fertility of the soil is destroyed by this incessant removal of phosphates and can only be restored by an equivalent supply . . .[18]

Liebig's arguments were supported by Chadwick, who, despite his recommendation to flush out London's ancient sewers, understood the value of fresh dung. Chadwick's own conversion to the uses of sewage had come on a trip to Edinburgh, where he had witnessed the prodigious fertility of a patch of farmland irrigated by the waters of one of the city's main outflows, the descriptively titled Foul Burn. In 1845, Chadwick had urged that London's sewers ultimately be reconfigured to create a 'hydrological ouroboros' that would, as he put it, 'complete the circle and realise the Egyptian type of eternity by bringing as it were the serpent's tail into the serpent's mouth'.[19] Although increasing awareness of pathogens made the use of night soil more problematic than of yore, the government was reluctant to give up on it altogether;

and two chemists, Messrs Hoffman and Will, were commissioned in 1857 to look into the practicality of converting London's sewage into manure – a practice that had gone on unofficially for centuries. But despite admitting that the nutritional value of the city's sewage was equivalent to Britain's entire annual imports of guano, the chemists ended up rejecting the idea:

> We have been taunted with the superior wisdom of the despised Chinese, who have no elaborate sewerage system, and who, instead of carrying away their floods of sewerage wealth into the sea . . . gather it every morning by public servant . . . and take it away to nourish agriculture. Our reply to these taunts is that people (adopting the vulgar superstition) who are as numerous as ants, and who have to live in boats because the land is too crowded to hold them with any comfort, must be often at their wits' end to procure food, and are, therefore, no models for a well-to-do civilised nation to copy.[20]

Just a few months after Hoffman and Will's verdict, the blazing hot summer of 1858 made the niceties of what a 'well-to-do civilised nation' ought to do with its sewage appear somewhat immaterial. As the summer wore on, a 'Great Stink' began to emanate from the black and poisoned river, causing a stench so unbearable that the windows of the House of Commons had to be draped with lime–chloride-soaked cloth, while choking MPs inside debated whether or not to decamp to the relative fragrance of Hampton Court.[21]

Heavy rains eventually dissipated the Stink, but by then it had accomplished its work. After centuries dabbling ineffectually with London's sewage, MPs were finally persuaded it was time for a Plan B. The Metropolitan Board of Works, set up to replace the Consolidated Commission of Sewers, was tasked with coming up with a solution that would deal with the problem once and for all. Submissions were invited from members of the public, whose various contributions, numbering 140 in all, covered the full gamut of possibility. London's sewage, according to one, should be conveyed to the countryside via a series of radiating drains like the spokes of a wheel, where it could be sold from small shops as fertiliser. Another suggested collecting the sewage in floating tanks and towing it out to sea; a third, building two enormous vacuum tubes capable of sucking all the waste from Westminster to the East End, where its fate remained unspecified. And so on.

In 1859, having received and rejected all 140 proposals, the Board finally plumped for a scheme put forward by its own engineer, Joseph Bazalgette. The scheme was based on one submitted 25 years earlier by the biblical painter John Martin, whose apocalyptic visions of doom and destruction seem to have given him an abiding interest in London's sewage. In 1834, Martin had published a pamphlet (illustrated with painterly finesse by the author) in which he proposed ridding the Thames of its pollution by building two 'interceptory' sewers to run either side of the river beneath graceful arcades, which would encourage the 'working population to indulge in the healthy exercise of walking'.[22] The sewers were to terminate at two large receptacles at Limehouse and Rotherhithe, where their contents would be converted into manure and sold on to farmers, as 'practised in China'. Despite the brilliance of Martin's vision, he lacked the engineering genius to turn his idea into reality. That was where Bazalgette came in. Bazalgette proposed five interceptory sewers in all, laid to gentle falls in order to harness the natural drainage of the Thames basin, intersecting with existing sewers and tributaries and carrying their contents downstream under the force of gravity. The system would terminate at two main outfalls, at Beckton to the north and Crossness to the south, where its contents would be held in vast storage tanks to await the high tide, when they would be discharged and so carried off to sea.

Bazalgette's method of disposal was a departure from Martin's scheme, and it put an end to any notion that London might extend its ancient habit of recycling its own waste. After the Great Stink, all the government was interested in doing was getting rid of the stuff, as quickly and effectively as possible. That was the task with which Bazalgette was charged, and the one which, triumphantly, he achieved. Completed within the astonishingly short space of just six years (including the wettest summer and coldest winter of the century), the project involved the excavation of 3.5 million cubic yards of earth and the use of 318 million bricks, the price of which rose by 50 per cent during construction. Eighty-five miles of interceptory sewers were built in all, each with graded egg-shaped cross-sections to maximise the speed of flow, whatever volume of fluid they were carrying. The network, which connected 450 miles of main sewers, was capable of shifting half a million gallons of sewage a day almost entirely by gravity. That 'almost' was where Crossness Pumping Station came in. Although Bazalgette used every ruse at his disposal to let gravity do its work, he still required four pumping stations (one north of the river and three to the lower-lying south) to raise the sewage to the correct height at the outfalls. Crossness, situated at the lowest section of the entire system, handled the greatest burden: that of raising half of London's sewage by up to 40 feet and storing it in vast underground reservoirs. That was the task that Victoria, Prince Consort and the others accomplished, and although the monsters are no longer on active duty, they serve as powerful testimony to the pride and skill it took to empty the bowels of the greatest nineteenth-century city on earth.[23]

Strolling along the Embankment today, few of us pause to think of what passes beneath our feet, or of the magnitude of Bazalgette's achievement. The network he built is still in operation, and although much of it is hidden, no building project has had a greater impact on London. The Thames, previously a ramshackle waterway bounded by shingle banks and rickety wharves, was transformed into the smooth, canalised thoroughfare we know today, while the city, long mired in the mephitic stench of filth and disease, was purged at last. Where the likes of Wren and Evelyn had failed, Bazalgette (with the assistance of several thousand flushing lavatories) finally succeeded. His feat was no less remarkable in its way than any carried out by his more glamorous contemporary, Isambard Kingdom Brunel, but Bazalgette's genius has never resonated in the public consciousness quite as powerfully as has that of his rival. People are never grateful for being made to think about their own shit.

Although the modern sewage treatment works at Crossness lack the charm of their Victorian predecessor, they continue to do a vital job for the city, processing some 700,000 cubic metres of waste water each day.[24] Getting rid of London's sewage has become a lot more complicated since Bazalgette's day, too. Before it can be released back into the wild, sewage must pass through a series of processes designed to remove all its polluting organic matter, so that what is left is water at least as pure as that of the river itself. The solid matter removed during purification (known collectively as 'sludge', the modern term for 'muck') was until recently taken by barge and dumped in the North Sea, so fulfilling the vision of at least one disappointed entrant from the 1858 competition. However, an EU directive in 1998 forbade the sea-dumping of sludge, since when Crossness has been consolidating and dehydrating it on site, baking it into cakes and burning it in its sludge-powered generator, a rather menacing-looking building with a swooping metal roof and tall chimney that dominates the site and provides it with three quarters of all its power.

With its primary digestion tanks, sludge-powered generator, aquabelt thickeners and so on (none of them, disappointingly, named Elizabeth, Duke of Edinburgh, Charles or Anne), Crossness represents the state of the art when it comes to treating human waste – the approach to it, at least, that sees sewage as a problem, not a resource. Despite the on-site incineration that was forced upon it, Crossness remains the product of the one-way approach to waste disposal typical of 'well-to-do civilised' nations ever since industrialisation. Contrary to the approach common among pre-industrial cities, commercial market gardeners and (as Will and Hoffmann noted) the Chinese, it is one that uses engineered solutions to find ways not of using waste better, but of getting rid of it more effectively. Yet as Herbert Girardet pointed out in his book *Cities, People, Planet*, the nutrients found in sewage are a finite commodity. Phosphates, one of the key ingredients of artificial fertiliser, are currently mined in North Africa, Florida and Russia, but when deposits run out in a few decades' time, human sewage will be their most easily available source.[25]

Societies have always differed in their attitudes towards waste; not just sewage (by its nature a highly provocative substance), but every by-product of their lives. What is wasted by society is the direct and opposite expression of what is valued. As a way of understanding the material basis of civilisations, nothing could be more telling.

The Problem of Waste

If our gold is so much waste, then, on the other hand, our waste is
so much gold.

Victor Hugo[26]

What is waste? Rubbish, detritus, effluent, excess, garbage, scrap: it has
so many names, and comes in so many different forms, that to try to
sum it up in a word can be misleading – even meaningless. Just about
the only thing that can be said about waste is that it is stuff that
someone, somewhere, does not want. However, that is not to say
that someone, somewhere else, might not want it. What is considered
waste – what is wasted – differs from one nation to another, from one
section of society to the next, from one man to his neighbour. Waste,
like beauty, is in the eye of the beholder.

Attitudes towards waste in the pre-industrial world were straightforward compared to those of today. Since most waste was organic
(either the direct or indirect by-product of the food chain), its re-use
was taken for granted. Cities formed part of an organic cycle in which
the food supply was fuelled by the waste it generated. Any inconvenience caused by the arrangement (not least its smell) was simply
something one had to put up with. Squeamishness in the pre-industrial
world was a luxury few could afford. But our attitudes in the post-
industrial West are very different. Much of the waste we produce today
is both non-organic and highly differentiated, ranging from material
with high embodied value (scrap paper, second-hand cars) to substances
so toxic they could kill us or our descendants on contact (nuclear
waste). In such a complex material landscape, waste has itself become a
highly differentiated industry, with its own logic, processes and
dilemmas. All of which tends to obscure the fact that a city's organic
inputs and outputs are vitally connected: that they constitute the cycle
of life itself.

A century and a half after London's decision not to recycle its
sewage, the British approach to waste remains essentially one-way. We
live in a consumer society in which everything is expendable: we throw
away cars and clothes, mobiles and computers, not because they have

260

worn out, but because they have reached their *cultural* 'use by' date. We have, in other words, lost the ability to distinguish between embodied and applied value. Wastefulness epitomises our way of life, not just in what we throw away, but in what we consume and how it is made. In those terms, we consume nothing more wastefully than we do food. Despite its obsession with 'efficiency', everything about the modern food industry is precisely the opposite: beef reared in feed lots instead of on grass, out-of-season produce raised in heated polytunnels, carbon emissions from subsidised aviation fuel, refrigerated containers on the international 'chill-chain' – the list goes on. Yet of all the forms of waste involved in modern food production, none is more damaging than that of food itself, because it contains all the others put together. When we waste food, we waste all the effort, labour, water, sunshine, fossil fuels – even life itself – that went into making it.

We may not be aware of much of the waste associated with industrial food production, but there is one part of it we can't pretend not to know about: our own. In Britain we throw away 6.7 million tonnes of household food a year – that is *one third* of all the food we buy.[27] Of course, such phenomenal levels of waste are only possible in a society that no longer values food – that has lost its sense of moral wrong in wasting it. A recent survey by the government-funded Waste and Resources Action Programme (WRAP) found that more than half of us are 'not concerned' about food waste, with 40 per cent saying that throwing food away is 'not a problem' because food is 'natural and biodegradable'.[28] Unfortunately, the 'natural and biodegradable' content of landfill, where most of our food waste ends up, is a highly toxic environmental hazard, poisoning watercourses with its fermented 'leachate' (the contaminated liquid that leaches from the waste), releasing carcinogenic dioxins into the atmosphere, and contributing more than a quarter of the UK's emissions of methane, a greenhouse gas 23 times more potent than CO_2.[29]

The same survey by WRAP identified a raft of reasons why we waste food. It found that the majority of us buy more than we need, because instead of making a shopping list or planning meals ahead, we wander around supermarkets in a dreamy haze, succumbing to 'BOGOFS' as we go.[30] Once we get the food home, our lack of knowledge in the art of household management compounds the problem. We misjudge the amount of food to cook at mealtimes, allow children to refuse whatever they don't want, and throw leftovers away because we lack the culinary skills to use them up. Last, but not least, we fail to notice when food is nearing its 'use by' date, or even throw it away before it has done so, because we don't understand what the labels mean, and don't trust our own judgement to tell whether or not it's off. One in five of those questioned by the survey said they 'would not take a chance' on food close to its 'best before' date even if it looked fine; in other words, they didn't know what 'best before' means. Another survey by the Food Standards Agency in 2005 came up with similar results, finding that only a third of us interpret food labels correctly – which means a staggering *two thirds* don't.[31] Even food labels themselves have to be adjusted to account for our incompetence. Once food has left the professional chill-chain, we are likely to subject it to all manner of daft things: leave it in the boot of a hot car, forget about it at the back of a too-warm fridge, put it within reach of the dog. Since food manu-facturers are forced to take our behaviour into account when they calculate 'use by' dates, food's potential shelf life is shortened before it even leaves the factory.[32]

Fear of Dirt

There is no such thing as absolute dirt.
Mary Douglas[33]

The reasons why we waste food all boil down to the same thing: our disconnected food culture. We live in a fog of ignorance about food, but the fact that we find it easier to throw the stuff away than determine whether or not it is safe to eat says more about us than that we are lazy or ill-informed. In our post-modern, clinical, hygiene-obsessed world, food makes us fearful – not just because it is so intimately connected with our bodies, but because, in Nanny State Britain, it is just about the only aspect of our health and safety for which we ourselves are still required to take responsibility. Dirt, like danger, is something we have tried to expel from our lives, yet the more remote we become from food and cooking, the less we are able to control either. Nuclear waste may be scary, but we are unlikely ever to come into contact with it – or to be required to exercise judgement over it if we do. However, food is something we have to confront every day. Faced with food of dubious edibility, we prefer to get rid of it – with a massive margin for error – rather than sniff it, prod it or – heaven forfend – nibble a bit to see whether it tastes OK. It is as if we fear the encounter itself – not just because something might happen to us if we were to venture into the realm of the semi-rotten, but because something about the very idea offends us.

In her 1966 book *Purity and Danger*, the anthropologist Mary Douglas analysed how rejected food comes to be classified as 'dirty'. There is no such thing as 'dirt' in nature, she argued, just various forms of matter. It is our habit of separating and categorising objects that creates dirt. It is simply 'matter out of place': something that threatens to undermine our human sense of order.[34] In order to illustrate her point, Douglas considered an item of food on a plate. At first, she said, the food is clearly 'good', since it belongs to the meal about to be consumed. But once it has been rejected and pushed to one side, its position becomes ambiguous. No longer clearly part of the meal, nor obviously waste, the food becomes 'dirty' – and dangerous – because it threatens to contaminate the rest of the food on the plate. However, once safely scraped off into the bin, good order is restored, because the food is now clearly rubbish, and can no longer be mistaken for what it is not. Matter is once again in its rightful place.

Douglas went on to contrast the way in which 'dirt' in primitive cultures is often adopted as part of a sacred structure, whereas in the West it is almost entirely 'a matter of hygiene or aesthetics'.[35] The fact that our idea of dirt is, as she put it, 'dominated by our knowledge of pathogenic organisms' gives us a strange relationship with it; a fear that renders us incapable of acknowledging its creative, even redemptive, power. Returning to the rejected item of food, Douglas described how it would be transformed by the 'long process of pulverising, dissolving and rotting' into a universal medium, capable, like water, of absorbing the past and generating new life.[36] As fecund organic mulch, its creative formlessness would render it as much a 'symbol of beginning and of growth as it is of decay'.[37] It is this regenerative property of dirt, she argued, that we are closed to in the West, because of our obsession with purity. For Douglas, the Western lifestyle was 'irremediably subject to paradox', since it denied the very life-forces that animated existence: 'It is part of our condition that the purity for which we strive and sacrifice so much turns out to be hard and dead as stone when we get it.'[38]

Douglas's arguments provide an insight into our problematic relationship with food, particularly when it comes to dealing with items we consider 'iffy'. Given our difficulty in telling the difference between good and bad food, nothing could be more threatening to us than that which appears – to our perception, at least – to be somewhere in between. Since 'dodgy' food refuses to be categorised, we find it easier to throw it away, rather than risk it contaminating other food in the fridge we *know* to be good, because we have just bought it.

Even more tellingly, Douglas touches on the way our fear of dirt is linked to our deeper fears about life itself. For well over a century, the foods we eat in the West, like the spaces we inhabit, have been designed to filter out any reminders of our own mortality. We have constructed a physical and mental cordon sanitaire around ourselves, from which anything redolent of death and decay, putrefaction and rottenness – anything, in short, that might once have been celebrated as Carnivalesque – has been excluded. As a result, we live in a theatre of anxiety: in a world that feels under constant threat from the very things necessary for sustaining life.[39] We recoil from our own waste, because it reminds us too closely of what we are.

The Immaculate City

Fear of dirt, and the corresponding quest for purity, has deep roots in the West. It can be traced back to the Enlightenment, when a series of scientific revelations (Newtonian physics, Galileo's astronomy, Harvey's circulation of the blood) shifted the very basis of human understanding about the natural world. Philosophers such as Descartes began to argue that man, suitably armed with scientific knowledge and a rational brain, could do more than merely explain the world about him, he could control it. Henceforth, it seemed, nothing – nature, society, the universe – would be beyond the grasp of man's reason. The Enlightenment made its mark on every aspect of Western culture; not least on cities, whose overcrowded and decrepit state now sprang sharply into focus. Just as human bodies were starting to be seen as objects of science, cities were viewed as diseased. Like sick bodies, they needed to be surgically operated on: their rotten parts removed so that the healthy flesh could be saved.

Not only were cities in the nineteenth century under constant threat of pollution and disease, they were also full of social anxiety. In his book *Paris Sewers and Sewermen*, Donald Reid described how material and social fears combined in post-revolutionary Paris to create a city fraught with the danger of disruption 'from below': from the under-world of rejects – animal, vegetable, mineral and human – that it sought to suppress. Clogged up, decaying and disease-ridden, the city's sewers were multiply threatening: not merely a source of pollution, but the realm of an unruly and murderous underclass that might rise up at any minute and overwhelm the city. For Victor Hugo, the sewers were redolent of the city's moral turpitude:

> The sewer . . . is the conscience of the town where all things con-
> verge and clash. There is darkness here, but no secrets. Everything has
> its true, or at least its definitive form. There is this to be said for the
> muck-heap, that it does not lie . . . Every foulness of civilisation,
> fallen into disuse, falls into that ditch of truth . . .[40]

Hugo was not alone in conflating physical degradation with moral abjection. Four years' immersion among London's poor was enough to convince Henry Mayhew of the closeness of the 'connection between physical filthiness in public matters and moral wickedness'.[41] Hugo's Paris and Mayhew's London were cities on the brink, whose social and physical decrepitude would soon lead, in Reid's words, to 'unprece-dented efforts . . . to control and transform the subterranean'.[42]

In the case of Paris, the efforts were chiefly those of Baron Georges Haussmann, Prefect of the Seine to Napoleon III, and the driving force behind arguably the most radical transformation ever visited on a European capital. Enjoined by his emperor to impose some sort of order on the city, Haussmann set about the task he described as that of making Paris 'the Imperial Rome of our time' with ruthless efficiency. He spent the years from 1852 to 1870 ripping the medieval city to shreds, slicing through its ancient fabric with a series of imposing neoclassical boulevards of truly epic proportions, each running above an equally impressive sewer. The mastermind behind the subterranean half of the enterprise was Haussmann's chief engineer Eugène Belgrand, who not only pioneered many of the techniques later used by Bazalgette, but faced a far sterner test than his British counterpart, since the flow of the Seine was too feeble to flush out his sewers. Consciously following the example of Marcus Agrippa, Haussmann worked with his engineer to construct a system of aqueducts (including, aptly enough, connections to several ancient Roman ones) so that the sewers could be flushed out artificially.

The 'Haussmannisation' of Paris was a remarkable achievement, but its engineered bravura hid a darker side. Haussmann's sweeping demolitions, ostensibly necessary to construct the sewer network, served the dual purpose of making the capital far easier to control, allowing troops to shoot down boulevards at long range, and seal off entire sections of the city from one another. What was apparently a scheme to establish material order in the city masked the imposition on it of a martial one.

Whatever the motives behind its transformation, the Paris of Haussmann marked the industrial city's coming of age. As the crumbling infrastructures of the *Ancien Régime* gave way, a new urban order was emerging – zoned, serviced, controlled – that would provide the blueprint for urban planning in the future: indeed, it formed the basis of the modern discipline. From now on, the constituent parts of cities would be separated out, so that those intended for work and play, rich and poor, clean and dirty would have their allotted places. The traditional mixed-use approach to city-building, in which all of human life existed on the same street, would be dismissed as old-fashioned, inefficient, *dirty*. With iron hearts and bowels of stone, cities would henceforth present themselves as rational, autonomous machines. Their inner workings, like those of the body, would remain hidden. Purged of their ordure, cities would be spared any reminder of their organic natures. In place of pigs and chickens in back yards, there would be landscaped parks and gardens: empty reminders of the natural world to bring the old pastoral fantasies back to life.[43]

Flawless Food

In the same way that Western cities have been purged of organic content, so the food we eat increasingly appears and behaves as if it were inorganic. Our quest for purity in the West has led to a demand for visually perfect food, and public acceptance of denatured, tasteless produce. Since that is what the food industry is ideally suited to producing, it is only too happy to indulge us, weeding out 'ugly' fruit and disguising bits of dead cow in order not to offend our sensibilities.

The removal from the food chain of what is perfectly edible food has created a whole secondary industry in the West. Our demand for meat with no discernible relationship to anything furry, feathery or fluffy, for instance, has spawned an industry entirely devoted to using up unwanted body parts, involving everything from the making of hamburgers (100 per cent 'pure' beef – just don't ask which bits) to the ultimate perversion of feeding dead animals back to themselves. As our willingness to pay for meat has dwindled along with our soaring demand, the livestock industry has increasingly relied on this secondary source of profit, finding ways to dispose of the meat and offal we refuse to eat, but which other cultures (and creatures) eat quite happily. The visual and conceptual sanitising of food is not limited to animals either: vegetables are also subjected to a beauty parade to ensure they match our aesthetic expectations. One report in the *Observer* found that in order to pass muster at Sainsbury's, Cox apples had to be between 60 and 90mm across and 30 per cent red, so that 12 per cent of perfectly good apples were rejected at source.[44]

Not only does our susceptibility to visual seduction create a vast amount of 'pre-waste' in the food chain, it creates waste at the other end too. We may no longer witness the slaughter of thousands of oxen at the dedication of a temple, but orgiastic food displays (with all the wastefulness that entails) still have the power to move us. In many ways, supermarket aisles overstuffed with goodies have replaced the groaning tables of banquets past. They rely for their effect, as did public feasts of old, on theatrical display, and a real or implied profligacy. Unlike street markets, where the selling-off of leftover food at the end of the day is all part of the theatre, supermarkets strive for the illusion of uniform, unsullied freshness. To admit that some of the food might be getting a bit 'iffy' would destroy the entire effect. Although some supermarkets do put food near its sell-by date discreetly on offer, most prefer to dispose of it on the quiet, either giving it away to charities, or, more commonly, simply throwing it away.

Even Whole Foods Market, the latest 'organic' food retail sensation to hit Britain from America, feels the need to display produce as if it were at a fashion show.[45] Its gleaming pyramids of flawless, polished aubergines and perfect, plump tomatoes look more like the food of immaculate conception than anything that might have come out of the ground. Despite the company's ethical roots and what it calls its 'uniquely mission-driven' stance, its great skill is in the theatre of superabundance, not in helping us get down and dirty with a knobbly carrot. The theme is carried through every aspect of the company's display techniques. In the flagship New York store, shelved foods, such as the myriad trays of packaged meats prepared 20 different ways, are invisibly replenished via sliding back-panels, from which white-gloved hands emerge to whisk away the old and bring in the new with conjuror-like legerdemain. The trays are kept full to the brim right until the store closes, sending out the message that this is food that will never run out, never go off, never let you down.

It is only when we get the food home that the illusion starts to wear off. Out of its carefully nurtured chill-chain, supermarket food rapidly starts to reassume its organic properties – and to reveal the effects of having had them suppressed. Soft fruit in particular does not lend itself well to the rigours of modern food delivery, and is often picked unripe so that it is not bruised in transit. As a result, visually stunning peaches that entice us with their comely blush turn out to have flesh like cannonballs, going straight from rock-hard to rotten without ever passing 'Go'. Untimely ripp'd from the bough, they are the fleshly victims of our desire for food that is beyond nature; that bears no scar of ever having lived.

Bin Bounty

Beautiful peaches you can't eat, wastebins full of things you could: something is rotten in the state of modern gastronomy. A quick glance downwards is enough to warn many of us that the way we eat is not doing our bodies much good; the fact that it is not doing the planet much good either is equally evident, once you know where to look. Not only are we chomping our way through reserves of oil, soil, forests and aquifers that have taken millions of years to develop, we are not even making good use of them as we do so. Almost *half* the edible food in the USA, worth an estimated $75 billion a year, is wasted; a worrying statistic whichever way you look at it, and one that doesn't take into account the most damaging waste of all: the food that people *do* eat, but would be much better off if they didn't.[46]

The modern food industry is a business; not the planet's caretaker. So long as its bottom line remains unaffected, it is content. Worse still, the industry is dedicated to overproduction, because it has discovered that, with a little persuasion, it can expand an apparently limited market just that little bit further. Viewed as a closed-loop system, all excess is waste. Viewed as a business opportunity, it is potential profit.

As termini of the industrial food supply chain, supermarkets are like badly designed valves. Since their scale allows them to buy food virtually at cost, a degree of operational wastage is preferable to losing customers because of empty shelves. The same applies to the food service sector. Caterers find it easier to buy cheap raw ingredients in bulk with a generous margin for error, rather than aim for higher quality and waste less. Hardly surprising, then, that British supermarkets sent half a million tonnes of edible food to landfill in 2005, and the food sector as a whole some 17 million tonnes.[47] In 1994, the homeless charity Crisis set up a subsidiary, FareShare, with the aim of redirecting some of that waste to the four million or so people in Britain who cannot afford to eat properly. In 2005, the charity managed to recover 2,000 tonnes of edible food from supermarkets and caterers – an impressive enough haul, but one that, when set against the millions of tonnes wasted in Britain, remains a drop in the ocean. Charities such as FareShare face an uphill struggle, not least because of the complexities of modern food logistics. Safety regulations mean they must reject certain foods such as shellfish outright, and they have to operate their meals-on-wheels service like emergency ambulance-drivers, rushing in order not to break the chill-chain that has kept the food they are trying to save 'fresh' from wherever in the world it has come from.

Not only are the scale and methods of modern food supply wasteful, they bedevil the attempts of those who would try to salvage something from the wreckage. However, for one group of urban consumers, the rules that govern food waste are there to be broken. In cities of old, the poor and sick once gathered at the gates of monasteries to be fed; now 'freegans' gather after dark in supermarket car parks to share out the bounty of the black bins.[48] In one sense, freeganism is nothing new – people have lived off other people's waste for centuries – but unlike their spiritual forebears, many freegans are highly educated, articulate individuals, whose way of life is a deliberate protest against the wastefulness of Western industrial society. The freegans' message is a powerful one, but as they themselves acknowledge, their approach presents no solution to the human dilemmas of scale. If we all ate like freegans, there would be nothing left for freegans to eat, and, *reductio ad absurdum*, there would be no cities, either. We would, literally, have to go back to living in forests.

One-Way Cities

As an environmental catastrophe, industrial civilisation is a work in progress: well on the way to meltdown, but not quite close enough yet to tarnish its gas-guzzling fatal attraction. It is not only the bosses of agribusiness who prefer to ignore the future. If life is good enough, we all have a tendency to fiddle while Rome burns. Quite where our one-way lifestyles will lead us remains to be seen; but luckily we do not have to wait to get a good idea, because we have the entire history of urban civilisation at our disposal.

The earliest Mesopotamian city-states provide what a geography teacher might describe as the perfect worked example of a one-way civilisation. Irrigating their otherwise barren hinterlands with mineral-rich water from the hills worked perfectly well for many centuries. But critically what Ur, Uruk and the rest failed to do was to drain their land sufficiently. As river water evaporated on the plains, it left behind salty deposits that over hundreds of years began to salinise the soil, gradually reducing its fertility. During the third millennium BC, the Sumerian diet shifted from wheat to barley, a crop more able to withstand a salty soil, and poets began to refer ominously to the 'whiteness of the fields'.[49] From that time on, surviving records reveal the cities' increasingly desperate struggle for food, with land put under continuous production rather than being allowed to lie fallow, and yields at just a fifth of what they had been 800 years before. By the seventeenth century BC, Sumerian city-states were all abandoned, and the world's first urban experiment was at an end.

The city-states of ancient Greece faced a similar problem to those of Sumeria, with local soils unsuited to the large-scale growing of grain. However, the Greeks faced the additional problem of hilly terrain. Initial forest clearances to make way for grazing during the Bronze Age had already caused a degree of soil erosion, but when heavier clearances were made in the fourth century BC in order to grow wheat, they denuded the landscape to such an extent that it became virtually barren. Surveying the Attican hills, Plato lamented the change in them he had witnessed in his own lifetime: 'What is left now,' he wrote, 'is, so to say, the skeleton of a body wasted by disease; the rich, soft soil has been carried off and only the bare framework of the district left.'[50] Had Athens had to rely on its local hinterland to feed it, it would have faced the same lingering death as its Mesopotamian predecessors. Athens, of course, was spared by the sea, across which it not only imported food, but exported people to found new colonies abroad.

In ancient Greece and Mesopotamia, what appeared at first to be successful strategies for survival turned out to have long-term defects impossible to reverse. In both cases, the catastrophe was clearly visible:

poets and philosophers gazing out from the city walls could see the denuded landscapes for themselves. But in the case of the greatest one-way city in history, things were rather different. The only physical evidence of his own consumption a Roman citizen would have seen from his back yard would have been the bulk of Mons Testaceus, Rome's 54-metre-high 'eighth hill' to the south of the city, made out of all the shattered amphorae and *testae* that brought oil and grain from Spain and Africa.[51] Far from being barren, the city's local hinterland flourished with all the fruit and vegetables, poultry and game the market-gardening practitioners of *pastio villatica* could squeeze out of it. It took an educated eye to see that all this luxury farming must have its invisible counterpart elsewhere. As the poet Martial drily observed, Egypt had once sent its winter roses to Rome; now Rome produced its own roses, and relied on Egypt for its grain.[52]

Due to its unparalleled command of logistics and military might, Rome found a way, for a while at least, of having its cake and eating it. It pioneered the expansionist model of urban consumption, spreading its load further and further afield as its needs increased. In the end, it was not the lack of food that did for Rome so much as a lack of interest: the effort of maintaining its overextended supply chains meant that at their furthest extremities they were manned by foreign soldiers who had never laid eyes on the city and frankly weren't bothered if they ever did. Having stretched itself to the furthest reaches of the map, the concept of Rome imploded like an overfilled balloon.

Rome's rise and fall have long been favourite topics among urban theorists. Opinions differ about the precise nature of the city's demise, but whatever its political and military position before its fall, the nutritional writing was already on the wall. Egypt and North Africa, Rome's breadbaskets for some 500 years, were nearing the end of their useful lives. Centuries of intensive monoculture had depleted their soils; deforestation had permanently altered their climates. Writing in AD 250, St Cyprian, Bishop of Carthage, described a land plundered to the point of exhaustion: 'The world has grown old and does not remain in its former vigour. It bears witness to its own decline . . . The husbandman is failing in his fields. Springs that once gushed forth liberally now barely give a trickle of water.'[53]

What makes Rome's experience so pertinent now is not the nature of its end, but its attitude towards feeding itself at its height. Its aberrational scale allowed Rome to act independently of the natural checks that governed other cities. Like a greedy child in a chocolate factory, it gorged itself unthinkingly, becoming consumed by the very act of consumption. No longer required by the mores of society, restraint and abstinence became a matter of individual choice. Like so many modern Hollywood stars, the great and powerful took to presenting themselves as having next to no appetite. The fourth-century AD *Historia Augusta*, an ancient exercise in political spin, insisted that Septimius Severus was 'partial to greens from his own land and occasionally enjoyed drinking wine; often he did not even bother to sample the meat that was served'.[54] Diet fads, like obesity, are symptoms of a food culture out of kilter.

Despite the many similarities between Roman patterns of consumption and our own, there is one crucial difference. Rome had the luxury of an expanding world; we don't. As it happens, Rome ran out of infrastructure before it ran out of food, but evidence suggests it was a close-run thing. To the inhabitants of late-eighteenth-century Britain, that was a sobering thought. The first nation in Europe to possess a capital comparable in size to Rome, the British were encountering food supply problems of a similar nature for the first time. Casting a mathematical eye over the swollen metropolises of his day, the English political economist Thomas Robert Malthus did a simple calculation, and came up with a gloomy prediction. In his 1798 *Essay on the Principle of Population*, he argued that 'population must always be kept down to the level of the means of subsistence', and that since human populations increased geometrically, while agricultural outputs only did so arithmetically, mankind would eventually run out of available land, and was so doomed to run out of food. Only some reduction in numbers, through war, pestilence or voluntary 'moral restraint' could save man from this inevitable end.

The impact of Malthus's pessimistic tract was widespread and profound. Among his many admirers was Charles Darwin, who later used Malthus's ideas to help formulate his own theory of natural selection, applying it not just to mankind, but to all living creatures. But not everyone was so impressed. Malthus's critics, whose ranks swelled almost from the moment his ink dried, argued that he had left something essential out of the equation: mankind's ingenuity. Man, they said, would not starve, because he would adapt, either by limiting his consumption for the common good, or by finding ways to increase agricultural yields. Since faith in artificial fertiliser was by no means universally shared (most notably not by its own inventor, Justus von Liebig), opinions differed as to quite how the latter was to be achieved. However, the cheery consensus was that somehow, man would be saved by his ability to think his way out of trouble.

Two centuries later, the debate continues. Malthus's detractors and supporters have both scored victories since his day. The mass starvation he predicted for the mid nineteenth century never took place, thanks largely to monocultural grain production fuelled by artificial fertiliser; on the other hand, the world's two most populous countries – India and China – have felt the need to adopt population-limiting policies aimed at effecting the same results as Malthus's 'moral restraint'. Opinions still differ over whether population control, technology or a new-found selflessness will save mankind. One thing, however, is clear. All that we have achieved by tearing up rainforests and dumping chemicals on the ground is to postpone the Malthusian question. What we have not done is make it go away.

'Pecunia Non Olet'

> We never exercise, or should never exercise a *besoin* as pure loss. It should be put to use as manure.
>
> Jeremy Bentham[55]

Of all bad habits, those to do with food can be the hardest to crack. The past is littered with examples of cities that one way or another have eaten themselves to death. Of course, civilisations fail for many reasons: lack of knowledge, climate change, shifting political allegiances, even sheer bad luck can spell their end. But as Jared Diamond argued in his recent book *Collapse*, it is often the choices people make in the light of clear evidence that seal their fate – even when the facts that could have saved them were staring them in the face.[56] What makes the study of past civilisations so grimly fascinating is the discovery that the dilemmas we face are nothing new. The struggle to survive is part of the human condition, along with a certain blindness to its consequences. Unless you happen to have shares in agribusiness, the signs that our industrialised food systems are flawed – that we are well on the way to Malthusian meltdown – are about as unambiguous as you could get. Yet like so many civilisations before us, we fail to see the problem, because we have trained ourselves for centuries not to see it.

In the same way that other people's doomed love affairs are easier to dissect than one's own, we can talk endlessly about how the Romans got it wrong, without seeing the same faults in ourselves. But not even the all-consuming Romans were blind to the value of their waste. *Popinae*, as we saw, were cookshops that sold leftover meat from temples, and Roman agronomists were enthusiastic about the benefits of using night soil as fertiliser. But the most blatant use of waste was by the emperor Vespasian, who raised funds by imposing a tax on urine from public latrines. Suetonius reports that when the emperor's son Titus complained that such a tax was not seemly, his father asked him to sniff the money to see whether it smelled bad. '*Pecunia non olet*' – money does not smell – became Vespasian's most famous axiom.[57]

Even post-industrial cities have occasionally shown an enlightened attitude towards waste. Nineteenth-century Cincinnati, dubbed 'Porkopolis' as we saw due to its meat-packing activities, gave its hogs the freedom of the city, allowing them to roam about at will, while citizens were required by law to throw their food waste into the middle of the street to make it easier for the hogs to eat. As one English visitor remarked in 1832, 'If I determined upon a walk up the main street, the chances were five hundred to one against my reaching the shady side without brushing by a snout fresh dripping from the kennel.'[58]

Yet of all nineteenth-century cities, the one that really bucked the trend was Paris. Although Haussmann's sewers purged the capital extremely effectively, the Seine did not flow strongly enough to carry the waste away, and for 45 miles downstream of the city it was a black and bubbling morass. The solution to this latest threat from 'below' would vindicate the pleadings of those such as Liebig and Chadwick who had argued in vain for the re-use of London's waste. Their French counterpart was Pierre Leroux, a prominent social philosopher whose 'circulus' theory of 1834 was written in direct refutation of Malthus. In it, Leroux declared that since humans were producers as well as consumers, if they would only recycle their own waste, they need never run out of food. Leroux's theory had long exposed him to ridicule in France, but while licking his wounds in exile in Jersey, he found a powerful convert in Victor Hugo, who became so convinced of Leroux's arguments that he broke off from the narrative thread of *Les Misérables* to philosophise on the subject:

> Do you know what all this is – the heaps of muck piled up on the streets during the night, the scavengers' carts and the foetid flow of sludge that the pavement hides from you? It is the flowering meadow, green grass, marjoram, thyme and sage, the lowing of contented cattle in the evening, the scented hay and the golden wheat, the bread on your table and the warm blood in your veins – health and joy and life.[59]

In 1867, five years after *Les Misérables* was published, the sanitary engineer A. Mille, already a convert to sewage filtration, persuaded his boss Eugène Belgrand to try it out in Paris. At an experimental farm at Clichy, Mille showed how irrigating the sandy soil with waste water not only filtered the water so effectively that it emerged purer than if it had been treated with chemicals, but rendered the land extremely fertile. Mille's first experimental crop, consisting of 27 varieties of vegetable, had a market value six times greater than the grain previously grown on the site, and was of such high quality that it earned compliments at the 1867 Universal Exposition. The results delighted Chadwick, who had supported Mille's experiments and defended him against those who objected to the idea of raising crops on sewage-enriched land:

> An Academician pronounced it to be gross, and unfit for the food of cattle. I appealed from the judgment of the Academician to the

judgment of the cow on the point. A cow was selected, and sewaged and unsewaged grass was placed before it for its choice. It preferred the sewaged grass with avidity, and it yielded its final judgment in superior milk and butter of increased quantity.[60]

Soon it was not only cows that approved of sewaged grass. With the discovery that porous sandy soil could both purify foul water and be made fertile in the process, political economists had found their philosopher's stone. It seemed that shit really could be turned into gold. In 1869, Mille and his assistant Alfred Durand-Claye set up the world's first municipal sewage treatment works at Gennevilliers, a sleepy little town across the river from Clichy. In order to overcome local resistance to the works, they offered 40 local farmers the chance to cultivate the irrigated land for nothing. By the following year, the engineers were inundated with requests from farmers for the right to irrigate their own land with sewage water. Results were so remarkable that Napoleon III felt compelled to make a visit to the sewage farm, arriving incognito, but leaving with armfuls of juicy vegetables. By 1900, there were 5,000 hectares of land under irrigation at Gennevilliers, each receiving 40,000 cubic metres of sewage water a day and capable of growing 40,000 heads of cabbage, 60,000 artichokes, or 200,000 pounds of sugar beet each per year. The water was used to soak the roots of crops, never touching their stems or leaves, and was found to be pure enough after filtration to be drawn off for domestic use. Gennevilliers was transformed from a one-horse town into Paris's horticultural supplier of choice, with the city's best hotels eager for its produce, and visitors coming out on day trips to marvel at the 'veritable gardens of Eden'.[61]

It is curious that Gennevilliers was the product of one of the most ruthless purges of any city in history – that the Haussmannisation of Paris should have demonstrated how the golden age of urban ecology could be replicated in the post-industrial era. Yet the fact that Paris's circulatory experiment was the combined result of military strategy, sanitary reform and the accident of geography did not detract from its underlying message. Contemporary authorities in Berlin didn't think so, anyway. In 1878, Berlin abandoned the chemical treatment of its waste in favour of sewage farms along Parisian lines. By the turn of the

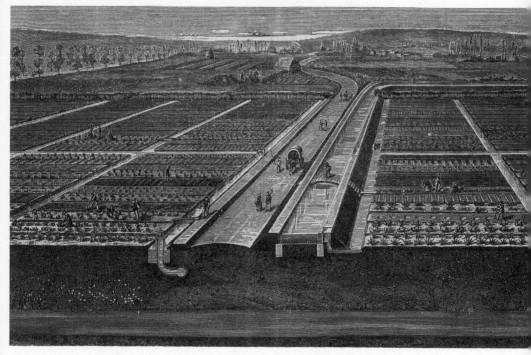

'Veritable gardens of Eden.' Gennevilliers in the 1870s.

century, the city had 6,800 hectares of municipal farms under irrigation, with 3,000 farmers and their families living in rent-free cottages on them.[62] Contemporary commentators declared the farms to be a living vision of utopia. Some are still in use today, as an integral part of Berlin's waste management and water purification systems.

Cyclical Cities

Living in the urbanised West, the fact that the cities we inhabit are part of an organic continuum can be hard to grasp. Since we appear to live independently of nature, worrying about our waste can seem irrelevant; cranky, even. In Britain, we have never been overly fussed by the matter in any case. Food and raw materials have come too easily to us; and the sea has always been there to dump stuff into when we're done with it. As a result, our throwaway culture is one of the most entrenched in Europe. In 2007, only Ireland and Greece sent more

278

waste per capita to landfill.[63] But however hard we try to ignore it, the issue of waste refuses to go away. Indeed, after a century or so of suppression, it is making a comeback in Western cities, threatening us once more with the danger of contamination 'from below'. As a House of Commons Select Committee put it in 2007:

> A little over ten years ago, 84 per cent of our municipal waste – the refuse councils collect from homes and businesses, parks and street bins – went to fill holes in the ground; a little over ten years from now, at present rates, there will, it is estimated, be no such holes left to fill.[64]

We need to change our ways in Britain; not just because of the lack of holes, but to avoid punitive fines from the EU Landfill Directive, which from 2010 will impose stiff penalties on us if its targets are not met.[65] But as the days of chucking stuff into the ground draw to a close in Britain, we find ourselves caught between a rock and a mushy place. Unlike nineteenth-century Berliners, we Britons have neither the zeal nor the infrastructure for recycling. The introduction in 2006 of fortnightly bin collections – the government's latest attempt to make us recycle more – simply caused widespread outrage, as the spectre of rat-infested, rotting garbage on the streets signalled a return to the horrors of the nineteenth-century city.

It is no accident that Austria, and not Britain, is the recycling champion of Europe. A landlocked, mountainous country, it has of necessity had to develop a very different attitude towards waste, and in the 1980s, the capital, Vienna, reached a point when its outgoings had nowhere left to go. The city began to collect biowaste separately, composting it in municipal depots and using it to fertilise suburban farming schemes, as well as handing the compost back to citizens for their own use. By 2000, the city was composting 90,000 tonnes of organic waste a year, enough to grow half the food for its hospitals, saving an estimated £5 million annually.[66] Today, 60 per cent of Austria's domestic rubbish is recycled, with every household obliged to sort it into four separate categories: glass, organic, paper and mixed. In Vienna, the remainder is burnt in a high-tech incinerator that by 2008 is expected to heat two thirds of the city's homes. The fact that the incinerator is as highly decorated as Crossness Pumping Station sends out its own message. For the Viennese, treating waste is once more a matter of municipal pride.

Contemporary Vienna, like nineteenth-century Paris, has had a waste epiphany. Faced with the horror of pollution in its own back yard, the city took a momentous decision, only to discover that what it feared most was in fact a cash cow in disguise. Because the city had clogged up, it experienced a seismic shift in thinking that has altered its entire relationship with waste. Donald Reid's remarks, referring to post-revolutionary Paris, could equally well describe Vienna's recent past: 'The danger to civilisation came from unthinking repression of waste; only by processing this waste could society conquer its anxieties and turn to profit the hidden worth of what it rejected.'[67]

It is no accident that the nineteenth century was the great age of debate about waste. Cities then were on the cusp; at a moment of transition from their pre-industrial, semi-rural status to their post-industrial, illusory autonomy. It was at that point that the scale of the issue became evident; that urban consumption revealed itself to be a global problem. Yet once the moment had passed, spirited away by bold engineering or temporary technologies, the crisis appeared to have been averted. A century and a half later, we know that not to have been the case.

Now that waste is back on the urban agenda, we face a tough physical challenge. The cities we live in do not lend themselves easily to recycling; on the contrary, most have been designed with the opposite in mind. Urban expansion has pushed up land values, making suburban market gardening economically unviable (those at Gennevilliers, for instance, ceased operation in the 1980s for that very reason). The fact that urban food supplies are no longer municipally controlled makes such schemes harder to replicate too. Then there is the organic purging of cities. Feeding scraps to pigs, the time-honoured method of choice, requires there to be pigs in the city – or at least nearby – to feed. Tottenham, for instance, used to be famous for its 'recycled' sausages, made from pigs fed on London scraps.[68] But there is little place for such cosy arrangements in modern food delivery. Even if the logistics could be made to work, EU regulations since the foot and mouth outbreak in 2001 have banned the practice of feeding leftovers to pigs, stipulating that food waste must either be composted or anaerobically digested, rather than fed directly to next Sunday's lunch. As with other aspects of the food chain, legislation geared towards industrial production often condemns small-scale practices that have worked perfectly well for centuries.

Waste is the by-product of life itself, and life these days has become mightily complicated. Yet, as the Austrians have demonstrated, with a bit of an effort, we can turn cities into reasonably effective recycling machines. We can invent new technologies to harness waste; make use of it to create new life. Yet when it comes to feeding cities, the real battle is not with what accumulates in them, but in controlling what arrives in the first place. The 'dirt' that pollutes our streets is as nothing to all the poison, pollution, destruction and depletion our food creates before it even reaches us – of which at least a third need never have taken place, since we don't even bother to eat the food when it gets here.

In the end, waste is a matter of attitude. It is in our nature only to value things we have to struggle for – what comes easily is easily tossed away. In Britain, our well-fed maritime lifestyles have allowed us to live oblivious to our place in the organic continuum; to pretend we play no part in a system that is both bigger and longer-lasting than ourselves. As was the case with ancient Rome, our part in the exchange is invisible to us – but that does not mean it is not there. In the global food chain, waste is the missing link: the vital element that makes or breaks the entire cycle. In order for the chain to function, every link must be joined, not just the last. Cities in the past were too aware of the value of food and its by-products to waste them. If they broke the organic cycle, it was because they lacked the knowledge to understand the long-term consequences of their consumption. We have no such excuses.

Chapter 7

Sitopia

'Digging for Victory', in 1942.

Dongtan, China

From the third-floor balcony of Shu-Li's flat in downtown Dongtan, I can see across the bay to the island of Heng Sha and beyond to the mainland city of Shanghai, its spiky skyline just discernible in the evening haze. Below me in the street, the neighbourhood is starting to come alive, as people return home from work, stopping at the food shops below to pick up something for dinner, or dropping in at the bar on the corner for a drink. Their voices carry up clearly from below, as does the spicy smell of fried fish, making me wish it was time for dinner. But apart from the friendly hubbub of trading, the street is relatively quiet. Most people here travel either on bike or on foot, and the one vehicle in the street – the electric tram – makes just a faint whine as it sets off for the suburbs on its rubberised wheels.

It is a typical July in Dongtan: steamy and humid, with just the slightest threat of thunder. Since it is not actually raining, I am under strict instructions from Shu-Li to water her plants, which are mainly vegetables: *hin choy*, or Chinese spinach, yard-long beans, and bitter melons. Standing on the balcony, I turn on the valve that will pipe nutrient-rich water to her plant-boxes. Shu-Li lives in one of the few downtown apartment blocks in Dongtan that has a food factory in its basement, which means she can receive the water directly from the municipality through a metered supply. The water used to be free of charge, but demand was so great that the city was forced to start charging for it. Leaning over the balustrade, I watch the last workers leave the building for the night: farmers emerging from the basement where they have spent the day tending the fruits and pulses that make up the bulk of factory-grown food in Dongtan.

I turn off the irrigator and get ready to go out – tonight I am meeting up with Shu-Li and some of her friends at the 'bunds', the sea defences that separate Dongtan from the wetlands that line its eastern seaboard. We are going to eat in one of the restaurants there that specialises in locally caught fish; a hangover from the days, not so long ago, when the only inhabitants of this part of the island were some local fishermen, a few farmers, and several hundred thousand nesting seabirds. The restaurant has a spectacular view, gazing out over the wetlands to the open sea, and I am looking forward to cooling off on its terrace. Opinions differ as to whether the giant offshore wind farm just to the north spoils the view. I must admit I was a bit shocked when I first saw it (the turbines are almost 70 metres tall), but now I am used to it, I find it rather beautiful. Somehow, when you visit Dongtan, you expect the unexpected. You know that you will be taking part in a working experiment: an exploration of low-carbon living never before attempted on such a scale. The first time I came, I remember some things seemed very strange – having to open the flat's passive cooling vents every night, sorting out the rubbish into six different streams, watering the plants with special water – but I soon got used to them. Other aspects of Dongtan continue to amaze me: its quietness, the amount of wildlife on the doorstep, and, of course, the super-fresh seafood . . .

OK, I confess. Dongtan doesn't really exist – at least not yet. But very soon it will. By the time its first phase is completed in 2020, it will be the world's first self-styled 'eco-city': an urban community of 80,000 souls, every detail of which will have been honed as far as possible to minimise its ecological impact. Commissioned by the Shanghai Industrial Investment Corporation (SIIC) in 2005, it is being designed by a London-based team at Arup, the engineering firm founded in 1946 by Ove Arup (the man responsible for, among other things, making the Sydney Opera House stand up), and now one of the largest inter-disciplinary design consultancies in the world. In terms of scale and ambition, Dongtan is arguably the most challenging project the firm has ever taken on. Apart from having to imagine what a twenty-first-century 'eco-city' might look like, the team are determined to preserve their environmentally sensitive site as far as possible. The eastern tip of Chongming island, 25 kilometres east of Shanghai, is one of the last remaining rural districts in the region, typical of the sort of landscape (and way of life) daily disappearing under the bulldozers all over China. But that won't be happening here. When Dongtan rises out of the ground, the farms, fishermen and birds are all staying put.

Dongtan is being designed according to the principles of what Arup calls 'integrated urbanism': a new approach to urban design that tries to balance the often competing demands of urbanisation – economic growth, social well-being, the environment – by creating 'virtuous cycles' that allow them to complement one another. A typical example is the 'village clusters' that form the basis of Dongtan's city plan, intended to encourage people to live, work and shop in the same neighbourhood, so reducing transport demands, as well as engendering the sort of mixed-use street life typical of traditional city centres. Another is the 'food factories' that will produce at least some of the city's food: multistorey buildings that will convert solar energy in order to power light-emitting diodes and grow several layers of crops at once, making use of nutrient-rich water recovered from the city's sewage. That is the theory, anyway – trials are still underway to find out quite how these high-rise farms à la Gennevilliers might work. With residential buildings up to eight storeys high, Dongtan will be relatively compact, with an average density of 75 dwellings per hectare: roughly that of a typical residential neighbourhood in central London.[1] The aim, in other words, is to make Dongtan both as eco-friendly and as pleasant to live in as possible, without sacrificing its essential urbanity: an aspiration that makes the city if not exactly utopian, at least a welcome contrast to the slash-and-burn approach to urbanisation taking place elsewhere in China and other parts of Asia.

So, how different will life in Dongtan be to that in a conventional city? Will its residents have to learn how to 'behave' properly in order for it to work? Not according to Alejandro Gutierrez, leader of the Arup design team, because by the time the city is built, the world will have become a different place. 'Two hundred years ago,' he says, 'people used to throw excrement into the street, and we laugh. In twenty years' time, we will say "People didn't have carbon credits?" and laugh.'[2] Apart from being extremely quiet due to all vehicles being electric, the city will also be noticeably verdant. A third of the buildings

Hope for a greener urban future? Dongtan Eco-City.

will have 'green roofs': roofs covered with vegetation to improve their thermal performance and help reduce rainwater run-off. Streets will also be planted with plenty of trees to provide shade. There are also plans to have food factories right in the city centre, so that, as Alejandro says, 'You will have agricultural workers coming into your building in the morning as you leave to go to work.' With a large offshore wind farm and photovoltaic cells mounted on rooftops, the city is expected to generate much of its own power. It also aims to become the world's first zero-waste city, with consolidation centres to strip out all incoming packaging and recycle it on the spot, and suburban eco-farms fertilised by municipal compost and waste water, the latter filtered through the gravel bunds that will fringe the coastal wetlands.

The first practical attempt to create a post-industrial city to exist in harmony with, rather than in opposition to, nature, Dongtan will create a new urban paradigm for the twenty-first century. Yet despite its eco-farms and food factories (not to mention its ready-made fishing fleet), there is one aspect of the city that its designers can't do as much about as they would like. Although some of Dongtan's food will be grown locally, the bulk of it will still have to come via conventional routes. The problem, according to the team's sustainability analyst Neil Grange, is that even if it were possible for the city to grow all its own food (which is doubtful) there would be no way of stopping people from buying cheaper food from elsewhere. In other words, although Arup is designing the physical fabric of Dongtan in great detail, it has little input into how the city will be run. 'Without being able to influence the management, there is a limit to what you can achieve,' says Grange. 'We would really like to make a greater link between design and operation – to have a sustainability management system in place – but that is up to the client, and the Chinese authorities.'[3] But management is not the only problem facing Arup in its struggle to reduce Dongtan's eco footprint. In order to build truly sustainably, Grange says, the team would need to be involved in the site selection process, so that it could analyse ecological efficiencies over an entire region.

And there is the rub. However low-carbon and idyllic Dongtan gets, the city will still be hooked up to a global supply system that is anything but. The city's residents will each have an ecological footprint of 2.4 global hectares: the area of land calculated to be necessary to provide all their food, water and energy needs, plus assimilate their waste emissions.[4] Although that is a lot less than the estimated 5.8 hectares currently required to sustain the average inhabitant of a conventional city (and a vast improvement on the 10 or so needed per urban American), it is still more than the 1.8 thought to be available for everyone on the planet.[5] Life in cities has always been more ecologically demanding than life lived directly on the land, not just because of our energy-hungry urban lifestyles, but because the food for cities necessarily has to come from elsewhere. The supply of food to European cities, for example, is currently estimated to account for up to 30 per cent of their total ecological footprint.[6] If we are to make cities really 'green', we need to rethink not just their physical form, but the way they are fed – no easy task in a globalised economy in which the food system is a highly consolidated, well-established, virtually autonomous network. Until we address that, building experimental food factories, while not exactly window dressing, is at best only dealing with part of the problem.

If even quasi-utopian cities like Dongtan can't get us living within our means, we are in trouble, because most cities currently being built are about as un-Dongtan-like as it is possible to get. Take Chongqing, for instance. Situated 1,600 kilometres west of Shanghai on the Yangtze River, Chongqing is China's fastest-growing municipality. With a population of 31 million it has more residents than Malaysia, and is gaining a further half a million every year.[7] Drawing energy from the controversial Three Gorges Dam, the city is an industrial powerhouse, churning out cars and electrical goods as if there were no tomorrow – which, if cities like it are to be the urban future, there probably won't be. Despite the nearby dam, many of Chongqing's factories are run on coal, and the city is blanketed in a choking smog that causes thousands of premature deaths every year. None of the city's 3,500 tonnes of daily rubbish is recycled, going instead to a vast landfill crater that swallows a volume of waste the size of two Albert Halls every week.[8] Set against Chongqing, Dongtan seems about as significant as the tiny fishing village it is itself about to swallow up. Which is not to say that Dongtan is not a Good Thing. Clearly, in the general run of things, it is. It is just a very *small* good thing in the midst of an evolving ecological catastrophe so vast that it has got even the Chinese authorities worried. As Zhenhua Xie, China's Minister of the State Environmental Protection Agency, put it, 'China's current development is ecologically unsustainable, and the damage will not be reversible once higher GDP has been achieved.'[9]

It is not the urbanisation of China that is tragic, but the manner of it. All the mistakes of the West repeated, but on a vastly greater scale and at 10 times the speed. Of course, not everyone in the world will end up living in cities. Somebody, after all, will have to do the farming. But unless we find a new urban model, we are soon going to run out of planet. This brings us back to the question this book started with – the question people have been asking themselves ever since someone had the bright idea of trying to eat grass. How on earth are we going to keep this thing going?

Utopia

Born of a new kind of food, the first cities represented man's emancipation from brute survival – the start of what we call civilisation. Yet the freedom they brought was never complete. Beneath the surface of urbanity, the contract between man and land never changed. As our chosen habitat, cities express the inner contradictions of the human condition. They provide us with shelter, but not sustenance. They give us space to dream, yet obscure our place in the natural order. Neither good nor evil, cities represent the messy imperfectability of human life. For better or worse, they are our common home, and it is up to us to make them work. Going back to living in forests is not an option.

How to satisfy our basic needs while leaving space for higher pursuits? How to share the burden and rewards of labour equably? How to achieve individual freedom and collective justice? These are the dilemmas that have taxed philosophers since ancient times, and they remain embedded in Western political thought. As abstractions, they also find tangible expression in the utopian tradition. 'Utopia' is a philosophical ruse; a parallel universe whose chief purpose is to ask what an ideal society, unfettered by the constraints of the real world, might be like. By its very nature, utopia is an unachievable paradigm, but it can be used to inspire a vision of a better society, set within real conditions.

The idea of utopia, meaning either 'no place' (from the Greek *ou-topos*) or 'good place' (from *eu-topos*), was first used by Plato, and was adopted by Sir Thomas More in 1516, as a deliberately ambiguous title for his fictional realm. More's Utopia was an island kingdom, accidentally discovered by a Portuguese mariner, consisting of 54 city-states all more or less the same, each arranged so as to give plenty of room to its neighbours, yet close enough so as to be no more than a day's walk away. The capital city, Amaurotum, was situated on a tidal river, and was square in plan, divided into quarters, each with its own market square. The city streets were broad and lined with terraced houses, arranged to form urban blocks with generous back gardens, in which the inhabitants loved to work:

They're extremely fond of these gardens, in which they grow fruit, including grapes, as well as grass and flowers. They keep them in wonderful condition – in fact, I've never seen anything to beat them for beauty or fertility. The people . . . are keen gardeners not only because they enjoy it, but because there are inter-street competitions for the best kept garden.[10]

The utopian obsession with growing things did not end there. Children were taught the art of farming from an early age, and all citizens – men, women and children – took turns working in the fields, spending a mandatory two years on the land during their lifetimes. Those who enjoyed farming (which many did) could volunteer to do extra time if they liked. All land and property was held in common, and working hours were short: Utopians laboured for just six a day, leaving plenty of time for other pursuits. Local communities were close-knit, and families came together regularly for communal meals in community halls, in which adults and children sat next to one another in table messes.

With its frugal work ethic and monkish dining arrangements, the monastic influence in *Utopia* is clear. But as well as being intensely religious, More was a humanist, and his Utopians were fond of a joke, regarding 'the enjoyment of life – that is, pleasure – as the natural object of all human efforts'.[11] More's mode of address – ironic, humorous and serious by turns – was partly a device to protect him. As he was well aware, questioning the status quo under Henry VIII was a potentially lethal pastime. Yet his *Utopia* not only succeeded in delivering a stinging critique of the injustices of his own day; it also painted a vision of a better society – compassionate, tolerant, communist in the broadest sense – that has influenced every utopian vision since.

Paradise Lost

One of the most intriguing aspects of utopianism is the consistency of issues under discussion. Land and farming, city and country, work and leisure – the basic building blocks of theoretical societies are universal.

Yet there is one sort of utopia from which they are absent: the mythical lost paradise, which in its various guises (Arcadia, the Gardens of Eden and Hesperides) is common to all three Abrahamic religions and the ancient civilisations that preceded them. As an image of human dwelling, the idyllic and bountiful garden is clearly not of this world: it is a vision of man freed from necessity and labour. In short, it is a vision of the heaven he hopes one day to regain. That the mythical utopian timeline should start and end with a garden tells us a great deal about urban civilisation. At best, it has only ever been seen as a compromise.

The tension between abstract perfection and imperfect reality underpins all utopian thought. Even Plato, whose interest in mundane necessity was never marked, divided his ideal city-state into urban and rural plots, so that each citizen would receive two patches of land, one in the city, the other in the country. Although neither he nor Aristotle had much truck with farmers (their ideal cities were fed, like the real one in which they lived, by slaves), both philosophers were concerned with urban self-sufficiency. On these grounds, Aristotle criticised Plato's *Republic* for being too big, since it would require a 'territory as large as Babylon, or some other huge site, if so many people are to be supported in idleness'.[12] By this remark Aristotle did not mean to criticise idleness: on the contrary, both he and Plato considered an ideal community to be one in which citizens – but only them – were freed from the burden of labour, and so able to lead a contemplative life.[13]

It was Christianity that put labour firmly on the utopian agenda, where it has remained ever since. The question for early Christians was not how to construct society so that a chosen few could enjoy a contemplative life, but how to combine toil and contemplation in a virtuous one. The change in attitude was articulated by St Benedict in his Rule: 'Idleness is an enemy of the soul. Because this is so the brethren ought to be occupied at specified times in manual labour, and in other fixed hours in holy reading . . .'[14] Work, sleep, study and prayer were the activities bound into the fabric of early Christian monasteries. However, since neither of the two founding fathers of Western monasticism (St Augustine and St Benedict) specified what physical form their monasteries should take, it was up to individual abbots to extrapolate their rules as best they could. Monastery design therefore became an act of personal interpretation; a series of attempts to reflect Heavenly Jerusalem on earth. In the St Gall Plan, a ninth-century ideal monastery scheme thought to be the work of Bishop Hatto, a leading figure in Charlemagne's court, we see the search for perfection in progress. The parchment shows a rectangular precinct with most of the typical monastic elements: church and cloister, library, school and infirmary, kitchens, dining halls, guesthouses and cemetery. But surrounding them are a series of buildings that prompted Wolfgang Braunfels to call the St Gall Plan a 'Noah's Ark of a monastery': cowsheds and stables for oxen and pregnant mares, sheds for goats, sheep, pigs, geese and hens, a barn, a threshing floor, brewery and bakery.[15] The earliest surviving example of a planned utopia, the St Gall Plan represents the paradigm of a Christian life on earth to which medieval city-states would later aspire, presenting a vision for an ideal community that seemed, for a brief period at least, as if it might actually be attainable.

Back to the Land

For every utopian dream of an ideal city, there have been plenty more based on a rural existence. As we saw in the first chapter, the right to subsist on the land has always exercised political philosophers, particularly during periods of land enclosure, such as those of seventeenth-century England. While thinkers such as John Locke grappled with the problem in the abstract, another more practical kind of utopian simply grabbed a spade and started digging. In 1649, a group calling themselves the True Levellers (soon dubbed the rather catchier Diggers), announced their intention to 'dig up, manure, and sow corn' on a patch of common land at George Hill in Cobham, Surrey. As the group's leader, Gerrard Winstanley, explained, their intention was to level not only the enclosures that were carving up the countryside, but the social divisions that they represented. Anticipating both Locke and Rousseau, Winstanley argued that since God had 'made the Earth to be a common treasury, to preserve beasts, birds, fishes, and man', and that 'not one word was spoken in the beginning, that one branch of mankind should overrule another', all men had a common right to land.[16] He therefore proposed that the people of England should organise themselves into a series of self-supporting agrarian communes – an idea that, unsurprisingly, did not go down too well in Parliament after seven years of bloody civil war. The New Model Army was dispatched to deal with the Diggers, but after deciding they were relatively harmless, left it to local landlords to get rid of them.

With land in England in increasingly short supply, a new breed of settler utopian began to look to the New World to found its ideal colonies. The Pilgrim Fathers' 1620 landfall aboard the *Mayflower* was just the first of a series of invasions from all over Europe, many of them by extreme religious sects for whom the 'virgin' territories of North America promised the opportunity to build utopia for real. Although some, such as the Swiss Amish, founded successful agrarian communities, the majority found that having unlimited amounts of farmland at one's disposal was not much use without a sufficient labour force to farm it. According to the historian Niall Ferguson, between one half and two thirds of all Europeans who crossed the Atlantic from 1650 to 1780 did so under a system of 'indentured labour', pledging a number of years' service in exchange for the cost of the voyage.[17] The New World might have seemed like paradise on earth to some, but, as Ferguson pointed out, it was built on the backs of settlers who were little more than 'slaves on fixed-term contracts'.[18]

With colonisation of the Americas creating the labour shortages that would eventually give rise to full-blown slavery, the onset of industrialisation back home was creating a new breed of manufacturing utopian. Foremost among them was Robert Owen, a Welsh craftsman's son who made his father-in-law's cotton mill at New Lanark on the River Clyde into a model working community. Within a few years of taking control in 1799, Owen had turned an unruly and unwilling workforce into an eager, efficient brigade, simply by reducing their hours, registering their performance on coloured 'monitors' mounted on looms, and rewarding their efforts with good-quality housing, a school, and a non-profit company shop. New Lanark soon began to receive a stream of illustrious visitors, and Owen's pamphlets were read by world leaders including King George III, Thomas Jefferson and supposedly even Napoleon in exile on Elba.

Convinced that he had discovered the answer to the relief of the urban poor, Owen presented plans to the House of Commons for a number of ideal communities, 'villages of unity and mutual cooperation' in which 1,200 people would live and work together, surrounded by 1,500 acres of farmland.[19] The settlements were to be somewhat like secularised, industrialised monasteries, containing blocks of family houses, communal dining halls, a school, guesthouse, meeting rooms and library. Unfortunately for Owen, the official enthusiasm that had greeted his plans soon waned when it became a question of having to pay for them. Disappointed by this lukewarm response, Owen headed off on the well-worn utopian trail across the Atlantic, plunging most of his considerable fortune into setting up a prototype community, New Harmony in Indiana, incorporating 30,000 acres of land bought with his own money. Around 1,000 disciples went with him, but unfortunately most of them, unlike Thomas More's farming-mad Utopians, were scientists and academics, who spent two years bickering about how their inappropriately named community should be run, before their founder finally ran out of cash.

Owen's experience was far from unique. His brand of utopianism, like those of his French contemporaries Charles Fourier and Henri de Saint-Simon, was forged in the afterglow of the Enlightenment, when it seemed that science and design could come together to create not just an ideal human settlement, but a perfect society to go with it. Their utopias were of a new kind, intended not merely as contemplative exercises or satirical critiques, but as blueprints for a better future.[20] While Saint-Simon looked to science and industry to create a new social order, Fourier spent a (disappointed) lifetime refining plans for his *phalanstères*: large hotel-like buildings surrounded by farmland in which the inhabitants would be motivated purely by pleasure, only performing tasks that suited their personalities.[21] All three 'socialist utopians', as they were later dubbed by Marx, would have a lasting influence on Western thought, yet for all their insights, their combined legacy was one of paradox. By seeming to suggest that paradise might be achievable on earth, they effectively folded the utopian timeline back on itself. Their optimistic formulations suggested that some trans-formational medium would come along – science, rationality, man's rediscovery of his inner 'noble savage' – and resolve all the dilemmas of human existence. There was just one problem. What everyone seemed to forget in the rush to build heaven on earth was that it is only in the celestial variety that *nobody* has to do the farming.

News from Nowhere

According to their keenest student and harshest critic Karl Marx, the socialist utopians' proposals were 'necessarily doomed to failure', because they attempted to create a perfect world, rather than change the existing one.[22] Marx dismissed their schemes as 'pocket editions of the New Jerusalem', going so far as to write an open letter to Etienne Cabet, a French Owenite who, with his mentor's encouragement, had tried to set up a proto-communist society in Texas in 1847. Marx warned Cabet that his project would fail because of its isolation: '. . . a few hundred thousand people cannot establish and continue a com-munal living situation without it taking on an absolutely exclusive and sectarian nature'.[23]

What Marx had put his finger on was the fundamental problem dogging all 'activist' utopias: scale. Arguably the most influential utopian thinker of all time, Marx did not consider himself to be one, because for him, the only true utopia would come when the entire world, not just one part of it, was transformed by revolution. Like Adam Smith before him, Marx foresaw the way in which improve-ments in transport and communication – 'the annihilation of space through time', as he put it – would lead inevitably to globalisation:

> The need of a constantly expanding market for its products chases the bourgeoisie over the whole surface of the globe . . . In place of the old wants, satisfied by the production of the country, we find new wants, requiring for their satisfaction the products of distant lands and climes.[24]

Since capitalism would lead inexorably to the concentration of wealth among just a few, the only route to collective justice was the gradual dismantling of the entire system. In his *Communist Manifesto*, written with Friedrich Engels in 1848, Marx listed the 10 measures necessary 'in the most advanced countries' to get the ball rolling, including 'The abolition of property in land . . . equal liability of all to labour . . . the establishment of industrial armies, especially for agriculture . . . the combination of agriculture with manufacturing industries, and the general abolition of the distinction between town and country.'[25]

After Marx, utopians would no longer attempt to flee the world, but would try to change it from the ground up. A new batch of literary utopians took to imagining life under communism, among them William Morris, a pioneering British socialist, as well as one of the most gifted artist-craftsmen of his generation. Morris's utopia took the form of a futuristic fantasy, *News from Nowhere*, in which a time-traveller (also called William) wakes up in an England transformed by a short, bloody revolution into a proto-communist state. He discovers that all land and means of production are now held in common, but instead of a single centralised authority, the country is organised into a federation of independent local democracies. Exploring his native London, William finds many landmarks have disappeared under 'pleasant lanes' and meadows, culverts have been restored to 'bubbling brooks', and Trafalgar Square has been transformed into a sloping sunny orchard full of apricot trees, from which the Dung Market (formerly the Houses of Parliament) can be glimpsed.[26] 'I fairly felt as if I were alive in the fourteenth century,' comments Morris's astonished time-traveller, who finds as he wanders though this Wen-turned-idyll that the 'sham wants' of capitalism no longer exist, and that most people work in agriculture or handicrafts, doing whatever suits them best. Thanks to their countrified, creative lives, the people have carefree countenances that are 'frankly and openly joyous', and when William asks one man what motivates them to work, he is told, 'The reward of labour is *life*. Is that not enough?'[27]

Part committed Marxist and part Romantic, Morris expressed the dilemmas of socialist utopianism perfectly. Fully prepared for the bloody revolution he believed to be necessary in order to create a better future, his vision of a pastoral, crafts-based, retro-medieval society was nevertheless about as fanciful as utopianism gets. The nearest it came to being realised was the distinctly un-revolutionary Guild of Handicrafts, set up by Charles Robert Ashbee in the picturesque Cotswold village of Chipping Campden in 1902. Like so many visionaries of his age, Morris's idealism was based on a fantasy in which his own talents and preferences would be shared by the world at large. Unfortunately for him, the world had other ideas. However, there was one man who shared enough of his vision to bring at least some of it to reality. That man was Ebenezer Howard, and his utopia was one of the vanishingly few ever to be even partially realised – the Garden City.

Garden Cities

Perhaps the best-known utopia after those of Plato and More, the Garden City is arguably the most consistently misinterpreted of the three. Frequently cited as the inspiration behind the leafy suburbia that spread through Britain like a virulent weed during the early twentieth century, Garden Cities were originally intended to be precisely the opposite: a network of small, independent, self-sufficient city-states, connected to one another by railway. So how did the confusion come about, and why has it stuck? The answer goes back to the crinkle in the utopian timeline created by the socialist utopians. Howard's use of the word 'garden' in his title simply triggered the Arcadian dream latent in every Victorian city-dweller, now seemingly brought within reach by the railways. Suburbia, for most people, *was* a garden city – at least as close to one as they cared to get. Howard's title overtook his vision, which is a shame, because 100 years on, *Garden Cities of To-morrow* remains one of the most persuasive and inspiring utopian tracts ever written.

A mild and modest man, Ebenezer Howard was an unlikely figure to bear the 'visionary' tag. After a formative period in America in his early twenties during which he discovered, among other things, that he was not cut out to be a farmer, he spent the rest of his life in London working as a parliamentary stenographer.[28] Hardly the stuff of legend;

yet arguably it was Howard's unshowy personality and day job that made him the perfect vessel to absorb all the influences of his age and combine them into a vision that had something in it for everyone. First outlined in a pamphlet of 1898 entitled *To-morrow: A Peaceful Path to Real Reform*, his Garden-City concept was an amalgam of almost every utopian idea going, from Plato and More, via Owen, to Marx and Morris. Remarkably, Howard managed to turn this improbable smorgasbord into a proposal of such coherence and appeal that it won the immediate backing of the sort of convert of whom most utopians can only dream: captains of industry with plenty of cash. Within months, Howard had set up his Garden Cities Association with the heavyweight support of Lord Leverhulme, Joseph Rowntree and the Cadburys.

In 1902, Howard republished his concept as *Garden Cities of To-morrow*, the title by which it would become both famous and commonly misapprehended. The book contained detailed proposals for what Howard called his 'town–country magnet': a Garden City that would combine the benefits of town and country living, while neutralising the disadvantages of both.[29] The 'magnet' was effectively a city-state that would occupy 6,000 acres of land, of which 1,000 would be built up and the rest cultivated. Crucially, all the land would be owned by the community and held in trust on its behalf, with all rents going to run the city and fund public works. This would mean that as land values rose, it would be the city, and not individual landowners, that would get rich. The close bond between city and country would ensure that there was a thriving agricultural estate, which would benefit from a secure market for its produce, as well as receiving waste from the town to increase the soil's fertility.[30]

Howard's economic ideas were radical, but it was his urban design that really caught the public imagination. Here was another irony: Howard, who was no designer, made it clear from the start that his plans were 'merely suggestive, and will probably be much departed from'.[31] Nevertheless, with the true instincts of a salesman, he took great pains to describe his ideal city, laid out in a spacious series of concentric rings, with boulevards of 'very excellently built houses', a large central public park bounded by a 'Crystal Palace' (a sort of circular winter-garden-cum-shopping-arcade), and a tree-lined Grand Avenue

150 metres wide. Despite all its open space, the city would be relatively compact: with an average 200 people per hectare in residential areas, it would have a density similar to that of central London; however, unlike London, it would also have a maximum population of 30,000, with a further 2,000 to work the land.[32] Once that number had been reached, a satellite city would be founded nearby, connected to the first by railway, a process that would repeat as the movement spread.

Right from the start, Howard made it clear that his vision rested on progressive land reform. Although his initial 'magnet' would be built on private property, further land was to be compulsorily purchased as the movement grew, and ceded to local control. In this way, a sort of incremental land enclosure in reverse would take place, gradually restoring the British landscape to something like its medieval form.

Although he had a Cobbett-like loathing of the choked-up metropolises of his day, Howard nevertheless recognised their social and cultural benefits. He argued that with his 'cluster of cities', which included a slightly larger Central City with a population of 58,000, the benefits of urban life – such as, for instance, the ability to put together a decent orchestra – need not be sacrificed:

> We should have a cluster of cities...each inhabitant of the whole group, though in one sense living in a town of small size, would be in reality living in, and would enjoy all the advantages of, a great and most beautiful city; and yet all the fresh delights of the country – field, hedgerow, and woodland – not prim parks and gardens merely – would be within a very few minutes' walk or ride.[33]

With its open-minded practicality, *Garden Cities of To-morrow* is a utopia for all seasons; a utopians' utopia that reads like a back catalogue of the entire genre. Howard's 'magnet' design is pure New Jerusalem, its limited population size Platonic. The plea for land reform is common to every utopian from More to Marx, the blending of urban and rural life likewise. Howard's network of compact, self-governing city-states is borrowed from More, Owen and Morris, as is his political structure, a federation of local democracies. Other classic utopian themes include closeness to nature (More, Fourier, Owen), the enjoyment of work (More, Fourier, Morris), shared labour and communal dining halls (St Benedict, More, Fourier, Owen, Morris . . .). One could go on.

Work on the first garden city began at Letchworth in 1903, to designs by the Arts and Crafts architects Barry Parker and Raymond Unwin. But although Letchworth gave architectural expression to Howard's concept, the land reform and social ambition that were its real basis failed to materialise. Despite its initial backers, Letchworth was underfunded from the start, struggling to attract investors and residents alike. The directors soon expelled Howard from the board, and reneged on the intended transfer of funds to the municipality, while the residents, instead of bonding with one another and cooking communal meals, kept mostly to themselves and commuted to a nearby corset factory for work.[34] Far from realising Howard's vision, Letchworth simply confirmed what More and Marx had always known. When it comes to building communities, there is no perfect formula; no instant 'good city mix' that works just by adding people.

Hero Architects

Even as Parker and Unwin perfected their fancy brickwork details at Letchworth, the motor age was about to make their Arts and Crafts hamlets seem terminally old-fashioned. Just as the railways had liberated cities from geography, cars and aeroplanes now signalled the arrival of modernism, offering seemingly limitless possibilities for human inhabitation. Le Corbusier's Ville Contemporaine of 1922 epitomised the new vision. All soaring skyscrapers and linear apartment buildings snaking through leafy parkland, it was, like virtually every utopia before it, an attempt to reconcile city and country.[35] What was new was the kind of city and country Le Corbusier had in mind.

Like the *maison citrohan*, his prototypical machine for living in, Le Corbusier's Ville Contemporaine was geared towards placing man within an abstract idea of nature. Sunlight and air, openness and greenery were all necessary to modern man's well-being; involvement with the 'other' nature (soil, earth, farmland) was not. Like Howard's

The utopian dream that spawned a nightmare. Le Corbusier's Ville Contemporaine.

Garden City, Le Corbusier's 'contemporary' one was filled with public parks and recreational spaces, made possible by tall buildings that released the ground plane ('crystal towers that soar higher than any pinnacle on earth'), and a segregated circulation system.[36] Despite advocating communal allotments in his outer 'Garden City' zone in concession to the needs of its humbler occupants, Le Corbusier's citizens of the future were far more likely to wield a tennis racket than a pitchfork. Although he later modified his plans in the Ville Radieuse of 1935 – even going so far as to include rural collectives, Fermes Radieuses, between his linear strips of city – it was Le Corbusier's earlier urban vision, with its relentless combination of tower blocks and inedible greenery, that stuck.

It is easy now to question how such a clinical cityscape could possibly have been imagined to work; how it could have engendered a sense of community, locality or identity – to say nothing of how it might have been fed. But at the time, nobody thought to ask. Le Corbusier was a new breed of utopian: one equally capable of dreaming up fantasy cities, selling them, designing and building them. He was an architect – and, like almost every contemporary member of his profession, convinced that he had the vision and the means to save the world through design. He was the kind of person in whom the utopian tendency finally fused with reality.

In Europe, where the availability of land was always an issue, Le Corbusier's 'crystal towers' seemed to offer at least some kind of spatial trade-off. But for the American architect Frank Lloyd Wright,

unlimited freedom of movement suggested a rather different opportunity: that of restoring man to his 'natural horizontality'.[37] Wright,
who like Le Corbusier was an uncontested genius when it came to
designing individual buildings, spent the last 30 years of his life refining
plans for his 'Broadacre City', best summarised as a proposal to scrap
North American urban civilisation and replace it with a coast-to-coast
patchwork of family smallholdings, each with its own spacious
'Usonian' house ('Usonia' was Wright's preferred term for his horizontal paradise).[38] Wright saw a return to the land as the means by
which Usonian man, 'the bravest and the best', would rediscover his
true nature. 'Of all the underlying forces working toward emancipation
of the city dweller,' he wrote, 'most important is the gradual
reawakening of the primitive instincts of the agrarian.'[38]

First published as *The Disappearing City* in 1932, the fully fledged
project emerged as *The Living City* in 1958, complete with a
meticulous 12-foot-square scale model showing how four square
miles of the project might look. The patchwork of one-acre plots was
to be connected by a network of hedge-lined highways that would be
noiseless and odourless, since all the traffic would be electric.
Although Usonians were expected to grow at least some of their food,
their efforts would be supplemented by specialist farmers, who would
take food 'fresh every hour' to roadside markets: vast pyramidal
structures that were to serve as the city's economic, social and cultural
hubs. Like every good activist utopian, Wright was convinced the
time for his vision was nigh: 'The whole swollen commercial
enterprise we call the City proceeds to stall its own engine,' he wrote.
'The day of reckoning is not so far away.'[40] Then the Broadacre
carpet would be ready to roll out, restoring man to the land, his 'true
line of human freedom on earth':

> . . . everywhere in America this warm upsurging of life is our
> heritage: a nation truly free to use its own great woods, hills, fields,
> meadows, streams, mountains and wind-blown sweeps of the vast
> plains all brought into the service of men and women in the name of
> mankind . . . This – to me – is the proper service to be rendered by
> the architects of our country . . .[41]

By Locke out of Jefferson with a hefty dash of Thoreau, *The Living City* reads like an Outward Bound manual one moment, a pitch for the job of jobs the next. What it never reads like, however, is a project that anticipated the planet running out of gas:

> . . . imagine man-units so arranged and integrated that every citizen may choose any form of production, distribution, self-improvement, enjoyment, with the radius of, say, ten to forty minutes of his own home – all now available to him by means of private car or plane, helicopter or some other form of fast public conveyance . . .[42]

Like all utopian visionaries, Corbusier and Wright were very good at seeing what was wrong with the world, and much less good at fixing it. They could see that urban civilisation posed some very big questions. What they could not see was that big questions don't always have big answers. Sometimes the questions themselves need to be broken down, or asked in a different way.

The Trouble with Utopia

If all utopian projects are doomed to fail and all 'activist' utopians deluded, why bother to look at utopia at all? The reason is that utopianism represents the nearest thing we have to a history of cross-disciplinary thought on the subject of human dwelling. Thinking in disciplines is what the Enlightenment taught us to do, and very useful it is too, up to a point. But two centuries of disciplined thought have given us architecture, planning, sociology, politics, economics, anthropology, geography, ecology and traffic engineering, each capable of operating in a virtual vacuum. What they have not given us is a way of thinking about dwelling holistically. Utopianism is at least an attempt to do that. You could say it brought us 'integrated urbanism' centuries before anyone at Arup came up with the term.

Taken on their own, activist utopias tend to come across as cranky, fanciful or flawed. Taken together, they reveal remarkable consistency. Their goals are often identical: bringing man close to nature, fusing town and country, the sharing of labour, a strong sense of community. The same is true of their dislikes: large conurbations, globalisation, the concentration of wealth, mindless serfdom. Teased out of their historical context, utopian themes start to read like a universal wish list for human happiness; dystopian ones like a description of modern post-industrial society. So why, if there is such a clear body of thought pointing towards the kind of life that might bring human happiness, have we gone so firmly in the opposite direction?

The problem lies in the nature of utopia itself. Utopia might be a 'good place', but it is also 'no place', because the real world can never be perfect. The mistake comes when we try to build a perfect world – when utopia stops being a philosophical ruse and becomes a practical mantra. That way lies delusion; the belief that the complexities of human existence can be manipulated as effectively as, say, cars at a roundabout. 'Social engineering' is one of the most unfortunate legacies of socialist utopianism. It has clouded our thinking about cities for 200 years, and despite the many lessons of modernism, it remains endemic to the discipline of urban planning. But cities, as numerous sink estates and windswept public plazas testify, don't work like that. One cannot capture the buzz of the Barcelona Ramblas by reproducing its proportions, nor knit communities together by giving people a piece of communal grass to sit on. Such gestures *can* work – but only as part of a deeper understanding of the social situation. In isolation, they are little better than urban phrenology.

By failing so consistently, utopianism teaches us some vital lessons. It warns us of the dangers of myopia, megalomania, monoculture. It shows us what can and cannot be achieved through design. It demonstrates the importance of scale, history, zeitgeist. It shows us that we can neither control the world, nor escape it. Most of all, it reminds us of our own limitations. Even when we try to change the world, we remain part of it. Ironically, its greatest lesson is the need to keep things real. We can't live in utopia, that much is clear. But once we accept that, we are in a much better position to address head-on the problem of dwelling. Perhaps the greatest barrier we face is the sheer scale and complexity of the problem. Urbanisation, capitalism, geopolitics, peak oil, hunger, global warming – faced with a list like that, where on earth does one start? It might strike us that there is something that does connect them all, not in an all-encompassing, *Gesamtkunstwerk* sort of way, but in a complex, messy one. That something is food. As a means of addressing the way we live, food shares with utopia the quality of being cross-disciplinary. But its great advantage is that it is grounded in reality. As we have seen in this book, food resists being contained and controlled. It embodies all the mess, chaos and dirt of the world, as well as its orderliness. Its rituals are specific in time and place and highly codified; yet food itself is inexorable, inevitable, universal. Most importantly of all, food is *necessary*, and so is very good at showing us what really matters.

Here, it seems, is what we have been looking for all along: a tool for shaping the world so ubiquitous and powerful, yet so obvious and simple, that it has somehow escaped our notice. So why, if it is so obvious, has food not been used as a design tool before? The answer, of course, is that it has – for millennia. But it has been done blindly. Those who have used food have generally wielded it like a weapon. Wars have been waged over it, continents conquered, landscapes transformed, regimes overthrown, treaties sealed. Food, the ubiquitous medium of civilisation, has always shaped the world, not always for the better. So what if we were to use food differently? To recognise that, while the atmosphere is what we breathe, the *sitosphere* (from *sitos*, the ancient Greek word for food) is what we live in?[43] To recognise that rather than trash the planet in order to produce food, we need to *plan* how we are to feed ourselves in order that we don't?

For a start, we would have to alter the power structures that currently control food; to stop using food as a weapon, and start sharing it as a force for good. That would require a revolution of sorts, but only in our minds. Change will come when we change the way we think. We have never seen food's true potential, because it is too big to see. But viewed laterally, it emerges as something with phenomenal power to transform not just landscapes, but political structures, public spaces, social relationships, cities. Its effects depend on those who control it. So who *does* control food? Farmers? Supermarkets? Government? Agribusiness? You and me? In the end, we all have a part to play, even those of us who never give food a second thought. Politicians need our votes, just like supermarkets need customers. They only have power because we give it to them. We can change the way they think and act by changing the way we do.

Eating the View

Once you start to see the world through food, everything changes. Seemingly unconnected things turn out to be closely linked; apparently confusing relationships spring into relief. Food, as we know, is one of the greatest forces shaping the world. So how might we use food to shape it better? Nowhere is the impact of food greater than in the countryside, so we might as well start there. We already know that you can't have countryside without farmers. Wilderness, yes; but not the manicured landscapes of 'Constable Country', 'Brontë Country' and the rest, with their hedgerows and meadows, vales and dales. As the Countryside Agency pointed out with its recent 'eat the view' campaign, the landscapes we love are often the product of farming.[44] Man has always eaten the view – or rather, has shaped the view according to his appetites. Things are no different today. When it comes to the land, food's influence is obvious and direct. If we want a beautiful planet – or even one capable of sustaining human life – we had better start changing the way we eat.

Britain is a verdant, varied, fertile land blessed with a temperate climate and reliable rainfall. It is also a crowded island that would struggle to feed itself entirely – but that is no reason not to maximise the amount of food we produce here, as long as we do it ecologically. Apart from the issue of food security, the ecological, political and social benefits of growing local, seasonal food are overwhelming. If we put our minds to it, we could have a thriving agriculture in Britain, as well as a beautiful landscape. Beef reared on Highland grass, lamb from the hills, dairy from specialist breeds such as Guernseys and Jerseys, apples from Kent. Precisely the sort of farming, in fact, that once evolved naturally in response to the landscape and to urban markets. It would all need paying for, of course, but no more than we are already paying for something infinitely worse.

Is such a vision reactionary, nostalgic? I would argue not. Responding directly to the land is never retrograde. On the contrary, it is our only hope of salvation. Permaculture is the farming of the future: farming that renews itself, that works with the land, not against it, that harnesses nature's own ecosystems, and crucially, that allows people to live on the land if they want to.[45] We need more farmers in the world, not fewer: people who will act as caretakers and custodians of the land, as well as harvest it on our behalf. Ironically, the greatest body of knowledge on the subject of permaculture belongs to the very nation whose urbanisation now threatens the planet: China. For thousands of years, the Chinese have been perfecting the art of closed-cycle farming – systems that use integrated biodiverse eco-cycles to maximise productivity and minimise waste. Land that is suitable for farming in China has always been scarce; yet now that it is scarce everywhere, we seem to be abandoning such techniques in favour of farming methods whose so-called 'efficiencies' are nothing of the kind.

It is symptomatic that there is no English word for *terroir*. We should either invent one or adopt the French word and apply it globally. That would not mean abandoning research into new technologies. *Terroir*, after all, has never excluded science. It is simply an ongoing search for the best way to harness the land – an exercise in the perfection of husbandry. The manufacture of genetically modified 'suicide genes' by companies such as Monsanto is utterly wrong; even wicked. But the problem lies with the cynical use of technology by such companies, not with science itself.[46] We need 'third way' agriculture that combines the best of ancient wisdom with modern technology.

The Food Network

If local farming is to survive, it must do so fairly, as part of an equable, balanced and internationally regulated market, in which all nations have equal access and say. That means addressing government policies, international trade agreements, the role of agribusiness – the whole shebang governing the global food system. Local small-scale and medium-scale farmers need our support, but international protectionism is not the way to deliver it. The most obvious way is simply to value what farmers do and pay them for it. In order to do that, we need more direct access to them. We need governments to intervene to prevent supermarkets from screwing them into the ground. Government should use its power to prevent monopolistic control of the food supply; not to encourage it.

Food is a form of dialogue. If we are to become what the founder of the Slow Food Movement Carlo Petrini calls 'co-producers', we need open lines of communication between consumers and producers – networks and channels that flow both ways. The global food super-highway is exactly what we don't need: a one-way system that delivers food as though the people at either end had no relationship with one another. It is a system based on profit, nothing else; one that only profits those who run it. As a diagram, it is what the architect Christopher Alexander calls a 'tree': a system in which many roots are channelled into a single trunk that then feeds many branches and lots of tiny leaves – us. Since the leaves can only get their nutrition through the trunk, the latter has a monopoly over their supply. If we want more influence over food, we need a different sort of system, one that joins the leaves directly to the roots. That would be what Alexander calls a semi-lattice: a complex network of interconnections – localised, personal, flexible, multi-directional – all of which can affect the other. As Alexander points out, that is closer to the way that cities themselves work.[47]

There is nothing wrong with a global food system per se, it is just a question of how you run it. Operated along current lines, the system is a social, economic and environmental catastrophe. But if we could put in place a more lattice-like global trading network, things could be very different. As initiatives such as Fair Trade have demonstrated, we in the West *can* deal equably with small farmers anywhere in the world, provided the right mechanisms are in place. Of course, we should only buy from them food that can be grown sustainably, and imported without threatening the planet (bring back sailing ships). For that, we need the help of food importers, whether they be supermarkets or other businesses. We need them to make the right choices for us – to 'choice edit' their products, so that *nothing* on their shelves is socially or environmentally damaging. Governments could insist upon it, if they had the will.

Above all, we need transparency in the food system – fair trade, not just for Colombian coffee-growers, but for small farmers everywhere, including Britain. Only then will we achieve true co-production. It all comes down to food sovereignty, defined by the international peasant movement La Via Campesina as 'the RIGHT of peoples, countries, and state unions to define their agricultural and food policy'. The movement, set up in 1993 to give those living on the land a voice, goes on:

> Food sovereignty organizes food production and consumption according to the needs of local communities, giving priority to production for local consumption. Food sovereignty includes the right to protect and regulate the national agricultural and livestock production and to shield the domestic market from the dumping of agricultural surpluses and low-price imports from other countries. Landless people, peasants, and small farmers must get access to land, water, and seed as well as productive resources and adequate public services. Food sovereignty and sustainability are a higher priority than trade policies.[48]

In the end, control of food is a question of liberty. In 1859, John Stuart Mill wrote a treatise on the latter; one that remains embedded in the British constitution and our concept of social justice. 'Over himself,' wrote Mill, 'over his own body and mind, the individual is sovereign.'[49] One need hardly add that without sovereignty over food, the concept becomes practically meaningless.

Grow your Own

The dream of every peasant has always been to be self-sufficient in food. That was also the aim of early city-states – and some, at least for a time, came close to achieving it. But of course the 'Wens' and 'Babylons' we inhabit today couldn't possibly manage it. They are the reason we have a global food economy in the first place, with its monolithic supply chains, monocultural wastelands and animal gulags.

But is there anything we could do to mitigate their effects? Could we, to some extent at least, grow our own food in them?

As we know, many pre-industrial city-dwellers produced some of their own food, as many in the developing world still do. A recent survey estimated that five million Egyptian families keep 'back yard birds': chickens raised either to be eaten at home or sold at market.[50] The chickens are often treated as family pets, and women feed them by chewing corn and blowing it into their beaks – a practice that dates back to the time of the pharaohs. We may not be ready for quite such an intimate relationship with lunch in Britain, but there are signs that we are at least warming to the idea of a home-grown breakfast. One of the surprise commercial hits of 2004 was the 'eglu': a high-tech urban chicken coop (complete with two organic hens and a fox-proof run), designed by four students from the Royal College of Art.[51] By 2007, over 10,000 eglus had been sold, and an estimated half a million British families now keep hens.[52]

Man cannot live on eggs alone, and there are signs of a resurgence of interest in growing other sorts of foods in Britain too. Allotments, first established in the eighteenth century as a means of compensating the rural poor for being turned off their land, are in greater demand now than at any time since the Second World War. A campaign led by the land reformer Jesse Collings (whose famous slogan 'Three Acres and a Cow' was later adopted by Joseph Chamberlain) led to local authorities being required by the Small Holdings and Allotment Act of 1908 to provide them for the benefit of the deserving poor, a requirement that remains in force today. Their charitable roots gave allotments something of an image problem in Britain, but that is starting to change, as middle-class foodies join the queues of people waiting for a patch of their own, and the chance to grow their own fruit and veg.

Most of those who grow their own food in Britain do so out of choice, but as the famous 'Dig for Victory' campaign showed during the Second World War, growing food in cities can be a much more serious business. The sight of London transformed by farming would no doubt have delighted William Morris had he lived to see it. Contemporary photographs of allotments next to the Albert Memorial and sheep grazing by the Serpentine look surreal today, but they serve as a reminder of the latent bounteousness of cities. By the end of the war, an estimated 1.5 million allotments in Britain were providing a tenth of the nation's food, and one half of all its fruit and vegetables.[53]

It often takes the disruption of normal food supplies to reveal a city's productive potential. During the 1970s, the failure of state-run agriculture in the Soviet Union drove millions of Russian city-dwellers to start growing their own food, cultivating fruit and vegetables on marginal land in the urban periphery. As time wore on, people began building themselves little huts on their strips in order to spend the weekends there – a habit that has outlasted the collapse of the Soviet regime. Today around a quarter of Russian city-dwellers have their own mini dachas – cut-price versions of the elegant summer residences of the eighteenth-century urban elite – and the May Day holiday has become an annual mass migration, as millions leave the city to plant crops for the following year.[54] St Petersburg is now the peri-urban farming capital of Europe, with two and a half million inhabitants engaged in agricultural activities of some sort, on either private dachas or community farms known as *sadovodstvos*, consisting of between 50 and 600 individual plots sharing common facilities.[55] Plenty of citizens also farm in their back gardens, in a sort of popular Russian version of *The Good Life*.[56]

Across the Atlantic, the collapse of the Soviet regime created an even more startling example of urban agriculture *in extremis*. The loss of its main trading partner turned Cuba from a dependent satellite into an isolated state virtually overnight.[57] With a US trade embargo in place, the island, where 80 per cent of the population lived in cities, was forced to rely on its own resources. Over the next decade, it underwent an extraordinary agricultural revolution, as government-sponsored agriculture converted suburbs into community-run farms, and cities including the capital Havana into a maze of *organopónicos*, high-yield market gardens inserted into every available open space and tended by local residents. State-owned land was parcelled out to anyone willing to cultivate it, with amateur farmers given government training, advice, seeds and equipment. Crucially, the government also departed from its communist principles in order to allow farmers to sell their produce on the open market. By 2003, over 200,000 Cubans were employed in urban agriculture, and although the island remained short of meat, grain and eggs, it was approaching self-sufficiency in vegetables, producing over three million tonnes annually – more than had been available before the crisis.[58]

Pies in the Sky?

The capacity of cities to grow at least some of their own food is beyond question. As the examples of London, St Petersburg and Havana demonstrate, even cities built on the assumption that their food will be coming from elsewhere can be adapted to become at least partially self-sufficient if the need is great enough. Since half of us already live in such cities, is there anything we can learn from them?

In Cuba, the accident of politics and geography combined to create a sort of urban-agrarian laboratory with many of the attributes – isolation, state ownership of land, strong community bonds – typical of utopia. Although the circumstances that brought it about could scarcely be called utopian, Cuba's agricultural revolution has been enough to persuade the UK-based architects André Viljoen and Katrin Bohn that something similar could be achieved in the West. Viljoen and Bohn propose that underused urban spaces such as brownfield sites, car parks and grassy verges are reclaimed in order to grow food in cities. The new farmland would be designed to link existing green spaces together to create what they call 'Continuous Productive Urban Landscapes' (CPULs), green corridors woven into the urban fabric, connecting the city to 'vegetation, air, *the horizon*'.[59] Viljoen and Bohn argue that, with the right government support, cities as open-textured as those in Britain could not only produce a significant proportion of their own fruit and vegetables with CPULs, but through them could create valuable new recreational space for local communities.

The Vertical Farm Project, led by Dickson Despommier at Columbia University, takes the idea of urban agriculture one step further, putting it right at the heart of the city.[60] The project's aim, as its name implies, is to explore ways of farming vertically: to develop specially designed buildings that can be inserted directly into existing cities in order to grow their food. Vertical Farms would effectively be high-rise 'food factories' such as those proposed for Dongtan, although on a much bigger scale: tall enough and high-tech enough to feed the entire urban population. Using data developed by NASA, Despommier and his team reckon that 30 square metres of intensively farmed land would be required per person using current technologies, although with true utopian optimism, they anticipate improving on those figures with the use of yet-to-be invented ones. On the basis of current data, Despommier believes that

one vertical farm with an architectural footprint of one square city block and rising up to 30 stories (approximately 3 million square feet) could provide enough nutrition (2,000 calories/day/person) to comfortably accommodate the needs of 10,000 people employing technologies currently available.[61]

Quite what London would look like with the necessary 1,000 vertical farms 100 metres square and 30 storeys high can only be imagined.[62] Nevertheless, Despommier makes a powerful case for the principle of vertical farming: zero food miles, on-site waste recycling, urban job opportunities, and an end to farming's oldest foe, the weather. For him, vertical farming is a way of freeing the countryside to return to something of its former state, restoring what he calls its 'ecosystem services and functions':

Vertical farms, many stories high, will be situated in the heart of the world's urban centers. If successfully implemented, they offer the promise of urban renewal, sustainable production of a safe and varied food supply (year-round crop production), and the eventual repair of ecosystems that have been sacrificed for horizontal farming.[63]

The Dutch architects MVRDV also believe high-rise farming is the answer, although in their case they propose building entire cities devoted to it. Their 2001 project Pig City took a hard look at one of the Netherlands' oldest industries, pig farming, which remains one of the most intensive farming systems in the world.[64] They worked out that if Dutch pork were produced organically at its current rate (16.5 million tonnes a year), it would take 75 per cent of the nation's land mass to achieve it. That, they argued, left only two options. Either we all become 'instant vegetarians', or we find better ways of raising pigs. Their resulting proposal – both playful and serious in the best utopian tradition – was to build a series of 'pig towers' 76 storeys high, each with floor plates 87 metres square to house the pigs in a high degree of comfort, in 'apartments' with plenty of bedding, access to large open-air balconies, and apple trees to rootle under. The towers would be powered by bio-gas digesters run on pig manure, and connected to a central abattoir to which the pigs would be moved by lift. Until that last fateful journey, the pigs would live much as many humans do now: freeing the countryside for other things. Pig City has gone down well in the Netherlands, and there is some official interest in taking the idea forward.

The Neo-Geographical Age

Whether or not vertical farming can be made to work remains to be seen. But for the foreseeable future, urban agriculture – or agricultural urbanity – can only ever be part of the solution to feeding humanity. City and country need one another, and their relationship is what we should really be addressing. That means thinking about cities differently; not just those we have already built, but those we are yet to build in order to house the three billion or so extra people expected to be living in them by 2050.

While projects like Dongtan are clearly a start, even the city's design team recognises the limitations of building eco-cities without being able to address their relationship with their regional and global hinterlands. It seems we have come full circle. We are entering a new geographical age; one in which our choices about where and how we live are becoming as critical for us as they were for our distant ancestors. Luckily, we have one advantage over them: hindsight. So what have

Porkers enjoying the high life in MVRDV's Pig City.

10,000 years of urban civilisation taught us? One could write endless books on the subject, but in the end they would all boil down to one thing: respect the land. For thousands of years, we have been building cities and letting the countryside take up the slack. What if we were to reverse the process? What if we were to return to the ancient custom of augury – in modern guise – as a way of choosing sites for our cities? The primary purpose of augury, after all, was to ensure that cities were built in favourable and sustainable locations through careful observation of the natural terrain.

For the Scottish biologist and geographer Patrick Geddes, that was precisely the right approach. Inventor of the word 'conurbation' (the professional term for large, urbanised blobs), Geddes was a keen student of the French geographer Élisée Reclus, whose concept of a 'natural region' inspired the Scot to create what now goes under the rather uninspiring title of 'regional planning'. The dull name is misleading, however, because for Geddes, the natural landscape was anything but boring. It was a vibrant, living thing that held the key to all human habitation. In 1905, he drew a diagram describing a universal 'valley section', stretching from mountain and forest to grassland and shore. Man's response to such natural terrain, he argued, has always formed the basis of human culture. Cities, such as they are, should take their cue from this 'active, experienced environment . . . the motor force of human development; the almost sensual reciprocity between men and women and their surroundings'.[65] Geddes believed that modern technology (the 'neotechnic era') would release people from having to live in large conurbations, allowing them to live closer to nature, with all their functional and cultural needs near at hand. As for the 'ink-stains and grease-spots' of existing conurbations, they should be blended with nature: 'We must bring the country to them . . . make the field gain on the street, not merely the street gain on the field.'[66]

Geddes, it will be recognised, was a utopian with the best of them. But there is something in what he says. Technology *has* released us from some of our geographical bonds – has at least opened up new possibilities for the way we live. The merging of city and country is far from a new idea; on the contrary, one could say it is endemic to civilisation. It is also one of the most enduring themes in utopian thought. So is there anything we can learn about how to go about it? As it happens, two utopians, Howard and Wright, provide us with two key paradigms, the compact and the spread. Howard gave us the post-industrial city-state, Wright suburbia; and when you consider the differences between the two men, it is not hard to see why. Howard was English; Wright American. Howard belonged to the age of steam; Wright to that of the motor car. Howard was no architect; Wright was. Howard was modest; Wright was not. And so on. No surprise, then, that Wright's utopia assumes limitless land and transport and is all designed by him, whereas Howard's assumes limited land and transport and is not.

Utopian visions tend to mirror their creators and contexts – so what does that tell us? All we have to begin with when we design cities are paradigms; notions of what might work and what might not. Until we actually try something, we can never know for sure how successful it will be, and even then, we might have to wait years before we find out. Building cities will always be a messy business. It is up to us to use our knowledge, experience and instincts, and respond to the situation as best we can. On that basis, it must be said that Howard's approach appears to have more practical applications for us today than does Wright's. In modern parlance, his garden city presents us with a low-carbon-footprint model; Broadacre City with a high one. Yet opinions are divided among architects and planners over whether we should be building 'cluster cities' or suburbia. In his 1997 book *Cities for a Small Planet*, the architect Richard Rogers advocated building as densely as possible, utilising existing 'brownfield' sites rather than allowing cities to spread on to green belts.[67] His arguments became enshrined in government policy through his work for the Urban Task Force in the late 1990s.[68] Yet 10 years on, housing in Britain is still being built at an average density of just 40 dwellings per hectare, and suburbia remains easily our most popular residential model.[69]

Whether we build densely or not, there is no doubt that we need to find ways of living more sustainably. The British government recently announced plans for the construction of 10 new 'eco-towns' with the intention that they be 'zero-carbon', although quite how that is to be achieved if the towns are plugged into the same food supply networks as the rest of us is anyone's guess. The Thames Gateway has also been named Britain's first 'eco-region', with a masterplan by the architect Terry Farrell, although so far the parkland with which new urban districts are to be merged is to be of the recreational rather than the productive sort. Despite the fact that much of the land being developed is highly fertile – including market gardens that once provided London with much of its fruit and vegetables – the issue of food production has yet to appear on our eco-regional radar.

Unless we address the political and socio-economic structures that govern cities, the question of what shape we build them, ecologically speaking, is of marginal importance. It is how cities function as organic entities that really matters. Building cluster towns in Kent is all very well, but if their inhabitants are still eating biscuits made with Bornean palm oil, their ecological credentials will always be com-promised. Although there is much that can be done design-wise to make cities more eco-friendly (and Dongtan is doing most of them), there is still a swathe of issues about the way we live that designers by themselves cannot address. That is where utopia still has much to teach us. Howard's eco-cities were surrounded by productive countryside; not recreational parkland. They addressed the entire urban eco-cycle, not just the energy needs of individual buildings. So why, if the Garden City was such a brilliant idea, did Howard's vision fail? The glib answer is that it was utopian. But there are other reasons. Just like Owen before him, Howard anticipated government support that never came. The really radical part of his plan called for political will; and that, as we know, is the hardest thing of all to obtain.

Small Answers

Contemplating the global meltdown that our post-industrial lifestyles appear to presage can be depressing. But it need not be. Once we confront what we're doing head-on, we can avert catastrophe and make our lives, and those of the people connected to us through food, a whole lot better in the process. It is not too late.

If we simply all *considered* food more, that would be a start. If we connected the peas on our plate to someone, somewhere, farming; the chicken in our sandwich to a living animal; related the taste, texture and colour of the food we eat to the weather and seasons. Food is the envoy of the countryside – a living part of the landscape where it was grown. Apart from making clear ecological sense, eating locally and seasonally is more *enjoyable*. In his book, *Slow Food*, Carlo Petrini had a great deal of trouble persuading his communist colleagues that the enjoyment of food was not in itself a sign of bourgeois decadence.[70] It isn't. Some of the best food in the world is what the Italians call *la cucina povera*: literally, 'the food of the poor', delicious because it is local, seasonal and simple. Most of us living in cities can't dream of eating as well as the average Italian peasant; but we can still make the link, as all peasants must, between what we eat and the land where it is grown. Once we have done that, we become what Petrini calls an 'ecological gastronome': someone who recognises the importance of food, and uses his or her knowledge in order to eat ethically.

In 1999, the Slow Food philosophy was extended to the concept of 'Cittaslow' (Slow Cities), towns where the way of life respects the value of locality, craftsmanship and history, and where people are, in the words of the Cittaslow manifesto, 'still able to recognise the slow course of the Seasons and their genuine products respecting tastes, health and spontaneous customs . . .'[71] It goes on:

> 'Living Slow' involves hastening slowly – *'festina lente'* as the Romans used to say. The Slow lifestyle respects tradition and quality, and seeks to use the best aspects of the modern world to enhance, preserve and enjoy the old ways of doing things, but not to the exclusion of progress and not for the sake of avoiding change.[72]

Towns wanting to join the Slow City movement must meet 60 different criteria (including having no more than 50,000 residents), and must commit to embedding the Slow Food philosophy in the running of the town. So far, 100 towns in 10 countries have qualified, including Ludlow, the first Slow City in the UK.

While the ideals of Cittaslow are overtly utopian (as the movement itself acknowledges), one does not have to live in a cute village in order to improve one's life through food. Whatever size and shape of city we live in, we can use food as a means of inhabiting it better. We can choose what food to buy, how we buy it and from whom; decide whether we cook or are cooked for; where we eat and when; with whom we eat and what we waste. All these things affect the places we live, from their physical appearance down to their social marrow. When we make time for food, we start to notice simple things: the sound in the room, the quality of light, the colour of walls, the noise in the street. If we want a rich and varied urban existence, we must embrace food in its totality; not just in order to live more ethically, but to engage with its manners and sociability.

Once you begin to recognise that we live in a sitosphere, city and country emerge as one continuous territory in which *terroir*, traditionally linked to the soil, is seen to transcend the urban–rural boundary. Locality, seasonality, identity, variety, tradition, knowledge, trust: all are as important for cities as they are for the countryside. London pubs, New York delis, Roman trattorias, Parisian cafés: all are examples of urban *terroir*. As is the food and drink they serve: steak and kidney pie; bagels and salt beef; pasta and pizza; croissants and *café au lait*. Whether you like them or not (and a characteristic of local foods is that not everybody does), they are what give urban life its flavour.

So if we were to design a city through food, what might it be like? A 'sitopic' city would have strong links with its local hinterland through a lattice-like food network, with active markets, local shops, and a strong sense of food identity. Its houses would be built with large, comfortable kitchens, there would be neighbourhood allotments, possibly a local abattoir. The local school would teach kids about food, and children would learn to grow and cook it from an early age. Above all, the city would celebrate food; use it to bring people together. The architecture could be as modern as you like, but it would not all be designed or built at once. The city plan would use food networks to 'seed the city', putting social and physical mechanisms in place that would evolve naturally over time. The city would thus, as cities were in the past, be partly shaped by food. Greater government protection from food monopolies would ensure the city enjoyed a high degree of food sovereignty, but it would also have access to medium-scale industrial food production, ethically managed and transparently monitored. There would be no formal limit to the size of the city, but its emphasis on food would ensure that, whatever its scale, it would be conceived from the start as an integral part of the local organic cycle. A city designed through food, in its ideal form, is clearly utopia. But we don't have to aim at perfection. By just seeing through food, we can go a long way. Sitopia is utopia grounded in reality.

Although no city has yet been deliberately designed through food, plenty of existing cities are starting to see food's design potential. Food, as we have seen, can be a powerful agent for urban renewal, and several British cities, including Bradford and Leicester, are now actively pursuing regeneration programmes through the strategic design and support of local food markets.[73] Other cities are using food as a tool for reducing the impact of urban consumption. 'Transition Towns' is a programme initiated by Rob Hoskins in Kinsale, Ireland, that creates 'Energy Descent Action Plans' for cities, strategies by which they can reduce their eco-footprints over time. 'Transition Town Totnes' (TTT) is the first working model, and it has a number of initiatives underway, including the strengthening of local food networks, the re-skilling of locals in the arts of cooking and vegetable-growing, and the creation of more space for allotments. The town also aims to raise its profile by becoming the 'Nut Tree Capital of Britain', planting a wide variety of edible nut trees in its streets. Like the Cittaslow movement, Transition Towns is an optimistic programme that sees the need to 'think globally, act locally' as a positive thing: 'The thinking behind TTT is simply that a town using much less energy and resources than we presently consume could, if properly planned for and designed, be more resilient, more abundant and more pleasurable than the present.'[74]

Who knows how food might shape cities in the future? As more of us do our shopping on the internet, out-of-town supermarkets might become redundant, and be converted to local food hubs with the function of dispatching our food to us by electric buggy, just as milk floats used to do.[75] Local food shops might be replaced by refrigerated locker rooms where we can go and collect our pre-ordered food parcels on the way home. Such systems might be an efficient way of delivering our food, but they would make for a pretty soulless street life.

How food shapes our lives in the future is up to us. Whoever we are and wherever we live, we can make choices that together would make an enormous cumulative difference. We can choose to eat ethically. Protect the countryside by 'eating the view'. Demand transparency in the food chain. Eat less meat and fish, and pay more for it when we do. Support local farmers through box schemes, farmers' markets, or community-supported agriculture.[76] Buy from our local food shops if we are lucky enough still to have them. Talk to shopkeepers about food; let them know we care. Demand that whoever we buy our food from, whether local grocers or supermarkets, they source their food ethically on our behalf. Get political about food. Demand government action. Learn to read food labels. Cook more. Invite our friends over for dinner. Get invited back. Eat with our kids. Buy them baby frying-pans for Christmas. Teach them to cook. *Enjoy* food more. Dig up the back garden. Start composting.

These things may sound trivial, but they're not. Food is all about networks; things that when connected together add up to more than the sum of their parts. Whether or not we care about food, the consequences of the way we eat are all around us. The global food system is a network in which we are all complicit. If we don't like the way it works, or the world it is creating, it is up to us to change it.

Man and corn – it all comes back to that. Cultivation and civilisation, city and country, paradise and hell: food has always shaped our lives, and it always will. Our legacy to those who inherit the earth will be determined by how we eat now – their future lies in our knives and forks and fingers.

Notes

Chapter 1 The Land

1   George Dodd, *The Food of London*, Longman Brown, Green and Longmans, London, 1856, p.1.
2   The programmes were broadcast on 19 December 2005.
3   Since the birds have been bred to develop prematurely, most struggle to support their own body weight in any case.
4   See Joanna Blythman, *Bad Food Britain*, Fourth Estate, 2006, p.132.
5   'Fuellies' are people who eat food simply as fuel in order to keep going. According to the IGD, 17 per cent of Britons are 'unhappy' about having to eat food at all. See http://www.igd.com/cir.asp?cirid=1873&search=1.
6   Food and Agriculture Organization of the United Nations (FAO) food balance sheets: http://faostat.fao.org/site/502/default.aspx.
7   According to Defra, there were 17.4 million hectares of farmland in the UK in 2006.
8   See *Feeding our cities in the 21st century*, Soil Association 60th Anniversary Conference press release, 12 September 2005.
9   Estimates by Philip M. Hauser, quoted in Norbert Schoenauer, *6000 Years of Housing*, W.W. Norton, New York, 2000, p.96.
10 *Livestock's Long Shadow*, UN Food and Agriculture Organization, Rome, 2006.
11 *Globalisation and Livestock*, Agriculture 21, Spotlight: 2005. See the FAO website: www.fao.org/ag/magazine/0504sp1.htm
12 FAO website, statistical archives, national food balance sheets.
13 Erik Millstone and Tim Lang, *The Atlas of Food*, Earthscan Publications Ltd, 2003, pp.34–5, and FAO, *Livestock's Long Shadow*, op.cit., p.xxi.
14 The environmental geographer Vaclav Smil reckons between 11 and 17 calories of feed are required to produce one calorie of flesh (beef, pork or chicken). Vaclav Smil, 'Worldwide transformation of diets, burdens of meat

production and opportunities for novel food proteins', *Enzyme and Microbial Technology* 30 (2002), p.309.

15 Jonathan Watts, the *Guardian*, 10 November 2005, and Gareth Chetwynd, the *Guardian*, 28 May 2004.

16 Adam Smith, *An Inquiry into the Nature and Causes of the Wealth of Nations*, ed. Edwin Cannan, Methuen, London, 1925, vol. 1, p.191.

17 For a general discussion of the origins of farming, see Reay Tannahill, *Food in History*, Penguin, 1988, pp.22–5.

18 See Joshua, Ch. 6, for the Old Testament version of Jericho's end. Archaeological evidence suggests that the town was destroyed by an earthquake around 1400 BC.

19 See Graham Lawton, 'Urban Legends', *New Scientist*, 18 September 2004.

20 See Tannahill, op.cit., p.47, and J.N. Postgate, *Early Mesopotamia: Society and Economy at the Dawn of History*, Routledge, London and New York, 1994.

21 See Richard Sennett, *Flesh and Stone*, Faber and Faber, 1996, p.71.

22 See Joseph Rykwert, *The Idea of a Town*, Faber and Faber, 1976, p.59.

23 Hesiod, *Works and Days*, trans. Richmond Lattimore, Ann Arbor, University of Michigan Press, 1959, p.31.

24 Caesar, *The Gallic War*, VI, 22, quoted in Massimo Montanari, *The Culture of Food*, trans. Carl Ipsen, Blackwell, Oxford, 1994, p.7.

25 Tacitus, *Germania*, Ch. 16, trans. M. Hutton, William Heinemann, London, 1970, p.155.

26 Seneca, *De Providentia*, *Dialogues* Book 1, quoted in Simon Schama, *Landscape and Memory*, Fontana Press, 1996, p.87.

27 In fact, the 'barbarian' reaction to Roman civilisation was mixed: some Germanic tribes became law-abiding members of the Empire.

28 Jean-Jacques Rousseau, *A Discourse on the Origin of Inequality* (1755), trans. G.D.H. Cole, (38), William Benton, London, 1952, p.348.

29 Postgate, op.cit., p.96.

30 Varro, *Res Rustica*, quoted in Neville Morley, *Metropolis and Hinterland*, Cambridge University Press, 1996, p.88.

31 Ibid., p.85.

32 Schama, op.cit., p.144.

33 'Feudalism', like 'city', is a hotly debated term. In its pure meaning it refers to a system in which a lord would lease a portion of land, known as a fief, to a tenant, known as a vassal, in exchange for military service – but I use it here in its broader sense, to refer to the practice of peasants or serfs working the land in return for annual labour or services.

34 Frank E. Huggett, *The Land Question and European Society*, Thames and Hudson, 1975, p.17.

35 See Wolfgang Braunfels, *Monasteries of Western Europe*, Thames and Hudson, 1972, p.31.

36 Henri Lefebvre describes the visual order of the Tuscan countryside, with its groups of *poderi*, peasant farmhouses clustered around landowners' villas and joined by radiating roads lined with cypresses, as anticipating the 'discovery'

of perspective in cities. See Henri Lefebvre, *The Production of Space*, trans. Donald Nicholson-Smith, Blackwell, 1998, pp.78–9.

37   The habit of deserting the city at harvest time even persisted into twentieth-century Britain: the Kent hop harvest was traditionally picked by migrant workers from the East End of London, who treated it as something of an annual holiday.

38   Quoted in Fernand Braudel, *Civilization and Capitalism 15th–18th Century* (3 vols.), trans. Siân Reynolds, Collins, London, 1981, vol.1, p.488.

39   Dodd, op.cit., pp.222–3.

40   Braudel, op.cit., vol.1, p.486.

41   Thomas Starkey, *Cyvile and Uncyvile Life*, quoted in Keith Thomas, *Man and the Natural World*, Penguin, 1984, p.247.

42   Hugh Latimer, *A Notable Sermon of the Plough* (1548), quoted in Xavier Baron, *London 1066–1914: Literary Sources and Documents* (3 vols.), Helm Information, East Sussex, 1997, vol.1, p.233.

43   Anon, quoted in Ian Dyck, *William Cobbett and Rural Popular Culture*, Cambridge University Press, 1992, p.53.

44   Quoted in Thomas, op.cit., p.250.

45   In fact the name was that of Penn's father, Admiral William Penn, to whom the land was bequeathed by Charles II in recognition of the elder Penn's services to the nation.

46   Thomas, op.cit., p.250.

47   Quoted in Jules Pretty, *Agri-Culture*, Earthscan, London, 2002, p.30.

48   John Locke, *An Essay Concerning the True Original, Extent and End of Civil Government* (1690) (Two Treatises of Government), in Ernest Barker (ed.), *Social Contract*, Oxford University Press, 1971, p.18.

49   See W.G. Hoskins, *The Making of the English Landscape*, Penguin, 1970, p.185.

50   Arthur Young, *Observations on the Present State of the Wastelands of Great Britain* (1773), quoted in Thomas, op.cit., p.255.

51   Quoted in Dyck, op.cit., p.51.

52   Political Register, 28 September 1833, p.827, quoted in ibid., p.53.

53   Political Register, 29 January 1831, p.288, quoted in ibid., p.3.

54   William Cobbett, *Rural Rides* (1830) (2 vols.), London, Reeves and Turner, 1885, vol.1, p.52.

55   See Huggett, op.cit., p.90.

56   Rousseau, op.cit., p.352.

57   See Rebecca L. Spang, *The Invention of the Restaurant*, Harvard, 2000, pp.57–9.

58   Although Edmund Burke's 1756 *Philosophical Inquiry into the Origin of Our Ideas of the Sublime and Beautiful* thrilled to the towering peaks and yawning chasms of 'sublime' nature, for Burke such wilderness remained 'terrible': decidedly (if enjoyably) 'other'.

59   Henry David Thoreau, *Walden, or Life in the Woods* (1854), Oxford University Press, 1997, p.84.

60   See Jules Pretty, op.cit., p. 42, and Schama, op.cit., p.7.

61 The problem was that Liebig assumed, incorrectly, that plants acquire all their nitrogen needs from the atmosphere, so failed to add it to his fertiliser. See Vaclav Smil, *Enriching the Earth*, MIT Press, 2004, pp.8–11.

62 Quoted in Craig Sams, *The Little Food Book*, Alastair Sawday Publishing, 2003, p.23.

63 Lady Eve Balfour, address given at a conference of IFOAM (International Federation of Organic Agriculture Movements) in Switzerland in 1977: www.journeytoforever.org.

64 Huggett, op.cit., p.129.

65 John Vidal, the *Guardian*, 17 May 2003.

66 United Nations Environment Programme (UNEP), http://www.who.int/ceh/publications/pestpoisoning.pdf.

67 Eddie 'the Eagle' Edwards was Britain's glasses-wearing representative in the ski-jump at the 1988 Winter Olympics.

68 The government recently announced plans to put stricter rules in place for regulating welfare standards of overseas producers. However, the difficulty of checking them at long distance remains.

69 The phrase was first used by the American Secretary of Defense, Donald Rumsfeld, speaking at a Defense Department Briefing, 12 February 2002.

70 Pretty, op.cit., p.28, and FAO Special Programme for Food Security, www.fao.org/spfs.

71 *Farming and Food: A Sustainable Future*, Report of the Policy Commission on the Future of Farming and Food, January 2002, chaired by Sir Donald Curry, p.68.

72 Ibid.

73 The court ruled that a microbiologist, Ananda Chakrabarty, could take out a patent for a genetically engineered bacterium he had created on the grounds that 'the fact that micro-organisms are alive is without legal significance for purposes of the patent law': http://caselaw.lp.findlaw.com/scripts/getcase.pl?court=us&vol=447&invol=303.

74 The talks took place at the Uruguay Round of GATT, the World Trade Organization General Agreements on Tariffs and Trade.

75 Vandana Shiva, speaking at the Soil Association One Planet Agriculture Conference, January 2007.

76 Vidal, as note 65 above.

77 Richard Heinberg, speaking at the Soil Association One Planet Agriculture Conference, January 2007.

78 E.F. Schumacher, *Small is Beautiful*, Vintage, 1973, p.3.

79 For a discussion of the issues surrounding peak oil, see Richard Heinberg, *The Party's Over*, New Society Publishers, 2006.

80 Heinberg, as note 77 above.

81 Smil, op.cit., p.xv.

82 In 2006, sales of organic food accounted for just 2 per cent of the food sold in Britain.

Notes

Chapter 2 Supplying the City

1　George Orwell, 'Charles Dickens' (1939), in *Critical Essays 1903–1950*, London, Secker & Warburg, 1946, p.35.

2　Pears are grafted on to quince rootstocks; apples on to crab apple.

3　*The Validity of Food Miles as an Indicator of Sustainable Development*, Defra, July 2005, p.6.

4　Ibid., p.7.

5　Quoted in Tim Lang and Michael Heasman, *Food Wars*, Earthscan, 2004, p.144.

6　*High Street Britain: 2015*, House of Commons All-Party Parliamentary Small Shops Group, 2006.

7　Joanna Blythman, *Shopped: The Shocking Power of British Supermarkets*, Fourth Estate, 2004, pp.73–82.

8　Defra, op.cit., p.ii.

9　From an interview with the author conducted in November 2005.

10　Neville Morley, *Metropolis and Hinterland*, Cambridge University Press, 1996, pp.63–5.

11　Quoted in Alex Forshaw and Theo Bergström, *Smithfield Past and Present*, Heinemann, London, 1980, p.34.

12　The real end came three years later, with the completion of the railway link between London and Great Yarmouth. See Richard Tames, *Feeding London: A Taste of History*, Historical Publications Ltd, 2003, pp.87–8.

13　See Malcolm Thick, *The Neat House Garden: Early Market Gardening Around London*, Prospect Books, 1998, pp.103–4.

14　Ibid.

15　Tobias Smollett, *The Expedition of Humphrey Clinker* (1771), ed. Lewis M. Knapp, Oxford University Press, London, 1966, p.122.

16　Fernand Braudel, *Civilization and Capitalism 15th-18th Century* (3 vols.), trans. Siân Reynolds, Collins, London, 1981, vol. 1, p.124.

17　Peter Hall (ed.), *Von Thünen's Isolated State*, trans. Carla M. Wartenberg, Pergamon Press, Oxford, 1966, p.7.

18　Derek Cooper, *Snail Eggs and Samphire: Dispatches from the Food Front*, Macmillan, London, 2000, p.2.

19　The term 'food miles' was first coined by the food policy expert Professor Tim Lang.

20　Neville Morley, *Metropolis and Hinterland*, Cambridge University Press, 1996, p.65.

21　A litre of unleaded petrol cost 80p in Britain in November 2000, 60p of which was tax. At the same period, a litre of air fuel cost just 18p. See *Eating Oil: Food Supply in a Changing Climate*, Sustain, 2001, p.30.

22　Some medieval Chinese cities probably reached a similar size. See Tertuis Chandler and Gerald Fox, *3000 Years of Urban Growth*, Academic Press, New York and London, 1974, p.363.

23　Morley, op.cit., p.13.

24 Geoffrey Rickman, *The Corn Supply of Ancient Rome*, Clarenden Press, Oxford, 1980, p.19.

25 Cassiodorus, *Variae*, VII, 29, quoted in Massimo Montanari, *The Culture of Food*, trans. Carl Ipsen, Blackwell, Oxford, 1994, p.51.

26 At Amarna, Akhenaten's capital 200 miles south of Cairo, regular festivals were held in which offerings of grain would be laid out on tables within the temple compound, after which the king would appear before his people at a special window, in order to ceremoniously redistribute what 'remained'.

27 Barry Kemp, *Ancient Egypt: Anatomy of a Civilization*, Routledge, London, 1989, p.195.

28 The population density of Imperial Rome has been estimated at 800 people per hectare: similar to modern-day Kolkata or Mumbai. See Morley, op.cit., p.34.

29 Rickman, op.cit., p.170.

30 Unfortunately, Brutus and friends also put paid to Caesar's plan to build a canal from Rome to Ostia, which might have saved his successors an awful lot of trouble.

31 Tacitus, *Annals*, I. 5, quoted in P.A. Brunt, 'The Roman Mob', in M.I. Finley (ed.), *Studies in Ancient Society*, Routledge and Kegan Paul, 1974, p.102.

32 Rickman, op.cit., p.2.

33 See Brunt in Finley (ed.), op.cit., pp.93–4.

34 Braudel, op.cit., vol.1, p.52.

35 Norman Davies, *God's Playground, A History of Poland* (2 vols), Oxford University Press, 2005, vol.1, p.204.

36 N.T.L. Des Essarts, *Dictionnaire Universel de Police Paris 1786–90*, quoted in Stephen Kaplan, *Provisioning Paris: Merchants and Millers in the Grain and Flour Trade During the Eighteenth Century*, Cornell University Press, Ithaca and London, 1984, p.24.

37 See Kaplan, op.cit., p.x.

38 Ibid., p.39.

39 Quoted in ibid., p.44.

40 Quoted in ibid., p.24.

41 Ibid., p.62.

42 See Rebecca L. Spang, *The Invention of the Restaurant*, Harvard University Press, 2000, pp.123–38.

43 Quoted in Felix Barker and Peter Jackson, *London: 2000 Years of a City and its People*, Macmillan, London, 1974, p.9.

44 The list is from Tames, op.cit., p.12.

45 See B.M.S. Campbell et al., *A Medieval Capital and its Grain Supply*, Historical Geography Research Series No. 30, 1993, p.47.

46 John Stow, *Survey of London* (1603), ed. Charles Kingsforde, Clarendon Press, Oxford, 1908, Vol.2, p.10.

47 See Niall Ferguson, *Empire: How Britain Made the Modern World*, Allen Lane, 2003, pp.2–4.

48   Quoted in ibid., p.3.

49   See Sidney Mintz, *Sweetness and Power*, Penguin, 1986, p.43.

50   Ibid., p.40.

51   Samuel Johnson (1709–84), *On the Trades of London*, published in *The Adventurer*, 1753, quoted in Xavier Baron, *London 1066–1914: Literary Sources and Documents* (3 vols.), Helm Information, East Sussex, 1997, vol.1, p.590.

52   Daniel Defoe, *The Review*, 8 January 1713, quoted in Dorothy Davis, *A History of Shopping*, Routledge and Kegan Paul, London, 1966, p.194.

53   Daniel Defoe, *Complete Tradesman*, ii, Ch. 6, quoted in George Dodd, *The Food of London*, Longman Brown, Green and Longmans, London, 1856, pp.110–11.

54   Adam Smith, *An Inquiry into the Nature and Causes of the Wealth of Nations*, ed. Edwin Cannan, Methuen, London, 1925 (2 vols.), vol. I, p.355.

55   Ibid., p.48.

56   Ibid., p.377.

57   Dodd, op.cit., frontispiece.

58   Ibid., p.2.

59   Ibid., p.101.

60   James P. Johnston, *A Hundred Years Eating: Food, Drink and the Daily Diet in Britain since the late Nineteenth Century*, Gill and Macmillan, McGill-Queen's University Press, 1977, p.59.

61   Ibid., p.3.

62   Charles Booth, 'Daily Bread', in *The Colony*, July 1868, quoted in LSE Charles Booth Online Archive, http:.//booth.lse.ac.uk/static/a/2.html.

63   See Edith Whetham, 'The London Milk Trade 1900–1930', in Derek J. Oddy and Derek S. Miller (eds.), *The Making of the Modern British Diet*, Croom Helm, London, 1976, Ch. 6.

64   Frank Trentmann, 'Bread, Milk and Democracy: Consumption and Citizenship in Twentieth-century Britain', in Martin Daunton and Matthew Hilton, *The Politics of Consumption: Material Culture and Citizenship in Europe and America*, Berg, Oxford, 2001, Ch. 7, pp.129–63.

65   *Power Hungry: Six Reasons to Regulate Global Food Corporations*, Action Aid International, 2004, p.4.

66   *Building Smiles*, Wal-Mart Annual Report, 2006, p.12.

67   Quoted in Lang and Heasman, op.cit., p.140.

68   Ibid., p.147.

69   *Power Hungry*, op.cit., p.21.

70   http://www.goodhousekeeping.co.uk/index.php/v1/British_dairy_farms _in_crisis.

71   Charles Fishman, *The Wal-Mart Effect: How an Out-of-Town Superstore Became a Superpower*, Allen Lane, 2006, pp.79–84.

72   Quoted in *Power Hungry*, op.cit., p.27.

73   Professor Heffernan's figures quoted in Lang and Heasman, op.cit., p.144.

74   *Power Hungry*, op.cit., p.4.

75   Fishman, op.cit., p.13.

76 *Power Hungry*, op.cit., p.25.
77 George Monbiot, *Captive State*, Macmillan, 2000, p.205.
78 Ibid., p.204.
79 Felicity Lawrence, the *Guardian*, 8 December 2005.
80 *Stop the Dumping! How EU agricultural subsidies are damaging livelihoods in the developing world*, Oxfam, 2002.
81 Ibid., p.4.
82 Defra, op.cit., p.6. By 2007, the figure was down to 58 per cent.
83 Spokesperson for Elliot Morley, quoted in *Science and Society*, Spring Newsletter 2006, http://www.i-sis.org.uk/isisnews/sis29.php.
84 George Bush, speech delivered on 25 April 2006, broadcast on *Newsnight*, BBC2.
85 FAO, Governing Body of the International Treaty on Plant Genetic Resources for Food and Agriculture, 3 May 2006.
86 *Power Hungry*, op.cit., p.21.
87 Felipe Fernandez-Armesto, the *Guardian*, 24 May 2003.
88 Fred Duncan, interviewed by the author in December 2005.
89 Quoted by Simon Cox in *The Silent Terrorist*, BBC Radio 4, 22 August 2006.
90 Lawrence Wein, *Analyzing a bioterror attack on the food supply: the case of botulinum toxin in milk* (with Y. Liu), Proceedings of the Natural Academy of Sciences, 2005, Vol.102, no.28, pp.9984–9, http://www.pnas.org/cgi/reprint/102/28/9984.pdf.
91 *The Silent Terrorist*, see note 89.

Chapter 3 Market and Supermarket

1 Victor Gruen and Larry Smith, *Shopping Towns USA, The Planning of Shopping Centres*, Reinhold Publishing Corporation, New York, 1960, p.267.
2 Tesco, Asda/Wal-Mart, Sainsbury's and Morrisons.
3 To get an idea of what a narrow squeak London had, take a look at the building at the top west corner of Drury Lane at High Holborn. That is what the whole of Covent Garden would look like now if the GLC had got its way.
4 The Covent Garden Community Association, which still exists, was set up in 1971 specifically to fight the GLC proposals. It was the first case of a community action changing the course of a planning enquiry in Britain. See http://www.coventgarden.org.
5 The area comprises Faneuil Hall and the neighbouring Quincy Market – by which name it is sometimes known.
6 Joanna Blythman, *Shopped: The Shocking Power of British Supermarkets*, Fourth Estate, 2004, p.6.
7 DETR, *Impact Of Large Foodstores On Market Towns And District Centres*, 1998, note 21.

8 *Ghost Town Britain: The Threat From Economic Globalisation To Livelihoods, Liberty And Local Economic Freedom*, New Economics Foundation, 2002, p.15.

9 Blythman, op.cit., p.20.

10 *Grocer* magazine, Vol.229, no.7753, 6 May 2006, p.35.

11 *The Money Programme*, Tesco: Supermarket Superpower, BBC2, 3 June 2005.

12 Jane Jacobs, *The Death and Life of Great American Cities*, Vintage, 1992, p.39.

13 Stale tampons.

14 George Dodd, *The Food of London*, Longman Brown, Green and Longmans, London, 1856, p.244.

15 Gillian Bebbington, *Street Names of London*, Batsford, London, 1972, p.82.

16 See Felix Barker and Peter Jackson, *London: 2000 Years of a City and its People*, Macmillan, London, 1974, p.76.

17 Quoted in Peter Burke, *Popular Culture in Early Modern Europe*, Temple Smith, London, 1978, p.179.

18 Aldo Rossi, *The Architecture of the City*, MIT Press, 1982, p.29.

19 Pier Luigi Fantelli and Franca Pellegrini (eds.), *Il Palazzo della Ragione in Padova*, Studio Editoriale Programma, Padova, 1990, p.20.

20 See R.E. Wycherley, *The Stones of Athens*, Princeton, 1979, p.93.

21 R. E. Wycherley, *How the Greeks Built Cities*, Macmillan Press, 1979, p.66.

22 Since citizenship was barred to women, slaves and foreigners, this aspect of the Agora was not fully inclusive.

23 Quoted in R.E. Wycherley, (1978), op.cit., p.91.

24 Aristotle, *Politics*, vii, 11, 2, quoted in Wycherley (1979), op.cit., p.67.

25 A separate senate house was eventually built on the Pnyx Hill. See Richard Sennett, *Flesh and Stone*, Faber and Faber, 1996, pp.52–67.

26 See Hannah Arendt, *The Human Condition*, University of Chicago Press, 1958, pp.22–78.

27 *Idios*, the ancient Greek root of our word 'idiot', indicated privacy as well as separateness, strangeness. See ibid., pp.38–49.

28 See Burke, op.cit., p.183.

29 Ibid.

30 Ibid., p.186.

31 Mikhail Bakhtin, *Rabelais and His World*, trans. Helene Iswolsky, MIT Press, 1968, p.6.

32 Ibid., p.25.

33 See Anthony Blunt, *Art and Architecture in France 1500–1700*, The Pelican History of Art, Penguin, 1973, pp.160–3.

34 *Punch*, 14 August 1880, quoted in Robert Webber, *Covent Garden: Mud-Salad Market*, J.M. Dent and Sons Ltd, 1969, pp.122–3.

35 The 'sermon' is attended every year by Punch and Judy men and women from all over the country.

36 Burke, op.cit., p.203.

37 Denis Diderot, *Oeuvres Complètes*, Paris, 1769, ed. Paris, 1969, 8:184, quoted

in Stephen Kaplan, *Provisioning Paris: Merchants and Millers in the Grain and Flour Trade During the Eighteenth Century*, Cornell University Press, Ithaca and London, 1984, p.185.

38 Dodd, op.cit., p.255.

39 Quoted in Forshaw and Bergström, *Smithfield Past and Present*, Heinemann, London, 1980, p.59.

40 Michel Foucault, 'Of Other Spaces' (1967), published in French journal *Architecture/Mouvement/Continuité*, October 1984, trans. Jay Miskowiec, www.foucault.info.

41 See Dorothy Davis, *A History of Shopping*, Routledge and Kegan Paul, London, 1966, pp.189–90.

42 G.K. Chesterton, *Wine, Water and Song*, London, 1915, quoted in James P. Johnston, *A Hundred Years Eating: Food, Drink and the Daily Diet in Britain since the Late Nineteenth Century*, Gill and Macmillan, McGill-Queen's University Press, 1977, p.70.

43 Ibid., p.76.

44 Ibid., p.78.

45 See http://www.pigglywiggly.com.

46 Quoted in Malcolm Gladwell, 'The Terrazzo Jungle', the *New Yorker*, 15 March 2004.

47 Victor Gruen, *Centres for the Urban Environment: Survival of the Cities*, New York, Van Nostrand Reinhold, 1973, p.158.

48 Victor Gruen, *The Heart of Our Cities*, Thames and Hudson, London, 1965, pp.248–50.

49 Gruen (1973), op.cit., p.74.

50 Ibid., p.37.

51 Johnston, op.cit., pp.61–2.

52 DETR, op.cit., introduction, paras 4 and 6.

53 See C.J. Chung, J. Inaba, R. Koolhaas, S. Leong (eds.), *Harvard Design School Guide to Shopping*, Taschen, 2001, p.642.

54 See ibid., pp.642–6.

55 See Blythman, op.cit., pp.29–30.

56 See the Tescopoly website, http://www.tescopoly.org/.

57 Friends of the Earth, *Calling the Shots: How Supermarkets Get Their Way in Planning Decisions*, January 2006, p.8.

58 Ibid., pp.21–2.

59 Blythman, op.cit., p.27.

60 Katherine Edwards, quoted in *Calling the Shots*, op.cit., p.23.

61 Building Design Partnership website, www.bdp.net.

62 Planning White Paper, 2007, Paragraph 7.54. See also the Friends of the Earth website, www.foe.co.uk.

63 Joseph F. Sullivan, 'Court Protects speech in Malls', *New York Times*, 21 December 1994, quoted by Sze Tsung Leong, '. . . And then there was Shopping', in Chung, et al., op.cit., p.152.

64 Ibid.

65 Public Eye: Art is a Battlefield, http://www.metroactive.com/papers/ metro/02.27.03/public-eye-0309.html.

66 Marc Augé, *Non-Places, Introduction to an Anthropology of Supermodernity*, trans. John Howe, Verso, New York, 1995, p.34.

67 Jacobs, op.cit., p.65.

68 *Measuring Access to Healthy Food in Sandwell*, The University of Warwick and Sandwell Health Action Zone, 2001, p.8.

69 London Development Agency, *Healthy and Sustainable Food for London, The Mayor's Food Strategy*, May 2006, p.49.

70 Nicholas Saphir, *Review of London Wholesale Markets*, Defra and the Corporation of London, 2002, p.55.

71 *The Mayor's Food Strategy*, op.cit., foreword by Jenny Jones.

72 An initial project to create a local food hub at New Covent Garden began in 2007.

73 Ibid., p.101.

74 Lady Caroline Cranbrook, interviewed by Patrick Barkham, 'The town that said no to Tesco', the *Guardian*, 28 June 2006.

75 *Queen's Market Development Agreement and Lease Summary*, Newham Council, 16 March 2006, p.3.

76 Marie Jackson, 'Can Paris Teach London a Lesson?', BBC News, 11 February 2005, news.bbc.co.uk/1/hi/england/london/4244609.stm.

77 Ibid.

78 From an interview with *Woman's Own*, 31 October 1987.

Chapter 4 The Kitchen

1 James Boswell, *Journal of a Tour of the Hebrides*, quoted in Michael Symons, *A History of Cooks and Cooking*, University of Illinois Press, 2004, p.34.

2 My visit to the Savoy took place several years ago, before the major refurbishment of 2008.

3 Grimod de la Reynière, *Almanach des Gourmands*, vol.4, p.47, quoted in Rebecca L. Spang, *The Invention of the Restaurant*, Harvard, 2000, p.163.

4 Emil Petrie, 'Feeding frenzy: convenient cuisine', *The Money Programme*, BBC2, 6 October 2006, http://news.bbc.co.uk/1/hi/business/5407472.stm.

5 See Carlo Petrini, *Slow Food Nation*, Rizzoli, 2007, pp.164–76.

6 From an interview with a product developer and food consultant to M&S in 2006.

7 Hydrogenated fats, otherwise known as trans fats, are chemically modified fats used widely in the food industry since the early 1900s. They are cheaper and have a longer shelf life than saturated fats, but have been linked to raised cholesterol and heart disease. In 2006, M&S and Waitrose removed hydrogenated fats from all their foods, and Sainsbury's announced its intention to phase them out. In December, Mayor Giuliani announced he was banning them from New York City – easier said than done.

8   I have never understood why so many chefs give recipes for roast potatoes that involve all sorts of 'tricks' to make them fluffy and crunchy without specifying the most important thing of all: the sort of potato you should use. King Edwards are perfect.

9   See http://news.bbc.co.uk/onthisday/hi/dates/stories/april/1/newsid_ 2819000/2819261.stm.

10   *Jamie's School Dinners*, Channel 4, 2005.

11   See Stephen Mennell, *All Manners of Food*, First Illinois Paperback, 1996, pp.309–10.

12   Leonard Woolley, *Excavations at Ur: a record of twelve years' work*, London, Ernest Benn, 1954, p.104.

13   Symons, op.cit., p.311.

14   William Fitzstephen, *Description of London* (c.1175), quoted in George Dodd, *The Food of London*, Longman Brown, Green and Longmans, London, 1856, p.26. See also Xavier Baron, *London 1066–1914: Literary Sources and Documents* (3 vols.), Helm Information, East Sussex, 1997, p.56.

15   Ned Ward, *The London Spy*, quoted in Edwina Ehrman, Hazel Forsyth, Lucy Peltz, Cathy Ross, *London Eats Out: 500 Years of Capital Dining*, Museum of London, 1999, p.40.

16   George Orwell, *Down and Out in Paris and London*, Penguin, 1986, p.67.

17   There are exceptions – for instance there is a strong tradition of professional female cooks from the seventeenth century onwards in England – but their work has generally been confined to household management and the keeping of inns – not haute cuisine. See Mennell, op.cit., pp.95–8.

18   The use of valuable ingredients such as sugar would, however, have been supervised by the mistress of the house.

19   See James P. Johnston, *A Hundred Years Eating: Food, Drink and the Daily Diet in Britain Since the Late Nineteenth Century*, Gill and Macmillan, McGill-Queen's University Press, 1977, p.13.

20   Bisto gravy powder (which stands for Browns, Seasons and Thickens all in One) was first manufactured in 1908. The TV adverts have run since the 1960s.

21   The social anthropologist Claude Lévi-Strauss attempted to analyse the social status of food by constructing a 'culinary triangle' consisting of the raw, the cooked and the rotten, and analysing the connections between them. See Claude Lévi-Strauss, 'The Culinary Triangle', 1966, *Partisan Review* pp.586–95.

22   Such domestic segregation still exists in Arabic cultures. See Richard Sennett, *Flesh and Stone*, Faber and Faber, 1996, p.74.

23   See Chapter 3.

24   For a detailed discussion of the Athenian *symposion*, see Oswyn Murray (ed.), *Sympotica: a Symposium on the Symposion*, Clarendon Press, Oxford, 1990.

25   Athenaeus, *The Deipnosophists*, 137f; 2:129, quoted in Symons, op.cit., p.35.

26 For a detailed social analysis of the Roman house, see Andrew Wallace-Hadrill, 'The Social Structure of the Roman House', *Papers of the British School at Rome*, 56 NS 43 (1988), pp.43–97.

27 See Mennell, op.cit., pp.102–3.

28 Maestro Martino, *The Art of Cooking: The First Modern Cookery Book*, Luigi Ballerini (ed.), trans. Jeremy Parzen, California Studies in Food and Culture 14, 2005, pp.77, 114.

29 Quoted in Mennell, op.cit., p.96.

30 *Relevés* were large dishes of stewed meat or fish; hors d'oeuvres accompaniments placed around them; entrées smaller savoury dishes; and *entremets* lighter sweet or savoury dishes served between courses.

31 Isabella Beeton, *The Book of Household Management*, London, Cassell & Co., 1861, reprint 2000, p.905.

32 J.E. Panton, *From Kitchen to Garrett*, quoted in Roy Strong, *Feast: A History of Grand Eating*, Jonathan Cape, London, 2002, p.293.

33 *Manners and Tone of Good Society, and Solecisms to be Avoided, by a Member of the Aristocracy*, Frederick Warne and Co., 1885, quoted in Strong, op.cit., p.294.

34 Quoted in Mennell, op.cit., p.309.

35 See Keith Thomas, *Man and the Natural World: Changing Attitudes in England 1500–1800*, Allen Lane, 1983, p.297.

36 See Tristram Stuart, *The Bloodless Revolution: Radical Vegetarians and The Discovery of India*, Harper Press, 2006, p.423.

37 Quoted in Thomas, op.cit., p.300.

38 John Ruskin, *Sesame and Lilies*, 1865, quoted in John Burnett, *A Social History of Housing, 1815–1970*, Methuen, London, 1986, p.197.

39 Robert Kerr, quoted in J.J. Stevenson, *House Architecture*, Macmillan, London, 1880, vol. 2, p.78.

40 Ibid., pp.82–3.

41 Robert Kerr, *The Gentleman's House*, John Murray, London (1864), 2nd edn, 1865, p.210.

42 See Burnett, op.cit., pp.70–7.

43 One alternative was 'catering flats' – blocks of flats that supplied catering services like those of a hotel. Residents could either choose to eat in a communal dining room, or take meals in their flats.

44 Catherine Beecher, *A Treatise on Domestic Economy*, Harper, 1842, p.62.

45 Ibid., p.143.

46 The Panopticon, with its underlying messages of observation, order and obedience, is discussed by Michel Foucault in *Discipline and Punish: The Birth of the Prison*, Peregrine Books, 1985.

47 Pasteur went on to invent one of the best-known processes in microbiology: pasteurisation, a process in universal use today.

48 Quoted in Annegret S. Ogden, *The Great American Housewife: From Helpmate to Wage-earner 1776–1986*, Greenwood Press, Westport, Connecticut and London, 1986, p.141.

49 Quoted in Barbara Ehrenreich and Deirdre English, *For Her Own Good: 150 Years of the Expert's Advice to Women*, Pluto Press, London, 1979, p.143.

50 Christine Frederick, *Efficient Housekeeping, or Household Engineering: Scientific Management in the Home*, George Routledge, 1915, p.22.

51 Ibid., p.46.

52 Ibid., p.93.

53 Nick Bullock, 'First the Kitchen: Then the Façade', *Journal of Design History*, Vol.1, No.3/4 (1988), pp.177–92.

54 Grete Lihotzky in *Schlesisches Heim (Silesian Home)*, 8/1921, p.217.

55 Le Corbusier, 'The Hour of Architecture', in *The Decorative Art of Today*, trans. James I. Dunnett, The Architectural Press, 1987, p.132.

56 Le Corbusier, *Towards a New Architecture*, Trans. Frederick Etchells, The Architectural Press, 1972, p.115; and Le Corbusier, *The Decorative Art of Today*, op.cit., p.188.

57 See Mark Wigley, *White Walls, Designer Dresses: the Fashioning of Modern Architecture*, MIT Press, London, 1995, pp.3–8.

58 Le Corbusier, *The Decorative Art of Today*, op.cit., p.188.

59 F.R.S. Yorke, *The Modern House*, The Architectural Press, London, 1934, p.32.

60 Lesley Jackson, *'Contemporary': Architecture and Interiors of the 1950s*, Phaidon, 1994, p.83.

61 Echoing the Victorian manual writers, Le Corbusier even suggests putting the kitchen on the roof to avoid smells: hardly the practical solution one would expect for a 'machine for living in'.

62 See Rayner Banham, *Theory and Design in the First Machine Age*, The Architectural Press, London, 1960, pp.305–19.

63 Jun'ichiro Tanizaki, *In Praise of Shadows* (1933), trans. Thomas J. Harper and Edward G. Seidensticker, Jonathan Cape, London, 1991, p.20.

64 See Harvey Levenstein, *The Paradox of Plenty: A Social History of Eating in Modern America*, Oxford University Press, 1993, p.34.

65 Ibid., p.32.

66 Ibid., p.37.

67 Ibid., p.102.

68 George Nelson and Henry Wright, *Tomorrow's House – A Complete Guide For the Home-builder*, Simon and Schuster, New York, 1945, p.72.

69 Ibid., p.75.

70 Pat Mainardi, *The Politics of Housework*, Redstockings, 1970, quoted in Joanna Blythman, *Bad Food Britain*, Fourth Estate, 2006, p.72.

71 Smash was instant mashed potato made popular by a brilliant TV ad in which a group of metallic 'aliens' mocked earthlings for their antiquated way of peeling potatoes, boiling them, and mashing them up with butter and milk.

72 IGD Convenience Retailing Market Overview factsheet, http://www.igd.com/CIR.asp?menuid=51&cirid=109.

73 Quoted in Andrew Seth and Geoffrey Randall, *The Grocers: The Rise and Rise of the Supermarket Chains*, Kogan Page, London, 1999, p.125.

74 *Eating Habits – Pan European Overview*, report by Mintel, December 2002.

75 *Eating Habits – Scratch vs Convenience Cooking*, report by Mintel, June 2005.

76 The Terra Madre (Mother Earth) conference is held in Turin every two years.

77 WRAP, *Understanding Food Waste*, March 2007, p.13.

78 Quoted in ibid., p.13.

79 Type B malnutrition is the new disease of the urban poor – see Chapter 5.

80 Mulholland Research & Consulting, *Perceptions of Privacy and Density in Housing, Report on Research Findings Prepared for the Popular Housing Group*, August 2003, p.100. See also *Housing Space Standards*, Mayor of London, August 2006, pp.47, 138.

81 *Housing Space Standards*, op.cit., Appendix 9, p.24.

82 PPG3 (1992), quoted in ibid., Appendix 9, p.2.

83 Mulholland Research & Consulting, op.cit., p.100.

84 Commission for Architecture and the Built Environment (CABE), *What Home Buyers Want: attitudes and decision making among consumers*, 2005, p.20.

85 *Housing Space Standards*, op.cit., p.42.

86 See the Joseph Rowntree Foundation website, http://www.jrf.org.uk/housingandcare/lifetimehomes/.

87 Blythman, op.cit., p.196.

88 http://www.waitrose.com/food_drink/foodexpertise/readymeals/index.asp.

89 Patricia Michelson, *The Cheese Room*, Penguin, 2001, p.16.

90 In January 2008, the government announced that compulsory cooking lessons for 11–14 year olds were to be re-introduced, although funding levels were minimal.

Chapter 5 At Table

1 Jean Anthelme Brillat-Savarin, *The Physiology of Taste* (*La Physiologie du gout*, 1825), trans. Anne Drayton, Penguin, 1970, p.13.

2 'Benchers' is short for Masters of the Bench; 'silks' are members of Queen's Counsel.

3 I am reliably informed that the food at Middle Temple has improved considerably since my meal there.

4 The inheritance is shared by Middle Temple's sister Inn, Inner Temple. Their chapel, Temple Church, gained international fame in 2004 thanks to its inclusion in Dan Brown's fantasy account of the Templar inheritance, *The Da Vinci Code*.

5 The Honourable Society of the Middle Temple, *Handbook* (2007), p.12.

6 See http://www.innertemple.org.uk/.

7 The Honourable Society of the Middle Temple, *Dining in Hall*, 1970, p.16.

8 According to the Institute of Grocery Distribution, 51.1 per cent of meals were eaten alone in 2006, compared to 34.4 per cent in 1994. IGD, *Grocery Retailing Report*, 2006.

9   See John Burnett, 'Time, place and content: the changing structure of meals in Britain in the 19th and 20th centuries', in Martin R. Schärer and Alexander Fenton (eds.), *Food and Material Culture*, Tuckwell Press, East Linton, Scotland, 1998, and Ch. 9, p.121; Office of National Statistics, *Family Spending 2002–3*.

10   In 2006, 48 per cent of meals in the USA were eaten outside the home.

11   Figures from the IGD website.

12   *The Times*, 4 June 2005, quoted in Joanna Blythman, *Bad Food Britain*, Fourth Estate, 2006, p.269.

13   For a detailed discussion of Seder, see Chaim Raphael, *A Feast of History*, Weidenfeld and Nicolson, 1972.

14   Brillat-Savarin, op.cit., p.162.

15   Although ritual halal and kosher slaughter is also carried out in Britain, it can only be done legally in licensed slaughterhouses.

16   The existence of diet clubs such as WeightWatchers emphasises how much we need to share our eating habits with others – even if those habits involve not eating.

17   *The Complete Works of Montaigne*, trans. Donald M. Frame, Hamish Hamilton, 1958, p.846.

18   Georg Simmel, 'Sociology of the Meal' (1910), trans. Michael Symons, *Food and Foodways*, Vol.5, No.4, 1994, pp.345–50.

19   The satisfyingly homophonic German equivalent, '*Der Mensch ist was er isst*', is attributed to the nineteenth-century philosopher Ludwig Andreas von Feuerbach.

20   Margaret Visser, *The Rituals of Dinner*, Penguin, 1991, p.87.

21   Homer, *The Odyssey*, trans. E.V. Rieu and revised by D.C.H. Rieu, Penguin, 1991, p.60.

22   See Visser, op.cit., pp.90–9.

23   Oscar Wilde, *A Woman of No Importance*, Act 2.

24   Visser, op.cit., p.17.

25   Ibid., p.92.

26   *Regional Eating and Drinking Habits*, Mintel, 2001, quoted in Sue Palmer, *Toxic Childhood*, Orion Books, 2006, p.34.

27   The survey was carried out by Brewsters restaurant chain, quoted in Palmer, op.cit., p.33. Of course, eating with your fingers is perfectly polite in other cultures.

28   Madhur Jaffrey, *An Invitation to Indian Cookery*, Jonathan Cape, 1987, p.21.

29   Blythman, op.cit., pp.87 and 217.

30   Athenaeus, *Deipnosophists* (6.228d), quoted in John Wilkins, David Harvey, Mike Dobson (eds.), *Food in Antiquity*, University of Exeter Press, 1995, p.197.

31   Anonymous, 1879, quoted in Visser, op.cit., p.69.

32   Xenophon, *Memorabilia* (3.14), quoted in Wilkins et al., op.cit., p.208.

33   See James Davidson, *Opsophagia: Revolutionary Eating at Athens*, in Wilkins et al., op.cit., pp.204–13.

34 Erasmus, *De Civilitate morum puerilium* (1530), trans. Brian McGregor, in *Collected Works of Erasmus*, ed. J.K. Sowards, University of Toronto Press, 1985, p.273.

35 Ibid., p.289.

36 Emily Post, *Etiquette in Society, in Business, in Politics and at Home*, Funk and Wagnalls, New York, 1922, pp.244 and 223.

37 Ibid., p.189.

38 Ibid., p.2.

39 Brillat-Savarin, op.cit., p.55.

40 Pliny, *Letters*, quoted in Roy Strong, *Feast: A History of Grand Eating*, Jonathan Cape, London, 2002, p.97.

41 Petronius, *The Satyricon*, trans. J.P. Sullivan, Penguin, 1981, pp.49–55.

42 Suetonius, *The Twelve Caesars*, quoted in Strong, op.cit., p.273.

43 For a discussion of attitudes toward excessive eating in Rome, see Chapter 6.

44 Michael Symons, *A History of Cooks and Cooking*, University of Illinois Press, 2004, p.268, and Strong, op.cit., p.8.

45 William Langland, *Piers Plowman*, quoted in Strong, op.cit., p.94.

46 Strong, op.cit., p.205.

47 Ibid., p.209.

48 Rebecca L. Spang, *The Invention of the Restaurant*, Harvard, 2000, p.96.

49 See Burnett, op.cit., pp.117–19.

50 Colin Clair, *Kitchen and Table*, Abelard-Schuman, London, 1964, p.105.

51 Burnett, op.cit., p.122.

52 Mary Douglas, 'Deciphering a Meal', in Carole Counihan, P. Van Esterik (eds.), *Food and Culture*, Routledge, New York, 1997, Ch. 4.

53 Thomas Decker, *Gull's Horn-Book* (1609), quoted in George Dodd, *The Food of London*, Longman Brown, Green and Longmans, London, 1856, p.87,

54 Hazel Forsyth, in Edwina Ehrman, Hazel Forsyth, Lucy Peltz, Cathy Ross, *London Eats Out: 500 Years of Capital Dining*, Museum of London, 1999, pp.34–40.

55 See John Schofield (ed.), *The London Surveys of Ralph Treswell*, London Topographical Society Publication No. 135, 1987, p.86.

56 Samuel Pepys' Diary, 1 August 1660, quoted by Forsyth, in Ehrman et al., op.cit., p.37.

57 Like restaurants today, taverns made most of their profits from stiff mark-ups on wine.

58 Ehrman et al., op.cit., p.46.

59 Mr Fairholt, *Percy Society's Publications* (1845), quoted in Dodd, op.cit., p.88.

60 See Jürgen Habermas, *The Structural Transformation of the Public Sphere* (1962), Polity Press, 1992, pp.89–102.

61 Quoted in Spang, op.cit., p.34.

62 Antoine Joseph Nicolas Rosny, *Le Péruvian à Paris* (1801), quoted in ibid., p.64.

63   See Stephen Mennell, *All Manners of Food: Eating and Taste in England and France from the Middle Ages to the Present*, First Illinois Paperback, 1996, pp.151–3.

64   William Blanchard Jerrold, *The Epicure's Year Book and Table Companion*, London, 1868, quoted by Edwina Ehrman in Ehrman et al., op.cit., pp.72–3.

65   Quoted in Harvey Levenstein, *The Paradox of Plenty: A Social History of Eating in Modern America*, Oxford University Press, 1993, p.228.

66   Ibid., p.51.

67   Quoted in ibid., p.229.

68   Ibid., p.233.

69   In exposing the iniquities of the fast-food industry, *Fast Food Nation* followed in the footsteps of *The Jungle* of a century earlier. In the film *Supersize Me*, the journalist Morgan Spurlock reported on the dangers of living on nothing but McDonald's for a month.

70   Reported by Reuters, September 2004.

71   McDonald's press release, 13 April 2007, http://www.mcdonalds.com.

72   See Levenstein, op.cit., pp.28–30.

73   George Orwell, *The Road to Wigan Pier* (1937), Penguin, 2001, p.92.

74   For a detailed discussion of the French 'decapitation' of English cookery, see Mennell, op.cit., pp.204–14.

75   Derek Cooper, *The Bad Food Guide*, Routledge and Kegan Paul, 1967, p.xvi.

76   Joanne Finkelstein, *Dining Out: A Sociology of Modern Manners*, Polity Press, Blackwell, 1989, p.3.

77   One tube advert for The Brunswick read, 'The Bloomsbury Set might have had culture, but they didn't have Waitrose.'

78   Yes, it contains coffee. But by the time it has been decaffeinated and had frothy milk, sugar and flavourings added, it effectively becomes a large, hot milkshake: a nursery drink.

79   See Naomi Klein, *No Logo*, Flamingo, 2001, pp.135–7.

80   Brillat-Savarin, op.cit., p.208.

81   See the splendidly named Barbara J. Rolls, 'The Supersizing of America, Portion Size and the Obesity Epidemic', *Nutrition Today*, Vol.38, No.2, March/April 2003, pp.42–53.

82   Greg Critser, *Fat Land*, Penguin, 2003, p.14.

83   Ibid., p.28.

84   Ibid.

85   Type B malnutrition describes of the effects of eating too many processed foods, leaving people simultaneously obese and undernourished, with a high risk of developing heart disease and Type 2 diabetes.

86   Paul Rozin, quoted in Levenstein, op.cit., p.256.

87   Banzhaf was also the first lawyer to sue tobacco companies on health grounds.

88   http://news.bbc.co.uk/1/hi/england/south_yorkshire/5349392.stm.

Notes

Chapter 6 Waste

1 Victor Hugo, *Les Misérables* (1862), trans. Norman Denny, Penguin, 1982, p.1065.

2 The engines were fabricated in 1856 by James Watt and Co. to designs by Joseph Bazalgette.

3 Richard Trench and Ellis Hillman, *London Under London*, John Murray, 1993, p.60.

4 Donald Reid, *Paris Sewers and Sewermen: Realities and Representations*, Harvard University Press, 1993, p.10.

5 Coventry Leet Book, quoted in Dorothy Davis, *A History of Shopping*, Routledge and Kegan Paul, 1966, p.24.

6 Estimates of London's size vary. See B.M.S. Campbell et al., *A Medieval Capital and its Grain Supply*, Historical Geography Research Series No.30, 1993, pp.9–11.

7 Trench and Hillman, op.cit., p.60.

8 Ibid., p.63.

9 Malcolm Thick, *The Neat House Gardens, Early Market Gardening Around London*, Prospect Books, 1998.

10 John Strype, *An Accurate Edition of Stow's Survey of London* (1720), quoted in Robert Webber, *Covent Garden: Mud-Salad Market*, J.M. Dent and Sons Ltd, 1969, p.31.

11 The first patented flushing WC was designed by Alexander Cummings in 1775. See Trench and Hillman, op.cit., p.64.

12 John Snow's discovery of germ theory was still two decades away.

13 Edwin Chadwick, *Inquiry into the Sanitary Conditions of the Labouring Population of Great Britain*, London, 1842, p.369.

14 Rome's sewers only served public buildings such as latrines and bath-houses. Most private houses made do with cesspits, while multistorey apartment buildings, *insulae*, had no means of sewage disposal. See Jérôme Carcopino, *Daily Life in Ancient Rome* (1941), Penguin, 1991, p.51.

15 According to some scholars, Rome was founded by the Etruscans. Certainly many Roman city-founding rites can be traced directly to Etruscan practice. See Joseph Rykwert, *The Idea of a Town*, Faber and Faber, 1976, p.29.

16 Carcopino, op.cit., p.51.

17 The Cloaca is still in use today, its mouth visible just downriver of the Ponte Rotto.

18 Justus von Liebig, *Agriculturchemie*, quoted in Herbert Girardet, *Cities, People, Planet: Liveable Cities for a Sustainable World*, Wiley Academy, 2004, p.77.

19 Reid, op.cit., p.56.

20 Trench and Hillman, op.cit., p.71.

21 Although John Snow made his discovery of the link between cholera and contaminated water in 1854, 'germ theory' was not yet fully understood. See Chapter 4.

22 Quoted in Trench and Hillman, op.cit., p.69.

23 One engine, Prince Consort, has been restored to full working order by the Crossness Engines Trust, and can be seen in action on 'steaming days'. See http://www.crossness.org.uk/.

24 http://www.thameswateruk.co.uk.

25 Girardet, op.cit., p.227.

26 Hugo, op.cit., p.1061.

27 WRAP, *Understanding Food Waste*, March 2007, p.4.

28 Ibid., p.19.

29 Defra, *Waste Strategy for England*, 2007, p.20.

30 WRAP, op.cit., p.9.

31 Ibid., p.12.

32 Walkers Midshire, one of Britain's largest food manufacturers, has a special lab dedicated to 'abusing' its products in various ways, and testing the outcome.

33 Mary Douglas, *Purity and Danger: An Analysis of the Concepts of Pollution and Taboo* (1966), Routledge, 1995, p.2.

34 Ibid., p.4.

35 Ibid., p.36.

36 Ibid., p.161.

37 Ibid.

38 Ibid., p.162.

39 The dilemma is captured in the double meaning of the English word 'soil', both a verb meaning 'make something dirty' and as a noun meaning earth; and the American usage of the word 'dirt', primarily referring to earth or soil.

40 Hugo, op.cit., p.1065.

41 Henry Mayhew, *London Labour and the London Poor*, quoted in Reid, op.cit., p.21.

42 Reid, op.cit., p.3.

43 Sometimes the transformation was direct: one of Paris's most fanciful parks, Buttes-Chaumont, was built on top of the city's notorious old rubbish tip at Montfaucon, made obsolete by the construction of the sewers and designed by Adolphe Alphand, another of Haussmann's chief sewer engineers.

44 'The food we eat – crops rot as supermarkets demand perfection', the *Observer*, 16 August 1998, quoted in *A Battle in Store?*, Sustain, 2000, p.11.

45 There has been some controversy in Britain over Whole Foods Market's 'organic' status, since rules governing the use of the term are less stringent in the US than they are in Britain.

46 Timothy Jones (2004), University of Arizona's Bureau of Applied Research Anthropology, http://www.foodnavigator-usa.com/news/ng.asp?id=56376 -us-wastes-half.

47 http://www.fareshare.org.uk/.

48 The word 'freegan' is a conflation of 'free' and 'vegan'.

49 J.N. Postgate, *Early Mesopotamia: Society and Economy at the Dawn of History*, Routledge, London and New York, 1994, p.181.

50 Plato, *Critias*, 111C, *The Collected Dialogues*, eds. Edith Hamilton and Huntington Cairns, Princeton University Press, 1987, p.1216.

51 The mound, now Monte Testaccio, remains intact. It was the city's main rubbish dump until the fourth century AD.

52 See Neville Morley, *Metropolis and Hinterland*, Cambridge University Press, 1996, p.88.

53 Quoted in Girardet, op.cit., p.46.

54 Quoted in Massimo Montanari, *The Culture of Food*, trans. Carl Ipsen, Blackwell, Oxford, 1994, p.10.

55 Jeremy Bentham, *Panopticon*, cited in Dominique Laporte, *History of Shit*, trans. Nadia Benabid and Rodolphe el-Khoury, MIT Press, 2000, p.119.

56 See Jared Diamond, *Collapse*, Penguin, 2005, p.11.

57 Suetonius, *Vespasian*, Book 23, quoted in Laporte, op.cit., p.77.

58 Frances Trollope, *Domestic Manners of the Americans*, 1832, quoted in John Clubbe, *Cincinnati Observed*, Ohio State University Press, 1992, p.88.

59 Hugo, op.cit., p.1061.

60 Quoted in Reid, op.cit., p.59.

61 Ibid., p.62.

62 Ibid., p.66.

63 Defra, op.cit., p.23.

64 House of Commons Communities and Local Government Committee on Refuse Collection, Fifth Report of Session 2006–07, p.4.

65 The EU Landfill Directive requires that the amount of biodegradable waste sent to landfill be reduced to 75 per cent of its 1995 levels by 2010, and 35 per cent by 2020.

66 Girardet, op.cit., p.209.

67 Reid, op.cit., p.4.

68 Robin Murray, *Creating Wealth from Waste*, Demos, 1999, p.4.

Chapter 7 Sitopia

1 In comparison, new housing developments in Britain between 1997 and 2001 were built at an average of just 25 dwellings per hectare.

2 From an interview with the author in August 2007.

3 Ibid.

4 The concept of an 'ecological footprint' was invented by the Canadian ecologist William Rees in 1992. Although its method of measurement is disputed, it remains a useful means of estimating and describing the impact of our lifestyles on the planet.

5 Living Planet Report, World Wildlife Fund, 2006, p.3.

6 European Commission, *Environmental Impact of Products (EIPRO)*, May 2006, p.17.

7 Jonathan Watts, 'Invisible City', the *Guardian*, 15 March 2006.

8   The approximate volume of the Albert Hall is 120,000 cubic metres; the volume of a tonne of municipal waste around 10.

9   Arup, Dongtan Eco-City, Shanghai, Presentation to PIA National Congress, Perth, Australia, May 2007.

10   Thomas More, *Utopia* (1516), trans. Paul Turner, Penguin, 2003, p.53.

11   Ibid., p.73.

12   Aristotle, *The Politics*, ed. Stephen Everson, Cambridge University Press, 1988 (Book 2, 1265a 14–16), p.30.

13   Fred D. Miller Jr, *Nature, Justice and Rights in Aristotle's Politics*, Clarendon Press, 1995, p.349.

14   St Benedict, *Rule*, Chapter 48, quoted in Wolfgang Braunfels, *Monasteries of Western Europe*, Thames and Hudson, 1972, p.233.

15   Ibid., p.42.

16   Gerrard Winstanley, et al., *The True Levellers Standard Advanced, or, The State of Community opened, and Presented to the Sons of Men*, London, 1649, p.6 (British Library Facsimile E.552.5).

17   Niall Ferguson, *Empire: How Britain Made the Modern World*, Allen Lane, 2003, p.69.

18   Ibid.

19   Frank and Fritzie Manuel, *Utopian Thought in the Western World*, Harvard University Press, 1979, p.679.

20   See Colin Rowe, *Collage City*, MIT Press, 1979, p.15.

21   Fourier's ingenious solution for the collection of rubbish was to organise children (who were naturally drawn towards dirt) into gangs and make it into a competition. See Joseph Rykwert, *The Seduction of Place: the History and Future of the City*, Oxford University Press, 2000, pp.63–4.

22   Karl Marx and Friedrich Engels, *The Communist Manifesto* (1848), trans. Samuel Moore, Penguin Classics, 2002, p.255.

23   Quoted in David Harvey, *Spaces of Hope*, Edinburgh University Press, 2000, p.30.

24   Marx and Engels, op.cit., p.223.

25   Ibid., p.244.

26   William Morris, *News From Nowhere and Other Writings*, ed. Clive Wilmer, Penguin Classics, 1993, pp.61 and 77.

27   Ibid., pp.61 and 122.

28   Howard had first-hand experience of the American Homestead Act of 1862, which allowed anyone to stake a claim to 160 acres of farmland for free, provided they built a house on it and proved themselves capable of farming it successfully for five years.

29   Identified by him as unsanitary overcrowding in towns and lack of services and opportunity in the countryside.

30   Ebenezer Howard, *Garden Cities of To-Morrow* (1902), MIT Press paperback edition, 1965, pp.60–2.

31   Ibid., p.51.

32   Density figures converted from Lewis Mumford, *The Garden City Idea and*

Modern Planning, in ibid., p.32.

33   Howard, op.cit., p.142.

34   See Peter Hall, *Cities of Tomorrow*, Blackwell, 2002, pp.97–101.

35   See Le Corbusier, *The City of To-morrow and its Planning* (*Urbanisme*, 1922), trans. Frederick Etchells, Dover Publications, New York, 1987.

36   Le Corbusier, *Oeuvres Complètes* I, p.118.

37   Frank Lloyd Wright, *The Living City*, Horizon Press, New York, 1958, pp.25 and 20.

38   'Usonia' was Samuel Butler's name for North America.

39   Wright, op.cit., p.62.

40   Ibid., p.60.

41   Ibid., pp.129–31.

42   Ibid., pp.118–19.

43   *Atmos* in ancient Greek means vapour, *sitos* food, and *sphaira* ball.

44   http://www.countryside.gov.uk/LAR/archive/ETV/index.asp.

45   The term 'permaculture' (from permanent + agriculture) was invented by the Australians Bill Mollison and David Holmgren, who outlined their vision of an eco-friendly sustainable agriculture in their book *Permaculture One* in 1978.

46   See Colin Tudge, *So Shall We Reap*, Allen Lane, 2003, pp.345–51.

47   See Christopher Alexander, *A City is Not a Tree*, Architectural Forum, vol.122, No.1, April 1965.

48   La Via Campesina website, http://www.viacampesina.org.

49   John Stuart Mill, *On Liberty*, John W. Parker and Son, London, 1859, p.22.

50   *File on Four*, BBC Radio, 13 March 2007.

51   Eglus are made by a firm called Omlet: http://www.omlet.co.uk.

52   'Hens rule the roost in suburbia', *The Sunday Times*, 5 April 2007.

53   David Crouch and Colin Ward, *The Allotment: Its Landscape and Culture*, Faber and Faber, 1988, p.76.

54   Raymond J. Struyk and Karen Angelici, 'The Russian Dacha Phenomenon', *Housing Studies*, Vol.II, Issue 2, April 1996, pp.233–50.

55   Oleg Moldakov, *Support for Urban Agriculture Needs Integration in St Petersburg*, RUAF, Resource centres on urban agriculture and food security, http://www.ruaf.org/node/174.

56   A 1970s BBC sitcom in which a suburban family, the Goods, scandalised their neighbours by digging up their suburban garden and turning it into a farm.

57   See Jorge Peña Díaz and Phil Harris, 'Urban Agriculture in Havana, Opportunities for the Future', in André Viljoen (ed.), *CPULs, Continuous Productive Urban Landscapes*, Architectural Press, 2005, p.137.

58   Sinan Koont, 'Food Security in Cuba', *Monthly Review*, vol.55, no.8, January 2004, http://www.monthlyreview.org/0104koont.htm.

59   Viljoen, op.cit., p.11.

60   http://www.verticalfarm.com.

61   Ibid.

62 Based on a population of 10 million, that is the number of vertical farms that would be needed to feed London, according to Despommier's figures.

63 http://www.verticalfarm.com.

64 http://www.mvrdv.nl/_v2/projects/181_pigcity/index.html.

65 Patrick Geddes, *The Valley Plan of Civilization*, *The Survey*, 54, pp.40–4, quoted in Hall, op.cit., p.149.

66 Patrick Geddes, *Cities in Evolution* (1915), Routledge, 1997, p.96.

67 Richard Rogers, *Cities for a Small Planet*, Faber and Faber, 1997, pp.32–3.

68 *Towards an Urban Renaissance*: Report of the Urban Task Force, Lord Rogers of Riverside (Chair), Department of the Environment, Transport and the Regions, 1999.

69 Susan Emmett, 'A new property map of England', *The Times*, 22 June 2007.

70 Carlo Petrini, *Slow Food: The Case for Taste*, Columbia University Press, 2001, p.10.

71 Cittaslow manifesto, http://www.cittaslow.net.

72 Ibid.

73 Bradford City Council website.

74 http://transitiontowns.org/Totnes/.

75 It is ironic that milk floats, by virtue of working for a virtual monopoly, actually delivered one of the 'greenest' food delivery systems yet.

76 Community-supported agriculture is a growing movement in both the USA and the UK, in which city-dwellers invest in local farms, guaranteeing them a market and even in some cases helping the farmer to work his land.

Bibliography

A Note on Sources

Books as broad in scope as *Hungry City* necessarily rely on the research and scholarship of others. Since it has not always been possible to do them full justice in the text, I have listed below the key works that have helped and inspired me through the writing of this book.

Massimo Montanari's *Culture of Food* formed the basis of my understanding of European food culture, and Fernand Braudel's *Civilization and Capitalism 15th–18th Century* that of its material life. *Man and the Natural World* by Keith Thomas is a scholarly analysis of attitudes towards nature in early modern England; Simon Schama's *Landscape and Memory* a penetrating exploration of man's relationship with wilderness. George Dodd's 1856 *The Food of London* is a remarkable survey of the Victorian capital's food supply; Stephen Kaplan's *Provisioning Paris* a similarly exhaustive account of the grain supply to that of eighteenth-century France. My analysis of the modern British food industry draws on the work of many campaigning food journalists, foremost among them Joanna Blythman and Felicity Lawrence, as well as on pioneering studies carried out by Sustain, the New Economics Foundation and Tim Lang at the City University Food Policy Unit. For anyone wishing to understand the roots of modern American food culture, Harvey Levenstein's *Paradox of Plenty* is essential reading, while

Stephen Mennell's *All Manners of Food* is equally indispensable on the subject of French and English cuisine. Margaret Visser's *The Rituals of Dinner* is the perfect introduction to the subject of table manners, while the Museum of London's publication *London Eats Out: 500 Years of Capital Dining* is full of detailed facts about the capital's historical eateries. Rebecca Spang's *The Invention of the Restaurant* is a scholarly study of the origins of restaurant dining in Paris and John Burnett's *A Social History of Housing* an equally insightful account of nineteenth- and twentieth-century domestic mores in Britain. Donald Reid's *Paris Sewers and Sewermen* provides an original critique of cultural attitudes towards waste in the nineteenth-century city and Peter Hall's *Cities of Tomorrow* a scholarly analysis of twentieth-century urban planning. My vision of a possible future for ethical agriculture is indebted to Jules Pretty's *Agri-Culture* and Colin Tudge's *So Shall We Reap*, and to the campaigning work of the Soil Association and the Slow Food Movement.

Select Bibliography

Arendt, Hannah, *The Human Condition*, University of Chicago Press, 1958

Atkins, Peter, Simmons, Ian and Roberts, Brian, *People Land and Time*, Hodder, 1998

Augé, Marc, *Non-Places: Introduction to an Anthropology of Supermodernity*, Trans. John Howe, Verso, 1995

Bakhtin, Mikhail, *Rabelais and His World*, Trans. Helene Iswolsky, MIT Press, 1968

Banham, Rayner, *Theory and Design in the First Machine Age*, The Architectural Press, 1960

Barker, Felix and Jackson, Peter, *London: 2000 Years of a City and its People*, Macmillan, 1974

Baron, Xavier, *London 1066–1914: Literary Sources and Documents*, 3 vols, Helm Information, 1997

Beecher, Catherine, *A Treatise on Domestic Economy*, Harper and Bros., 1842

Beeton, Isabella, *The Book of Household Management*, Cassell & Co., 2000; 1861

Benton, Tim, *The Villas of Le Corbusier*, Yale University Press, 1987

Blythman, Joanna, *Shopped: The Shocking Power of British Supermarkets*, Fourth Estate, 2004

———, *Bad Food Britain*, Fourth Estate, 2006

Booth, Charles, *Life and Labour of the People in London*, Macmillan, 1903

Braudel, Fernand, *Civilization and Capitalism 15th–18th Century*, 2 vols Trans. Siân Reynolds, Collins, 1981

Braunfels, Wolfgang, *Monasteries of Western Europe,* Thames and Hudson, 1972

Brillat-Savarin, Jean Anthelme, *The Physiology of Taste* (*La Physiologie du goût),* Trans. Anne Drayton, Penguin Classics 1994; 1825

Burke, Peter, *Popular Culture in Early Modern Europe*, Temple Smith, 1978

Burnett, John, *A Social History of Housing, 1815–1970*, Methuen, 1986

Campbell, B.M.S., Galloway J.A., Keene D. and Murphy M.A., *A Medieval Capital and its Grain Supply: Agrarian Production and Distribution in the London Region c.1300*, Historical Geography Research Series No.30, 1993

Carcopino, Jérôme, *Daily Life in Ancient Rome*, Penguin, 1991

Chadwick, Edwin, *An Inquiry into the Sanitary Conditions of the Labouring Population of Great Britain*, Poor Law Commission, 1842

Chandler, Tertuis and Fox, Gerald, *3000 Years of Urban Growth*, Academic Press, 1974

Chung, C.J., Inaba, J., Koolhaas, R. and Leong S.(eds.), *Harvard Design School Guide to Shopping*, Taschen, 2001

Clair, Colin, *Kitchen and Table*, Abelard-Schuman, 1964

Clubbe, John, *Cincinnati Observed*, Ohio State University Press, 1992

Cobbett, William, *Rural Rides*, 2 vols, Reeves and Turner, 1885; 1830

Coffin, David R., *The Villa in the Life of Renaissance Rome*, Princeton University Press, 1979

Cooper, Derek, *The Bad Food Guide*, Routledge and Kegan Paul, 1967

Counihan, Carole and Van Esterik, P. (eds), *Food and Culture*, Routledge, 1997

Critser, Greg, *Fat Land*, Penguin, 2003

Crouch, David and Ward, Colin, *The Allotment*, Faber and Faber, 1988

Davis, Dorothy, *A History of Shopping*, Routledge and Kegan Paul, 1966

Defoe, Daniel, *A Tour Thro' the Whole Island of Great Britain*, Frank Cass & Co., 1968; 1720

Dennis, Michael, *Court and Garden: From the French Hôtel to the City of Modern Architecture*, MIT Press, 1986

Diamond, Jared, *Collapse*, Penguin, 2005

Dodd, George, *The Food of London*, Longman, Brown, Green and Longmans, 1856

Dyck, Ian, *William Cobbett and Rural Popular Culture*, Cambridge University Press, 1992

Douglas, Mary, *Purity and Danger: An Analysis of the Concepts of Pollution and Taboo,* Routledge, 1995; 1966

——, 'Deciphering a Meal', in *Daedalus* 101, 1972

Ehrenreich Barbara and English, Deirdre, *For Her Own Good: 150 Years of the Expert's Advice to Women*, Pluto Press, 1979

Ehrman, Edwina, Forsyth, Hazel, Peltz, Lucy, and Ross, Cathy, *London Eats Out, 500 Years of Capital Dining*, Museum of London, 1999

Eltis, Walter, *The Classical Theory of Economic Growth*, Palgrave, 2000

Erasmus, *De Civilitate morum puerilium*, Trans. Brian McGregor, in *Collected Works of Erasmus*, ed. J. K. Sowards, University of Toronto Press, 1985; 1530

Ferguson, Niall, *Empire: How Britain Made the Modern World*, Allen Lane, 2003

Fernández-Armesto, Felipe, *Food, A History*, Macmillian, 2001

Finkelstein, Joanne, *Dining Out: A Sociology of Modern Manners*, Polity Press, 1989

Finley M.I.(ed.), *Studies in Ancient Society*, Routledge and Kegan Paul, 1974

Fishman, Charles, *The Wal-Mart Effect: How an Out-of-Town Superstore Became a Superpower,* Allen Lane, 2006

Flandrin, Jean-Louis and Montanari, M., *Food: A Culinary History*, Trans. Albert Sonnenfeld, Columbia Press, 1999

Forshaw, Alec and Bergström, Theo, *Smithfield Past and Present*, Heinemann, 1980

Foucault, Michel, *Madness and Civilization*, Random House, 1965

——, *Discipline and Punish: The Birth of the Prison*, Peregrine Books, 1985

Frankfort, Henri, *Kingship and the Gods*, University of Chicago, 1978

Frederick, Christine, *Efficient Housekeeping, or Household Engineering: Scientific Management in the Home*, George Routledge, 1915

Geddes, Patrick, *Cities in Evolution*, Routledge 1997; 1915

Girardet, Herbert, *Cities People Planet: Liveable Cities for a Sustainable World*, Wiley Academy, 2004

Girouard, Mark, *Cities and People*, Yale University Press, 1985

Goody, John R., *Cooking, Cuisine and Class*, Cambridge University Press, 1982

Gruen, Victor, *Centres for the Urban Environment: Survival of the Cities*, Van Nostrand Reinhold, 1973

——, *The Heart of Our Cities*, Thames and Hudson, 1965

——, *Shopping Towns USA: The Planning of Shopping Centres*, Reinhold Publishing Corporation, 1960

Habermas, Jürgen, *The Structural Transformation of the Public Sphere: an Inquiry into a Category of Bourgeois Society*, Polity Press, 1992; Darmstadt, 1962

Hall, Peter, *Cities of Tomorrow: An Intellectual History of Urban Planning and Design in the Twentieth Century*, Blackwell, 2002

——, (ed.), *Von Thünen's Isolated State*, Trans. Carla M. Wartenberg, Pergamon Press, 1966

Hartley, Dorothy, *Food in England*, Little Brown and Company, 1999; Macdonald, 1954

Harvey, David, *Spaces of Hope*, Edinburgh University Press, 2000

Heinberg, Richard, *The Party's Over: Oil, War, and the Fate of Industrial Societies*, New Society Publishers, 2006

Hesiod, *Works and Days*, Trans. Richmond Lattimore, University of Michigan Press, 1959

Hoskins, W.G., *The Making of the English Landscape*, Penguin, 1970

Howard, Ebenezer, *Garden Cities of To-Morrow*, MIT Press Paperback Edition,1965; London, 1902

Huggett, Frank, *The Land Question and European Society*, Thames and Hudson, 1975

Hugo, Victor, *Les Misérables*, Trans. Norman Denny, Penguin, 1982; Paris, 1862

Jackson, Lesley, *'Contemporary': Architecture and Interiors of the 1950s*, Phaidon, 1994

Jacobs, Jane, *The Death and Life of Great American Cities*, Vintage, 1992; 1961

Johnston, James P., *A Hundred Years Eating: Food, Drink and the Daily Diet in Britain since the Late 19th Century*, Gill and Macmillan, McGill-Queen's University Press, 1977

Kaplan, Stephen, *Provisioning Paris: Merchants and Millers in the Grain and Flour Trade during the 18th Century*, Cornell University Press, 1984

Kemp, Barry, *Ancient Egypt: Anatomy of a Civilization*, Routledge, 1989

Kerr, Robert, *The Gentleman's House*, 1865

Klein, Naomi, *No Logo*, Flamingo, 2001

Lang, Tim and Heasman, Michael, *Food Wars*, Earthscan, 2004

Laporte, Dominique, *History of Shit*, Trans. Nadia Benabid and Rodolphe El-Khoury, MIT Press, 2000

Lawrence, Felicity, *Not on the Label*, Penguin, 2004

Le Corbusier, *Towards a New Architecture (Vers une Architecture)*, Trans. Frederick Etchells, The Architectural Press, 1972; Paris, 1923

——, *The Decorative Art of Today (L'Art Décoratif d'Aujourd'hui)*, Trans. James L. Dunnett, The Architectural Press, 1987; Paris, 1925

——, *The City of Tomorrow and its Planning, (Urbanisme)*, Trans. Frederick Etchells, Dover, 1987; Paris, 1922

Lefebvre, Henri, *The Production of Space*, Trans. Donald Nicholson-Smith, Blackwell, 1998

Levenstein, Harvey, *The Paradox of Plenty: A Social History of Eating in Modern America*, Oxford University Press, 1993

Lévi-Strauss, Claude, *The Raw and the Cooked*, Jonathan Cape, 1969

Locke, John, *An Essay Concerning the True Original, Extent and End of Civil Government* (Second Treatise on Civil Government), in Ernest Barker (ed.), *Social Contract*, Oxford University Press, 1971; 1690

Manuel, Frank E. and Manuel, Fritzie P., *Utopian Thought in the Western World*, Harvard University Press, 1979

Marx, Karl and Engels, Freidrich, *The Communist Manifesto*, Trans. Samuel Moore, Penguin Classics 2002; London, 1848

Mennell, Stephen, *All Manners of Food*, First Illinois Paperback, 1996

Michelson, Patricia, *The Cheese Room*, Penguin, 2001

Millstone, Erik and Lang, Tim, *The Atlas of Food*, Earthscan Publications Ltd., 2003

Mintz, Sidney, *Sweetness and Power*, Penguin, 1986

Mollison Bill and Holmgren, David, *Permaculture One: A Perennial Agriculture for Human Settlements,* Doveton Press, 1990; Transworld, 1978

Monbiot, George, *Captive State: The Corporate Takeover of Britain*, Macmillan, 2000

Montanari, Massimo, *The Culture of Food*, Trans. Carl Ipsen, Blackwell, 1994

More, Thomas, *Utopia*, Trans. Paul Turner, Penguin, 2003; 1516

Morley, Neville, *Metropolis and Hinterland: The City of Rome and the Italian Economy 200 B.C.–A.D. 200,* Cambridge University Press, 1996

Morris, William, *News From Nowhere and Other Writings*, edited by Clive Wilmer, Penguin Classics, 1993

Mumford, Lewis, *The City in History*, Penguin, 1961

Murray, Oswyn (ed.), *Sympotica: A Symposium on the Symposion,* Clarendon Press, 1990

Nelson, George and Wright, Henry, *Tomorrow's House: A Complete Guide for the Home-Builder*, Simon and Schuster, 1945

Oddy, Derek J. and Miller, Derek S. (eds.), *The Making of the Modern British Diet*, Croom Helm, 1976

Ogden, Annegret S., *The Great American Housewife: From Helpmate to Wage-earner 1776–1986*, Greenwood Press, 1986

Orwell, George, *Down and Out in Paris and London*, Penguin, 1986; Victor Gollancz, 1933

——, *The Road to Wigan Pier*, Penguin, 2001; Victor Gollancz, 1937

Palmer, Sue, *Toxic Childhood*, Orion Books, 2006

Pepys, Samuel, *Diary*, 10 vols, edited by R. Latham and W. Matthews, HarperCollins, 2000

Petrini, Carlo, *Slow Food: The Case for Taste*, Columbia University Press, 2001

——, *Slow Food Nation: Why Our Food Should be Good, Clean and Fair*, Trans. Clara Furlan and Jonathan Hunt, Rizzoli, 2007

Petronius, Titus, *The Satyricon*, Trans. J.P. Sullivan, Penguin, 1981

Pollan, Michael, *The Omnivore's Dilemma*, Bloomsbury, 2006

Post, Emily, *Etiquette in Society, in Business, in Politics and at Home*, Funk and Wagnalls, 1922

Postgate, J.N., *Early Mesopotamia: Society and Economy at the Dawn of History*, Routledge, 1994

Pretty, Jules, *Agri-Culture: Reconnecting People, Land and Nature*, Earthscan, 2002

Raphael, Chaim, *A Feast of History*, Weidenfeld and Nicholson, 1972

Rassmussen, Steen Eiler, *London, The Unique City*, MIT Press, 1982; 1934

Reader, John, *Cities*, Vintage, 2005

Reid, Donald, *Paris Sewers and Sewermen: Realities and Representations*, Harvard University Press, 1993

Rickman, Geoffrey, *The Corn Supply of Ancient Rome*, Clarendon Press, 1980

Rogers, Richard, *Cities for a Small Planet*, Faber and Faber, 1997

Rossi, Aldo, *The Architecture of the City*, MIT Press, 1982

Rousseau, Jean-Jacques, *A Discourse On the Origin of Inequality* (1755), Trans. G.D.H.Cole, William Benton, 1952

Rowe, Colin, *Collage City*, MIT Press, 1979

Rykwert, Joseph, *The Idea of a Town*, Faber and Faber, 1976

——, *The Seduction of Place*, Oxford University Press, 2000

Sams, Craig, *The Little Food Book*, Alistair Sawday Publishing, 2003

Schama, Simon, *Landscape and Memory*, Fontana Press, 1996

Schärer, Martin R. and Fenton Alexander (eds.), *Food and Material Culture*, Tuckwell Press, 1998

Schlosser, Eric, *Fast Food Nation*, Allen Lane, 2001

Schoenauer, Norbert, *6000 Years of Housing*, W.W. Norton, 2000

Schofield, John (ed.), *The London Surveys of Ralph Treswell*, London Topographical Society Publication No. 135, 1987

Schumacher, E.F., *Small is Beautiful*, Vintage, 1973

Sennett, Richard, *The Fall of Public Man*, Faber and Faber, 1986

——, *Flesh and Stone*, Faber and Faber, 1996

Seth, Andrew and Randall, Geoffrey, *The Grocers: The Rise and Rise of the Supermarket Chains*, Kogan Page, 1999

Simms, Andrew, *Tescopoly: How One Shop Came Out On Top and Why it Matters,* Constable and Robinson, 2007

Sinclair, Upton, *The Jungle,* Penguin Classics, 1986; Doubleday, 1906

Smil, Vaclav, *Enriching the Earth: Fritz Haber, Carl Bosch, and the Transformation of World Food Production,* MIT Press, 2004

Smith, Adam, *An Enquiry into the Nature and Causes of the Wealth of Nations,* 2 vols, E. Cannan (ed.), Methuen, London 1925; 1776

Spang, Rebecca L., *The Invention of the Restaurant: Paris and Modern Gastronomic Culture,* Harvard University Press, 2000

Stevenson, J.J., *House Architecture,* 2 vols., Macmillan, 1880

Stow, John, *Survey of London,* 2 vols, Charles Kingsforde (ed.), Clarendon Press, 1908; 1603

Strong, Roy, *Feast: A History of Grand Eating,* Jonathan Cape, 2002

Stuart, Tristram, *The Bloodless Revolution: Radical Vegetarians and The Discovery of India,* Harper Press, 2006

Symons, Michael, *A History of Cooks and Cooking,* University of Illinois Press, 2004

Tacitus, *Germania,* Trans. M. Hutton, Heinemann, 1970

Tames, Richard, *Feeding London: A Taste of History,* Historical Publications Ltd, 2003

Tanizaki, Jun'ichiro, *In Praise of Shadows,* Trans. Thomas J.Harper and Edward. G. Seidensticker, Jonathan Cape, 1991; 1933

Tannahill, Reay, *Food in History,* Penguin, 1973

Thick, Malcolm, *The Neat House Gardens: Early Market Gardening Around London,* Prospect Books, 1998

Thomas, Keith, *Man and the Natural World: Changing Attitudes in England 1500–1800,* Penguin, 1984

Thomson, E.P., *The Making of the English Working Class,* Penguin, 1980; 1963

Thoreau, Henry David, *Walden, or Life in the Woods,* Oxford University Press, 1997; 1854

Trench, Richard and Hillman, Ellis, *London Under London,* John Murray, 1993

Tudge, Colin, *So Shall We Reap,* Penguin, 2004

Viljoen, André (ed.), *CPULs: Continuous Productive Urban Landscapes,* The Architectural Press, 2005

Visser, Margaret, *The Rituals of Dinner*, Penguin, 1991

Webber, Robert, *Covent Garden: Mud-Salad Market*, J.M. Dent and Sons Ltd., 1969

White, Eileen (ed.), *Feeding a City: York: The Provision of Food from Roman Times to the Beginning of the Twentieth Century*, Prospect Books, 2000

Wigley, Mark, *White Walls, Designer Dresses: The Fashioning of Modern Architecture*, MIT Press, 1995

Wilkins, John, Harvey, David and Dobson, Mike (eds.), *Food in Antiquity*, University of Exeter Press, 1995

Wilson, Anne (ed.). *Luncheon, Nuncheon and Other Meals: Eating with the Victorians*, Alan Sutton Publishing, 1994

Winstanley, Gerrard. *The True Levellers Standard Advanced, or, The State of Community opened, and Presented to the Sons of Men*, London, 1649

Woolley, Leonard, *Ur of the Chaldees*, edited by P.R.S. Moorey, Cornell University Press, 1982; 1929

Wright, Frank Lloyd, *The Living City*, Horizon Press, 1958

Wrigley, E.A., *People, Cities and Wealth: The Transformation of Traditional Society*, Blackwell, 1987

Wycherley, R.E., *The Stones of Athens*, Princeton, 1978

——, *How the Greeks Built Cities*, Macmillan Press, 1979

Yorke, F.R.S., *The Modern House*, The Architectural Press, 1934

Young, Arthur, *Observations on the Present State of the Wastelands of Great Britain*, London, 1773

Reports

Action Aid, *Power Hungry: Six Reasons to Regulate Global Food Corporations* (2006), www.actionaid.org

Commission for Architecture and the Built Environment (CABE), *What Home Buyers Want: Attitudes and Decision-making Among Consumers* (2005), www.cabe.org.uk

Department for Environment, Food and Rural Affairs (Defra), *The Validity of Food Miles as an Indicator of Sustainable Development* (2005), www.defra.gov.uk

——, *Environmental Impacts of Food Production and Consumption* (2006)

——, *Waste Strategy for England* (2007)

Defra and The Corporation of London, *Review of London Wholesale Markets* (2002), Nicholas Saphir (author), www.defra.gov.uk

DETR (Department of the Environment, Transport and the Regions, *Impact Of Large Foodstores On Market Towns And District Centres* (1998), www.communities.gov.uk

——, *Towards an Urban Renaissance,* Report of the Urban Task Force (1999), Lord Rogers of Riverside (Chair), www.urbantaskforce.org

European Commission, *Environmental Impact of Products (EIPRO: 2006)*, http://ec.europa.eu

Demos, *Creating Wealth from Waste* (1999), Robin Murray (author), www.demos.co.uk

Friends of the Earth, *Calling The Shots: How Supermarkets Get Their Way In Planning Decisions* (2006), www.foe.co.uk

Greenpeace Environmental Trust: Zero Waste (2002), Robin Murray (author), www.greenpeace.org.uk

HM Treasury, *The Economics of Climate Change* (2006), Sir Nicholas Stern (chair), www.hm-treasury.gov.uk

House of Commons All-Party Parliamentary Small Shops Group, *High Street Britain: 2015* (2006), www.nfsp.org.uk

Intergovernmental Panel on Climate Change (IPCC), *Climate Change 2007: The Physical Science Basis* (2007), www.ipcc.ch

Institute of Grocery Distribution, *Grocery Retailing Report* (2006), www.igd.com

Joseph Rowntree Foundation, *Preferences, Quality and Choice in New-build Housing* (2004), www.jrf.org.uk

——, *Markets as Sites for Social Interaction: Spaces of Diversity* (2006), Sophie Watson and David Studdert (eds.)

London Development Agency, *Healthy and Sustainable Food for London: The Mayor's Food Strategy* (2006), www.lda.gov.uk

——, *Housing Space Standards* (2006)

Mulholland Research & Consulting, *Popular Housing Group: Perceptions of Privacy and Density in Housing* (2003), www.mch.co.uk

New Economics Foundation, *Ghost Town Britain: The Threat From Economic Globalisation To Livelihoods, Liberty And Local Economic*

Freedom (2002), www.neweconomics.org

——, *Clone Town Britain: The Survey Results on the Bland State of the Nation* (2005)

——, *The World on a Plate: Queens Market. The economic and social value of London's most ethnically diverse street market* (2006)

Royal Institute of Chartered Surveyors, *What Kind of World Are We Building? The Privatisation of Public Space* (2006), Anna Minton (author), www.rics.org

Oxfam, *Stop the Dumping! How EU Agricultural Subsidies Are Damaging Livelihoods in the Developing World* (2002), www.oxfam.org.uk

Policy Commission on the Future of Farming and Food, *Farming and Food: A Sustainable Future* (2002), Sir Donald Curry CBE (Chair), http://archive.cabinetoffice.gov.uk/farming

Sustain: The Alliance for Better Food and Farming. *City Harvest: The Feasibility of Growing More Food in London* (1999), Tara Garnett (author), www. sustainweb.org

——, *How Green Are Our Apples? A Look at the Social and Environmental Effects of Apple Production* (1999), Rosemary Hoskins (research)

——, *A Battle in Store? A Discussion of the Social Impact of the Major UK Supermarkets* (2000), Corinna Hawkes (author)

——, *Eating Oil: Food Supply in a Changing Climate* (2001), Andy Jones (author)

United Nations Food and Agriculture Organisation (FAO), *Livestock's Long Shadow* (2006), www.fao.org

World Wildlife Fund, *Living Planet Report* (2006), www.world wildlife.org

Waste and Resources Action Programme (Wrap), *Understanding Food Waste* (2007), www.wrap.org.uk

Other Useful Websites

Big Barn: a network providing information on sources of local food, www.bigbarn.co.uk

Common Ground: an organisation dedicated to promoting links between nature and culture, www.commonground.org

Bibliography

The Food Climate Research Network: an interdisciplinary research network looking at the impacts of food on climate change, www.fcrn.org.uk

The Food Ethics Council: an organization that challenges government, business and society to make choices that will lead to better food and farming, www.foodethicscouncil.org

Local Food Shop: a local food network linking farmers to consumers by their postcode, www.localfoodshop.co.uk

Slow food: an international network promoting traditional values and ways of life associated with local food cultures, www.slowfood.com

Soil Association: the leading UK organisation promoting ecologically sustainable organic farming, www.soilassociation.org

Tescopoly: a site dedicated to raising public awareness about the damaging impact of Tesco's dominance on local businesses and communities, www.tescopoly.org

The UK Food Group: the leading UK network for non-governmental organisations (NGOs) working on global food and agriculture issues, www.ukfg.org.uk

The Vertical Farm Project: an interdisciplinary research and design programme based at Columbia University dedicated to finding solutions for 21st century global agriculture, www.verticalfarm.com

Transition Towns: a UK network dedicated to planning in response to peak oil and climate change, www.transitiontowns.org

Acknowledgements

Every idea has its sources; every book its mentors. I am greatly indebted to Dalibor Vesely and Peter Carl, whose inspirational teaching at the Department of Architecture at Cambridge University opened my eyes (along with those of countless others) to the true horizons of our discipline. To have had their continued friendship and support through the writing of *Hungry City* has been a great joy. I hope they won't mind my saying that I consider them to be its intellectual godfathers. For persuading me I was capable of writing a book, David Bass and Rowan Moore deserve all my thanks. Rowan's early advice and encouragement were invaluable, while David has been my chief sounding-board and critic throughout. I could not have wished for two better mentors for my first book, and their wit and intelligence is woven into its pages. I am also greatly indebted to Wendy Pullan, who invited me to create my first lecture series on *Food and the City* at the Department of Architecture at Cambridge. Her leap of faith and continued support have meant a great deal.

Finding a literary agent was a grisly process, so when Jonny Pegg of Curtis Brown responded to my proposal with a resounding 'Yes!', it was one of the best moments of my life. I am extremely grateful to Jonny for his unstinting enthusiasm, and for sticking with me through the arduous process of finding a publisher with similarly lateral vision. Our search came to an end when Chatto & Windus took me on, and I am hugely grateful to Alison Samuel and my editor Poppy Hampson, for taking a punt on a first-time writer with such uncharted subject matter. I would like to thank Poppy especially for all her enthusiasm and encouragement, her patient handling of me and uncomplaining hard work. One could not wish for a more sympathetic editor.

The arguments within *Hungry City* have evolved over many years, and through countless conversations. My warmest thanks to all those who have selflessly given their time and energy to reading drafts of the text and giving me their comments: Charisse Amand, Matthew Barac, David Bass, Cressida Bell, Claire Bennie, Nick Bullock, Lulu Chivers, Chris Dawe, Dominik Dlouhy, Neil Grange, Nick Horsley, Richard Nightingale, Robert Kennett, Georgia Lowe, Rowan Moore, Jeremy O'Sullivan, Stefan Schlobach, Stanley Steel, Max Steuer, Dalibor Vesely and Stephen Witherford. Grateful thanks also to all those whose debate and engagement have contributed so much to shaping the book: Cany Ash, Peter Carl, Sam Causer, Liz Dowler, James Fisher, Jane Fisher-Hunt, Simon Fujiwara, Mark Hewitt, Stephen Hunt, Alex Laird, Tim Lang, Helen Mallinson, Michael Mallinson, Anna Minton, Juliet Odgers, Arthur Potts-Dawson, Polly Russell, Robert Sakula, David Sawer, Liz Stretch, Simon Tucker, Brian Vermeulen, Nick Warner, David Willink and Roger Zogolovitch. Roger may be last in the list, but he is first in essence, since it was during a conversation with him that the idea for *Hungry City* first took shape. In addition, I would like to thank all those who have generously offered their professional insight and expertise, in particular Peter Clarke of Kingcup Farm, who gave up many hours of his time to share his extensive knowledge of farming and the food industry with me. Many thanks also to Zeenat Anjari and Ben Reynolds at Sustain, Keith and Liz Bennett of Stockings Farm, Cheryl Cohen of London Farmers' Markets, Simone Crofton of Borough Market, Fred Duncan of Grampian Country Food Group, Mick Evans and Steve Crawford of Walkers Midshire Foods, Neil Grange and Alejandro Gutierrez of Arup, Kevin Hand of Pennine Foods, and Claire Pritchard of Greenwich Co-operative Development Agency.

One of the most unexpected and delightful aspects of writing *Hungry City* has been the many friends I have made along the way; an astonishing number through Claire Hartten, whose open-spirited *Dirt*

Café project is a table society for the modern age. Its meetings, generously hosted by Patricia Michelson and Sarah Bilney at *La Fromagerie* in Marylebone (London's only political cheese shop), provided a wonderful forum for debate and sharing at a time when I was first feeling my way in the world of food. My heartfelt thanks to all of them for their hospitality and support. Special thanks also to Nick Horsley, Karen Gilbert and Susan and Julian Elias, for inviting me to wonderful dinners and allowing me to describe them in the book. Particular thanks also to Richard Nightingale, who has put up with my multi-faceted career for many years, and has always been hugely generous in his friendship and advice. Thanks also to Simon Monkman and Elissa Schlanker for keeping my work safe, to Marion Houston for her administrative help, and to my dear brother Brian, who talked me out of the trees several times through various hi-tech nightmares, and memorably rescued an unrepeatable day's work from the oblivion of computer meltdown.

I am most grateful to the Arts Council, whose grant in 2006 helped me to write *Hungry City* full time, and to the Royal Society of Literature and the Jerwood Foundation, whose prize for non-fiction was awarded to *Hungry City* in 2006. To have the approbation of such august judges as Hilary Spurling, Moris Farhi and Roland Chambers so early in my writing career was a great boost.

The constant help and encouragement I have received through the writing of this book (including those of many people not specifically mentioned here) has moved me more than I can say. One person, however, requires a further mention. The unfailing support of David Bass, his insight and judgement, humour and companionship, have made the writing of *Hungry City* feel more of a shared effort than a solo one. DB, thank you from the bottom of my heart – I really can't think how I would have done this without you.

List of Illustrations

1. Ambrogio Lorenzetti, *The Effects of Good Government on City and Country* (1338). Detail from *The Allegory of Good Government*, Palazzo Pubblico, Siena. (The Bridgeman Art Library)
2. Map of the Fertile Crescent. (Drawn by the author, with thanks to Matt Seaber)
3. George Robertson, *A North View of the Cities of London and Westminster with part of Highgate* (1780). (The Bridgeman Art Library)
4. Hoisting hogs on a Hurford revolving wheel (c.1906), Chicago. (Courtesy of Hagley Museum and Library)
5. Albert Bierstadt, *Yosemite Valley* (1868). (The Bridgeman Art Library)
6. Christmas fatstock show at Shipston-on-Stour, Warwickshire. Photo, early 20th century. From *The Land*, by John Higgs, Readers Union, 1965.
7. Map of the food supply to ancient Rome. (Drawn by the author)
8. Ramesseum (the mortuary temple of Rameses II). Plan after U. Hölscher. (With the kind permission of Barry Kemp)
9. The *Grève*, or *Port aux Blés*, in Paris, looking toward the Pont Marie. 17th century engraving. (Courtesy of Getty Images/Roger Viollet)
10. *The Great Western Railway at Kelston Bridge Near Bath*. Lithograph from *Illustrations of the Great Western and Bristol and Exeter Railways*, L. Hague, 1840.

11. *Palazzo della Ragione and Piazza delle Frutta*, Padua. 20th century photograph. (The Civic Museum, Padua)

12. John Ogilby, *A Large and Accurate Map of the City of London* (1676). Detail from facsimile published by the London and Middlesex Archaeological Society (1894). (Annotated by the author)

13. Pieter Bruegel, detail from *The Fight Between Carnival and Lent* (1559). (Courtesy of the Kunsthistorisches Museum, Wien)

14. Smithfield Market (c.1830). Aquatint by R.G. Reeve after James Pollard. (The Bridgeman Art Library)

15. Southdale Shopping Centre, Minnesota. Photograph of the interior, 1956. (Courtesy Victor Gruen Papers, American Heritage Center, University of Wyoming)

16. Joris Hoefnagel, detail from *A Fête at Bermondsey* (c.1570). (The Bridgeman Art Library)

17. *Fetching Home the Christmas Dinner*. Engraving from the *Illustrated London News*, 1848. (Courtesy of ILN/Mary Evans Picture Library)

18. Cooking in a small country kitchen. Photograph from Christine Frederick, *Household Engineering*, 1915.

19. Le Corbusier, Villa Stein-de Monzie, Garches. Photograph of the kitchen. (© FLC/ADAGP, Paris and DACS, London 2008)

20. *A View of the Inside of Guildhall as it appeared on Lord Mayor's day, 1761*. Detail of engraving from *The Gentleman's Magazine*, December 1761. (The Bridgeman Art Library)

21. Detail of a place set at a formal dinner table of a great house. Photograph from Emily Post, *Etiquette in Society, in Business, in Politics and at Home*, 1922.

22. Interior of a London coffee house. Aquatint signed and dated A.S.1668. (The Bridgeman Art Library)

23. Photo of first Cincinnati, Ohio White Castle, 1927. (The White Castle images and materials and the "WHITE CASTLE®" mark are the exclusive property of White Castle Management Co. and are used under license. No use, reproduction or distribution is allowed)

24. The Thames Embankment under construction. Detail of engraving from the *Illustrated London News*, 1867. (Courtesy of ILN/Mary Evans Picture Library)

Every effort has been made to trace or contact all copyright holders, and the publishers will be pleased to correct any omissions brought to their notice at the earliest opportunity.

Index

Index

www.vintage-books.co.uk